THE PRINCE

A NORTON CRITICAL EDITION

≫ A NORTON CRITICAL EDITION ≪

NICCOLÒ MACHIAVELLI

THE PRINCE

A NEW TRANSLATION
BACKGROUNDS
INTERPRETATIONS

≫≪

Translated and Edited by
ROBERT M. ADAMS
UNIVERSITY OF CALIFORNIA AT LOS ANGELES

W · W · NORTON & COMPANY · INC · *New York*

"The Setting of *The Prince*," reprinted from *Machiavelli and Renaissance Italy*, by J. R. Hale, English Universities Press (1961). Reprinted by permission.

"The Humanist Concept of the Prince and *The Prince* of Machiavelli," reprinted from the *Journal of Modern History* 11:4 (December 1939), pp. 449–83. Reprinted by permission of The University of Chicago Press, Chicago, Illinois, and Felix Gilbert.

"Implications of the New Theory of the State," reprinted by permission of Yale University Press from *The Myth of the State*, by Ernst Cassirer. Copyright © 1946 by Yale University Press.

"Machiavelli the Immoralist," from the Introduction to *Thoughts on Machiavelli*, by Leo Strauss (1958), pp. 9–14. Reprinted by permission of the University of Washington Press.

"The Economy of Violence," reprinted from *Politics and Vision: Continuity and Innovation in Western Political Thought*, by Sheldon S. Wolin, pp. 220–35, 470–73. Copyright © 1960 by Little, Brown and Company. Reprinted by permission.

"On Machiavelli's Use of *Ordini*," reprinted from *Discourses on Machiavelli*, by J. H. Whitfield (1969), chapter 9, pp. 141–62. Permission to reprint granted by J. H. Whitfield, Serena Professor Emeritus of Italian Language and Literature, University of Birmingham.

"The Origins of Evil" from *Niccolò Machiavelli, Storia del Sue Pensiero Politico* by Gennaro Sasso (1958), pp. 290–303. Reprinted by permission of Gennaro Sasso.

"In Search of Machiavelli's Virtù" by John Plamenatz. Reprinted from *The Political Calculus: Essays on Machiavelli's Philosophy*, edited by Anthony Parel, by permission of University of Toronto Press. Copyright © University of Toronto Press (1972).

"Morals as Fossilized Violence" from *The Genealogy of Morals* by Nietzsche, translated by Francis Golffing. Copyright © 1956 by Doubleday and Company, Inc. Reprinted by permission of the publisher.

"What Is Authority?" from *Between Past and Future* by Hannah Arendt, pp. 136–41. Copyright © 1961 by Hannah Arendt. All rights reserved. Reprinted by permission of Viking Penguin, Inc. British rights granted by Faber & Faber Ltd. of London.

"The Modern Prince" from *The Modern Prince and Other Writings* by Antonio Gramsci, translated by Louis Mark, Publishers, Lawrence & Wishart Ltd., 46 Bedford Row, London W.C.1. Reprinted by permission.

Library of Congress Cataloging in Publication Data
Machiavelli, Niccolò, 1469–1527.
  The prince: a new translation, backgrounds, interpretations.
  (A Norton critical edition)
  Bibliography: p.
  Includes index.
  1. Political science—Early works to 1700.
  2. Political ethics. I. Adams, Robert Martin, 1915–
11. Title
JC143.M38 1977   320.1   77–3581
ISBN 0-393-04448-3
ISBN 0-393-09149-X pbk.

FIRST EDITION

1 2 3 4 5 6 7 8 9 0

Contents

Historical Introduction

For as long as rulers have been ruling, they have been receiving —from laymen and clergy, from nobles and commons, from their predecessors and those who would like to be their replacements, masters, or successors—advice on how to do their jobs. Most of these manuals for statesmen and handbooks for sovereigns, since they simply rephrase, codify, and make applications of the common wisdom of the day, enjoy only an ephemeral existence. Rulers rarely read them, and even more rarely make use of their precepts; the typical manual for rulers seems to be chiefly of interest to other writers of manuals, and after a while only to students of manual writing. The major exception to all these cynicisms is a little booklet written, but not published, by Niccolò Machiavelli, citizen of Florence, in 1513. *The Prince* is not far from its 500th birthday, and it continues as vital, as much discussed, as influential, as any book only a tenth of its age.

Many of the reasons for this exceptional vitality are apparent to the most casual reader of Machiavelli's text. They are literary, dramatic, and moral qualities that stand out boldly on the page. They are implicit in the personality and voice of Machiavelli himself. But Machiavelli and his book were very much the product of their times, and it may be useful for the reader to have in mind a minimal outline sketch of the historical circumstances that formed both.

Machiavelli was born in 1469 and died in 1527; he was a Florentine. The city of Florence, straddling the Arno in northwest Italy, was in those days both a commercial center of European importance and the politico-military capital of the surrounding district, known as Tuscany. The Tuscans are a story all by themselves: they think themselves, and probably are, smarter than most other Italians. They tend to be ironic if not cynical, and rather proud of the fact that nobody likes them—which they take to be evident proof of their superior intelligence. Dante's is a characteristically Tuscan imagination—dry, clear, proud, and severely logical in its poetry. Machiavelli's mind has many of the same traits

During the Renaissance, the Florentines exercised direct or indirect power over a great many other Tuscan cities, such as Prato, Pistoia, Pisa, Lucca, San Gimignano, and Siena. Like it or not, and many did not, these cities, and many of the country folk in the surrounding countryside, were ruled by the smart, quick Florentines.

The city proper had been a republic as far back as historical records reached (before the year A.D. 1,000), though with occasional intervals when a particular family or individual gained enough power to set up, uneasily and temporarily, as ruler. Thus the struggle between rich and poor, between centralized authoritarian rule and more popular, participatory forms of government, was a constant feature of Florentine history. During Machiavelli's lifetime, the chief family menacing the republican institutions of Florence was the Medici. Relevant portions of their family tree are outlined in the genealogical table on page ix.

Cosimo, Piero, and Lorenzo, three successive generations of the Medici, ruled over Florence through the greater part of the fifteenth century, without altogether abolishing representative government, yet while clearly dominating it. They did so through a combination of force, persuasion, leniency, deception, and social astuteness. But the skills required to manage, without actual dictatorship, so restive and independent a city were exceptional, and without them even a Medici was helpless. When Lorenzo died in 1492, his son Pietro proved quite incapable, and within two years he and his supporters were forced into exile. A republican government replaced him. Machiavelli was then just twenty-three years old, and for the next eighteen years, until just before the writing of *The Prince*, it was a republican government under which he lived and for which he worked.

This is no place to describe the detailed machinery of Florentine city government and politics; a vivid impression of its working will be found in Jean Lucas-Dubreton, *Daily Life in Florence in the Time of the Medici*, chapter II. What cannot fail to amaze a modern reader is the extraordinary intensity of political life in this moderately sized city of 100,000 or so inhabitants. Even under the Medici, and to a much greater degree under the republic, Florence was like a swarm of political bees. Because they feared that administrations long in power would become entrenched and tyrannical, the Florentines limited most of their officials to short terms in office: a man might be elected to some major bodies for a term as brief as two months. As a result, the city was constantly involved in election campaigns, and politics was a constant preoccupation of every citizen. There were parties based upon ancient though nebulous principles, like the old Guelfs, who were tolerant of papal power and anti-German; they opposed the Ghibellines, who tended to favor the Holy Roman emperor, a German, and to distrust the pope. There were religious reformers, notably the Dominican monk Savonarola, who preached up a storm during the years 1494–98, till Alexander VI caused him to be burned in the public square. These were massive public events. But down among the grass roots—or at

Medici Family Tree—A Rough Diagram

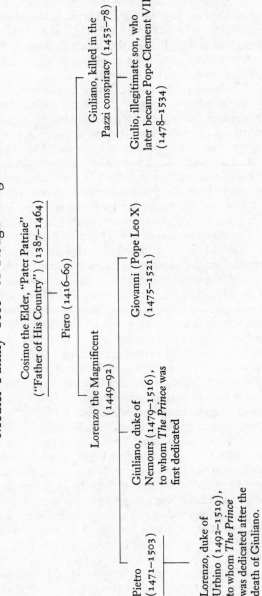

least in the narrow, cobblestoned alleys of the walled city—Florence was in constant ferment. The various wards and districts were in political conflict with one another; the rich and poor were often at each other's throats; the various families gathered and broke up into factions; the guilds and trades were politically active; and because they were all crowded together in a tight little town behind walls, the Florentines were subject to gusty rumors and surges of passion which sent them raging through the streets to howl or hammer at the high towers and massive palazzi within which lay hidden their heroes or hated enemies of the moment.

The systematic chaos here described was modified, however, by some stabilizing institutions. In 1502 a widely respected and constitutionally moderate man named Piero Soderini was elected for life to the highest office of the republic (gonfalonier); it was a deliberate effort to confer stability on the regime. On another level entirely, the family structures were strong forces making for stability. Young men were trained in politics by the elders of their family and party; only after a long period of initiation and trial in minor offices did men become eligible to run for major ones. And in areas where experience and continuity were essential, as in foreign policy, there was an ongoing bureaucracy of trained civil servants. At the age of twenty-nine, Machiavelli joined this staff, and he remained a valued servant in the diplomatic corps till the events of 1512 brought about the downfall of the republic as a whole, and the return of the Medici. Sometimes he served in the home office, transmitting instructions to, and receiving messages from, ambassadors abroad; on several occasions of no slight importance he was himself dispatched to represent the republic at the court of some foreign power. This work constituted his training to write *The Prince*, and we provide, in the Backgrounds section (pp. 79–92) a sampling of the reports he wrote on these missions. He knew his business well; his reports were much admired, and he himself rose in the service to be a valued agent of Piero Soderini.

The chief interest of Machiavelli's professional life was foreign policy, and not surprisingly the subject bulks large in *The Prince*. It behooves us therefore to know something of the world within which he and his employers had to operate. Florence, the city from which he saw everything, and in whose interests he always wrote, was neither large nor warlike; it was not protected by the sea, like Venice, nor was it an international center of religious authority, like Rome. To a great extent it depended on the skill of its craftsmen, the shrewdness of its merchants and bankers, and the political astuteness of its leaders. Until the death of Lorenzo in 1492, it survived and competed successfully in the little world of Italian power politics. Partly this was because of its strong points, noted above, and partly it was because the world of Italian politics was indeed a fairly autonomous world. There were five chief power units on the peninsula, consisting, in addition to Florence, of Milan, Venice, the Papal States (an unruly district of semi-autonomous chieftains under the theoretical dominion of the pope in Rome), and the kingdom of Naples, also known sometimes as the kingdom of the Two Sicilies, or just the Kingdom. Because they had fairly well defined areas of interest, because no one of them was ever strong enough to dominate the other four, and because their wars were fought largely by professional soldiers who had no great interest in making things tough on one another, these five units managed to maintain, throughout the fifteenth century, an uneasy balance of power, tempered by frequent squabbles but never seriously shaken. They were not, after all, very much like modern nations. Ethnically, they were very similar; they all called themselves Italians. In religion, they were all Catholics, who accepted at least nominally the authority of the pope. They all spoke dialects of the same language. Socially, they were not too different. The kingdom of Naples was a royal state of sorts, though its dynastic affairs were an incredible tangle, with the French, the Spanish, and the papacy all laying claim to the royal power via various pretexts. The doge of Venice and the pope in Rome were elected to their offices, though by very different procedures. Milan was for many years under the command of the Visconti, local tyrants; they were replaced in 1450 by their former employee, Francesco Sforza, who was a professional soldier by trade, and the son of another professional soldier, who began life as a peasant. All these rulers were, for Machiavelli and his contemporaries, "princes"; it was a catchall term. But not one of them was the head of a nation in the modern sense.

Such nations did exist, however, and just two years after the death of Lorenzo, they began to intrude into Italy's little world of small-power political balances and neighborly squabbles. All through the fifteenth century, the kings of France had been consolidating their territories, taking over independent duchies like Burgundy and Brittany, and reducing the feudal lords to the service of a centralized monarchy. Much the same thing happened in Spain, though by a different process. The marriage of Ferdinand of Aragon with Isabella of Castile in 1469 led directly to the final expulsion of the Moors from Spain and a whole series of foreign adventures in Europe and the New World, to which the formidably centralized bureaucracy of Spain contributed support on an unprecedented scale. To put it with Machiavelli's bluntness, Ferdinand was always ready to start a new military adventure because he had a ruthlessly efficient system of tax collection. In Germany, centralization of power did not take the same form or proceed quite as far as in France and Spain; but under the Holy Roman emperor Maximilian I, the Germans were able to muster from their vast territories armies of tough professional soldiers (Landsknechte), before which the small Italian armies were ultimately helpless.

The influx of foreign armies into Italy was triggered by Ludovico Sforza of Milan. He invited the French, under Charles VIII, to invade Italy in order to assert their claim to the kingdom of Naples. This they in fact did (1494), and though they were forced to withdraw almost at once (by a coalition that included the treacherous Sforza himself), the ease with which they advanced the length of the peninsula alerted the other European powers to the fact that Italy was a plum for the picking. In 1499 the French were back again, this time under Louis XII—first to seize Milan from their old friend Sforza, then to assert their claim to Naples. And this time it was the Venetians who half encouraged the French invasion, as a way of getting back at their old enemies the Milanese; but the pope helped too, because he wanted French troops to support his bid for temporal power. Seeing Naples on the point of falling to the French, the Spanish moved in to cut them off; by the Treaty of Granada (1500) they got a share of Naples, and three years later they grabbed the whole thing. And thus the various Italian states began struggling to get themselves powerful foreign allies, and to protect themselves by hiring more and more foreign mercenaries— Swiss, Germans, Albanians, Gascons, Croatians, any bloodthirsty thugs whatever. Everybody deplored the arrival of these brutal freebooters, but the fact was that they won battles. In the last chapter of *The Prince*, Machiavelli recites a mournful litany of battles lost by Italian armies to invading foreigners; over a period of twenty years, he lists seven major battles lost or cities destroyed, and could have doubled or tripled the list without difficulty.

For Florence—rich, without natural protection, lying on the main road south, and without either a big army or a strong military tradition—things were particularly difficult. In the very first French invasion, Florence lost control of Pisa, which guarded the mouth of the Arno and thus was vital to Florentine trade. The struggle to get Pisa back was infinitely painful, expensive, and frustrating. Meanwhile, every gang of soldiers that appeared before the city gates meant a new levy on the citizens. Florence had to pay so many powerful "friends" to protect it, and powerful "enemies" not to attack it, that the difference between friends and enemies evaporated altogether. In the end, the Florentine republic suffered more as a result of its traditional loyalty to the French than from its traditional enemies. With blind obstinacy, and despite Machiavelli's repeated objections, the republic insisted on reaffirming its loyalty to its French allies, at the very moment when they were on the point of packing up and leaving Italy altogether. Their departure, in 1512, left the Florentines at the mercy of a hostile pope who was under the influence of the exiled Medici and allied with the tremendous power of Spain. For years Machiavelli had been calling for a citi-

zens' army or militia, which would make the city independent of
the hated and treacherous mercenaries. He had actually recruited
and begun training this body. But in 1512, they came up prema-
turely against some veteran Spanish infantry, who smashed them
with contemptuous ease. The republic fell, and Machiavelli with it;
the Medici returned; and Machiavelli, after an uncomfortable interval during which he was tortured in connection with a suspected
plot, was allowed to retire to the country, where he composed *The
Prince*. His retirement from active politics did not of course stop
the terrible process of decay and disintegration against which he
had protested. Mercenaries continued to pour into Italy, the city-
states continued to fight one another instead of the invaders, and
the climactic act of the whole squalid drama came in 1527, the year
of Machiavelli's death. This was the infamous Sack of Rome, when
a huge, disorderly mob of mercenary soldiers, mostly German and
many Lutheran, but completely out of control by their officers or
anybody else, surrounded, besieged, captured and for an entire
summer looted, raped, murdered, burned, smashed, and vandalized
the Holy City. Pope Clement VII was forced to seek shelter in the
Castel San Angelo and pay a giant ransom to regain his liberty. The
humiliation of Italy was complete.

In this entire story, one institution peculiar to the Italian scene
played a constant part, that calls for a bit of extra explanation: this
was of course, the papacy. *The Prince* weaves the story of the various popes so deftly into the texture of its argument, and alludes to
them so lightly, that it may be useful to have here a list of them,
covering the period of Machiavelli's life:

Sixtus IV (Francesco della Rovere), pope from 1471 to 1484
Innocent VIII (Giovanni Battista Cibo), pope from 1484 to 1492
Alexander VI (Rodrigo Borgia), pope from 1492 to 1503
Pius III (Francesco Todeschini-Piccolomini), pope for eight weeks in 1503
Julius II (Giuliano della Rovere, nephew of Sixtus IV, above), pope from
  1503 to 1513
Leo X (Giovanni de' Medici), pope from 1513 to 1521
Adrian VI (Adrian Dedel), pope from 1522 to 1523
Clement VII (Giulio de' Medici, cousin of Leo X above), pope from 1523
  to 1534

All these popes were alike in combining enormous spiritual power
with a certain measure of temporal power. It's customary to date
the beginning of the Lutheran revolt from 1517; before that the
spiritual power of the popes was largely unquestioned; and even
after that, in most of the Latin countries, it remained supreme, as a
practical matter. On the other hand, the temporal power of the
popes varied enormously, depending on Italian circumstances; and
its application varied enormously, depending on the pope who occu-

pied the seat of Peter, and his concerns. Machiavelli estimates the average life span of a sitting pope at about ten years, and as will be seen from the dates above, that figure is high. So changes of policy were inevitable and very frequent. Three strong, ambitious popes among the first five listed above embroiled the papacy deeply in the Italian political process that Machiavelli was trying to teach his prince to master. But as they took very different lines, and each policy was cut short in mid-career by the death of its maker, the papacy had an erratic, inconsistent influence on Italian politics that Machiavelli bitterly deplores.

Sixtus IV, the first of the three restless and ambitious popes, came to the office with little diplomatic or ecclesiastical experience, because he was the newest of the cardinals when they elected him pope. He began by arranging large international adventures, like an expedition against the Turks and a reconciliation with the Russian Church, but turned to Italian politics, as more feasible, and involved his Papal States in successive wars against the Florentines and the Venetians. To finance his military campaigns, his building programs (including the Sistine Chapel, made famous later by Michelangelo), and a whole flock of hungry relatives, he began the process of milking the church's power to extract money from believers by the sale of indulgences, and the promulgation of new taxes, direct and indirect, on the faithful.

Alexander VI, the second of the activist popes, calls for more specific discussion. Like his predecessor Sixtus, he strained the money-gathering powers of the church to their absolute limits and beyond; like his predecessor Sixtus, he was a lavish and shameless nepotist, pouring money on his relatives. But those relatives were not just nieces and nephews; they were his own illegitimate children. And one of them, Cesare Borgia, Duke of Valentino, is of central importance to Machiavelli's book.

Cesare seems originally to have been destined for the Church; through his father's influence, he was made an archbishop and a cardinal at the age of seventeen. But after only five years he gave up these offices "for the good of his soul," as he said; in fact, he was a reckless, violent man, with a deep streak of personal cruelty. Whether or not all the stories of incest, fratricide, poisoning, and so on that are told about the domestic life of the Borgias are true, we need not decide here. That Cesare Borgia was a formidable fellow in an age of very hard cases indeed, is apparent from the record. And from the first he was the agent of his father's political schemes. These can be roughly outlined as follows. In October 1498, Cesare went to France as legate (agent) for his father; he brought with him a papal bull entitling Louis XII to set aside his first wife and marry Anne of Brittany, thereby completing the unification of France.

Louis also got papal permission, if not encouragement, to assert his claim to the dukedom of Milan at the expense of Ludovico Sforza. In exchange, Cesare got the dukedom of Valentinois in France (hence the Italians always called him Duke Valentino), and a promise of French assistance in his own military affairs in Italy. These affairs called first of all for the unification and strengthening of the Papal States; and then, though Louis was not told this, and would not have liked it had he guessed, for the unification of all Italy under the leadership of Cesare Borgia.

The Papal States comprised a large group of semi-feudal domains and semi-independent cities across the middle of the Italian peninsula. In two campaigns which are carefully described in *The Prince* (they took place in 1499 and 1500–1501), Cesare subdued this area, known as the Romagna. In 1502 a conspiracy was raised against him, by the petty war lords of the district and the powerful Roman family of the Orsini, who saw too late that he was threatening their independent survival. But he put down the conspiracy, trapped its leaders in the little town of Sinigaglia, and on the last day of December 1502, had the two most dangerous of them strangled in their dungeon. As spring turned to summer of 1503, Cesare and his father Alexander stood on the verge of success in their bold and venturesome scheme. One more campaign in northern Italy would enable Cesare to dictate terms to the Italian states, and then to deal on more or less equal terms between France and Spain. But at that crucial moment, Alexander unexpectedly died, just at the time when Cesare himself was deathly ill. Everything depended on the choice of Alexander's successor; and though Cesare was able to manipulate one stopgap pope into office, the wretched man did not live a month; and in the next election, Julius II was named without opposition. He was an old and inveterate enemy of all the Borgias; without support in the Vatican, Cesare was doomed, and he faded away, to die a few years later in an obscure scuffle in Spain.

Meanwhile, though Julius, the third activist pope, retained many of the same general objectives as his predecessor, he pursued them in an entirely different way. Headstrong and volatile, he bullied the Florentines and made war on the Venetians in order to persuade them to join with him driving the French out of Italy. In many of his projects he was successful, partly because nobody expected to see a graybearded Vicar of Christ campaigning at the head of his army through winter mud and snow. But because he was committed to a wholly new set of feuds and loyalties, Julius built his policies at complete cross-purposes with those of the Borgias. Where they had tried to use the French against the Spanish, he tried to use the Spanish against the French, and enlisted the Swiss against both; where they had tried to crush the Orsini family and the magnates of the Romagna, Julius raised many of them up. And as he was sixty years old when he became pope, it was apparent to one and all that his policies would almost certainly be soon reversed by a successor. Hence the fatal conclusion described above, the total prostration of Italy, less than fifteen years after his death.

This, then, in bare outline, is the school in which Machiavelli learned his trade. His was a lean, acute mind to begin with; years of struggle against complex and dangerous circumstances honed it to razor sharpness. Two other influences on it should perhaps be cited. Machiavelli was a learned man; he read widely in the classical authors, especially the historians of the republics, reading Greek authors in Latin translations and Latin authors in the original. He was proud of his learning, and often used it, after the manner of his day, to buttress a contemporary argument. At the same time, he was an instinctive dramatist, and one of the dramatic effects he most enjoyed producing was shock and outrage. Even when writing in private to his friends, he often chose to depict himself in more villainous colors than he could have used, and professed more desperate opinions than he really held. Like a great many Tuscans, he had a horror of being taken for a dupe, and to avoid that appearance did not mind sometimes being considered a monster. The reader who has carefully studied *The Prince* will be able to make his own estimate of Machiavelli's character; but when he has studied the *Discorsi* and the other writings as well, he will be able to make a better one.

Robert M. Adams

Translator's Note

Readers of *The Prince* who study it in Italian after first becoming acquainted with it in English translation are likely to be a little surprised at the complex and various quality of Machiavelli's prose. It is not of a piece throughout, as translations make it seem. There are indeed epigrams and aphorisms with the brief, cruel point of a stiletto; there are also, and more characteristically, complex sentences overburdened by modifiers, laden with subordinate clauses, and serpentine in their length. Machiavelli likes to balance concepts and phrases, to build the structure of his thought out of elegantly juxtaposed contrasts, and draw out the tenor of his thought through a long, linked, circumstantial sentence. By contrast with the Ciceronianisms of his humanist contemporaries, Machiavelli's periods may have seemed brutally swift and abrupt; but standards have changed, and I have not thought it improper to render, on occasion, one of my author's poised yet labyrinthine periods, by four or five separate English sentences. Given a choice between the lucid poise of Machiavelli's ideas, and their close syntactical knotting, I have generally opted for the former. It is, after all, partly a matter of convention; in some ways, Machiavelli used the full stop as we use the paragraph (which was not at his disposal), and the only way to preserve his main intention is to alter the convention by which he punctuated. Besides, a modest advantage really does attach, in translation, to readability. So I have sinned like most of my predecessors, and surrendered one of my author's many qualities in the hope of making the others shine forth more cleanly.

For a couple of crucial words in *Il Principe*, modern English has no true equivalent. The pair *principe-principato* is of course perfectly easy to translate as "prince-principality"; but neither equivalent is very accurate. Machiavelli's prince is not our prince by a long shot—he may, for example, be what we would call a king or he may be a mercenary soldier; he may be elected, like a doge, or be a churchman like a pope. A "principality" in English doesn't include a kingdom or a baronial fief, as "principato" does in Italian; but its worst defect is that it is a learned, cautious word, a kind of neutral word in English. A "principality" is what a "prince" governs, and he is defined chiefly as not a king, not a duke, not a president, not a pope, not a condottiere—not even a prince, really, because in English usage a prince (like the Prince of Wales) doesn't govern, and that's one thing that Machiavelli's *principe* emphatically does. "Prince" and "principality" are chiefly defined in English by negatives, whereas for Machiavelli they are nothing if not positive and inclusive. I have generally translated *principe* as "prince," simply for lack of a better term, though I have turned occasionally to "ruler" or "governor"; and *principato* has become a variety of words, depending on circumstances—"principate," "princedom," "princely state," or just plain "state" when the context has permitted. Further dilemmas arise in translating the words *stato, dominio, paese, provincia, regno, città,* and *patria* (but never *nazione*), which I have had to adjudicate with nothing more decisive than tact. A last, long-standing problem in translating Machiavelli is posed by the word *virtù*, which can mean anything from "strength," "ability," "courage," "manliness," or "ingenuity" to "character," "wisdom," or even (last resort) "virtue." I have translated it in all of these senses and several others; but to preserve an awareness that it's really the same original word behind all these manifestations, I have retained it (in brackets, in the original Italian) next to each different translation.

This diphthong effect (which must be exaggerated if it's to be caught at all) suggests another special stylistic quality of Machiavelli's prose, which is bound to cost a translator a few extra twinges. This is his trick of using adjectives or nouns in carefully distanced pairs, so that one undercuts as well as complements the other. Cesare Borgia, for instance, was gifted with "tanta ferocità e tanta virtù" that with a little luck he might have survived the catastrophe of his father's death. The débâcle of Louis in Lombardy is described as no miracle, but "molto ordinario e ragionevole"—where both adjectives imply, though from different points of view, a wonderfully remote and serene perspective. A virtuoso performance on the double adjective is that which begins with the description of Remirro de Orco's murder as having left the people both "satisfatti e stupidi"; the phrase is picked up, in intricate counterpoint, twelve chapters later, when Septimius Severus is said to have rendered the soldiers "attoniti e stupidi," while leaving the people "reverenti e satisfatti." One translates here for a finely mingled concord and discord: the words are isometric, so to speak.

Another oddity in the original, which there's no reason to do more than mention in passing, is Machiavelli's habit of titling his chapters in Latin and using occasional Latin words in his text, above all when defining logical relationships. *Praeterea, in exemplis, tamen, quodam modo,* and so forth— they give the treatise a slightly dry and schoolmasterish tonality. At the same time, Machiavelli is not above slang and popular metaphors, as when Charles took Italy "with chalk" (*col gesso*); and he is capable of extended passages of rather broad irony, as in his description of the felicity of ecclesiastical states. Among other pleasures of the translator's task is the swift dexterity with which Machiavelli can sketch a story like that of Oliverotto da Fermo, in chapter VIII, with its magnificently climactic last word, *strangolato*; or slash an argument down to the dimensions he has chosen for it:

> E perchè e' non può essere buone legge dove non sono buone arme, e dove sono buone arme conviene sieno buone legge, io lascerò indrieto il ragionare delle legge e parlerò delle arme.

> ("And since there can't be good laws where there aren't good soldiers, and where there are good soldiers there are bound to be good laws, I shall set aside the topic of laws and talk about soldiers.")

Since the question of laws would never have come up if Machiavelli himself hadn't raised it, the ruthless speed with which he here disposes of it suggests a certain impatience with pedagogic formulae which is itself profoundly pedagogic. A prince must learn to look under the surface of antithetical constructs (such as Machiavelli himself has used freely in the first chapters of his book) in order to distinguish the mere formula (the either-or for its own sake) from genuine alternatives. In addition to practical precepts, Machiavelli's language offers the prince a severe model of the lean Tuscan style.

But these are pleasures to be appreciated in the text itself. A book so lucid and taut in its phrasings offers relatively few problems to the translator who has opted for a plain style. The book has been many times rendered, and while some versions are better than others, the spectrum of their variation is not particularly wide, as it generally is in translations of lyric poetry. The problems of Machiavelli's text lie less in its verbal complexities than in its practical implications and applications.

R.M.A.

The Text of

The Prince

Niccolò Machiavelli to the Magnificent Lorenzo de' Medici[1]:

It is a frequent custom for those who seek the favor of a prince to make him presents of those things they value most highly or which they know are most pleasing to him. Hence one often sees gifts consisting of horses, weapons, cloth of gold, precious stones, and similar ornaments suitable for men of noble rank. I too would like to commend myself to Your Magnificence with some token of my readiness to serve you; and I have not found among my belongings anything I prize so much or value so highly as my knowledge of the actions of men, acquired through long experience of contemporary affairs and extended reading in those of antiquity. For a long time I have thought carefully about these matters and examined them minutely; now I have condensed my thoughts into a little volume, and send it to Your Magnificence. Though I know it is unworthy to enter your presence, still I hope you will be graciously pleased to accept this work; since I could give no greater gift than this, which will enable you to grasp in short order everything I have learned over many years and come to understand through many trials and troubles. My book is not stuffed with pompous phrases or elaborate, magnificent words, neither is it decorated with any form of extrinsic rhetorical embroidery, such as many authors use to present or adorn their materials. I wanted my book to be absolutely plain, or at least distinguished only by the variety of the examples and the importance of the subject.

I hope it will not be thought presumptuous if a man of low social rank undertakes to discuss the rule of princes and lay down principles for them. When painters want to represent landscapes, they stand on low ground to get a true view of the mountains and hills; they climb to the tops of the mountains to get a panorama over the valleys. Similarly, to know the people well one must be a prince, and to know princes well one must be, oneself, of the people.

Will Your Magnificence, then, deign to accept this little gift in the same spirit that I send it? If you will read it over and study it carefully, you will recognize in it my most earnest desire that you may achieve that summit of grandeur to which your happy destiny and your other capacities predestine you. And if from that summit Your Magnificence will occasionally glance down at these humble places, you will recognize how unjustly I suffer the bitter and sustained malignity of fortune.

1. When he first wrote it, Machiavelli dedicated his book to Giuliano de' Medici, third son of Lorenzo the Magnificent; after Giuliano's death in 1516, he rededicated it to Lorenzo, duke of Urbino, one of the original Lorenzo's grandsons. See the genealogical table in the Historical Introduction, p. ix.

The form of the dedication reveals Machiavelli's devotion to antiquity; it is an imitation of the Address to Nicocles by the ancient Greek rhetorician Isocrates.

I

DIFFERENT KINDS OF STATES, AND THE DIFFERENT WAYS TO GET THEM

All the states and governments that ever had or now have power over men were and are of two sorts: either republics or princely states. And princely states also are of two sorts: either hereditary, where the family of the ruler has been in control for a long time, or else new. And the new ones are either brand-new, as Milan was for Francesco Sforza,[2] or they are like grafts freshly joined to the hereditary state of a prince who has acquired them, as the kingdom of Naples was to the kingdom of Spain.[3] New acquisitions of this sort are either accustomed to living under a prince, or used to being free; they may be acquired either by force of other people's arms or with one's own, either by fortune or by strength [*virtù*].

II

ON HEREDITARY PRINCIPATES

Setting aside republics, about which I have spoken at length elsewhere,[4] I shall concern myself only with princely states; and, following the outline set down above, I shall describe how these states may be governed and kept in hand.

Let me say, then, that hereditary states which have grown used to the family of their ruler are much less trouble to keep in hand than new ones are; it is simply a matter of not upsetting ancient customs, and of adjusting them instead to meet new circumstances. Hence, if a prince is just ordinarily industrious, he can always keep his position, unless some unusual or excessive act of force deprives him of it. And even if he is dethroned, the slightest mistake by the usurper will enable him to get it back.

We have an Italian example in the duke of Ferrara,[5] who stood

2. Francesco Sforza (1401–66), second of the name. The father, originally named Giacomo or Muzio Attendolo, was a tough peasant who when he became a professional soldier took the name of Sforza, implying energy and ambition. His bastard son Francesco was also a professional soldier for many years, often on both sides of the same feud. When the ancient line of the Visconti expired in Milan (1447), he first defended, then betrayed the republic that replaced it, and in 1450 had himself declared duke of Milan.
3. As noted in the Historical Introduction, the kingdom of Naples, including southern Italy and Sicily, had a tangled succession to which practically everybody in Europe had some sort of claim. After being partitioned between France and Spain by the Treaty of Granada (1500), it was captured for Spain and King Fer-

dinand by brute force of arms (1503). This is the annexation to which Machiavelli alludes. See chapters III and XVIII.
4. In book I of the *Discorsi* on Livy's history, Machiavelli discusses, among other things, republics.
5. Two dukes of Ferrara were involved in the two assaults. Ercole d' Este (1471–1505) had to yield a district of his territory to the Venetians in 1484 as a result of a scuffle over a tax on salt. His successor, Alfonso (1486–1534), refused to join the Venetians and the pope in a holy league against the French, and had to defend himself against both of them. He too lost a couple of cities, but held out, and was ultimately able to regain them. The house of Este had been established in Ferrara for four centuries, but Machiavelli's point would have been less clear-cut had he told us that Al-

up against attacks from the Venetians in 1484, and those of Pope Julius in 1510,[6] for no better reason than that his family had ruled in that district for a long time. Since a prince by birth has fewer reasons and less need to offend his subjects, it follows that he should be better liked; if he has no extravagant vices to make him hateful, it is only natural that he should be popular with his own people. And in the antiquity and continuity of the government, people forget not only the reasons for innovations, but their very existence, because every new change provides a footing to build on another.[7]

III

ON MIXED PRINCIPALITIES

But it is the new state that makes troubles. To begin with, if it is not entirely new but like a graft freshly joined to an old kingdom (so that the two bodies together may be considered mixed), its problems derive from a natural difficulty, common to all new states, which is that all men are ready to change masters in the hope of bettering themselves. In this belief they take up arms against their master, but find themselves deceived when they discover by experience that instead things have got worse. And the reason for this is another natural and ordinary necessity, which is that a new prince must always harm those over whom he assumes authority, both with his soldiers and with a thousand other hardships that are entailed in a new conquest. Thus you have as enemies all those you have harmed in seizing power, and you cannot stay friends with those who put you in power, because you can never satisfy them as they expected. Nor can you use strong medicines against them, because you are under obligations to them. However strong your armies may be, you always need the backing of local people in order to take over a province. This was why Louis XII of France took Milan quickly and lost it just as quickly. The first time, Ludovico's[8] own troops were able to take it back without any help, because those who had opened the gates to Louis were deceived in their hopes, disappointed in the rewards they had expected, and so refused to put up with the annoyances of the new prince.[9]

fonso d' Este was a wily diplomat, a master strategist, a superb gunner, and one of the most skilled soldiers in Europe. His conflating of the gentle, culturally minded Ercole with the tough, resourceful Alfonso makes more impressive his point that a long-established regime is a stable one.

6. Julius II, the pope who attacked Alfonso, was the most warlike Vicar of Christ ever to hold the office. Machia-

velli summarizes his rash, adventurous character in chapter XXV.

7. Machiavelli uses the technical term *l'addentellato* ("crenellation") to express the way in which one policy of a long-continuing government can deliberately be designed to provide a footing on which to construct the next.

8. Ludovico Sforza's.

9. The calamitous story of how the French were first called into Italy by Lu-

It is true, of course, that once lands which have rebelled are conquered a second time, they are not so easily lost, because the ruler who has learned from the revolt will be less hesitant about securing his position by punishing culprits, exposing suspects, and strengthening his own weak points. So that though France could be driven out of Milan the first time by nothing more than Duke Ludovico blustering on the borders of the territory, the second time it was necessary for the whole world to unite against her, destroying her armies or chasing them out of Italy.[1] The reasons for this difference were stated above. In any case, Milan was taken away from France the second time as well as the first.

I have described the general reasons for the first loss; I must now describe the reasons for the second, and see what devices were available to Louis, or to someone else in his position, to keep better hold on his new possessions than the French king did. Let me say, then, that new states which are acquired by, or annexed to, an already existing state are either of the same district and language, or else not. When they are, it is perfectly easy to hold onto them, especially when they are not used to independence. To keep a secure hold, it suffices to have extinguished the line of the previous prince, because in other matters, as long as you keep their old way of life and do not change their customs, men will live quietly, enough. And this has been demonstrated in the cases of Burgundy, Brittany, Gascony, and Normandy, which have been joined with France for so long.[2] There is indeed some difference of language, but the customs are much the same, and so they have been able to get along easily. Whoever has acquired such lands and wants to hold onto them must keep just two things in mind: one is to wipe out the line of the previous prince, and the other is to avoid changing either the laws or the taxes, so that the new acquisitions may become incorporated, in the shortest possible time, with the old kingdom as one single body.

---

dovico Sforza is sketched in the Historical Introduction. The historical details to which Machiavelli is referring are that Louis XII took Milan in the fall of 1499, that Ludovico recovered it on February 5, 1500, and lost it for the second time only a couple of months later. Ludovico ended his life gloomily, a prisoner in remote exile at the lovely but alien castle of Loches, not far from Tours.
1. After the French captured Milan for a second time (April 1500), they held it for more than a decade, and could be dislodged only by Julius II's Lega Santa. Effectively, this was a coalition of papal troops with those of Spain and Venice; on paper it also included the emperor

Maximilian I and Henry VIII of England—hence Machiavelli's phrase, "the whole world." (It was Alfonso d' Este's refusal to join this league that led to Pope Julius's attack on him, see chapter II, note 5, p. 4.)
2. Normandy became part of France in 1204, but the other semi-independent duchies and provinces were all incorporated with France over the last half of the fifteenth century—Gascony in 1453, Burgundy in 1477, and Brittany in 1491. The last of these annexations took place in connection with the marriage of Charles VIII to Anne of Brittany. By completing the consolidation of France, it paved the way for Charles's and Louis's Italian adventures.

But when one acquires new possessions in a district that differs from one's own in language, customs, and laws, that is where troubles arise, and where one needs good luck and plenty of resolution to hold onto them. One of the best and most effective policies is for the new possessor of territories to go there and live. This would make his possession more secure and longer-lasting, as it did for the Turks in Greece.[3] These people would never have been able to hold onto their new possessions, whatever precautions they took, if they had not gone there to live themselves. When you are on the spot, you can see troubles getting started, and take care of them right away; when you do not live there, you hear of them only when they have grown great and there is no longer a cure. Besides this, the new province will not be looted by your officials, and the citizens will be satisfied because they have easy access to the prince. If they want to be good citizens, they have more reason to love him, and if they do not, they have more reason to fear him. Any foreigner who thinks of attacking that state will think twice about it; for the prince who lives on his new possessions can be deprived of them only with the greatest difficulty.

Another, and even better policy, is to set up colonies in one or two places which will serve, so to speak, as the shackles of the state. If he does not do this, the prince will have to maintain immense forces of cavalry and infantry. Colonies are not expensive; for little or nothing you can send them out and keep them up. The only people hurt are those who lose their houses and fields to the new possessors, and they are a very small part of the new state. The ones who are actually hurt, being poor and scattered, cannot possibly do any harm. All the others remain untouched, which is a persuasion to keep quiet; yet they also become fearful of making a mistake and suffering like those who have already been despoiled. I conclude that these colonies are cheaper, do better service, and commit less damage than any other method. Those whom they harm can take no reprisals, because they are left poor and scattered, as I said. And in this connection it should be remarked that men ought either to be caressed or destroyed, since they will seek revenge for minor hurts but will not be able to revenge major ones. Any harm you do to a man should be done in such a way that you need not fear his revenge. If you maintain an army instead of colonies, the expense will be much greater, so that you may have to spend all the money you get from a state in standing guard over it: the profit may even turn to a loss. An army is also much more offensive to the subjects, because the whole state is harmed when the prince drags his army

3. After the Turks captured Constantinople in 1453, under Muhammad II, "the Conqueror," their power was rapidly extended, not only over modern Greece but throughout the Balkans; by deliberate policy, the new occupiers settled onto the land, not to be uprooted till the nineteenth century.

about with him from place to place. Everyone feels this inconvenience, every man becomes an enemy; and these are enemies who can do harm, because, even though beaten, they remain in their own homes. On every count, then, defense by armies is useless, as defense by colonies is useful.

In addition, the man who comes into an alien province of this sort ought to set up at once as head and protector of his weak neighbors, should try to weaken his strong neighbors, and should make sure at all costs that no foreigner gets in who is as powerful as he is. You can always count on the foreigner's being invited in by those who are discontented, through either excess ambition or fear, as was seen long ago when the Aetolians[4] first brought the Romans into Greece. Wherever the Romans went in other provinces, they were always sent for by the local inhabitants. The rule is that as soon as a powerful foreigner enters a district, those in the area who are least powerful flock to him, out of hatred of the strong man who has been ruling over them. Thus the foreigner need be at no pains to gain over these people, because they will quickly and gladly join in the new state he has acquired. He need only take care not to let them have too much strength and authority of their own; then, with his own strength and their support, he can easily put down the powerful men of the district, to become master of the province in all things. Anybody who does not follow this line will quickly lose what he has acquired, or as long as he manages to keep it will find it a source of infinite problems and annoyances.

Whenever the Romans took over a province, this was the policy they followed; they sent out colonies, indulged the less powerful without increasing their strength, broke the powerful, and never allowed any strong foreigners to pick up a following in their lands. I will limit my examples to the Romans in their dealings with the province of Greece, where they indulged the Achaeans and Aetolians, humbled the kingdom of Macedon, and drove Antiochus out of the land.[5] Yet they never let the merits of the Achaeans and Aetolians gain them any authority in the region, never let Philip talk them into being friends till they had reduced his strength, and never let the power of Antiochus gain any foothold in their territory. In each of these instances, the Romans did just what every wise ruler ought to do: you have to keep an eye, not only on pres-

4. In 211 B.C. the Aetolians, a relatively weak confederacy of cities and states in north and central Greece, called in the Romans to help them against Philip of Macedon. Once established in Greece, the Romans easily controlled a balance of power, by means indicated below.

5. The Achaeans were a federal league, similar to the Aetolians and opposed to them. Antiochus III of Syria, invited by the Aetolians and incited by Hannibal (who had taken refuge in the Middle East after his defeat in the Second Punic War), invaded Greece in 196 B.C.; he provided a natural counterweight to Philip V of Macedon. The decisive battle in which the Romans gained control of Greece by defeating Philip was that of Cynoscephelae (197 B.C.); seven years later they destroyed the power of Antiochus at Magnesia in Asia Minor.

ent troubles, but on those of the future, and make every effort to avoid them. When you see the trouble in advance, it is easily remedied, but when you wait till it is on top of you, the antidote is useless, the disease has become incurable. What doctors say about consumption applies here: in the early stages it is hard to recognize and easy to cure, but in the later stages, if you have done nothing about it, it becomes easy to recognize and hard to cure. That is how it goes in affairs of state: when you recognize evils in advance, as they take shape (which requires some prudence to do), you can quickly cure them; but when you have not seen them, and so let them grow till anyone can recognize them, there is no longer a remedy.

Thus the Romans, who could see troubles at a distance, always found remedies for them. They never allowed a trouble spot to remain simply to avoid going to war over it, because they knew that wars don't just go away, they are only postponed to someone else's advantage. Therefore they made war with Philip and Antiochus in Greece, in order not to have to fight them in Italy. At the time, they could have avoided both wars, but they chose not to. They never went by that saying which you hear constantly from the wiseacres of our day, that time heals all things. They trusted rather to their own character [*virtù*] and prudence—knowing perfectly well that time contains the seeds of all things, good as well as bad, bad as well as good.

But, returning to France, let us see if she did any of the things we have described; and I shall talk of Louis rather than Charles, because he controlled Italy for a longer period of time and wrote a more considerable record.[6] You will see that he did exactly the opposite of what should be done to control an alien province.

King Louis was brought into Italy by the ambition of the Venetians, who expected by his coming to get control of half the state of Lombardy. I don't mean to blame the king for his part in the scheme; he wanted a foothold in Italy, and not only had no friends in the province, but found all doors barred against him because of King Charles's behavior.[7] Hence he had to take what friendships he could get; and if he had made no further mistakes in his other arrangements, he might have carried things off very successfully. By taking Lombardy, the king quickly regained the reputation lost by Charles. Genoa yielded, and the Florentines turned friendly; the marquis of Mantua, the duke of Ferrara, the Bentivogli (of Bol-

6. Charles VIII, a thoroughly impractical, visionary fellow, was in Italy for little more than a year (1494–95). Neither Charles nor Louis, both of whom were unprepossessing men physically and intellectually, could have failed to impress Machiavelli. If national organization could raise men like these to positions of power and authority, what could it

not do for Cesare Borgia?
7. Starting from his idea of claiming Naples, Charles dreamed of recapturing Constantinople from the Turks and then advancing through the East like another Alexander; no sooner had he actually appeared in Italy than the Italians joined with Maximilian I, the Holy Roman emperor, to drive him out.

ogna), the countess Forlì, the lords of Faenza, Pesaro, Rimini, Camerino, Piombino, and the people of Lucca, Pisa, and Siena all sought him out with professions of friendship.[8] At this point the Venetians began to see the folly of what they had done, since in order to gain for themselves a couple of districts in Lombardy, they had now made the king master of a third of Italy.

Consider now how easy it would have been for the king to maintain his position in Italy if he had observed the rules laid down above, and become the protector and defender of his new friends. They were many, they were weak, some of them were afraid of the Venetians, others of the Church, hence they were bound to stick by him; and with their help, he could easily have protected himself against the remaining great powers. But no sooner was he established in Milan than he took exactly the wrong tack, helping Pope Alexander to occupy the Romagna. And he never realized that by this decision he was weakening himself, driving away his friends and those who had flocked to him, while strengthening the Church by adding vast temporal power to the spiritual power which gives it so much authority. Having made this first mistake, he was forced into others. To limit the ambition of Alexander and keep him from becoming master of Tuscany, he was forced to come to Italy himself.[9] Not satisfied with having made the Church powerful and deprived himself of his friends, he went after the kingdom of Naples and divided it with the king of Spain.[1] And where before he alone had been the arbiter of Italy, he brought in a rival to whom everyone in the kingdom who was ambitious on his own account or dissatisfied with Louis could have recourse. He could have left in Naples a caretaker king of his own, but he threw him out, and substituted a man capable of driving out Louis himself.[2]

It is perfectly natural and ordinary that men should want to acquire things; and always when men do what they can, they will be praised or not blamed; but when something is beyond them and they try to get it anyhow, then they are in error, and deserve blame. If France could have taken Naples with her own power, she should

8. Machiavelli's list of Louis's friends deliberately includes both big and little *signori*, the rulers of important cities like Bologna and of very little towns indeed, people from every area of northern Italy. In throwing away their support, Louis weakened himself everywhere.

9. Alexander VI was Rodrigo Borgia, father of Cesare and Lucrezia. The armies of Louis XII, led by Gian Giorgio Trivulzio during the first expeditions against Ludovico Sforza, required the presence of the king himself in August, 1502, as a result of Cesare's menacing presence.

1. Charles VIII's claim to the throne of Naples was based on dynastic arguments involving his connection with the house of Anjou; but Naples, as the most remote of the Italian states, was obviously the hardest for a French army to annex or defend. Ferdinand II of Spain was the king with whom Louis arranged (by the treaty of Granada, in 1500) to share Naples.

2. He could have left Frederick of Aragon, the original ruler, in Naples, taking the real power from him but leaving him nominal command of his kingdom; instead, he installed Ferdinand, who promptly drove him out. The modern historian, summarizing the treaty of Granada, assigns most of the disgrace to Ferdinand, most of the folly to Louis: John S. Bridge, *History of France* (Oxford, 1929), III, 137–40.

have done so; if she could not, she should not have split the kingdom with the Spaniards. The division of Lombardy that she made with the Venetians was excusable, since it gave Louis a foothold in Italy; the division of Naples with Spain was an error, since there was no such necessity for it.

Thus Louis committed these five errors: he put down the weaker powers; he increased the strength of a major power; he introduced a very powerful foreigner in the midst of his new subjects; he never took up residence among them; and he never set up any colonies. And yet all these mistakes, if he had lived, might not have ruined him, if he had not made a sixth, in depriving the Venetians of their power.[3] Indeed, if he had not previously made the Church powerful, or brought Spain into Italy, putting down the Venetians might have been perfectly reasonable and necessary. But when he had taken the other steps, he should never have agreed to their ruin, because while they remained powerful, they would have kept everyone else out of Lombardy. The reason is simply that the Venetians would never have let anyone else into Lombardy unless they were in control; nobody would have wanted to take Lombardy from France just to give it to the Venetians; and nobody would have had courage enough to attack the two of them together. And if someone puts up the argument that King Louis gave the Romagna to Pope Alexander, and the kingdom of Naples to Spain, in order to avoid a war, I would answer as I did before: that you should never let things get out of hand in order to avoid war. You don't avoid such a war, you merely postpone it, to your own disadvantage. And if someone else should cite the oath that the king swore to the pope,[4] promising to undertake this enterprise in exchange for the annulment of his marriage and the post of cardinal for Rouen, my answer will be given later on, when I discuss the promises of princes and how they should be kept.

Thus King Louis lost Lombardy because he did not observe any of the rules established by others who have taken provinces and tried to keep them. None of this is in any way miraculous, but perfectly ordinary and reasonable. And I talked over this whole subject at Nantes with the cardinal of Rouen when Valentino (as people

3. When he joined in the League of Cambrai (1508) under the leadership of Julius II to take part in a war against the Venetians, Louis sealed his own doom. The victory of Vailà or Agnadello (May 14, 1509), which put the Venetians out of circulation on the mainland, led directly to the formation of the Lega Santa (see note 1, page 6), in which they were allowed to take a subordinate part for purposes of driving the French from Italy.
4. In order to retain possession of Brittany by marrying Anne of Brittany, widow of Charles VIII (see note 2, page

6), Louix XII had to get a dispensation from Alexander VI to divorce his first wife, Joanne. In addition, he wanted his favorite, George d'Amboise, archbishop of Rouen, to be made cardinal. In exchange for these papal favors, Louis agreed with Alexander VI to help the pope get the Romagna, and to undertake the expedition against Naples—to which both pope and king asserted an historic claim. Louis felt he had to honor this promise—which, as made to Alexander, might have been merely very dangerous—with his successor Julius II, with whom it was disastrous.

generally called Cesare Borgia, the son of Pope Alexander) was occupying the Romagna.[5] Actually, the cardinal told me that Italians knew nothing about war, and I told him that the French knew nothing about politics; since, if they knew the first thing about it, they would never allow the Church to grow so great. It has been our experience in Italy that the Church and Spain have grown powerful through the influence of France, and that their power caused her ruin. From this we can draw a general rule, which never fails or only rarely: the man who makes another powerful ruins himself. The reason is that he gets power either by shrewdness or by strength, and both qualities are suspect to the man who has been given the power.

IV

WHY THE SUCCESSORS OF ALEXANDER AFTER HIS DEATH DID NOT LOSE THE KINGDOM HE HAD CONQUERED FROM DARIUS

Seeing how hard it is to hold onto a newly acquired state, somebody might wonder why after the death of Alexander, when he had conquered Asia in just a few years and had barely settled into power, the land did not rebel, as you might have thought it would; on the contrary, Alexander's successors kept their hold on it, and had no problems in keeping it other than those arising from their own ambitions and consequent difficulties with one another.[6] I answer that all kingdoms of which we have any knowledge are governed in one of two ways: either by a single prince with everyone else as servants, who by his appointment and permission assist him in the task of ruling; or by a prince with the aid of barons, who hold that rank, not by the prince's grace, but by right of birth in an ancient family. Barons of this sort have states and subjects of their own, who recognize them as masters and are naturally fond of them. States governed by a prince and his servants grant the prince more authority because in the whole district there is nobody who can claim real power except the prince; when other people are obeyed, they are obeyed as ministers and officials, and command no affection in their own persons.

Contemporary examples of these two different sorts of government are to be found in Turkey and France. The whole monarchy of Turkey is governed by a single master; everyone else is his serv-

5. Machiavelli was on a diplomatic mission to France in 1500, i.e., just when Cesare Borgia and his father were starting to gain control of the Romagna, and must have talked with George d'Amboise, the cardinal of Rouen, at that time.

6. When Alexander died abruptly in 323 B.C., power was divided among his main lieutenants, Antipater, Antigonus, Ptolemy, and Perdiccas. As these men had already been granted wide governmental as well as military power (they were satraps of districts as well as generals of the army), they adapted easily to independent rule. The exception which Machiavelli makes (in saying the only trouble they got into came from their own quarrels) is accurate but it is not insignificant; their quarrels were continuous, immensely complex, and brutally destructive.

ant; he divides his kingdom into districts, sending different administrators to each, and changing them around as he thinks best.[7] But the king of France is placed in the midst of a great many noblemen of long standing, each recognized by his own subjects in his own district, and held in esteem by them. They have their different privileges; the king himself cannot meddle with these, except at his peril. Comparing the two states, anyone can see that, though conquering the Turkish state might be hard, once conquered, it would be easy to hold. On the other hand, to take the state of France would be relatively easy in some ways, but to hold onto it would be very hard.

The problem in gaining control of Turkey is that you cannot hope to be invited in by the district rulers, or to make use of a palace revolt in gaining a foothold. The reasons are given above: since they are all the slaves of their master and obliged to him, there is no easy way of corrupting them; and even if you succeeded, there is not much advantage to be hoped from it, because the man you corrupt cannot bring along many followers, as noted above. Hence, anyone who attacks the Turks may expect to find them completely united, and had better count on his own strength rather than any internal disorders. But once they are thoroughly beaten, and crushed so their army cannot reform, there is nothing more to fear except the family of the prince; once his line is extinct, there is no other danger, since nobody else has any standing with the people; and as the victor before his victory could expect no help from them, so, after it, he has nothing to fear from them.

Quite the other way in a kingdom like France, which you can easily get into by winning over to your cause some baron of the kingdom; one or another of them will always be discontented or restless for a change.[8] As I said before, these people can open the way for you, and make your victory an easy one. But after that, holding onto the power will involve you in infinite difficulties, both with those who helped you in and with those you have beaten. Extinguishing the royal house will not suffice, because those local nobles will remain to head up new rebellions against you; and since you can neither make them happy nor wipe them out completely, you will lose control at the first unlucky accident.

Now, if you ask yourself what kind of government Darius had, you will find it very much like that of Turkey, and so Alexander

7. Two great sultans ruled Turkey in Machiavelli's time: Muhammad II the Conqueror (1451–81) and Bayezid II (1481–1512). The first instituted and the second consolidated a highly efficient organization of centralized government, and both made use of the newly created elite corps of janizaries to control enemies at home and abroad. Machiavelli evidently equates their government with that of Darius as hard to take but easy to hold.
8. Henry V of England had, for example, made expert use of the dukes of Burgundy to gain a foothold in France early in the fifteenth century; even as Machiavelli wrote, the duke of Savoy was intriguing with Austria for protection against annexation by France.

had to smash the whole thing, and take control of the country. But when that was done, and Darius was dead, the state was securely in Alexander's hands, for the reasons described above. And if his successors had remained united, they could have ruled the empire at their leisure, because the only disorders that arose were those they stirred up themselves. But states organized like that of France cannot possibly be held so easily. Hence the frequent rebellions of Spain, France, and Greece against the Romans—they were due to the many local powers in those districts.⁹ As long as the memory of those powers persisted, the Romans were always uneasy in their control of the provinces; they became secure masters only after memories faded in the course of the empire's long duration and as a result of its great strength. Even afterward, when the Romans began fighting among themselves, each one was able to attract a following in the provinces, depending on the authority he had built up there; and the provinces, once the family line of their former rulers was extinct, refused to recognize anyone but Romans. All these things considered, no one should be surprised at the ease with which Alexander grasped the whole government of Asia, nor at the difficulties other men have had in maintaining possession, like Pyrrhus and many others.¹ Success in this matter depends not on the greater or lesser skill [*virtù*] of the conqueror, but on the different circumstances of the vanquished.

V

HOW CITIES OR STATES SHOULD BE RULED WHICH LIVED BY THEIR
OWN LAWS BEFORE BEING TAKEN

When states are acquired, as I've said, which have got in the way of living at liberty and under their own laws, there are just three ways to hold onto them: the first is to destroy them;² the second is

9. Spain was a long time being Romanized, and resisted (especially among the mountain tribes) well into the empire. But Gaul, after its conquest by Caesar, was almost a model of docility—there were few and only short-lived revolts against the Roman power; and Greece, apart from the Mithridatic incursion of 88–84 B.C., was almost as well behaved. Historical inaccuracy is unusual in Machiavelli and his several overstatements here suggest that he may be concerned to make a categorical distinction between oriental dynasties (Darius, the sultans) and European governments (less centralized and more like a confederation of local powers).

1. Pyrrhus of Epirus (died 272 B.C.) was a Greek kinglet related to Alexander the Great. He was called to Italy in 281 by the city of Tarentum, to help defend Magna Graecia against encroaching Roman power. Both in Greece and in Italy, he mounted dashing and momentarily successful military campaigns, but could strike no permanent roots anywhere.

2. What Machiavelli means by this deliberately bitter phrase is not quite unequivocal. He could mean physical demolition of the captured cities and dispersal of their inhabitants; and instances of this sort of thing are cited below. But there is no example of anything like that happening during the Renaissance, in Italy; and Machiavelli is particularly unlikely to have recommended this policy "seriously" because all through this chapter it is apparent that Florence herself (as a city still vibrant with republican instincts) is the city he has in mind. Writing to a Medici, he would recommend the demolition of Florence only as a way of saying, "*unless* you go to live there, you may actually have to destroy your city."

to go there and live in person; and the third is to let them continue living under their own laws, levying tribute on them, and creating a government of a few people who will keep the state friendly toward you. Such a government, being the prince's actual creation, knows it cannot stand without his friendship and power; therefore it will do anything to maintain him in authority. And a city which is used to freedom can be held more easily by means of its own citizens than in any other manner—always supposing you want it to survive at all.

Examples are to be found among the Spartans and Romans. The Spartans held onto Athens and Thebes by creating oligarchies there, though in the end they lost both cities.[3] The Romans, in order to hold onto Capua, Carthage, and Numantia, destroyed them, and therefore never lost them.[4] They wanted to hold Greece in about the same way the Spartans did, making it free and leaving it under its own laws, but they were not successful; so that in the end, they had to destroy many cities in the province in order to hold it. And in fact there is no sure way to hold onto cities except to destroy them. Any man who becomes master of a city accustomed to freedom, and does not destroy it, may expect to be destroyed by it. Because such a city, when it rebels, can always call on the name of liberty and its ancient ordinances, which no passage of time or bestowal of gifts can ever cause to be forgotten. No matter what measures one takes for the present or future, if one does not divide or disperse the inhabitants, they will never forget that name or those ordinances; and, at the slightest incident, they will instantly have recourse to them. That was what happened in Pisa a full hundred years after it had first been placed in subjection to the Florentines.[5] But when cities and provinces are used to living under a prince, and his line is destroyed, they fall on great difficulties: on the one hand, they are used to obeying, yet they no longer have their old prince; they cannot agree among themselves to set up a new prince, yet they do not know how to live in freedom. As a result, they are slow to take up arms, and a prince can easily take them over and make

3. After the fall of Athens in 405 B.C., a briefly oligarchy under Spartan control replaced the previously democratic government, and Sparta's relation to Thebes, previously amicable, changed sharply. In 382 B.C., a Spartan force occupied the citadel of Thebes, and held possession for three years.
4. These three cities, Capua in Italy (211 B.C.), Carthage in Africa (146 B.C.), and Numantia in Spain (133 B.C.) were captured after long and desperate sieges, and actually dismantled as municipalities: the physical plant was torn down, the population dispersed, the laws and constitutions abrogated. All three were later reconstituted, but from scratch.

It is possible that behind the appar-

ently classical reference to Capua, a potent contemporary allusion may lie. In the course of the Neapolitan war between France and Spain, Capua was captured on July 24, 1501 by a French army under D'Aubigny and Cesare Borgia. While the city was not exactly "destroyed," estimates place the number of casualties in the general massacre, orgy, and looting spree that followed capitulation, at about 7,000.
5. Pisa, purchased by Florence in 1405, subjugated in 1406, and very harshly treated through the fifteenth century, asserted its liberty as a result of the invasion of Charles VIII in 1494; after four bitter campaigns and sieges, the Florentines finally won it back again in June, 1509.

himself sure of them. But in republics, you will find greater life, greater hate, more desire of revenge; memories of ancient liberties cannot and will not give them any rest; so that the safest way with them is either to wipe them out or to settle among them.

VI

ABOUT NEW PRINCEDOMS ACQUIRED WITH ONE'S OWN ARMS AND ENERGY [*Virtù*]

No one should be surprised if, in talking about states completely new in their rulers and constitutions, I make use of the very greatest examples. Men almost always prefer to walk in paths marked out by others and pattern their actions through imitation. Even if he cannot follow other people's paths in every respect, or attain to the merit [*virtù*] of his originals, a prudent man should always follow the footsteps of the great and imitate those who have been supreme. His own talent [*virtù*] may not come up to theirs, but at least it will have a sniff of it. Thus he will resemble skilled archers who, seeing how far away the target lies, and knowing the strength [*virtù*] of their bow, aim much higher than the real target, not because they expect the arrow to fly that far, but to accomplish their real end by aiming beyond it.

Let me say, then, that a new prince taking charge of a completely new kingdom will have more or less trouble in holding onto it, as he himself is more or less capable [*virtuoso*]. And since this transition, from private citizen to prince, presupposes either skill [*virtù*] or luck, it would seem that either one or other of these two qualities might ease some of the difficulties, at least partly. Still, the less one trusts to chance, the better one's hope of holding on. It helps, too, if the prince is forced, for lack of other states, to come and live personally among his new subjects. Turning to those who have become princes by their own powers [*virtù*] and not by accident, I would say that the most notable were Moses, Cyrus, Romulus, Theseus, and a few others.[6] And though we should not consider Moses, because he was simply an agent sent by God to do certain things, he still should be admired, if only for that grace which made him worthy of talking with God. But let us turn to Cyrus and the others who acquired or founded kingdoms. You will find them all deserving of admiration; and if you consider their individual actions and decrees, they will be found not much different from those of Moses, who had such a great teacher. When we look into their actions and their lives, we will find that fortune provided nothing for them but

---

6. The heroes on whom Machiavelli proposes that the realistically minded prince pattern his behavior are all more or less mythical; they all founded, not simply national organizations, but enduring civilizations. Machiavelli plants these great, vague prototypes here, at least in part, for the rhetorical effect he will get from reinvoking them in chapter XXVI.

an opportunity; that gave them material, on which they could impose whatever form they chose.[7] Without the opportunity their strength [*virtù*] of mind would have been vain, and without that strength [*virtù*] the opportunity would have been lost.

Hence it was necessary for Moses to find the children of Israel in Egypt, enslaved and oppressed by the Egyptians, so that they should be disposed to follow him, in order to escape from that servitude.[8] For Romulus it was necessary that he not remain in Alba, but should be exposed at birth, so that he might become ruler of Rome and founder of that country.[9] It was necessary that Cyrus should find the Persians unhappy with the rule of the Medes, and the Medes soft and effeminate from years of peace.[1] Theseus could never have exercised his energy [*virtù*] if he had not found the Athenians in confusion.[2] Specific occasions brought these happy men to power, and their unusual abilities [*virtù*] enabled them to seize the occasion and so to make their countries noble and very fortunate.

These men and men of this sort, who become princes through their own strength of character [*per vie virtuose*] may have troubles gaining the power, but they find it easy to hold onto. Their troubles in getting power derive partly from the new laws and measures they have to adopt in order to set up their state and secure themselves. And it is worth noting that nothing is harder to manage, more risky in the undertaking, or more doubtful of success than to set up as the introducer of a new order. Such an innovator has as enemies all the people who were doing well under the old order, and only halfhearted defenders in those who hope to profit from the new. This halfheartedness derives partly from fear of opponents who have the law on their side, and partly from human skepticism, since men don't really believe in anything new till they have had solid experience of it. This is why, whenever the enemies of a new state have occasion to attack it, they do so furiously, while its friends come only languidly to its defense, so that the whole venture is likely to collapse.[3]

7. The scholastic distinction of *materia* and *forma* carried with it the overtone that the former was feminine, the latter masculine; the male provided shape and soul for what, without him, would be mere inchoate shape or mass (*mola*). Thus the prince's *virtus* is the male principle of the marriage between ruler and people.

8. On the bondage of the children of Israel, see Exodus 2–6.

9. The story of Romulus is familiar from the first books of Livy and from Plutarch.

1. Herodotus, notoriously devoted to fables, is one major authority for the life of Cyrus; Xenophon's *Cyropaedia* is also full of moral purpose and hence of pious legend.

2. Theseus, who is even more fabulous than any of the others, is known to us through the collection of legends summarized by Plutarch—who makes the comparison with Romulus.

3. It is a surprisingly rational view of human nature that Machiavelli takes here; actually, men often attribute strictly irrational values to things of which they have no experience at all—as Machiavelli explicitly recognizes in the *Discorsi*, I, 53.

Still, if we are to discuss the matter thoroughly, we shall have to ask if these innovators stand on their own feet, or depend on the help of others—that is, whether they have to go begging in order to carry out their work, or can use force of their own. In the first case, they are bound to fail without accomplishing anything; but when they depend on their own energies and can make use of force, then they hardly ever come to grief. This is why armed prophets always win and unarmed prophets lose. Apart from all the factors considered above, it is the nature of people to be fickle; to persuade them of something is easy, but to make them stand fast in that conviction is hard. Hence things must be arranged so that when they no longer believe they can be compelled to believe by force.[4] If Moses, Cyrus, Theseus, and Romulus had had no weapons, they could never have imposed their institutions on their peoples for so long. In our own times, there is the example of Fra Girolamo Savonarola, who collapsed with all his new ordinances as soon as the people ceased to believe in him; he had no way of keeping the backsliders in line or of converting the doubters.[5] Such men meet with great difficulties in their rise to power; all their dangers are on the way up, and must be overcome by their talents [*virtù*]; but once they are on top, once they are held in veneration, and have destroyed all their envious rivals, they remain powerful, secure, honored, and happy.

To these exalted examples, I'd like to add a lesser one; but it parallels the others, in a way, and may stand for a whole class. It is Hiero of Syracuse.[6] When he rose from a private citizen to prince, he owed nothing to fortune except the opportunity; the Syracusans were oppressed, and elected him general, then raised him to prince when he proved worthy. He was a man of such character [*virtù*], even as a private citizen, that somebody said of him "the only thing he needs to be a ruler is a kingdom." He abolished the old army and formed a new one, broke the old alliances and formed new ones; and, when he had his own soldiers and his own allies, he could build on that foundation any structure he wanted. For him too the throne was hard to acquire but easy to keep.

4. Practically the first act of Moses when he descended from Sinai with the tablets was to get the sons of Levi to massacre three thousand worshippers of the Golden Calf; see Exodus 32: 19–28. Romulus murdered Remus and his associate Titus Tatius, acts which Plutarch describes and Machiavelli warmly endorses in the *Discorsi*, I, 9.
5. Savonarola was undone, less by the fickleness of his followers, than by the hostility of Alexander VI and the great houses of Florence, among whom, primarily, were the Medici. Given the sort of followers to whom Savonarola appealed, it is doubtful if force on his part would have persuaded them of anything: Machiavelli himself condemns as self-destructive the one infraction of the law that Savonarola condoned (*Discorsi*, I, 45).
6. This was Hiero II of Syracuse who lived in the third century B.C., and about whom Machiavelli could have learned in Livy XXI, 49–51, and in Polybius I, 8, and VII, 7; but the phrase that he quotes is from the historian Justin.

VII

ABOUT NEW STATES ACQUIRED WITH OTHER PEOPLE'S ARMS AND BY GOOD LUCK

When simple good luck raises private citizens to the rank of prince, they have little trouble in rising, but plenty in holding their positions. They have no troubles along the way, because they are practically flying; all the problems arise when they are in place. These are the people who get control of a state either by buying it, or as a gift from someone. Such things happened often in Greece, in the cities of Ionia and Hellespont, where Darius created a great many princes to augment his own glory and security;[7] and some Roman emperors attained that rank after starting as private citizens, by corrupting the soldiers.[8] Men of this sort depend entirely on the good will and good fortune of those who raised them up, and these are two extremely volatile, unstable things. The new rulers do not know how to hold what they have been given, and they could not do it if they did know. They don't know because, unless they are men of great shrewdness and vigor [*virtù*], they cannot be expected to have the knack of command after living all their lives as private citizens. And they cannot, because they have no troops of their own, which are devoted to them and trustworthy. Besides, states which spring up suddenly, like everything else in nature which springs up in a day, cannot have a network of roots and branches; they are destroyed by the first storm that strikes. Of course it may be that men who become princes overnight have so much natural astuteness [*virtù*] that they quickly prepare themselves to preserve what fortune has showered on them; the foundations that other men construct before becoming princes, they may be able to construct afterwards.

I'd like to illustrate these two ways of becoming prince, by strength [*virtù*] or by luck, with two examples taken from our own times: they are Francesco Sforza and Cesare Borgia. Francesco started as a private citizen, and used the appropriate means with great shrewdness [*virtù*] to become duke of Milan: he won power in the teeth of a thousand difficulties, and maintained it with little effort.[9] On the other hand, Cesare Borgia, popularly called Duke Valentino, acquired authority through his father's fortune and lost it in the same way: he did so in spite of the fact that he used every means and took all the precautions that a wise and able [*virtuoso*]

---

7. Darius the Great (died 485 B.C.) created many local princedoms and satrapies throughout his extensive realms: see Herodotus, III.
8. Reviewing the Roman emperors in chapter XIX, Machiavelli particularly emphasizes Septimius Severus as one who rose to power and maintained his rule by gratifying the soldiery.
9. On Francesco Sforza, see above, chapter I, note 2, p. 4.

man should, to root himself in those states which had been granted him by the arms and fortune of others. As I noted above, the man who does not lay his foundations in advance may with great effort [*virtù*] build them later—but he will always do so with inconvenience to the architect and danger to the structure. If, then, we consider all the duke's proceedings, we shall see that he laid strong foundations for future power; and I don't consider it irrelevant to describe them, since I can't imagine better advice to give a new prince than the example of his actions. If he didn't profit by his own measures, the fault was not his, but resulted from an extraordinary and extreme piece of bad luck.

When Alexander VI set out to make his son the duke a great man, he faced many difficulties, both immediate and long-term. First, he saw no way to make him master of any state except one of those belonging to the Church; and, looking over the Papal States, he realized that the duke of Milan and the Venetians would never consent to that, because Faenza and Rimini were already under the protection of the Venetians.[1] Besides, he saw that the armies of Italy, especially those that he might have been able to use himself, were under the control of those who had reason to fear the Pope's power and whom he therefore could not trust—members of the Orsini and Colonna families, and their allies.[2] Therefore he was first obliged to upset existing arrangements and create disorder among the Italian states in order to gain secure control over some of them. This was easy enough because he found that the Venetians, for reasons of their own, had decided to let the French back into Italy. Far from opposing this project, the pope hastened it along by dissolving the first marriage of King Louis.[3] Thus the king entered Italy with the help of the Venetians and the consent of Alexander; and he was no sooner in Milan than the pope got from him troops for the conquest of the Romagna, which he quickly overcame with the help of the king's reputation.[4]

Now when the duke was possessed of the Romagna, and the Colonna people were beaten, he wanted to keep his winnings and

1. On Cesare Borgia, natural son of Pope Alexander VI, see the Historical Introduction.
2. The Orsini and Colonna families were famous Roman tribes or gangs, in immemorial feud with one another; on the Pope's traditional trouble in putting down one without exalting the other, see chapter XI.
3. Cesare was the papal legate who, in a spectacularly lavish expedition (October-December 1498) brought Louis papal permission to set aside his first wife Jeanne in order to marry Anne of Brittany. Many basic decisions about the future of Italy must have been reached during the visit, but we must guess at

them from the tangled and perhaps unintended results.
4. Cesare Borgia made two formal campaigns in the Romagna, the first May 1499 to February 1500; his army consisted mostly of French, Gascon, and Swiss troops, and with these forces he captured Imola (Nov. 24) and Forlì (Dec. 17). The second campaign was October 1500 to June 1501, with a larger army, better equipped and better disciplined, and including a good many Italian mercenaries among the usual miscellaneous cosmopolites. At the head of this crowd he took Rimini (Oct. 10), Pesaro (Oct. 27), and Faenza after a longer siege (April 25, 1501).

push ahead, but two things held him back: one was that his army did not seem trustworthy, and the other was the French position. That is, the Orsini troops he had been using might play him false, endangering not only his new projects but his old winnings; and the king also could not be trusted. He had a hint of the mood among the Orsini when, after storming Faenza, he attacked Bologna, and found them very halfhearted in the assault. As for the king, he learned his mind when, after taking Urbino, he moved on Tuscany, and the king made him pull back from that enterprise.[5] Hence the duke decided he would no longer depend on the weapons and fortune of others. So first he moved to weaken the Orsini and Colonna factions in Rome, by recruiting to his cause all their followers who were of noble rank, enrolling them in his party, and giving them generous pensions and posts, according to their station, in the army or the government. In a few months, therefore, all factional enthusiasm faded from their minds, and their devotion turned toward the duke. After this he watched for a chance to wipe out the Orsini family, as he had already broken up the house of Colonna. A good occasion turned up, and he made even better use of it. For when the Orsini realized, too late, that the power of the duke and the Church was making for their ruin, they called a gathering of the clan at La Magione near Perugia.[6] This was the reason why Urbino rebelled and all those disorders occured in the Romagna, with infinite peril to the duke; but he overcame them all, with the aid of the French. Once he had regained his reputation, he put no furthur trust in the French, nor in any other outside forces, since he found them too risky; so he turned to trickery. And he was so skillful in disguising his intentions that the Orsini themselves sought to be reconciled with him through the mediation of Signor Paolo,[7] whom the duke tried to placate in every way conceivable, giving him money, fine clothes, and horses. Thus the simple-mindedness of the Orsini brought them to Sinigaglia, and into the duke's hands. And when he had killed all the leaders, and won over their followers to be his friends, the duke had laid excellent foundations for his power, since he possessed the entire Romagna, along with the duchy of Urbino; most important of all, he not only controlled the

---

5. After the fall of Faenza, Bologna was menaced in late April and early May, but never put to the assault. Urbino fell to the duke in June 1502; on May 15 Florence had had to hire the duke as its general and "protector" (promising him 36,000 ducats a year for three years) in order to preserve its independence. But Florence was already, supposedly, under the "protection" of the king of France. "Protection" seems to have meant in Renaissance Italy very much what it means today to a New York bookmaker or brothel keeper.

6. Present at the gathering at La Magione near Perugia in early October 1502 were various Orsini, Pandolfo Petrucci of Siena, Ermete Bentivoglio, and various Baglioni of Perugia.

7. Signor Paolo is Paolo Orsini, head of the house; Vitellozzo Vitelli and Oliverotto da Fermo were strangled at Sinigaglia on the last day of December 1502; the duke of Gravina and Paolo Orsini a few days later.

Romagna, but controlled it as a friend, and won over the people of the district as soon as they began to savor the benefits of his rule.

The next point is worthy of special note, and of imitation by others; I don't want to pass lightly over it. When the duke took over the Romagna, he found it had been controlled by impotent masters, who instead of ruling their subjects had plundered them, and had given them more reason for strife than unity, so that the whole province was full of robbers, feuds, and lawlessness of every description. To establish peace and reduce the land to obedience, he decided good government was needed; and he named Messer Remirro de Orco, a cruel and vigorous man, to whom he gave absolute powers. In short order this man pacified and unified the whole district, winning thereby great renown. But then the duke decided such excessive authority was no longer necessary, and feared it might become odious; so he set up a civil court in the middle of the province, with an excellent judge and a representative from each city. And because he knew that the recent harshness had generated some hatred, in order to clear the minds of the people and gain them over to his cause completely, he determined to make plain that whatever cruelty had occurred had come, not from him, but from the brutal character of the minister. Taking a proper occasion, therefore, he had him placed on the public square of Cesena one morning, in two pieces, with a piece of wood beside him and a bloody knife.[8] The ferocity of this scene left the people at once stunned and satisfied.

But, to return from our digression, let me say that the duke now found himself powerful, fairly safe from immediate dangers, and in charge of his own armies; he had largely destroyed those forces which, if they were near, might have destroyed him. But he still had to look to the king of France, before going on with his program; because he knew that the king, who had belatedly recognized his error, would not now support him. For this reason, he began to look for new alliances and to temporize with the French during their expedition toward the kingdom of Naples against the Spaniards who were besieging Gaeta. His intention was to gain Spanish support; and he would quickly have done it, if Alexander had lived.[9]

Such were his policies with regard to present matters. As for the future, he had to be concerned lest a new successor to the Church prove hostile to him, and try to take back what Alexander had given. Against this possibility he tried to secure himself in four

8. Remirro de Orco (or Ramiro de Lorqua, to call him by his native Spanish name) was appointed lieutenant general of the Romagna March 1500, imprisoned December 22, 1502, and put to death the morning after Christmas day.

9. Gaeta, a few miles north of Naples, was a first center of fighting between French and Spanish troops after the breakdown of the Treaty of Granada. Alexander VI died August 18, 1503, of a sudden fever, and Pius III was not elected till September 22.

ways: first he planned to wipe out all the families of those noble-men he had ruined, so the pope would not be able to use them as pretexts to strike at him; second, he proposed to enlist all the gentry of Rome, as I said before, and use them to keep the pope in check; third, to make the College of Cardinals his own creatures, so far as he could; and fourth, to acquire so much power of his own, before the pope died, that he could resist a first onslaught. Of these four projects, by the death of Alexander, he had completed three, and the fourth he was still working on. He had killed as many of the ruined nobles as he could, and very few escaped; he had all the Roman bravos; and in the College, he controlled a good majority. As for new power, he had plans to control Tuscany, and he was already master of Perugia and Piombino, while Pisa was under his protection. And since he no longer needed to be concerned with France (because the French had already been stripped of Naples by the Spaniards, so that both of them now needed his friendship), he was ready to grasp at Pisa.[1] After that, Lucca and Siena would quickly have given in, partly to spite the Florentines, and partly from fear; and the Florentines could never have done anything about it. If he had carried this off (and in fact he was doing so in the very year when Alexander died), he would have had such strength and prestige that he could have stood alone, depend-ing no longer on other people's fortunes and forces, but only on his own power and skill [*virtù*]. But Alexander died just five years after the duke first drew his sword, leaving him with the govern-ment of Romagna in good order, but with all the rest up in the air, between two very powerful hostile armies; and the duke himself was deathly sick. Yet the duke was a man of such savagery and courage [*virtù*], and he understood so perfectly how to win men over or ruin them, and the foundations were so strong that he had laid down in so short a period, that if he hadn't had those armies on his back, or hadn't been sick himself, he would have pulled through all his difficulties. And that his foundations were solid was obvious, since the Romagna waited more than a month for him; in Rome, even when he was half-dead, he was safe from attack; and though the Baglioni, the Vitelli, and the Orsini came to Rome, they could not raise any force against him.[2] Perhaps he could not have made pope the man he wanted, but he could have kept from the office anyone he did not want. If he had been in good health the day of

1. Perugia came under Cesare's control in February 1503; Piombino had been his since September 3, 1501; Pisa was under his "condotta" because, having de-clared itself independent of Florence, it had looked to France for protection, and when the French position became unten-able (because the Spaniards had driven them out of Naples), only Cesare could restrain the Florentines.

2. Cesare had many enemies, and when he was sick they all came to finish him off; but indeed they could make little headway against him. Pius III, who suc-ceeded Alexander, was moribund when elected, and survived his coronation by a matter of only ten days (October 8–18, 1503).

Alexander's death, everything would have been easy for him. He told me himself, on the day Julius II was made pope, that he had thought of everything which could happen at his father's death, and had found a solution for everything; only he never thought that when his father was dying he too would be at death's door.

Looking over all the duke's actions, then, I find nothing with which to reproach him; rather I think I'm right in proposing him, as I have done, as a model for all those who rise to power by means of the fortune and arms of others. Being a magnanimous man of lofty ambitions, he was bound to govern in that way; and the only obstacles to his plan were the cutting short of Alexander's life and his own illness. Any man coming into a new state, therefore, who finds it necessary to guard against enemies and win friends, to over-come by force or fraud, to make himself loved and feared by the people, followed and respected by his troops—if you have to destroy those who can or might hurt you, revamp old laws with new mea-sures, be severe and indulgent, magnanimous and liberal, disband old armies and replace them with new, meanwhile managing your rela-tions with other princes and kings in such a way that they will be glad to help you and cautious about harming you, you can find no better recent examples than those of his career. His only error lay in making Julius pope, where he simply made a bad choice; because, as I said, though he couldn't make his own man pope, he could keep anyone else from the office.[3] And he should never have allowed any cardinals to become pope whom he had injured, or who, on their election, might have had reason to fear him. For men injure others either through fear or hate. Those whom he had already injured were, among others, San Pietro in Vincoli, Colonna, San Giorgio, and Ascanio; all the others, if elected, would have had reason to fear him, except for Rouen and the Spaniards.[4] The latter were all bound to him by nationality and obligation; the former had nothing

3. In the elections of September 1503, which led to the brief papacy of Pius, there were originally fifteen votes for Carvajal (a Spaniard), fourteen for della Rovere, and thirteen for Rouen; Pius was elected as a compromise candidate when all three leaders agreed to with-draw. In the October elections which re-sulted in the election of Julius II, there was no significant division, since Rouen had given up hope; thus Julius was elected on the first ballot.

4. Cardinals may be known by the Roman church to which they are as-signed, by their family names, or even by their given (Christian) names:

San Pietro in Vincoli was Giuliano della Rovere (later Julius II); his uncle had been Sixtus IV, who appointed him early to eight or ten major ecclesiastical offices.

Colonna was Giovanni Colonna, of the great Roman house, named cardinal in 1480, died in 1508.

San Giorgio was Raffaello Riario, a nephew of Sixtus IV and patron of the arts, born in 1451, died in 1521.

Ascanio was Ascanio Sforza, son of Francesco and thus brother of Lodovico Il Moro. Captured by the French in the collapse of Milan, he was released by in-fluence of the cardinal of Rouen, who wanted his vote to be made pope. He was devoted to his brother, whose fond-ness for an opulent life-style he shared.

Rouen was George d'Amboise, favored adviser of Louis XII. Machiavelli thinks Cesare might have controlled the eleven Spanish cardinals in the college, since the Borgias were of Spanish origin; but the clerics were beyond sentiments of that sort, and never worked with him as a bloc.

to fear, being closely bound to the king of France. And so the duke, first and foremost, should have tried to make a Spaniard pope, and if he could not do that, should have accepted Rouen and not San Pietro in Vincoli.[5] Anyone who thinks that recent benefits make great people forget old injuries is simply deluding himself. Thus the duke made a mistake in this election, and it was the cause of his final ruin.

VIII

ON THOSE WHO HAVE BECOME PRINCES BY CRIME

But as there are two other ways to rise from private citizen to prince which cannot be laid to either luck or ability [*virtù*], I cannot omit them, even though one could be handled more fully in a discussion of republics. These are: ascent to princely power by some criminal or evil conduct; and the rise of a private citizen to supreme authority in his land through the choice of his fellow citizens. In describing the first, I will use just two examples, one ancient, one modern, without further declaiming on the method itself, since I think the examples will suffice for anyone who needs to follow them.

Agathocles the Sicilian became prince of Syracuse, not simply from the rank of a private citizen, but from a base and abject position in life.[6] Born the son of a potter, he led a life of complete iniquity at every stage of his career; yet he joined to his villainies such powers [*virtù*] of mind and body that after enlisting in the army he rose through the ranks to become military governor of Syracuse. Once settled in this post, he decided to make himself prince, and take violent possession, without obligation to others, of what had already been freely granted to him. First he told his plan to Hamilcar the Carthaginian, who was campaigning in Sicily with his armies; then one morning he convoked all the people and the full senate of Syracuse, as if he had some announcement of public concern to make. At a prearranged signal, he then had his soldiers butcher all the senators and the richest of the people; and after they were dead, he took and kept the office of prince over that city without the slightest public protest. And even though the Carthaginians twice defeated him, and at last brought his city under siege, he was

5. Giuliano della Rovere, who became Julius the Second, had cherished his grudge against the Borgias during ten years of bitter exile in France (1494–1503). His election after the death of Pius III was a foregone conclusion; but Machiavelli is of opinion that Cesare might have done more for Rouen (obviously by manipulating the Spanish faction) during the elections of September, thus forestalling the elections of both Pius and Julius. The French king agreed; when he heard of the election of Pius, he is said to have shouted, "That son of a whore [Cesare] has kept Rouen from the papacy!"

6. The story of Agathocles the tyrant of Syracuse (361–289 B.C.) was known to Machiavelli through the historians Justin and Diodorus Siculus; the latter is himself scandalized at the misdeeds of the tyrant.

not only able to defend his city; but, leaving some of his people to defend against the besiegers, he led the others off to assault Africa. In short order, he was able to lift the siege of Syracuse and reduce the Carthaginians to desperate straits; and in the end, they had to come to terms with him, content themselves with their African possessions, and leave Sicily to Agathocles.

Considering the deeds and career of this man, one finds little or nothing that can be attributed to luck; for, as I noted above, he did not come to power through anyone's help, but rose through the ranks of the army, passed through a thousand hardships and perils to become prince, and held onto the office by the spirited and dangerous means described. Yet it certainly cannot be called "virtue" [*virtù*] to murder his fellow citizens, betray his friends, to be devoid of truth, pity, or religion; a man may get power by means like these, but not glory. If we consider simply the courage [*virtù*] of Agathocles in facing and escaping from dangers, and the greatness of his soul in sustaining and overcoming adversity, it is hard to see why he should be considered inferior to the greatest of captains. Nonetheless, his fearful cruelty and inhumanity, along with his innumerable crimes, prevent us from placing him among the really excellent men. For we can scarcely attribute to either fortune or virtue [*virtù*] a conquest which he owed to neither.

In our own days, during the papacy of Alexander VI, there is the example of Oliverotto da Fermo.[7] His father having died when he was young, he was raised by a maternal uncle named Giovanni Fogliani, and sent off as a young man to soldier with Paolo Vitelli, so that he might learn the discipline and qualify for a good post in the army. After Paolo's death, he served under Vitellozzo his brother; and before long, being clever and a gallant fellow in mind as well as body, he advanced to head of the army. But as he considered it slavish to depend on others, he plotted with various citizens of Fermo who preferred to see their native land enslaved rather than free; and they resolved, with Vitellozzo's help to capture Fermo. Therefore he wrote to Giovanni Fogliani, saying that as he had been away from home for several years, he would now like to see his uncle and his native town, in addition to looking over his estate there. And he added that since he had sought only honor and would like his fellow citizens to see that he hadn't altogether failed of it, he would

7. Oliverotto da Fermo killed, in the coup of Fermo, not only his uncle Giovanni Fogliani, but Giovanni's son Gennario, his son-in-law Raffaello della Rovere, and four other persons. Paolo Vitelli had been killed by the Florentines in 1499 on suspicion of double-dealing in their campaigns against Pisa; see below, chapter II, note 5, p. 37. Cesare Borgia, when he allowed Vitellozzo Vitelli to take Arezzo from the Florentines (June 1502), explained to the Florentines (including their ambassador, Machiavelli himself) that Vitellozzo was acting on his own, to revenge his brother. But nobody believed this story. As indicated above (chapter VII, note 5, p. 21), Cesare was blackmailing the Florentines into naming him their chosen, and very well paid, "protector." See pp. 84–85.

like to make a state visit, and bring along a hundred of his friends and followers on horseback. He hoped the people of Fermo would give them an honorable reception, one that would bring credit not only to Oliverotto but to his former guardian. Giovanni, on his part, omitted no ceremony that would gratify his nephew; he persuaded the people of Fermo to receive him in high style, and took him into his own house. After he had been there a few days, and made all those secret preparations necessary for his crime, Oliverotto announced a splendid banquet to which he invited Giovanni Fogliani and all the most important men of Fermo. When the meal was finished, and the entertainments usual on such occasions were completed, Oliverotto deliberately raised certain grave topics, speaking of Alexander's greatness and that of Cesare, his son, and of all their undertakings.[8] When Giovanni and the others ventured certain comments, he rose abruptly, saying that these were things to be discussed in a less public place; and he moved to another room, followed by Giovanni and the other citizens. No sooner were they all seated than soldiers appeared from secret places where they lay concealed; they killed Giovanni and all the rest. After this slaughter, Oliverotto mounted his horse, rode through the city, and blockaded the town council in their palace, terrorizing them into obedience and forcing them to form a government of which Oliverotto became chief. Once everyone was dead whose discontent might have been dangerous, he strengthened his position with new laws and regulations, to such effect that in the single year of his rule, he not only secured the city of Fermo, but became the terror of his neighbors. Getting rid of him would have been as hard as getting rid of Agathocles, if he hadn't let himself be tricked by Cesare Borgia when he trapped all the Orsini and Vitelli at Sinigaglia, as described above. There he was taken, along with the others, just a year after he committed the parricide, and there, along with Vitellozzo, who had been the teacher, both of his craft [*virtù*] and of his crime, he was strangled.[9]

Somebody might wonder how it happened that Agathocles and others of his ilk, after they had committed so many acts of treachery and cruelty, could live long, secure lives in their native cities, defend themselves from foreign enemies, and never be conspired against by their fellow citizens. And yet many other princes were unable, because of their cruelty, to maintain their power, even in time of peace, not to speak of the troubled times of war. I believe this depends on whether the cruelty is used well or badly. Cruelty can be described as well used (if it's permissible to say good words about something which is evil in itself) when it is performed all at

---

8. At the time of this story, both Oliverotto and Vitellozzo were in the service of Cesare; the date, if it was just a year before the trap at Sinigaglia, must have been late 1501.

9. Cf. chapter VII, note 7, p. 21.

once, for reasons of self-preservation; and when the acts are not repeated after that, but rather are turned as much as possible to the advantage of the subjects. Cruelty is badly used, when it is infrequent at first, but increases with time instead of diminishing. Those who use the first method may find some excuse before God and man for their state, as Agathocles did; the others cannot possibly stay in power.

We may add this note that when a prince takes a new state, he should calculate the sum of all the injuries he will have to do, and do them all at once, so as not to have to do new ones every day; simply by not repeating them, he will thus be able to reassure people, and win them over to his side with benefits. Whoever believes otherwise, either through fearfulness or bad advice, must always keep his knife in hand, and he can never count on his subjects, because their fresh and recurring injuries keep them suspicious of him. In a word, injuries should be committed all at once, because the less time there is to dwell on them, the less they offend; but benefits should be distributed very gradually, so the taste will last longer. Above all, a prince should live with his subjects on such terms that no accident, whether favorable or unfavorable, can force him to change his conduct. When misfortune strikes, harsh measures are too late, and the good things you do are not counted to your credit because you seem to have acted under compulsion, and no one will thank you for that.

IX

ON THE CIVIL PRINCIPATE

Turning now to the other alternative, when a private citizen becomes a prince, not through crimes or other intolerable violence, but by the choice of his fellow citizens (and this may be called a civil princedom, success in which depends neither completely on skill [*virtù*] nor completely on fortune, but rather on a kind of lucky shrewdness), let me say that one rises in such a state either by the favor of the people or by that of the nobles. In every city there are two different humors, one rising from the people's desire not to be ordered and commanded by the nobles, and the other from the desire of the nobles to command and oppress the people. From these two different impulses we get one of three consequences: either the rule of a prince, or liberty, or license.

The rule of a prince results either from the power of the people or that of the nobles, depending on which has a chance to prevail. When the nobles see they cannot resist the people, they start to build up one of their own, and make him prince so that in the shadow of his power they can satisfy their own wants. In the same way, the people, when they see they can't resist the nobles, build up one of *their* own, and make him prince to have his authority as a shield. The man who becomes prince with the help of the nobles has more trouble holding onto his power than the man who rises with the aid of the people, because as prince he is surrounded by many who think themselves his equals, and for this reason he cannot give orders or manage his agents as he would like. But the man who becomes prince by popular favor reaches the pinnacle alone, and finds no one around him, or very few, who are not prepared to take orders. Apart from this, you cannot satisfy the nobles honestly and without harming others, but you certainly can satisfy the people. In fact, the aim of the common people is more honest than that of the nobles, since the nobles want to oppress others, while the people simply want not to be oppressed.[1] Besides, a prince can never be sure of his position when the people are against him, because there are so many of them; but he knows where to find hostile nobles, because they are few. The worst thing a prince can expect from a hostile population is that they will abandon him; but hostile nobles may not only abandon him, but attack him directly. They are more farsighted and shrewder, taking timely steps to protect themselves and ingratiate themselves with the man they expect to win. Besides, the prince must always live among the same people, but he can do very well without a particular set of noblemen, since it's in his power to make or unmake them every day, abolishing honors or creating them, just as he pleases.

And to make this point clearer, let me say that noblemen can be seen as essentially of two sorts: either they manage their affairs in such a way as to be entirely at your disposal, or they don't. Those who are devoted to you and who are not greedy, you should honor and cherish; those who are not devoted to you may again be seen in two ways. They may hold back from pusillanimity and innate lack of spirit; then you should make use of them, especially as counsellors, since in times of prosperity they will hold you in honor, and in times of adversity there is no need to fear them. But when they deliberately refuse to commit themselves for reasons of ambition, that is a clear sign they are thinking more of themselves than of you; and the prince should beware of men like this, and fear them as if they were open enemies, because in times of adversity they will certainly join in trying to ruin him.

Of course a man who becomes prince through the good will of the people ought to keep them well disposed toward him; and this should not be hard, since all they ask is not to be oppressed. But

1. Machiavelli's strong democratic and popular feelings here are echoed in that unit of the *Discorsi* showing that a prince is more likely to be ungrateful than are the people (I, 29); "ungrateful" in this context equates with "untrustworthy."

even a man who becomes prince against the will of the people, with the aid of the nobles, should try above all things to win over the populace; he can do this quite easily by taking them under his protection. And because men, when they receive benefits from a prince whom they expected to harm them, are especially obliged to him, such a prince's subjects may feel more warmly toward him than if he had risen to power with their help. The prince can earn the good will of his subjects in many ways, but as they vary according to circumstances, I can give no fixed rules and will say nothing of them. One conclusion only can be drawn: the prince must have people well disposed toward him; otherwise in times of adversity there's no hope.

Nabis, prince of Sparta, held out against the attacks of all the rest of Greece and a Roman army that had always been victorious, defending his country and his state against them; and when danger threatened, there were very few Spartans against whom he had to protect himself.[2] If he had had the people against him, his measures would never have sufficed. And let nobody pretend to answer me with that trite proverb that "The man who counts on the people builds his house on mud." That may be true when a private citizen plants his foundations amid the people and lets himself think that the people will come to his aid when he is in trouble with his enemies or the magistrates. In such a case one can easily find himself deluded, as happened in Rome with the Gracchi and in Florence with Messer Giorgio Scali.[3] But if it is a prince who puts his trust in the people, one who knows how to command, who is a man of courage and doesn't lose his head in adversity, if he will make the necessary practical preparations and can rouse his people to action by his own example and orders, he will never find himself betrayed, and his foundations will prove to have been well laid.

These principalities are generally in most danger at the moment when they are just passing from a civil to an absolute form of government. In such circumstances, a prince commands either in his own person or through the magistrates; in the latter case, his position is much weaker and more dangerous, because he depends entirely on the good will of those citizens who have been put in office. Especially in time of trouble, they can easily depose him, either by opposing him directly or simply by not obeying him. And

---

2. Nabis, tyrant of Sparta from 205 to 192 B.C., was a very crude fellow; what Machiavelli probably has in mind is the story that before engaging in his first war with Flamininus the Roman, he had eighty suspected citizens murdered in Sparta; Livy XXXIV, 27.
3. The two Gracchi, Tiberius and Gaius, were popular Roman reformers of the second century B.C., who both met violent ends as a result of bitter aristocratic resistance. Giorgio Scali took part in the so-called "revolt of the Ciompi" (wool carders) in 1378; after a brief success, he and his fellow leaders were thrown out of power, and Scali was beheaded. In his *History of Florence* (III, 5), Machiavelli makes much of Giorgio Scali's complaints against the fickleness of the people.

the prince has no chance to seize absolute command once his rule is endangered, because citizen-subjects who are used to obeying the magistrates will not take orders from him in times of crisis. At crucial moments a prince always finds himself short of trustworthy men. This is why a prince should never count on what he sees in times of quiet, when the citizens find the state useful to them, and everyone pushes forward, making big promises and professing readiness to die for the prince—as long as death is far away; but when times are tough, when the state really needs its citizens, few are to be found. And a crisis of this sort is particularly dangerous, as a prince never experiences it a second time. Thus a wise prince will think of ways to keep his citizens of every sort and under every circumstance dependent on the state and on him; and then they will always be trustworthy.

X

HOW TO MEASURE THE STRENGTH OF ANY PRINCE'S STATE

There is one other consideration to bear in mind regarding these civil principates; that is, whether a prince is strong enough to stand on his own feet in case of need, or whether he is in constant need of help from others. And to make the matter clearer, let me say that in my opinion princes control their own destiny when they command enough money or men to assemble an adequate army and make a stand against anyone who attacks them. I think princes who need outside protection are those who can't take the field against their foes, but have to hide behind their walls and defend themselves there. I've already mentioned the first class,[4] and will save whatever else I have to say about them till later. As for the others, all I can say is that they should keep their cities well fortified and well supplied, and pay no heed to the surrounding countryside. Whenever a man has fortified his city strongly, and has dealt with his subjects as I described above and will describe further below, people will be slow to attack him; men are always wary of tasks that seem hard, and it can't seem easy to attack a prince whose city is in fine fettle, and whose people do not hate him.

In Germany the cities are perfectly free, though their territories are small; they obey the emperor when they feel like it, and have no fear of him or any other neighbors, because they are so well fortified that everyone realizes it would be slow, hard work to capture them. They all have moats and walls of good size, plenty of artillery, and in the public warehouses food, drink, and fuel for a full year;

4. The "first class" seems to consist of those who, like Cesare Borgia, have no army of their own, but go out to get one; that group is described in chapter VII. The second group is those who don't have an army of their own, and don't even try to get one; they lurk behind walls, and to them alone Machiavelli directs the advice that follows.

besides which, to keep the workers occupied without draining the public treasury, they always hold in reserve a year's supply of raw materials for the crafts which are the city's vital nerves—the industries by which the common people make a living. They also respect military training, and have many ordinances to keep people active in this way.[5]

Thus a prince who has a strong city and does not earn his people's hatred cannot be attacked, or if he were, that attacker would be driven off to his own disgrace; because the way things keep changing in this world, it's almost impossible for a prince with his armies to devote an entire year to a siege while doing nothing else. Maybe someone will object: when the people see their possessions outside the walls being burnt up, they will get impatient; a long siege and their own self-interest will make them forget the prince.[6] But to this I answer that a brave, strong prince will overcome all these problems, giving his subjects hope at one minute that the storm will soon pass, stirring them up at another moment to fear the enemy's cruelty, and on still other occasions restraining those who seem too rash. Besides, the enemy will generally do his burning and ravishing of the countryside as soon as he begins the siege, when men's minds are still passionate and earnest for the defense; thus the prince has less reason to worry, because, after a few days, when tempers have cooled, the harm will already have been done, the losses inflicted, and there will clearly be no cure. At that point, the people will rally even more strongly behind their prince, because they will feel he owes them something, since their houses were burnt and their fields ravaged in defense of his cause. Indeed, men are so constructed that they feel themselves committed as much by the benefits they grant as by those they receive. Hence, all things considered, it should not be hard for a prudent prince to keep his subjects in good spirits throughout a siege, as long as he does not run short of food or weapons.

XI

OF ECCLESIASTICAL STATES

It remains for us now only to discuss ecclesiastical states, which present their worst difficulties before one takes possession of them;

5. In 1507 Machiavelli had been sent by the Florentines to treat with Maximilian, and had ventured into Austria perhaps as far as Innsbruck, writing (perhaps some years later) a little *Portrait of Things of Germany*. The cities he saw were thus Swiss and Tyrolean, though he called them all German; and their self-sufficiency is the quality he emphasizes.

6. In a classic passage (II, 6, 21) Thucydides describes the rage of the Athenians when they saw the lands outside their walls being ravaged; but Machiavelli probably had in mind the more immediate instance of the Pisans, from whose city the Florentines in their fury once actually tried to divert the river Arno.

for though they are gained either by virtue [*virtù*] or fortune,[7] they can be held without either one of those qualities. They are sustained by the ancient principles of religion, which are so powerful and of such authority that they keep their princes in power whatever they do, however they live. These are the only princes who have states that they do not defend and subjects that they do not govern; the states, though undefended, are never taken from them, and the subjects, though ungoverned, neither protest, nor try to break away, nor could revolt if they had a mind to. These, then, are the only safe and happy governments. But since they are ruled by a heavenly providence to which human reason cannot reach, I shall say nothing of them. Instituted as they are by God, and sustained by him, it would be a rash and imprudent man who ventured to discuss them.[8]

Still, someone might wonder how it happened that the Church became so powerful, since before Alexander's time, the rulers of Italy—and not just those who were known as potentates, but every minor baron and lord down to the smallest—had little respect for its temporal power. Yet now a king of France trembles before it, and the papacy was actually able to throw him out of Italy and ruin the Venetians at the same time[9]—in view of which, well known though the events are, I do not think it superfluous to recall some of them to memory.

Before Charles, king of France, came into Italy, this part of the world was divided between the pope, the Venetians, the king of Naples, the duke of Milan, and the Florentines. These rulers were bound to keep two principal ends in view: one, to ensure that no foreign armies entered Italy; the other, to ensure that none of the five became overly powerful.[1] The two most to be feared were the pope and the Venetians. To hold the Venetians in check, a union of all the others was required, such as was formed for the defense of Ferrara.[2] And to keep the pope down, the nobles of Rome were very useful; they were divided in two factions, the houses of Orsini and Colonna, which always had good reason to feel hostile toward

7. With Alexander VI and Julius II in mind, it might be inappropriate to translate the word *virtù* in this passage as "virtue." But as Leo X was pope when Machiavelli wrote (a Medici and a decent man, if not especially holy), if Machiavelli had had to separate the meanings of *virtù* he would probably have opted for "virtue" here.
8. Machiavelli's bitter view of the Church in politics found fullest expression in *Discorsi*, I, 12 (see pp. 102–4).
9. Julius II defeated the Venetians at Vailà (or Agnadello) May 14, 1509; he drove the French out of Italy in 1512,

and was assembling at the time of his death the Fifth Lateran Council, which proposed to condemn both the French Church and the French king.
1. Guicciardini's *History* opens with a long and eloquent picture of the peace and prosperity prevailing in Italy at the moment when Lorenzo the Magnificent died.
2. In 1484 the pope (Sixtus IV), the king of Naples, the duke of Milan, and the Florentines all combined to help defend Ferrara against the Venetians in the so-called "war of salt." See chapter II, note 5, p. 4.

one another, and thus stood armed to the teeth under the pope's very nose, keeping him weak and impotent. Occasionally, no doubt, a pope of courage came along, like Sixtus, but neither fortune nor wisdom could free him from this predicament.[3] One reason for this was simply the shortness of papal lives; because in ten years, which is all the average pope lives, he might barely put down one of the factions, but then when he had about put down the Colonnas, for example, in would come another pope hostile to the Orsini, and in raising one faction he would not have time to put down the other.

For these reasons, the temporal power of the pope was little respected in Italy. Then Alexander VI was raised to the papacy, and he showed, more than any other pope that ever was, how much can be done in that office with money and arms. Using Duke Valentino as his instrument and the coming of the French as his occasion, he did all those things that I described above in talking of the duke's actions. His intent, to be sure, was to aggrandize the duke and not the Church; still, what he did served the Church's ends; and after his death, when the duke was out of the way, the Church profited from his efforts. Pope Julius followed, and he found the Church in flourishing estate, controlling the whole of the Romagna, with the Roman nobles crushed and the two factions beaten down by Alexander. What was more, he found handy ways of accumulating money, that before Alexander had never been used.[4] Julius not only followed his predecessor but pushed beyond him; he planned to take Bologna, crush the Venetians, and drive the French out of Italy. In fact he accomplished all these things, and what is even more to his credit, he did them all for the benefit of the Church and not of any private individual.[5] Moreover, he kept the Orsini and Colonna factions in the same lowly condition in which he found them; and though among these one leader or another has since tried to stir things up, two things kept them quiet: one was the power of the Church, which awed them; and the other was that they had no cardinals, who start most of the quarrels between them. As long as they have cardinals, these factions will never be at ease; the churchmen stir up trouble, inside Rome as well as outside it, and then the barons have to back them up; thus ambitious prelates inflame quarrels and tumults among the barons. These are the rea-

3. Sixtus IV, pope from 1471 to 1484, was a member of the aggressive family of della Rovere; Julius II, his nephew, inherited his disposition and a number of his quarrels.
4. Alexander pronounced 1500 a special jubilee year, and created cardinals wholesale in order to support his son Cesare's campaigns in the Romagna; Julius also sold Church offices and indul-gences, perhaps less spectacularly, but on a wider scale.
5. Even his enemies agreed that Julius II wanted money for political, not personal purposes; though known before his elevation as a lavish man, he followed as pope the policies recommended in Machiavelli's chapter XVI, as Machiavelli himself indicates.

sons why his present holiness Pope Leo has found the papacy so strong; and we may hope that as his predecessors made it great by force of arms, he by his generosity and countless other talents [*virtù*] will make it even greater and more to be revered.[6]

XII

ON DIFFERENT KINDS OF TROOPS, ESPECIALLY MERCENARIES

Now that I have described in detail the natures of the various states that are my topic; now that I have considered some of the reasons for their prosperity and decline, and have shown how they have often been won and held—I must discuss in general the offensive and defensive actions that princes may be called on to undertake. I said before that a prince must lay strong foundations, otherwise he is bound to come to grief. The chief foundations on which all states rest, whether they are new, old, or mixed, are good laws and good arms. And since there cannot be good laws where there are not good arms, and where there are good arms there are bound to be good laws, I shall set aside the topic of laws and talk about arms.

Let me say, then, that the armies with which a prince defends his state are either his own or are mercenaries, auxiliaries, or mixed. Mercenaries and auxiliaries are useless and dangerous. Any man who founds his state on mercenaries can never be safe or secure, because they are disunited, ambitious, undisciplined, and untrustworthy— bold fellows among their friends, but cowardly in the face of the enemy; they have no fear of God, nor loyalty to men. They will protect you from ruin only as long as nobody assaults you; in peace you are at their mercy, and in war at the mercy of your enemies. The reason is that they have no other passions or incentives to hold the field, except their desire for a bit of money, and that is not enough to make them die for you. They are all eagerness to be your soldiers as long as you're not waging war; when war breaks out, they either turn tail or disappear. And this should not be hard to believe, because the present ruin of Italy is caused by nothing else than its having trusted for so long to mercenary armies. For some individuals they were indeed useful, and they seemed fierce enough when they had only one another to fight; but when outsiders appeared, they showed themselves for what they were. For this reason Charles of France was allowed to take Italy "with chalk."[7] And the man

<hr/>

6. The compliment is barely polite; writing to a Medici about a Medici pope, Machiavelli could hardly say less.
7. Charles VIII took Italy "with chalk" and without fighting by simply marking the doors of houses requisitioned as quarters for his troops. Alexander VI made the remark about chalk being the only weapon he needed. Savonarola was the man who attributed the French invasion to Italian sinfulness.

who said our sins were the cause said the truth; but they weren't the sins he thought, they were those I described, and because princes committed them, princes have suffered for them.

To demonstrate further the ill effect of these troops, let me say that either mercenary leaders are skilled soldiers, or they are not; if they are, they cannot be trusted, because they will always be trying to increase their own authority, either by attacking you, their employer, or by oppressing people with whom you have no quarrel. But if your mercenary is not a brave [*virtuoso*] leader, he will ruin you with his incompetence. And if you object that any leader may do this, whether mercenary or not, my answer is that armies are controlled by either a prince or a republic. The prince should go to war in his own person, and assume the captain's post; the republic has to send its citizens. When one of those it sends does not prove a valiant leader, it must change him; when he does well, it must check him with laws, to keep him in line. Experience teaches that independent princes and well-armed republics accomplish great things, but mercenary armies do nothing but lose; and a republic with its own armies holds out longer against the tyranny of one of its citizens than does a republic with foreign armies. For many centuries the Romans and the Spartans were well armed and free; the Swiss are heavily armed and live in the greatest freedom.

The Carthaginians are an example from antiquity of a people who used mercenary armies: even though they had Carthaginian leaders, those armies nearly overran the city after the first war with the Romans.[8] After the death of Epaminondas, the Thebans appointed Philip of Macedon head of their armies; he won a victory for them, and took away their liberty.[9] After the death of Duke Philip, the Milanese used Francesco Sforza against the Venetians; after he had beaten the enemy at Caravaggio, he joined with them to put down the Milanese, his employers.[1] When Sforza his father was soldiering for Queen Joanna of Naples, he deliberately left her unprotected on one occasion, so that, to keep from losing her kingdom, she was forced to throw herself on the mercies of the king of Aragon.[2] No doubt the Venetians and the Florentines have recently increased their empires by means of mercenary armies, the leaders of which didn't make themselves prince, but defended their employ-

---

8. In the so-called ·"servile war" which broke out in 241 B.C., directly after the First Punic War, the Carthaginian mercenaries turned on their own masters. This struggle provides the background for Flaubert's novel, *Salammbô;* Machiavelli read of it in the less gaudy pages of Polybius.

9. The Thebans accepted help from Philip of Macedon (Alexander's father) against the Phocians, and less than ten years later he took away their liberty at the battle of Chaeronea (338 B.C.).

1. Duke Philip was the last of the Visconti line: he died in 1447. The republic that followed in Milan employed Francesco Sforza, with the results indicated. See above, p. 4.

2. The tangled relationships between Joanna II of Naples and Sforza the elder included an erotic episode, in the course of which, as part of a lovers' quarrel, Sforza deliberately left the lady at the mercy of her enemies.

ers. But I answer that the Florentines were just lucky in this matter; because the good leaders whom they might have had to fear sometimes were not victorious, sometimes had rivals, and sometimes turned their ambition elsewhere. Giovanni Acuto was not victorious, and for that reason we cannot tell how he would have kept his word; but everyone concedes that if he had won a victory, the Florentines would have been at his mercy.[3] Sforza always had the Braccio crowd as his rivals, and they kept an eye on one another. Francesco[4] turned his ambition against Lombardy, while Braccio went against the Church and the kingdom of Naples.

But let us turn to events of recent history. The Florentines made Paolo Vitelli their military leader; he was a very shrewd man, who had risen from private life to a position of the greatest renown. If he had taken Pisa, there is no denying that the Florentines would have had to stick with him; since if he had taken service with their enemies their cause would have become hopeless, and as long as they kept him they had to obey him.[5] As for the Venetians, if we consider their career, we will see that they made steady, splendid progress with their own people, before they began to fight on land; using their own gentry and armed populace, they campaigned very successfully [*virtuosissamente*]. But when they began to fight on land, they abandoned these good customs [*virtù*], and began to follow the military traditions of Italy. When they first began to expand on land, because their country was still small and their reputation great, they had no special need to fear their captains; but as they expanded in power under the leadership of Carmagnola,[6] they got a sniff of their danger. They knew he was a man of great ability [*virtuosissimo*], and recalled that under his leadership they had beaten the duke of Milan; on the other hand, they saw that he was cooling in his conduct of the war. Thus they judged that they could not win the war with him, because he did not want to win; yet they could not dismiss him either, for fear of losing what they had won. So, finally, to be sure of him they had to have him murdered. Thereafter they had as their captains Bartolomeo da Bergamo, Roberto da San Severino, the count of Pitigliano, and suchlike—men who gave them more reason to worry over losses than gains. That

3. Sir John Hawkwood (1320–94), originally of England but known in Italy as "Giovanni Acuto," served the Florentines for many years, with his "White Company." Braccio da Montone and Sforza the elder were contemporaries, fellow-students, and professional rivals among the condottieri of the early fifteen-century Romagna.
4. Francesco Sforza.
5. Paolo Vitelli, who commanded the Florentine armies against Pisa but did not make satisfactory progress with that enterprise, was accused of treason and

executed in 1499. It was his brother Vitellozzo, who had never forgiven the Florentines, who was strangled three years later at Sinigaglia by Cesare Borgia.
6. Francesco Bussone, count of Carmagnola (ca. 1380–1432), was not in reality as successful as Machiavelli describes him; during most of his later campaigns, he was either inept or deliberately dilatory. The Venetians chose the second horn of that dilemma, and had him executed.

happened shortly at Vailá,[7] where in a single day they lost everything that their incessant labors over eight hundred years had
earned them. Armies of this sort make only slow, weak, late conquests; their losses are sudden, amazing.

As these examples have all brought me to the consideration of
Italy, which for many years has been controlled by mercenary
armies, I would like to look into the backgrounds, so that when we
have seen the origin and progress of this warfare, we can take steps
to change it. I must explain, then, that when the empire began to
lose its hold on Italy and the pope's temporal power began to
increase, Italy was divided into several states. Many of the big cities
took arms against their nobles who previously, with the help of the
emperor, had kept them under. The Church favored these risings as
a way of increasing its temporal power; and thus private citizens
became princes in many cities. Thus almost all Italy came into the
hands of the Church and of a few republics; and since neither
priests nor ordinary citizens know much about military matters,
they began to hire foreigners. The first to bring this sort of soldiering into reputation was Alberigo da Conio, from the Romagna.[8]
Among those trained in his school were Braccio and Sforza, who in
their day were arbiters of Italy. After them came the whole crew
who have directed Italian armies down to the present day; and the
result of their prowess [*virtù*] has been that Italy has been overrun
by Charles, sacked by Louis, raped by Ferdinand, and disgraced by
the Swiss.

Their policy was, first of all, to raise their own reputation by diminishing that of the infantry. They did this because they had no
estates or native lands, but lived on salaries; a few infantry would
have given them little prestige, and a large number they could never
have supported. So they limited themselves to cavalry, a moderate
number of which could give them both strength and high repute.
And before long, they had so arranged things that in an army of
twenty thousand soldiers, not two thousand infantrymen were to
be found. Besides, they went to great lengths to avoid disturbing
themselves or their soldiers with work or danger, never killing one
another in skirmishes, but only taking one another prisoner and
never asking any ransom. They never attacked a fortification at
night, and the besieged never counterattacked; around their camps

7. Bartolomeo Colleoni da Bergamo, a
relatively able commander, is best known
now for the splendid equestrian statue
by Verrocchio erected by the Venetians
after his death in 1475. The other Venetian generals mentioned by Machiavelli
were his associates and subordinates.
The battle of Vailà (also known as Agnadello, also known as Ghiaradadda)
was fought against forces assembled by
Pope Julius II, on May 14, 1509; in this
engagement the Venetians lost their entire land empire—which was not, indeed,
all they had gained in 800 years of
struggle, but, in conjunction with their
recent losses at sea to the Turks, represented a staggering blow.
8. Alberigo da Barbiano, count of Conio
(? –1409) founded the first Italian mercenary company, and gave instruction in
the art of mercenary warfare to both
Braccio da Montone and Sforza the
elder (see note 3 above).

they built neither palisades nor ditches; and they never campaigned in winter. All these things were permitted by the rules of their warfare, and deliberately contrived, in order to avoid work and danger, as we said; so that they have brought Italy to a state of slavery and contempt.

XIII

ON AUXILIARY TROOPS, MIXED TROOPS, AND YOUR OWN TROOPS

Armies of auxiliaries, the other useless sort, are the kind that come when you ask a powerful neighbor to help with his soldiers in your defense. Pope Julius tried this only recently; he had learned a gloomy lesson at Ferrara as a result of using mercenary troops, and now turned to auxiliaries, getting Ferdinand, king of Spain, to help with his soldiers and armies.[9] Troops of this sort may be perfectly good and useful in their own right, but to the man who calls them in they are almost always harmful, because when they lose they carry your cause down with them, and when they win, you remain their prisoner. And though ancient history is full of instances, I don't want to set aside the fresh example of Pope Julius. His behavior could scarcely have been more ill-advised: just because he wanted Ferrara, he put his whole destiny in the hands of a foreigner. Only his good luck enabled him to escape the consequences of his bad judgment, through the operation of a third force. For when his auxiliaries had been beaten at Ravenna, the Swiss suddenly appeared and drove off the victors, much to his surprise and everyone else's.[1] So he was not captured either by his enemies, because they had fled, or by his auxiliaries, because he was victorious through the efforts of somebody else. Likewise the Florentines, when they had no arms of their own, brought ten thousand Frenchmen to attack Pisa; and this project of theirs brought greater dangers upon them than any of their other tribulations.[2] The emperor of Constantinople, in order to put down his neighbors, brought into Greece an army of ten thousand Turks; when the war was over, they refused to leave, and thus began the enslavement of Greece by the infidels.[3]

9. Julius assaulted Ferrara in 1510, using troops of several different nationalities, including 300 Spanish lances supplied by Ferdinand. As noted above in chapter II, note 5, p. 4, Alfonso, duke of Ferrara, who stood off this attack, was one of the great soldiers of Europe.
1. At the desperate battle of Ravenna, on April 11, 1512, the French defeated Julius and his auxiliaries; but in May, twenty thousand Swiss descended on Italy, compelling the victorious French to retreat. Machiavelli is forcing his case here; though defeated at Ravenna, the Spaniards fought like lions, inflicting crippling losses on the French even before the Swiss invasion.
2. Gascon and Swiss troops, borrowed by the Florentines from the French king for use against Pisa in the summer of 1500, mutinied for more pay, so the whole enterprise collapsed; Machiavelli himself was one of the commissioners who had to explain the fiasco to Louis XII.
3. For his third example, Machiavelli leaps back more than 150 years; it was 1353 when Emperor John V Cantacuzene first made the fatal error of inviting the Turks to help him against his European enemies.

Anyone who wants to make dead sure of not winning, then, had better make use of armies like these, since they are much more dangerous than mercenaries. In these you get your ruin ready-made; they come to you a compact body, all trained to obey somebody else. Mercenaries after a victory need a little time and a better occasion before they attack you, since they are not a unified body, but a group of individuals picked and paid by you. Hence a third party, even if you name him as head, cannot immediately gain enough authority to do you serious harm. In a word, when you have mercenaries, their cowardice is most dangerous to you; when you have auxiliaries, it is their courage [*virtù*] you must fear. Hence a wise prince has always kept away from troops like these, and made use of his own, preferring to lose under his own power than to win with other people's troops—since it isn't a real victory when alien armies win it for you. I am never reluctant to cite Cesare Borgia and his deeds. The duke entered the Romagna with auxiliary troops, consisting entirely of Frenchmen; and with them he took Imola and Forlì.[4] But then when he found they were not to be trusted, he adopted mercenaries as less dangerous, and hired the Orsini and Vitelli. When he found they too were undependable, treacherous, and dangerous to his service, he got rid of them, and turned to troops of his own. And you can easily see the difference there is between these various armies by the difference in the duke's reputation when he had only French soldiers, when he had the Orsini and Vitelli, and when he had his own soldiers and could stand on his own feet. His reputation grew steadily more impressive, and it never stood higher than when everyone saw he was the complete master of his own troops.

Though I don't want to stop using Italian examples which are fresh in mind, I cannot omit Hiero of Syracuse, whom I mentioned earlier. When the Syracusans made this man head of their armies, as I said before, he recognized at once that mercenary soldiers were useless, being formed on the same pattern as our Italian condottieri; and since he couldn't safely keep them, nor yet let them go, he had them cut to bits, and after that he made war with his own armies, not with those of other people.[5] I'd like also to call to mind a parable from the Old Testament which bears on the point. When David volunteered before Saul to fight with Goliath the Philistine challenger, Saul, to give the young man courage, offered him his

---

4. Cf. above chapter VII, note 4, p. 20. When he says "it is not a real victory when alien armies win it for you," Machiavelli isn't invoking the rules of sportsmanship or fair play; he means that prizes gained by other peoples' energies belong to them, when they are strong enough to hold onto them.

5. The mercenaries with whom Hiero had to struggle were known as Mamertines; actually, they were first hired by Agathocles. Hiero had to attack them, not because they were ineffectual, but because they were threatening his rule of Syracuse. See Polybius, I, 7–9. The story of Saul and David is found in I Samuel 17: 38–39.

own royal armor. But David, after trying it on, refused, saying he could never do himself justice in that armor. He preferred to meet the enemy armed simply with his own sling and a knife. In a word, other men's armor will either slip off your back, or weigh you down, or constrict your actions. When Charles VII, father of King Louis XI, had freed France from the English by his own energy [*virtù*] and good luck, he realized how necessary it was to have his own armies, and established laws in his kingdom for training cavalry and infantry. But afterwards his son, King Louis, gave up the infantry and began to hire Swiss;[6] that mistake was followed by others, and brought the country into the dangers which we can now observe. By giving the Swiss a great reputation, he lowered that of his own armies; he abolished all his own infantry, and forced his cavalry into dependence on outsiders—for when they became accustomed to fight with the help of Swiss infantry, they began to suppose they could not win without them. And now the French are no longer strong enough to oppose the Swiss, while without Swiss in their ranks they cannot stand up to anyone else. Thus the French armies have become mixed, part mercenary and part native troops. Taken all in all, these troops are much better than mere auxiliaries or mere mercenaries, but they are much inferior to armies of one's own people. The example already given will suffice; the kingdom of France would be invincible if the laws of Charles had been kept in force or strengthened. But shortsighted men undertake policies for their immediate advantage, paying no heed to the slow poison hidden within them, as I said before regarding consumptive fevers.

So a prince who does not recognize the evils of a state the minute they are born is not really wise; and such ability to look ahead is given to very few. If you try to seek out the basic reason for the fall of the Roman Empire, you will find it began with the hiring of Goths as soldiers; from that moment, the force of the Roman Empire began to grow slack, and all the energy taken from it accrued to them.

I conclude, then, that unless it has its own armies, no principality is really secure; in that case, it depends entirely on fortune, having no power [*virtù*] to defend itself dependably in times of trouble. Wise men have always thought and said "that nothing is so weak and unstable as a reputation for power not founded on strength of one's own."[7] Your own armies are defined as those composed of

---

6. In a Renaissance army, everyone wanted to be a horseman because the pay was better. Charles VII, made king of France by Joan of Arc, had to reform the French army to end the war with England. He formed a kind of national militia, but in 1474 his successor, Louis XI, repealed the ordinance and began hiring Swiss mercenaries. The dangers facing the French in 1513 grew out of their losses at Ravenna (1512) and Novara (1513), which Machiavelli attributes to their poor infantry.

7. The quotation is from Tacitus, *Annals*, XIII, 19.

your own subjects, citizens, or dependents: all others are either mercenary or auxiliary. You will have no trouble creating your own armies if you study the ordinances of the four men noted above,[8] and note how Philip, father of Alexander the Great, levied and organized his armies. Many other republics and kingdoms have done the same; and to their precedents I refer you without further remark.

XIV

MILITARY DUTIES OF THE PRINCE

A prince, therefore, should have no other object, no other thought, no other subject of study, than war, its rules and disciplines; this is the only art for a man who commands, and it is of such value [*virtù*] that it not only keeps born princes in place, but often raises men from private citizens to princely fortune. On the other hand, it is clear that when princes have thought more about the refinements of life than about war, they have lost their positions. The quickest way to lose a state is to neglect this art; the quickest way to get one is to study it. Because he was a soldier, Francesco Sforza raised himself from private citizen to duke of Milan; his successors, who tried to avoid the hardships of warfare, became private citizens after being dukes.[9] Apart from the other evils it brings with it, being defenseless makes you contemptible. This is one of the disgraces from which a prince must guard himself, as we shall see later. Between a man with arms and a man without them there is no proportion at all. It is not reasonable to expect an armed man to obey one who is unarmed, nor an unarmed man to be safe among armed servants; because, what with the contempt of the former and the mistrust of the latter, there's no living together. Thus a prince who knows nothing of warfare, apart from his other troubles already described, can't hope for respect from his soldiers or put any trust in them.

Therefore the prince should never turn his mind from the study of war; in times of peace he should think about it even more than in wartime. He can do this in two ways, by training the body and training the mind. As for physical training, apart from keeping his troops well disciplined and exercised, he should do a great deal of hunting, and thus harden his body to strenuous exercise, meanwhile learning to read terrain. He will see how the mountains rise, how the valleys open out, and how the plains lie; he will know about

8. The examples make a curious quartet: Cesare Borgia, Hiero of Syracuse, King David, and Charles VII of France. The point seems to be that the rule holds good whatever the moral status of the person to whom it's applied.
9. The Sforzas passed, with spectacular abruptness, from barbarism to decadence in a generation; Machiavelli's exhortations, however necessary he supposed them, were not borne out by Medici history—they generally lost by warfare what they gained by diplomacy and trade.

rivers and swamps—and to this study he should devote the greatest attention. What he learns will be doubly useful; first, he will become acquainted with his own land, and understand better how to defend it; and then, because he knows his own country thoroughly, he can easily understand any other country that he is forced to look over for the first time. For example, in Tuscany the hills, valleys, plains, and swamps are pretty much like those in other provinces, so that, knowing one, you can easily get to know the others. Any prince who lacks this experience lacks the main thing a captain should have, that is, a knowledge of how to find the enemy, pick a campsite, draw up an army, prepare it for battle, and organize sieges for his own advantage.

Among the other good things that historians report of Philopoemon, prince of the Achaeans, they say that in peacetime he thought of nothing but how to make war;[1] and when he was in the country with his friends, he would sometimes stop and ask them: "Suppose there were enemies up in those hills, and we were here with our army, who would have the advantage? How could we get at them, without breaking ranks? If we wanted to get away, how would we do it? If they tried to get away, how could we cut them off?" Thus, as they traveled along he would raise every tactical problem that could confront an army; he listened to their opinions and put forth his own, supporting them with reasons. As a result of this constant practice, no unexpected circumstance could ever arise, when he was at the head of his army, for which he did not have a ready remedy.

As for exercising the mind, a prince should read history and reflect on the actions of great men. He can see how they carried themselves during their wars, and study what made them win, what made them lose, so that he can imitate their successes and avoid their defeats. Above all, he should do as great men have done before him, and take as a model for his conduct some great historical figure who achieved the highest praise and glory by constantly holding before himself the deeds and achievements of a predecessor. They say Alexander the Great imitated Achilles, Caesar imitated Alexander, and Scipio imitated Cyrus. Anyone who reads Xenophon's life of Cyrus must realize how closely Scipio modelled himself on Cyrus, how much that imitation contributed to his glory, and how closely he conformed, in temperance, affability, humanity, and liberality to the things that Xenophon wrote about Cyrus.[2]

1. The story of Philopoemon, leader of the Achaean league, and his single-minded strategic training program is told by Plutarch among the *Parallel Lives*, where the Greek general is compared with the Roman Flamininus; and also by Livy XXXV, 28.
2. These various stories of classical figures imitating other classical figures are all taken from books—the story of Alexander imitating Achilles from Plutarch, the story of Caesar imitating Alexander from Suetonius, the story of Cato imitating Cyrus from a passage of Cicero. Even Xenophon's ostensible "life" of Cyrus is really a didactic novel, with only the slightest basis in historical fact.

Such are the rules that a wise prince should observe. He must never idle away his days of peace, but vigorously make capital that will pay off in times of adversity; thus, when fortune changes, it will find him in a position to resist.

XV

ON THE REASONS WHY MEN ARE PRAISED OR BLAMED—ESPECIALLY
PRINCES

It remains now to be seen what style and principles a prince ought to adopt in dealing with his subjects and friends. I know the subject has been treated frequently before, and I'm afraid people will think me rash for trying to do so again, especially since I intend to differ in this discussion from what others have said. But since I intend to write something useful to an understanding reader, it seemed better to go after the real truth of the matter than to repeat what people have imagined. A great many men have imagined states and princedoms such as nobody ever saw or knew in the real world,[3] for there's such a difference between the way we really live and the way we ought to live that the man who neglects the real to study the ideal will learn how to accomplish his ruin, not his salvation. Any man who tries to be good all the time is bound to come to ruin among the great number who are not good. Hence a prince who wants to keep his post must learn how not to be good, and use that knowledge, or refrain from using it, as necessity requires.

Putting aside, then, all the imaginary things that are said about princes, and getting down to the truth, let me say that whenever men are discussed (and especially princes because they are prominent), there are certain qualities that bring them either praise or blame. Thus some are considered generous, others stingy (I use a Tuscan term, since "greedy" in our speech means a man who wants to take other people's goods; we call a man "stingy" who clings to his own);[4] some are givers, others grabbers; some cruel, others merciful; one man is treacherous, another faithful; one is feeble and effeminate, another fierce and spirited; one humane, another proud; one lustful, another chaste; one straightforward, another sly; one harsh, another gentle; one serious, another playful; one religious, another skeptical, and so on. I know everyone will agree that among these many qualities a prince certainly ought to have all those that

3. Plato's *Republic* was certainly in Machiavelli's mind; More's *Utopia* was not yet published. But Machiavelli was doubtless thinking, as well, of previous books giving advice to princes, which dealt in idealistic terms with impractical situations. Egidio Colonna had said, for example, that to lack just one of the princely virtues was to lack them all.

4. The two words in Italian are *avaro* and *misero*. Machiavelli seems to derive the first by mistaken etymology from the verb *avere*, ("to possess"); the "avaro" is he who "per rapina desidera di avere." The "misero," by contrast, is the true miser; and that's a legitimate etymological link.

are considered good. But since it is impossible to have and exercise them all, because the conditions of human life simply do not allow it, a prince must be shrewd enough to avoid the public disgrace of those vices that would lose him his state. If he possibly can, he should also guard against vices that will not lose him his state; but if he cannot prevent them, he should not be too worried about indulging them. And furthermore, he should not be too worried about incurring blame for any vice without which he would find it hard to save his state. For if you look at matters carefully, you will see that something resembling virtue, if you follow it, may be your ruin, while something else resembling vice will lead, if you follow it, to your security and well-being.

XVI

ON LIBERALITY AND STINGINESS

Let me begin, then, with the first of the qualities mentioned above, by saying that a reputation for liberality is doubtless very fine; but the generosity that earns you that reputation can do you great harm. For if you exercise your generosity in a really virtuous way [*virtuosamente*],[5] as you should, nobody will know of it, and you cannot escape the odium of the opposite vice. Hence if you wish to be widely known as a generous man, you must seize every opportunity to make a big display of your giving. A prince of this character is bound to use up his entire revenue in works of ostentation. Thus, in the end, if he wants to keep a name for generosity, he will have to load his people with exorbitant taxes and squeeze money out of them in every way he can. This is the first step in making him odious to his subjects; for when he is poor, nobody will respect him. Then, when his generosity has angered many and brought rewards to a few, the slightest difficulty will trouble him, and at the first approach of danger, down he goes. If by chance he foresees this, and tries to change his ways, he will immediately be labelled a miser.

Since a prince cannot use this virtue [*virtù*] of liberality in such a way as to become known for it unless he harms his own security, he won't mind, if he judges prudently of things, being known as a miser. In due course he will be thought the more liberal man, when people see that his parsimony enables him to live on his income, to defend himself against his enemies, and to undertake major projects without burdening his people with taxes. Thus he will be acting liberally toward all those people from whom he takes nothing (and

5. This phrase marks one extreme in Machiavelli's handling of the word *virtù*. It means here, not simply doing a charitable thing, but doing it without ulterior motives, from a sincere, inward, and personal sense of "caritas." Contrast phrases like "tanta ferocità e tanta virtù" (chapter VII) or "maestro delle virtù e scelleratezze sua" (chapter VIII).

there are an immense number of them), and in a stingy way toward those people on whom he bestows nothing (and they are very few). In our times, we have seen great things being accomplished only by men who have had the name of misers; all the others have gone under. Pope Julius II, though he used his reputation as a generous man to gain the papacy, sacrificed it in order to be able to make war; the present king of France has waged many wars without levying a single extra tax on his people, simply because he could take care of the extra expenses out of the savings from his long parsimony.[6] If the present king of Spain had a reputation for generosity, he would never have been able to undertake so many campaigns, or win so many of them.

Hence a prince who prefers not to rob his subjects, who wants to be able to defend himself, who wants to avoid poverty and contempt, and who doesn't want to become a plunderer, should not mind in the least if people consider him a miser; this is simply one of the vices that enable him to reign. Someone may object that Caesar used a reputation for generosity to become emperor, and many other people have also risen in the world, because they were generous or were supposed to be so. Well, I answer, either you are a prince already, or you are in the process of becoming one; in the first case, this reputation for generosity is harmful to you, in the second case it is very necessary. Caesar was one of those who wanted to become ruler in Rome; but after he had reached his goal, if he had lived, and had not cut down on his expenses, he would have ruined the empire itself. Someone may say: there have been plenty of princes, very successful in warfare, who have had a reputation for generosity. But I answer: either the prince is spending his own money and that of his subjects, or he is spending someone else's. In the first case, he ought to be sparing; in the second case, he ought to spend money like water. Any prince at the head of his army, which lives on loot, extortion, and plunder, disposes of other people's property, and is bound to be very generous; otherwise, his soldiers would desert him. You can always be a more generous giver when what you give is not yours or your subjects'; Cyrus, Caesar, and Alexander were generous in this way. Spending what belongs to other people does no harm to your reputation, rather it enhances it; only spending your own substance harms you. And there is nothing that wears out faster than generosity; even as you practice it, you lose the means of practicing it, and you become either poor and

6. Louis XII, though afflicted like his predecessor Charles VIII with a mania for foreign conquest (a work for which both were largely incompetent), ran a thrifty shop at home. Starting with an empty treasury, he accumulated within a year after his accession enough money to support two years of war in Italy; and, as Machiavelli remarks, he imposed no new taxes. Ferdinand of Spain was equally prudent in money matters; and though he is not mentioned here, Henry VII of England was as famous for stinginess as his son Henry VIII was for extravagance.

contemptible or (in the course of escaping poverty) rapacious and hateful. The thing above all against which a prince must protect himself is being contemptible and hateful; generosity leads to both. Thus, it's much wiser to put up with the reputation of being a miser, which brings you shame without hate, than to be forced— just because you want to appear generous—into a reputation for rapacity, which brings shame on you and hate along with it.

XVII

ON CRUELTY AND CLEMENCY: WHETHER IT IS BETTER TO BE LOVED OR FEARED

Continuing now with our list of qualities, let me say that every prince should prefer to be considered merciful rather than cruel, yet he should be careful not to mismanage this clemency of his. People thought Cesare Borgia was cruel, but that cruelty of his reorganized the Romagna, united it, and established it in peace and loyalty. Anyone who views the matter realistically will see that this prince was much more merciful than the people of Florence, who, to avoid the reputation of cruelty, allowed Pistoia to be destroyed.[7] Thus, no prince should mind being called cruel for what he does to keep his subjects united and loyal; he may make examples of a very few, but he will be more merciful in reality than those who, in their tender-heartedness, allow disorders to occur, with their attendant murders and lootings. Such turbulence brings harm to an entire community, while the executions ordered by a prince affect only one individual at a time. A new prince, above all others, cannot possibly avoid a name for cruelty, since new states are always in danger. And Virgil, speaking through the mouth of Dido, says:

> Res dura et regni novitas me talia cogunt
> Moliri, et late fines custode tueri.[8]

Yet a prince should be slow to believe rumors and to commit himself to action on the basis of them. He should not be afraid of his own thoughts; he ought to proceed cautiously, moderating his conduct with prudence and humanity, allowing neither overconfidence to make him careless, nor overtimidity to make him intolerable.

Here the question arises: is it better to be loved than feared, or vice versa? I don't doubt that every prince would like to be both; but since it is hard to accommodate these qualities, if you have to make a choice, to be feared is much safer than to be loved. For it is

---

7. In 1501–2 the Pistoians broke out in a small but desperate civil war between two factions, the "Panciatichi" and the "Cancellieri"; though the nearby Florentines were in control of the city, and actually sent Machiavelli to investigate, they were afraid to intervene effectually, and so the townspeople hacked one another to pieces.

8. "Harsh pressures and the newness of my reign / Compel me to these steps; I must maintain / My borders against foreign foes. . . ." (*Aeneid*, II, 563–4). [*Editor's translation.*]

a good general rule about men, that they are ungrateful, fickle, liars and deceivers, fearful of danger and greedy for gain. While you serve their welfare, they are all yours, offering their blood, their belongings, their lives, and their children's lives, as we noted above —so long as the danger is remote. But when the danger is close at hand, they turn against you. Then, any prince who has relied on their words and has made no other preparations will come to grief; because friendships that are bought at a price, and not with greatness and nobility of soul, may be paid for but they are not acquired, and they cannot be used in time of need. People are less concerned with offending a man who makes himself loved than one who makes himself feared: the reason is that love is a link of obligation which men, because they are rotten, will break any time they think doing so serves their advantage; but fear involves dread of punishment, from which they can never escape.

Still, a prince should make himself feared in such a way that, even if he gets no love, he gets no hate either; because it is perfectly possible to be feared and not hated, and this will be the result if only the prince will keep his hands off the property of his subjects or citizens, and off their women. When he does have to shed blood, he should be sure to have a strong justification and manifest cause; but above all, he should not confiscate people's property, because men are quicker to forget the death of a father than the loss of a patrimony. Besides, pretexts for confiscation are always plentiful; it never fails that a prince who starts living by plunder can find reasons to rob someone else. Excuses for proceeding against someone's life are much rarer and more quickly exhausted.

But a prince at the head of his armies and commanding a multitude of soldiers should not care a bit if he is considered cruel; without such a reputation, he could never hold his army together and ready for action. Among the marvelous deeds of Hannibal, this was prime: that, having an immense army, which included men of many different races and nations, and which he led to battle in distant countries, he never allowed them to fight among themselves or to rise against him, whether his fortune was good or bad. The reason for this could only be his inhuman cruelty, which, along with his countless other talents [*virtù*], made him an object of awe and terror to his soldiers; and without the cruelty, his other qualities [*le altre sua virtù*] would never have sufficed. The historians who pass snap judgments on these matters admire his accomplishments and at the same time condemn the cruelty which was their main cause.[9]

When I say, "His other qualities would never have sufficed," we can see that this is true from the example of Scipio, an outstanding

9. Among the historians who applauded Hannibal's feats but deplored the "inhuman cruelty" that made them possible was Livy himself, whom Machiavelli admired, but not uncritically.

man not only among those of his own time, but in all recorded history; yet his armies revolted in Spain, for no other reason than his excessive leniency in allowing his soldiers more freedom than military discipline permits.[1] Fabius Maximus rebuked him in the senate for this failing, calling him the corrupter of the Roman armies. When a lieutenant of Scipio's plundered the Locrians, he took no action in behalf of the people, and did nothing to discipline that insolent lieutenant; again, this was the result of his easygoing nature. Indeed, when someone in the senate wanted to excuse him on this occasion, he said there are many men who knew better how to avoid error themselves than how to correct error in others.[2] Such a soft temper would in time have tarnished the fame and glory of Scipio, had he brought it to the office of emperor; but as he lived under the control of the senate, this harmful quality of his not only remained hidden but was considered creditable.

Returning to the question of being feared or loved, I conclude that since men love at their own inclination but can be made to fear at the inclination of the prince, a shrewd prince will lay his foundations on what is under his own control, not on what is controlled by others. He should simply take pains not to be hated, as I said.

XVIII

THE WAY PRINCES SHOULD KEEP THEIR WORD

How praiseworthy it is for a prince to keep his word and live with integrity rather than by craftiness, everyone understands; yet we see from recent experience that those princes have accomplished most who paid little heed to keeping their promises, but who knew how craftily to manipulate the minds of men. In the end, they won out over those who tried to act honestly.

You should consider then, that there are two ways of fighting, one with laws and the other with force. The first is properly a human method, the second belongs to beasts. But as the first method does not always suffice, you sometimes have to turn to the second. Thus a prince must know how to make good use of both the beast and the man. Ancient writers made subtle note of this fact when they wrote that Achilles and many other princes of antiquity were sent to be reared by Chiron the centaur, who trained them in his discipline.[3] Having a teacher who is half man and half

1. In balancing Hannibal, the great Carthaginian commander, with his chief antagonist, Scipio Africanus, Machiavelli seems to be imitating the method of Plutarch, but he got most of his details from Livy.
2. The city of Locri in southern Italy was captured by Scipio in 205 B.C. and placed under Q. Pleminius. Livy tells

how he outdid even the Carthaginians in wanton brutality without suffering so much as a minor rebuke from Scipio.
3. In allegorizing Chiron as he does, Machiavelli is relatively original. If the mythographers know any such moral for the myth, they have hidden it in very remote places. A later writer, like Natale Conti (1568), follows Machiavelli.

beast can only mean that a prince must know how to use both these two natures, and that one without the other has no lasting effect.

Since a prince must know how to use the character of beasts, he should pick for imitation the fox and the lion. As the lion cannot protect himself from traps, and the fox cannot defend himself from wolves, you have to be a fox in order to be wary of traps, and a lion to overawe the wolves. Those who try to live by the lion alone are badly mistaken. Thus a prudent prince cannot and should not keep his word when to do so would go against his interest, or when the reasons that made him pledge it no longer apply.[4] Doubtless if all men were good, this rule would be bad; but since they are a sad lot, and keep no faith with you, you in your turn are under no obligation to keep it with them.

Besides, a prince will never lack for legitimate excuses to explain away his breaches of faith. Modern history will furnish innumerable examples of this behavior, showing how many treaties and promises have been made null and void by the faithlessness of princes, and how the man succeeded best who knew best how to play the fox. But it is a necessary part of this nature that you must conceal it carefully; you must be a great liar and hypocrite. Men are so simple of mind, and so much dominated by their immediate needs, that a deceitful man will always find plenty who are ready to be deceived. One of many recent examples calls for mention. Alexander VI never did anything else, never had another thought, except to deceive men, and he always found fresh material to work on. Never was there a man more convincing in his assertions, who sealed his promises with more solemn oaths, and who observed them less. Yet his deceptions were always successful, because he knew exactly how to manage this sort of business.

In actual fact, a prince may not have all the admirable qualities we listed, but it is very necessary that he should seem to have them. Indeed, I will venture to say that when you have them and exercise them all the time, they are harmful to you; when you just seem to have them, they are useful. It is good to appear merciful, truthful, humane, sincere, and religious; it is good to be so in reality. But you must keep your mind so disposed that, in case of need, you can turn to the exact contrary.[5] This has to be understood: a prince, and especially a new prince, cannot possibly exercise all those virtues for which men are called "good." To preserve the state, he often has to do things against his word, against charity, against humanity,

---

4. Machiavelli perhaps had in mind the folly of Louis XII of France in trying to honor with one pope a pledge he had made to another: see chapter III, note 4, p. 11. But truth to one's word was not the usual fault of princes in the Renaissance.
5. This recommendation that the prince should deliberately play the hypocrite has perhaps done more than any other passage of *The Prince* to darken Machiavelli's reputation. But it says nothing worse than what youthful Cyrus was required to learn in the first book of Xenophon's *Cyropaedia*.

against religion. Thus he has to have a mind ready to shift as the winds of fortune and the varying circumstances of life may dictate. And as I said above, he should not depart from the good if he can hold to it, but he should be ready to enter on evil if he has to.

Hence a prince should take great care never to drop a word that does not seem imbued with the five good qualities noted above; to anyone who sees or hears him, he should appear all compassion, all honor, all humanity, all integrity, all religion. Nothing is more necessary than to seem to have this last virtue. Men in general judge more by the sense of sight than by the sense of touch, because everyone can see but only a few can test by feeling. Everyone sees what you seem to be, few know what you really are; and those few do not dare take a stand against the general opinion, supported by the majesty of the government. In the actions of all men, and especially of princes who are not subject to a court of appeal, we must always look to the end. Let a prince, therefore, win victories and uphold his state; his methods will always be considered worthy, and everyone will praise them, because the masses are always impressed by the superficial appearance of things, and by the outcome of an enterprise. And the world consists of nothing but the masses; the few have no influence when the many feel secure. A certain prince of our own time, whom it's just as well not to name,[6] preaches nothing but peace and mutual trust, yet he is the determined enemy of both; and if on several different occasions he had observed either, he would have lost both his reputation and his throne.

XIX

ON AVOIDING CONTEMPT AND HATRED

Now that I have talked in detail about the most important of the qualities mentioned above, I'd like to discuss the others briefly under this general heading: that the prince should try to avoid anything which makes him hateful or contemptible, as was suggested above.[7] When he has avoided actions that will have this effect, he has done his best, and he will run no risks from his other vices. What makes him hated above all, as I said,[8] is his confiscating the property of his subjects or taking their women. He must not commit these acts, since most men, if you don't touch their property or their honor, will live contentedly. Then you have only to contend with the ambition of the few, which can easily be checked in a number of ways. What makes the prince contemptible is being considered changeable, trifling, effeminate, cowardly, or indecisive;

6. The not-very-covert allusion is to Ferdinand of Spain, a political animal who is said to have boasted toward the end of his life that he had deceived Louis XII twelve times hand running. Machia- velli actively disliked Ferdinand, calling him a shifty, shameless, tricky ruler, rather than a proper prince.
7. See chapter XVI.
8. See chapter XVII.

he should avoid this as a pilot does a reef, and make sure that his actions bespeak greatness, courage, seriousness of purpose, and strength. In the private controversies of his subjects, he should be sure that his judgment once passed is irrevocable; indeed, he should maintain such a reputation that nobody will even dream of trying to trick or manage him.

Any prince who gives such an impression is bound to be highly esteemed, and a man with such a reputation is hard to conspire against, hard to assail, as long as everyone knows he is a man of character and respected by his own people. For a prince must be on his guard in two directions: domestically, against his own subjects; and abroad, against foreign powers. From the latter he can defend himself with good weapons and good friends; if he has good weapons, he will never lack for good friends. And domestic affairs will always be secure, as long as foreign policy is successful, unless the situation is disturbed by a conspiracy. Indeed, even when foreigners turn on him, if he has organized his defenses and his life as I suggested, and does not lose his head, he will withstand every assault, just as I said Nabis the Spartan did.[9]

As for one's own subjects; even when no outside disturbance occurs, there is danger they may form a secret conspiracy; from such a plot the prince's best protection lies in not being hated or despised, and keeping himself in popular favor. In a previous passage I explained the necessity for this at length.[1] One of the strongest counters that a prince has against conspiracies is not to be hated by the mass of the people, because every man who conspires always thinks that by killing the prince he will be pleasing the people. But when he thinks his act will enrage them, he no longer has any stomach for the work, because the problems of a conspirator are enormous at best. Experience teaches us that, of many conspiracies attempted, few turn out successfully; because a man who conspires can hardly do so alone, and can take as co-conspirators only those whom he judges to be discontented. Yet as soon as you explain your plot to a malcontent, you have furnished him with a means to be very content indeed. For he has everything to gain by giving you away; and when he has everything to gain one way, and so much danger and loss the other way, he must be either a very special friend of yours or a bitter enemy of the prince, if he is to keep faith with you. In a word, there is nothing in the conspirator's life but fear, jealousy, and the awful prospect of punishment; while the prince is defended by the majesty of his office, by the laws, by the help of his allies, and by the state itself. And if to all this you add the good will of the people, it is impossible that any man will be

9. See chapter IX.
1. See chapters XV–XVIII. These sev- eral references to previous chapters of the book suggest review and summary.

rash enough to conspire against you.[2] Every conspirator is bound to live in fear before he executes his plot; but the man who conspires against a popular prince must also be fearful after his crime is committed—since then he will have the whole people against him, and from their hate he can hope for no refuge whatever.

I could give innumerable examples of this point, but one will suffice, that took place within the memory of our fathers. Messer Hannibal Bentivoglio, grandfather of the present Messer Hannibal, was murdered when he was prince of Bologna by a conspiracy of the Canneschi; he left behind only Messer Giovanni, then in his swaddling bands.[3] Immediately after the prince's murder, the people rose up and massacred all the Canneschi. The reason for this was simply the people's devotion to the house of Bentivogli, which was so great at that time that, when nobody was left in Bologna who could rule the state after Hannibal's death, the Bolognesi went to Florence to seek out a man of the Bentivogli family (though he had previously been regarded as the son of a blacksmith), and entrusted him with the governing of their city. He governed it till Messer Giovanni was of age to rule.

Thus I conclude that a prince should not worry too much about conspiracies, as long as his people are devoted to him; but when they are hostile, and feel hatred toward him, he should fear everything and everybody. Well-ordered states and prudent princes have made every effort to keep the aristocracy from desperation and to satisfy the populace by making them happy; this is one of the most important of a prince's duties.

Among the well-ordered and -governed kingdoms of our time is that of France, where one can observe a great many good institutions making for the liberty and security of the king. Outstanding among these is the parliament, and its authority.[4] The founder of the kingdom, clearly knowing the ambition of the nobility and their insolence, saw the necessity of putting a bit in their teeth by which they could be managed. At the same time he understood the hatred of the common people for the nobles, a hatred grounded in fear, and tried to reassure them. Yet he did not want this to be a particular responsibility of the king, lest he be accused of partiality—by the nobles for favoring the people, or by the people for favoring the

2. Machiavelli who dismisses conspiracies rather lightly here, is more impressed by them elsewhere; *Discorsi*, III, 6 is an extended analysis of several different historical conspiracies, and of the elements involved in them.

3. The murder of Hannibal Bentivoglio took place in 1445; his son Giovanni did not come of age till seventeen years later, in 1462. Santi Bentivoglio, who filled the gap, was probably a bastard son of Hercules, Hannibal's cousin; but

for the Bolognesi a left-handed Bentivoglio was clearly better than none.

4. Machiavelli's ideas on the form and function of the French Parliament are not very historical. It began under the early Capets as a court of law, where the king in person gave judgment in the presence of his vassals. The idea of using it to balance off the various estates did not occur till later, and certainly never had the importance that Machiavelli assigns it.

nobles. Thus he established a third judicial force which, while it was not the king's direct responsibility, could hold down the nobility and favor the commons. There could hardly be a better or more prudent arrangement than this, nor one serving better to promote the security of king and kingdom. And from this we can draw another notable lesson: princes should delegate unpleasant jobs to other people and reserve the pleasant functions for themselves.[5] Again let me conclude by saying that a prince should respect his nobles, but not let himself be hated by the people.

Many people who have studied the lives and deaths of the Roman emperors may think that they provide examples contrary to this opinion of mine, since some of them lived exemplary lives and showed great strength [*virtù*] of mind, yet lost the empire or were killed by subjects who conspired against them. By way of answering these objections, let me describe some of these emperors and show the reasons for which they came to grief; they will not be found much different from those I proposed. In passing, I will try to point out the most notable events in the history of those times, but I will limit myself to those emperors who came to the purple between Marcus the philosopher and Maximin. They were Marcus himself, Commodus his son, Pertinax, Julian, Severus, Antoninus Caracalla his son, Macrinus, Heliogabalus, Alexander, and Maximin.[6]

Now the first thing to note is that, unlike other princes who had to contend only with the ambition of nobles and the insolence of the people, the Roman emperors had a third difficulty: they had to cope with a cruel and avaricious soldiery. Satisfying both the soldiers and the populace at the same time proved so difficult that it cost many of the emperors their thrones. For the people generally wanted quiet, and thus were pleased with unambitious princes, while the soldiers loved a prince of warlike spirit, who was domineering, greedy, and cruel; they wanted to see these qualities exercised on the people, because that meant double wages for them, and satisfied their cruelty as well as their greed. These were the reasons why those emperors who had not a great reputation (granted by nature or acquired by political practice) could not keep the two factions in hand, and so came invariably to grief. Most of them, especially when they were new in office, recognized that they could not reconcile these two humors, so they chose to please the soldiers at the cost of doing harm to the people. This was a choice they had to

5. The somewhat cynical principle that Machiavelli is recommending here, to let nasty jobs be done by expendable agents, can be found as early as Xenophon's *Hiero*, a dialogue on the tyrant; it is a timeless piece of common sense.
6. This period of Roman history, from the accession of Marcus Aurelius (A.D. 161) to the death of Maximin (A.D. 238) is later than that covered by the great Roman historians. The fragmented history of Dio Cassius and that of Herodian (both in Greek) and the Latin biographies of the six *Scriptores historiae Augustae* are the chief authorities for the seventy-year period that Machiavelli covers; he used primarily Herodian, probably in Poliziano's Latin version.

make; because when princes cannot help being hated by someone, they ought first of all to try to avoid universal hatred, and when they cannot do this, they should try as hard as they can to avoid the hatred of the most powerful group around. Thus emperors who were new in office and needed special support, turned to the soldiers rather than the people, that policy serving them well or badly according to whether they maintained control over their troops or not.

These are the reasons why Marcus, Pertinax, and Alexander, who were all men of decent lives, lovers of justice, enemies of cruelty, humane, and benevolent, all came to bad ends—except for Marcus. Marcus alone lived and died in the highest honor, because he came to the purple by the law of heredity, and had nobody to thank for it, either soldiers or people. Besides, his many virtues [*virtù*], which made him an object of reverence to all, enabled him to keep both factions within bounds, as long as he lived, and he was never hated or despised. But Pertinax was created emperor against the will of the army; the soldiers were accustomed to a licentious life under Commodus, and could not endure the honest life toward which Pertinax tried to direct them. In this way he made himself hated, and to hate was added contempt because he was old, and this ruined him at the very beginning of his administration.

And here it should be noted that hatred may be earned by doing good just as much as by doing evil; and so, as I said above, a prince who wants to keep his state, is often bound to do what is not good. Because when that group is corrupt whose support you think you need—whether the people or the army or the nobility—then you have to follow their humors to satisfy them; and in that case, good deeds are harmful to you. But let us now consider Alexander, who was such a good man that, among his other praises, this one is recorded: that in the fourteen years of his reign, no man was ever put to death by his orders without a trial. Yet, being considered effeminate and under his mother's thumb, he fell into contempt, the army conspired against him, and murdered him.[7]

Turning now for contrast to the emperors Commodus, Severus, Antoninus Caracalla, and Maximin, you will find that they were extremely cruel and rapacious men; to satisfy their soldiery, they condoned every sort of lawlessness against the people; and yet they all came to a wretched end, except for Severus. The reason was that Severus was a man of such character [*tanta virtù*] that, by keeping the soldiers friendly to him, and oppressing the people, he was able

7. Pertinax was forced to become emperor in his old age and against his will; he lasted just three months in the job. Alexander Severus was just fourteen years old when the murder of Heliogabalus propelled him to the purple. But Machiavelli is making points to which these untidy individual circumstances are irrelevant.

to reign in prosperity all his life long: his talents [*virtù*] made him so remarkable, in the eyes of the people as well as the soldiery, that the former remained awestruck and appeased, the latter astonished and abashed.[8]

And since his actions were so striking and worthy of study by a new prince, I would like to show in brief what good use he made of the fox and the lion; which are the two natures that I said above must be imitated by a successful prince. When Severus realized that the Emperor Julian was a weakling, he persuaded the army he was leading in Sclavonia[9] that it was a good idea to go to Rome, in order to avenge the death of Pertinax, who had been killed by the Praetorian Guards. Under this pretext, and without any indication that he aspired to the purple, he led his army against Rome, and was in Italy before anyone there knew he had set out. As soon as he reached Rome, the senate, acting out of fear, elected him emperor and ordered Julian killed. After taking this first step, Severus faced two other difficulties in making himself master of the entire state: one was in Asia, where Pescennius Niger, leader of the Asiatic armies, had had himself proclaimed emperor, and the other was in the west, where Albinus also aspired to the empire. Seeing it would be rash to engage both these enemies at once, he decided to attack Niger and deceive Albinus. So he wrote the latter, saying that though the senate had elected him emperor, he wanted a partner in that dignity; he hailed him as Caesar and got the senate to declare him a colleague. Albinus took all this at face value. But then when Severus had defeated Niger, killed him, and pacified the East, he went back to Rome and complained in the senate that Albinus, unmindful of all the benefits showered on him, had treacherously tried to murder him. For this reason, Severus was bound to seek him out and punish his ingratitude. Whereupon, he hunted him down in France, deprived him of his authority, and took his life.

Whoever examines carefully the actions of this man will find that he was a most ferocious lion and a very clever fox; he was feared and respected by all, and his army did not hate him. Even though

8. The virtues [*virtù*] of Severus, which amounted to cold and ruthless decisiveness, are perceptibly different from the virtues [*virtù*] of Marcus Aurelius; in thus deliberately equating them, Machiavelli is in effect declaring that the moral qualities of a prince are virtues or vices only as they help or hinder his political functioning.

9. Severus was at Carnuntum, not far from modern Vienna; it was a frontier post on the Danube, where Marcus Aurelius had composed some of his *Meditations*. The year was A.D. 193. In estimating the reasons for Severus's success, the following circumstances may be useful to recall. He was forty-seven years old, son of a North African civil servant, and trained in administration from earliest youth. He had commanded legions; he had governed provinces. His hour struck just when the provincial legions, in whom the real military power resided, were growing restive at the continual empire making and empire breaking of the Praetorian Guard. Under the circumstances, it may have been a particular piece of luck for Severus that Latin was not his native language; his first tongue was Punic, and he appealed to the ragtag legionaries, who for centuries had been resentfully fighting along the distant, dangerous frontiers, as one of themselves.

he was a new man, it's no wonder that he could successfully hold
onto so great an empire, since his splendid reputation always protected him from that popular hatred which might have been the
consequence of his looting.[1] His son, Antoninus Caracalla, was also
a man of great talents, well suited to make him admirable in the
eyes of the people and popular with soldiers; he was a man of arms,
who could stand any kind of fatigue or hardship, who despised fine
food and all sorts of delicate living; and this made him very popular
with the army. But his cruelty was so ferocious, so unheard-of (after
endless individual murders, he killed most of the population of
Rome and the entire population of Alexandria), that he became
hateful to everyone, and even his intimate associates began to fear
him—so that he was finally murdered by a centurion in the middle
of his army. We should note here that assassinations of this sort,
long meditated by a fanatical mind, are impossible for a prince to
avert, because anyone who does not fear to die himself can carry
out such a deed. But since such episodes are very rare, the prince
need not be too much concerned about them. He ought only to beware of inflicting serious injury on any of his personal servants or
those who are employed near him in the service of the state. That
was the mistake of Antoninus, who had imposed a shameful death
on a brother of this centurion, and threatened the man himself
every day, though he still kept him in his bodyguard; this was a
rash thing to do, and, as it happened, brought about the emperor's
death.

Now let us come to Commodus, who found the empire easy to
acquire, since it descended to him by hereditary right, as son of
Marcus Aurelius; and if he had simply been content to follow his
father's footsteps, he would have satisfied both the populace and
the soldiers. But he was a cruel and beastly man, who, to exercise
his rapacity on the people, indulged his armies to the limit, and
directed them to license. On the other hand, he took no care for his
own dignity, descending many time into the theater to fight with
gladiators, and doing other completely vulgar things unworthy of
imperial majesty, till at last he became contemptible to his own soldiers. Then, when he was hated by one faction and despised by the
other, a conspiracy was formed against him, and he perished.

It remains now to describe Maximin. He was a man much prac-

---

1. Machiavelli omits any mention of Severus's ruthless terrorizing of the Roman
senate. As he himself had created a law
punishing anyone who murdered a sena-
tor, he was careful to expel his enemies
from the senate first, and then murder
them when they were no longer senators.
This did a good deal for his splendid
reputation. His son Caracalla seems to
have been more than half insane; having
murdered his brother Geta in their
mother's arms, he turned over the government to her, and spent the last years
of his life wandering from one remote
military frontier to another, seeking the
death with which his own soldiers at last
obliged him. Macrinus, who murdered
him and thereby gained the throne, retained it for less than a year.

ticed in war; and as the armies were disgusted by the effeminacy of Alexander, whom we described above, after his death they elected Maximin emperor. He was not long in power, because two things caused him to be hated and despised: one was his base birth (he had once been a shepherd in Thrace, everyone knew it, and it was much held against him); the other was his delay in entering Rome at the beginning of his reign to take possession of the royal throne. His prefects in Rome and other parts of the empire meanwhile carried out many harsh acts; and these gave everyone an impression of terrible personal cruelty. Thus everyone turned against him, some because of his base birth, others for fear of his bloodthirstiness; Africa was first to rebel, then the senate and all the Roman people followed, and all Italy conspired against him. Even his own army joined in; they were besieging Aquileia, found the assault difficult, were disgusted with his cruelty, feared him the less because he had so many enemies, and thus killed him.

I shall say nothing of Heliogabalus, Macrinus, and Julius because everyone despised them, and so they were quickly done away with. To conclude this discourse, let me say that the princes of our day have less trouble in satisfying by extraordinary means the demands of the soldiers under their command; though you have to have some concern for them, the conflicts are easily resolved, because modern princes do not have armies involved with provincial governments and administrations, like the armies of the Roman Empire. At that time, it was necessary to gratify the soldiers rather than the people, because the soldiers represented the greater power; nowadays, it is necessary to gratify the people rather than the soldiers, because the people have more power, except in the lands of the Turk and the sultan.[2] I except the Turk here, because he always keeps near the court twelve thousand infantry and fifteen thousand cavalry, on whom the strength and security of his rule depend; and, before anything else, he must keep these armies satisfied. So too with the realm of the sultan, which is all under military rule; he also has to keep the soldiers on his side without regard to the people. And it is to be noted that the sultan's state is unlike all others in one respect, where it most resembles the Christian pontificate. It cannot be called a hereditary monarchy, nor yet a new monarchy, because the sons of the old prince do not inherit the throne and assume command; instead a man is elected to the office by those who have authority to do so. Since the system is traditional, the monarchy

2. "The Turk" is the hereditary monarchy of the Ottoman Empire, under the direction, as it happened, of successive sultans—Muhammad II the Conqueror, Bayezid II, Selim I, son regularly succeeding father. By "the sultan" Machiavelli evidently means the caliphate, as established by Muhammad the prophet in the pattern of an elective monarchy, but radically modified, in its latter Egyptian manifestations, by frequent assassinations, insurrections, depositions, and efforts by the caliphs to get their sons appointed to succeed them.

cannot be called a new one; it has none of the difficulties inherent in new regimes, for even though the prince himself may be new, the laws of the state are old, and are set up to receive him just as if he were a hereditary monarch.

But, to return to our topic, let me say that whoever studies the record described above will see that either hatred or contempt was the ruin of the Roman emperors we mentioned; and he will understand how the very different paths they took led each of them to his destined end, whether happy or unhappy. For Pertinax and Alexander, since they were new princes, it was useless and harmful to imitate Marcus Aurelius, who was emperor by hereditary right; so too it would have been fatal for Caracalla, Commodus, and Maximin to imitate Severus, since they had not sufficient character [*virtù*] to follow in his footsteps. Thus a new prince, coming to power in a new state, cannot imitate the actions of Marcus Aurelius, nor indeed is he bound to follow after Severus; but he should take from Severus those elements of his conduct that are necessary to found his state, and from Marcus those that are useful and creditable in preserving a state already stabilized and secure.[3]

XX

WHETHER BUILDING FORTRESSES AND OTHER DEFENSIVE POLICIES OFTEN ADOPTED BY PRINCES ARE USEFUL OR NOT

In order to keep a tight grasp on the state, some princes have disarmed their subjects; others have tried to control their captured cities by dividing them into factions; still others have deliberately formented hostilities against themselves; others again have made a point of winning over those who were suspect at the beginning of their reign; some have built new fortresses, others have torn down old ones. And though there is no formulating a definite rule about these many alternatives without knowing the particular circumstances of the state to be suited, still I will discuss these topics as generally as the nature of the subject allows.

There never was a new prince who disarmed his subjects; on the contrary, when he found them without weapons, he always armed them. The reason is that when you arm them, their arms become yours; those who were suspect become your faithful supporters, and those who were faithful before continue so, and from merely being

---

3. This perfunctory and superficial chapter concludes with some perfunctory and superficial moral generalities. In reality the downfall of Alexander Severus had nothing to do with his being a new prince: he was not, and the virtues fatal to him contributed to the success of Marcus Aurelius. The judgment about Caracalla, Commodus, and Maximin is an obvious begging of the question; if they had acted like Severus, Machiavelli would have concluded that they had his *virtù*. Finally, it is apparent that in all these judgments, Machiavelli is making liberal use of historical hindsight, and tailoring his account of the different men's careers to the different fates he knows they met.

your subjects become your partisans. Naturally, you can't arm all your subjects, but when those whom you've armed are well treated, you can consider yourself safer from the others. Those you select for special favor will think themselves obliged to you, and the others will forgive you, judging that men deserve special rewards when they assume special risks and obligations. But when you disarm them, you begin to alienate them; you advertise your mistrust of them, which may come from your suspecting them of cowardice or treachery; both these insinuations will raise hatred against you. And since you cannot remain unarmed yourself, you will have to turn to mercenary armies, the quality of which was discussed above: even if they were good, they couldn't possibly defend you from powerful enemies and treacherous subjects. Therefore, as I've said, a new prince in a new kingdom has always armed the citizens; the histories are full of examples. But when a prince acquires a new state and attaches it, like a fresh graft, on his old state, then the new acquisition must be disarmed, except for those who actively helped you acquire it; even those people, as time and occasions allow, must be rendered soft and compliant. Things have to be arranged so that all the arms in your new state are in the hands of your own soldiers, who used to live in your own state, under your eye.

The so-called wise men among our ancestors used to say that Pistoia was to be held by factions and Pisa by fortresses; on this principle, they encouraged factionalism in various cities that they possessed, in order to control them more easily.[4] In those days, when a kind of balance of powers prevailed in Italy, this may well have been a good idea; but I don't believe we can take it as a precedent nowadays. As a matter of fact, I don't think factions ever did any good; on the contrary, it is inevitable, when an enemy approaches, that divided cities will collapse immediately, since the weaker faction will join with the invader, and the stronger faction will not be able to hold out against them both.

It was on this logic, I suppose, that the Venetians fostered the Guelf and Ghibelline parties in the cities they controlled; and though they never let matters come to bloodshed, still they encouraged the quarrel, thinking that when the citizens were occupied in their feuds, they would not unite against the Venetians. But things did not turn out according to their plan, as everyone knows; after their defeat at Vailà, one of the factions took fire and snatched the whole state from them.[5] Besides, these policies are an argument of weakness in the prince. In a strong state, divisions of this sort would

4. Machiavelli is often impatient with wise saws and ancient adages, and particularly this one about Pistoia, since he had seen first-hand the consequences of factional rioting there: see chapter XVII, note 7, page 47.
5. After the defeat at Vailà, the Venetians were not exactly overrun by a faction; for a mixture of selfish and generous reasons, they released their tributary cities to their own devices, and tried to equivocate for themselves between pope and emperor.

never be permitted. They serve only in times of peace, when indeed subjects can be managed more easily; but when war breaks out, the weakness comes to the surface.

Princes become great, no doubt about it, by overcoming the difficulties and obstacles placed in their way; thus fortune, when it wants to favor a new prince (who has more need of gaining a personal reputation than a hereditary prince), gives him enemies who are active against him, so that he can overcome them and climb even higher on the ladder that his enemies have brought to him. For this reason, many hold that a shrewd prince will, when he can, subtly encourage some enmity to himself, so that by overcoming it he can augment his own reputation.[6]

Especially when they are new, princes have often found more fidelity and serviceability in men who at first were suspect than in men who originally enjoyed the royal confidence. Pandolfo Petrucci, prince of Siena, ruled his state more with men he did not trust than with men whom he did.[7] But there is no general rule in this matter, because it varies with circumstances. I shall say only this: that if the men who at the beginning of a regime are considered its enemies are in need of support to maintain themselves, the prince will have no trouble at all in winning them over. They are the more deeply obliged to serve him faithfully because they know that only good service will cancel the bad impression he had of them. Thus the prince always gets better service from them than from men who feel too sure of their jobs, and so neglect his interests. In connection with this matter, I feel impelled to remind princes who have acquired a new state with the help of the local inhabitants, that they should consider carefully what motives stirred their supporters. If it was not native affection for the new prince, but just discontent with the previous state, then he will have great difficulty keeping them friendly, because he will not be able to satisfy them. Considering carefully the principle at work here, in the light of ancient and modern examples, you will see that it is much easier to gain as friends those men who were satisfied with the earlier state, and therefore were hostile to the conqueror, than those men who, because they were discontented in the earlier state, looked with favor on the new prince and helped him take over.[8]

6. Machiavelli passes no judgment on the princely practice of fomenting insurrections in order to make a reputation by crushing them. What he describes is the functioning of the agent provocateur, familiar in repressive regimes of all sorts, and serving many different functions.

7. Pandolfo Petrucci, leader of the aristocratic faction in Siena, may well have ruled with the aid of men he did not trust, but no other historian records this judgment. In making the point, Machiavelli can scarcely have been unaware that the Medici, to whom he was addressing his book, did not much trust *him*, Machiavelli. Petrucci, highly respected, very successful, and only recently dead, provided good precedent for an action in which Machiavelli had a certain interest.

8. The major principle set forth here (that revolutionary regimes, once established, depend for their survival, not on revolutionaries, but on managerial types) has been many times verified, as in the English, French, and Russian revolutions.

It has been customary for princes who want to keep a tight grasp on their states to build fortresses for use as a checkrein on those who might want to rise against them, and as a place of secure refuge against a first attack. I approve of this policy, because it has been used since ancient times; yet in our own days Messer Niccolò Vitelli has been observed to demolish two fortresses in Città di Castello as a means of holding onto that state. Guidobaldo, duke of Urbino, when he returned to his kingdom after being driven out by Cesare Borgia, razed all the fortresses in the kingdom to the ground, and thought himself much less likely to lose his kingdom a second time without them; the Bentivogli did the same thing when they returned to Bologna.[9] Thus fortresses may be useful or otherwise, according to circumstances; if they help you one way, they hurt you another. And the matter may be summarized as follows: the prince who fears his own people more than he does foreigners ought to build fortresses, but a prince who is more afraid of foreigners than of his own people can neglect them. The castle that Francesco Sforza built in Milan has been and will be the cause of more disturbance to the house of Sforza than anything else in that state.[1]

Actually, the best fortress of all consists in not being hated by your people. However many fortresses you hold, if the people hate you, the forts will not save you, because once the people have taken up arms, they will never lack for foreigners to come to their aid. In our own day, the only prince who profited by forts was the countess of Forlì, when her husband Count Girolamo died; by taking refuge in the fortress she was able to escape the rising of the people, hold out till aid came from Milan, and thus regain her state. At that time, there were no foreign powers around who could come to the aid of the people. But later on her forts were of little value when Cesare Borgia attacked her, and her people in their hostility joined with the outsider. So on both occasions, it would have been safer for her if, instead of trusting to fortresses, she had managed not to be hated by her people.[2]

All things considered, then, I may approve of those who build

9. These various instances of fortress razing point somewhat different morals. Niccolò, father of Vitellozzo and Paolo Vitelli, destroyed castles at Città di Castello at a time when he had just returned from exile—as a gesture of confidence in his people. Guidobaldo, duke of Urbino, destroyed fortifications because he found by bitter experience that they were more useful to an invader than to him. The Bentivogli when they got back Bologna in 1511 destroyed a castle that Pope Julius had built there to command the city—destroying thus an emblem of the invader's power. In each instance, smashing the fortress meant something different, politically.

1. Francesco Sforza built the Castello, which still stands, shortly after becoming duke of Milan; within Machiavelli's recent memory, Ludovico had lost it twice without a shot being fired.

2. The countess of Forlì was Caterina Sforza, niece of Il Moro. After her husband was murdered in 1488, Caterina held out in the fortress till help came from her uncle. But in 1500 Cesare Borgia, in the course of his first campaign, compelled her to surrender. Machiavelli admired her courage but deplored her lack of popular support.

fortresses or of those who do not, depending on the circumstances; but it is a foolish man who, because he puts his trust in fortresses, thinks he need not worry about the enmity of his people.

XXI
HOW A PRINCE SHOULD ACT TO ACQUIRE REPUTATION

Nothing gives a prince more prestige than undertaking great enterprises and setting a splendid example for his people. In our day we have Ferdinand of Aragon, the present king of Spain.[3] He may be considered a new prince, since from being a weak king he has risen to become, for fame and glory, the first prince of Christendom; and if you consider his actions, you will find all of them very great and some of them extraordinary. At the beginning of his reign he attacked Granada, and that enterprise was the cornerstone of his reign. For some time he carried on the siege in a leisurely way, and without any outside distractions; he kept all the barons of Castille preoccupied with it, and while they were thinking of the war, they never considered the changes he was making in the state. Thus he acquired reputation and authority over them without their being aware of it. Money from the Church and the people enabled him to recruit big armies, and in the course of this long war to build a military establishment which has since won him much honor. Apart from this, he made use of the pretext of religion to prepare the way for still greater projects, and adopted a policy of pious cruelty in expelling the Moors from his kingdom and despoiling them; his conduct here could not have been more despicable nor more unusual.[4] On the same pretext, he attacked Africa; he carried out a campaign in Italy; and finally he assaulted France.[5] Thus he has always been planning and carrying out some great design which has enthralled and preoccupied the minds of his subjects, and kept them fascinated with the outcome of his schemes. And his various projects have risen one out of the other, so that they have never allowed men leisure to take concerted action against him.

It is also helpful for a prince to give special evidence of his ability

3. Admiration mingles with repugnance in this sketch of Ferdinand the Catholic. Ferdinand was a "new prince" in a sense not explicitly noted by Machiavelli, since the throne of Castille really belonged to Isabella; the unification of Aragon and Castille was what some Castilian barons might have objected to, if he had not distracted them with a series of wars. Ferdinand's boldness was thus even greater than it seemed.
4. The adjectives are *miserabile* and *raro*. The expulsion of the Moors (and simultaneously of the Jews) deprived Spain of two energetic and intelligent minorities, who might have done some-

thing to avert the blight that fell on Spain after her golden age.
5. Dates here suggest the pace of Ferdinand's activity and the casualness of Machiavelli's chronology. The conquest of Granada was completed after ten years of war in 1492; the expulsion of the Moors in 1502; the Italian campaign begun in 1495 culminated in the war with France over Naples 1502–4 and the assault on Navarre in 1512; the conquest of Tripoli took place in 1510. In most of these undertakings Ferdinand made a mighty show of religious motives, but it was hardly more than a show.

in internal affairs, as we hear about Messer Bernabò of Milan;[6] whenever anyone did anything special affecting the state, whether for good or evil, he chose a way of rewarding or punishing him that gave rise to comment. It should be a prince's major concern in everything he does to give the impression of being a great man and of possessing excellent insight.

A prince will also be well thought of when he is a true friend or an honest enemy, that is, when, without any hedging, he takes a stand for one side and against another. It is always better to do this than to stand on one's neutrality; because if two of your powerful neighbors come to blows, they are either such people that you have to fear the winner, or they are not. In either case, it will be better for you to assert yourself and wage open war; because, in the first case, when you do not take sides, you are bound to be the prey of the winner, to the pleasure and satisfaction of the loser. Then you have no excuse, nothing to defend you, nobody to take you in; a winner never wants doubtful friends, who would not support him in adversity, and a loser will not take you in because you were not willing to take your chances with him, sword in hand.

When Antiochus came into Greece, brought there by the Aetolians to drive out the Romans, he sent ambassadors to the Achaeans to persuade them to neutrality; meanwhile the Romans were persuading the Achaeans to take up arms on their side. The matter came up for consideration in the Achaean council, and when Antiochus's envoy had spoken for neutrality, the Roman ambassador answered: "What these people tell you about not getting mixed up in a war could not be more opposed to your real interests; if you do that, whatever the outcome of the war, you will fall prey to the victors, without any hope of mercy."[7]

As a general thing, anyone who is not your friend will advise neutrality, while anyone who is your friend will ask you to join him, weapon in hand. Weak-minded princes who want to avoid present dangers generally follow the path of neutrality and generally come to grief. But when the prince declares himself like a man in favor of one side, even if this ally wins and becomes so powerful that you are at his mercy, still he owes you something, he is your friend. Men are never so dishonest that they will show gross ingratitude by turning immediately on their helpers. Besides, victories are never so decisive that the victor does not have to maintain some moderation,

6. Bernabò Visconti divided rule of Milan in the late fourteenth century with his nephew (later to become his executioner) Gian Galeazzo. All the Visconti were infamous for the hideous ingenuity and cruelty of their punishments but Messer Bernabò was the worst; in addition, he sired over thirty children, legitimate and illegitimate, whom he tended to marry off for their advantage or his own. Machiavelli may have had this profuse generosity in mind when he selected Bernabò to exemplify skill in internal affairs, "e governi di dentro."

7. The episode is described by Livy XXXV, 48.

some show of justice. But even if your ally loses, you will still be dear to him; he will help you as long as he can, and be a staunch ally when your fortune rises again.

As for the second case, when neither of the two powers who are at odds is so strong that you have to be afraid of his winning, it is all the more sensible for you to take sides, since you are now able to ruin one with the aid of the other, who would have saved him if he had any sense. The winner, whoever he is, will be at your mercy, and the side to which you throw your weight is bound to win. And here let me say that a prince should never ally himself with someone more powerful than himself in order to attack a third party, except in cases of absolute necessity. As I said before, when your ally wins, you remain his prisoner; and princes ought to avoid, as far as they can, being under the control of other people. The Venetians joined with the king of France against the duke of Milan;[8] they could perfectly well have avoided this alliance, which led directly to their ruin. There are of course times when an alliance cannot be avoided (for example, the Florentines had to join in when the pope and the king of Spain sent armies to subdue Lombardy),[9] and then the prince must take sides, for the reasons given above. No leader should ever suppose he can invariably take the safe course, since all choices involve risks. In the nature of things, you can never try to escape one danger without encountering another; but prudence consists in knowing how to recognize the nature of the different dangers and in accepting the least bad as good.

A prince ought also to show himself an admirer of talent [*virtù*], giving recognition to men of ability [*uomini virtuosi*] and honoring those who excel in a particular art. Moreover, he should encourage his citizens to ply their callings in peace, whether in commerce, agriculture, or in any other business. The man who improves his holdings should not be made to fear that they will be taken away from him; the man who opens up a branch of trade should not have to fear that he will be taxed out of existence. Instead, the prince should bestow prizes on the men who do these things, and on anyone else who takes the pains to enrich the city or state in some special way. He should also, at fitting times of the year, entertain his people with festivals and spectacles. And because every city is divided into professional guilds and family groupings, he should be inward with these people, and attend their gatherings

8. In 1499, when Louis XII first expelled Lodovico from Milan.
9. In 1512, when Julius II and Ferdinand united to drive out the French. Machiavelli discreetly avoids saying that the Florentine government with which he was involved backed the wrong horse, holding to the French alliance and thus bringing about the defeat of Machiavelli's militia by Spanish regulars at Prato, and the return of the Medici. The platitudes which follow, about choosing the lesser of two evils, date back at least to Cicero, *De officiis*, III, i, 3.

from time to time, giving evidence of his humanity and munifi-
cence, yet avoiding any compromise to his dignity, for that must be
preserved at all costs.[1]

XXII

ON A PRINCE'S PRIVATE COUNSELORS

Choosing his ministers is a matter of no small importance to a
prince, since they will be good or bad, depending on his judgment.
The first notion one gets of a prince's intelligence comes from the
men around him; when they are able and loyal, you may be sure he
is wise, because he knew enough to recognize their ability and command their loyalty. When they are otherwise, you can always form
a poor opinion of the prince, because he made an error in his very
first choice.

Nobody who knew that Messer Antonio da Venafro was a minister of Pandolfo Petrucci, prince of Siena, could fail to consider Pandolfo a thoroughly worthy man, since he had this sort of minister.[2]
There are, in fact, three sorts of brains: one understands on its own,
another understands what others tell it, and the third understands
neither itself nor other people. The first sort is superb, the second
sort very good, the third sort useless.[3] Thus it necessarily followed
that if Pandolfo was not of the first sort, he must have been of the
second; since a man who has wit enough to discern good words and
deeds from bad ones, even if he could not invent the good himself,
can tell his minister's good ideas from his bad ones, encourage the
former and correct the latter. The minister cannot hope to deceive
such a master, and so continues to serve well.

There is one way for a prince to judge of a minister that never
fails. When you notice that your minister is thinking more of himself than of you, and that everything he does serves his own interest, a man like this will never make a good minister; you cannot
possibly trust him. The man who holds a prince's kingdom in his
hand should think, not of himself, but of the prince; he should not
even be aware of anything but his master's business. And on the
other hand, the prince who wants to keep his minister obedient
should think of his welfare, honor him, enrich him, load him with
honors and offices. Thus the minister will not be able to stand without the prince, the many honors will keep him from looking else-

1. In his advice about how the prince
should seek popularity among his subjects, Machiavelli is largely repeating
commonplace wisdom of his own day
and of antiquity. The last part of the
paragraph paraphrases Xenophon, *Hiero*,
chapter IX.
2. Antonio da Venafro was a lawyer

long in the employ of Pandolfo Petrucci,
prince of Siena; Machiavelli's friend,
Francesco Vettori, says he was the most
persuasive man he ever heard. See chapter XX, note 7, p. 61.
3. The three sorts of mind are described
in Livy XXII, 29, but the distinction was
commonplace, even in Livy's day.

where for more honor, the many riches will keep him from thinking of more riches, and the many offices will give him reason to fear changes. When the prince and his minister stand on these terms, they can have complete confidence in one another; when things are otherwise, they always turn out badly, either for one or the other.

XXIII

HOW TO AVOID FLATTERERS

I don't want to omit an important point on which princes find it hard to avoid error unless they are extremely prudent and choose their advisers very wisely. Courts are always full of flatterers; men take such pleasure in their own concerns, and are so easily deceived about them, that this plague of flattery is hard to escape. Besides, in defending against flattery, one runs the further risk of incurring contempt. For there is no way to protect yourself from flattery except by letting men know that you will not be offended at being told the truth. But when anyone can tell you the truth, you will not have much respect. Hence a prudent prince should adopt a third course, bringing wise men into his council and giving them alone free license to speak the truth—and only on those points where the prince asks for it, not on others. But he should ask them about everything, hear his advisers out, and make his decision after thinking things over, according to his own style. In dealing with his advisory councils and every member of them, he should make clear that the more freely they speak their minds, the better he will like it. But apart from these counselors he should not listen to anyone; he should go straight to the matter under discussion and stand firmly by his decision. Any prince who behaves differently will either be subject to the importunings of flatterers or will waver between different views of the subject, as a result of which he will be little respected.

In this connection, I'd like to propose a modern example. Father Luca, a servant of Maximilian, the present emperor,[4] in speaking of His Majesty, said that he never took counsel with anyone, and never did anything the way he wanted to. The reason for this was that he went about things in a way exactly contrary to that described above. The emperor is a secretive man, he communicates his plans to nobody, he accepts no advice; but when his plans become publicly known, as they start to be put into effect, then

4. Pre' = Prete = Father Luca Raimondi was one of the chief agents of Maximilian I (1459–1519), the Holy Roman emperor. Machiavelli got to know Raimondi during his legation to the emperor in 1507–08; about this experience he wrote several reports, never failing to emphasize the way Maximilian's erratic and wavering conduct rendered ineffectual his many good qualities as soldier and statesman.

they start to be contradicted by his ministers; and the emperor, who is easy to push around, gives up on them. Thus whatever he does one day he undoes the next; nobody understands what he really wants or plans to do; and there is no way of counting on his decisions even when they are made.

A prince should always take counsel, then, but when *he* wants advice, not when other people want to give it. On the contrary, he should prevent anyone from offering him uncalled-for advice. But he should also be a liberal questioner, and afterwards a patient hearer of the truth regarding whatever he has asked about. Many people think that a prince who is considered prudent gets that reputation, not on his own merits, but because he has good counselors around him. That's completely wrong. For this is a general and unfailing rule: that a prince who is not shrewd himself cannot get good counseling, unless he just happens to put himself in the hands of a single able man who makes all the decisions and is very knowing. In such a case, an ignorant prince might rule well, but it could not last, because in short order the counselor would take over supreme power. If he consults with several different advisers, a prince without wisdom will never get the different opinions coordinated, will never make a policy. Each of the ministers will think of his own interests, and the prince will not know how to recognize them for what they are, or how to make them pull together. Ministers are bound to act this way, because men will always turn out badly for you unless they are forced to be good. Hence I conclude that the prince's wisdom does not come from having good policies recommended to him; on the contrary, good policy, whoever suggests it, comes from the wisdom of the prince.

XXIV

WHY THE PRINCES OF ITALY HAVE LOST THEIR DOMINIONS

The precepts given above, if properly observed, will help a new prince appear like an old one, and quickly make him more secure and better established on his throne than if it had been his for years. For the actions of a new prince are watched much more sharply than those of an hereditary prince; and when they are recognized as shrewd [*virtuose*], they do more to win men over and attract a deeper commitment than anything done by an established regime. Men are much more attracted by immediate than by remote events; when they find things going well in the here and now, they are pleased, and think of nothing else. Indeed, they will defend a new prince boldly as long as he himself does not let them down elsewhere. And so he will have double glory, from establishing a new state and then from having enriched and strengthened it with good laws, good armies, and good examples. Just so, the prince will suffer a double disgrace if he was born to the purple and then through his own lack of good sense lost it.

And if we consider those Italian lords who have lost their dominions in our day, like the king of Naples, the duke of Milan, and others, we shall find that they all made that first mistake which was described at length above,[5] of not maintaining their armed forces; and besides, some of them had the people against them, and others, who had the people on their side, could not protect themselves against the nobles. If a state has power enough to field an army, it can be lost only through errors like these. Philip of Macedon, not the father of Alexander, but the one who was defeated by Titus Quintius, had no great state, compared with the power of the Greeks and Romans who attacked him; but because he was a military man who knew how to win the favor of the people and keep the loyalty of the nobles, he held out against his enemies for several years, and even though in the end he lost a couple of cities, still he kept his kingdom.[6]

Thus these princes of ours, who, after holding power for many years, finally lose it, should not blame fortune, but rather their own sloth; they never thought, during quiet times, that things could change (and this is a common failing of men: they never think of storms so long as the sky is blue). Then when the tempest breaks, their first thought is to run away, not to defend themselves; they hope that the people, when they are tired of the arrogance of their conquerors, will call them back.[7] Maybe when there is no other recourse, this policy will work; but to abandon other remedies for this one is complete foolishness. There is never any point to falling simply in the hope of finding somebody else to pick you up. Whether this comes to pass or not, it never makes for your security,

5. Though he mentions Frederick of Aragon (the King of Naples), and gestures at "others," Machiavelli has primarily in mind, throughout this brief chapter, Ludovico Sforza, duke of Milan. He was a luxurious, lazy, dissolute, deceitful prince, no warrior and no leader of men. It is a fair argument that if he had been half the soldier his father was, the French would never have taken Milan so easily or held it so long. But Frederick is a different case altogether. He was dispossessed through the collusion of the two greatest powers on the continent, France and Spain; the perfidy of his kinsman Ferdinand was a stab in the back that he had no reason to suspect; and no force that he could conceivably have mustered from his little kingdom would have sufficed against Ferdinand and Louis, combined.

6. Philip V of Macedon (221–179 B.C.) fought two wars against the Romans under Titus Quintus Flamininus. But though he struggled manfully, Machiavelli overstates the degree of his success. Livy tells us (XXXIII, 30) that after his final defeat at Cynoscephalae (197 B.C.), he was practically wiped out as an independent prince.

7. Once again, Machiavelli glances at Ludovico Il Moro; after the first invasion he ran away, but was recalled, when the populace rose against the French; after he was deposed a second time, there was no question of recall; he died in a French jail. See chapter III, note 9, pp. 5–6.

since it is a cowardly kind of defense that does not depend on your own efforts. The only good, safe, and dependable defenses are those that you control yourself with your own energy [*virtù*].

XXV

THE INFLUENCE OF LUCK ON HUMAN AFFAIRS AND THE WAYS TO COUNTER IT

I realize that many people have thought, and still do think, that events are so governed in this world that the wisdom of men cannot possibly avail against them, indeed is altogether useless.[8] On this basis, you might say that there is no point in sweating over anything, we should simply leave all matters to fate. This opinion has been the more popular in our own times because of the tremendous change in things during our lifetime, that actually is still going on today, beyond what anyone could have imagined. Indeed, sometimes when I think of it, I incline toward this opinion myself. Still, rather than give up on our free will altogether, I think it may be true that Fortune governs half of our actions, but that even so she leaves the other half more or less, in our power to control. I would compare her to one of those torrential streams which, when they overflow, flood the plains, rip up trees and tear down buildings, wash the land away here and deposit it there; everyone flees before them, everyone yields to their onslaught, unable to stand up to them in any way. This is how they are; yet this does mean that men cannot take countermeasures while the weather is still fine, shoring up dikes and dams, so that when the water rise again, they are either carried off in a channel or confined where they do no harm. So with Fortune, who exerts all her power where there is no strength [*virtù*] prepared to oppose her, and turns to smashing things up wherever there are no dikes and restraining dams. And if you look at Italy, which is the seat of all these tremendous changes, where they all began, you will see that she is an open country without any dikes or ditches. If she were protected by forces of proper valor [*virtù*], as are Germany, Spain, and France,[9] either this flood would never have wrought such destruction as it has, or it might

8. We today are likely to think this sort of loose, defeatist opinion could be held only by uneducated "popular" thinkers; but Fortuna was a very real force in Renaissance philosophy, with plenty of classical precedent; she was often identified with Nature, with Fate, with Nemesis, or (under the epithet Panthea) with all the other gods combined. Her omnipotence was a cliché, the variations on which are listed by Natale Conti in his *Mythologiae* (IV, 9).

9. Machiavelli had previously (chapter

IV) described France as easy to take though hard to hold precisely because it was divided by political dikes and dams. What he seems to envisage as ideal is a political arrangement combining local loyalties and traditions with an overall central authority. It is interesting that he does not distinguish Germany, in this respect, from France and Spain—though, as late as the nineteenth century, Germany would be legendary for the divisions of its petty princedoms.

not even have occurred at all. And let this much suffice on the general topic of opposing Fortune.

But coming now to the particulars, let me observe that we see a prince flourishing today and ruined tomorrow, and yet no change has taken place in his nature or any of his qualities. I think this happens, primarily, for the reasons discussed at length above, that is, that a prince who depends entirely on Fortune comes to grief immediately she changes. I believe further that a prince will be fortunate who adjusts his behavior to the temper of the times, and on the other hand will be unfortunate when his behavior is not well attuned to the times.[1] Anyone can see that men take different paths in their search for the common goals of glory and riches; one goes cautiously, another boldly; one by violence, another by stealth; one by patience, another in the contrary way; yet any one of these different methods may be successful. Of two cautious men, one will succeed in his design, the other not; so too, a rash man and a cautious man may both succeed, though their approaches are so different. And this stems from nothing but the temper of the times, which does or does not accord with their method of operating. Hence two men proceeding in different ways may, as I've said, produce the same effect; while two men proceeding in the same way will vary in their effectiveness, one failing, one succeeding. This too explains the variation in what is good; for if a prince conducts himself with patience and caution, and the times and circumstances are favorable to those qualities, he will flourish; but if times and circumstances change, he will come to ruin unless he changes his method of proceeding. No man, however prudent, can adjust to such radical changes, not only because we cannot go against the inclination of nature, but also because when one has always prospered by following a particular course, he cannot be persuaded to leave it. Thus the cautious man, when it is time to act boldly, does not know how, and comes to grief; if he could only change his nature with times and circumstances, his fortune would not change.

In everything he undertook, Pope Julius proceeded boldly; and he found the times and circumstances of his life so favorable to this sort of procedure, that he always came off well. Consider his first campaign against Bologna, when Messer Giovanni Bentivogli was still alive.[2] The Venetians were unhappy with it, and so was the king of Spain; he held conversations about it with the French; but Julius, with his usual assurance and energy, directed the expedition

1. See *Discorsi*, III, 8 (pp. 118–20) and the letter to Piero Soderini (pp. 127–30) for a further statement of Machiavelli's truly cynical view that success in government is a matter of adapting oneself to circumstances.

2. Writing at the time (1506), Machiavelli was very conscious of Pope Julius's rashness in gambling on French support. His reports from the field, collected as *Legazione seconda alla corte di Roma* compare well with his historical hindsight, as in *Discorsi*, III, 44.

in person. His activity kept the Spanish and the Venetians uneasy and inactive; the former were afraid, and the latter thought they saw a chance to recover the entire kingdom of Naples. Finally, the pope drew the king of France into his enterprise, because when the king saw what he was doing, and realized that he needed the pope's friendship to put down the Venetians, he judged that he could not deny the support of his troops without openly offending him.[3] Thus Julius carried off, in his rash and adventurous way, an enterprise that no other pope, who exercised the greatest human prudence, could successfully have performed. If he had waited before leaving Rome till all the diplomatic formalities were concluded, as any other pope would have done, he would never have succeeded. The king of France would have found a thousand excuses, and the other powers would have given him a thousand reasons to be afraid. His other actions can be omitted, as they were all like this one, and all turned out well. The shortness of his life prevented him from having the opposite experience; but in fact if circumstances had ever required him to act cautiously, he would have been ruined at once; he could never have varied from the style to which nature inclined him.

I conclude, then, that so long as Fortune varies and men stand still, they will prosper while they suit the times, and fail when they do not. But I do feel this: that it is better to be rash than timid, for Fortune is a woman, and the man who wants to hold her down must beat and bully her.[4] We see that she yields more often to men of this stripe than to those who come coldly toward her. Like a woman, too, she is always a friend of the young, because they are less timid, more brutal, and take charge of her more recklessly.

XXVI

AN EXHORTATION TO RESTORE ITALY TO LIBERTY AND FREE HER FROM THE BARBARIANS

Considering, therefore, the matters discussed above, I ask myself whether at present the hour is ripe to hail a new prince in Italy, if there is material here that a careful, able [*virtuoso*] leader could mold into a new form which might bring honor to him and benefits to all men; and I answer that all things now appear favorable to a new prince, so much so that I cannot think of any time more suit-

---

3. Pope Julius took to the field against the Baglioni of Perugia and the Bentivogli of Bologna, on August 26, 1506; he took Perugia on September 13, and Bologna on November 11. During most of Julius's campaign, Machiavelli was with the papal court as Florentine legate, and could thus observe at first hand the diplomatic indecision of the Spaniards and Venetians.

4. The ninth story of Boccaccio's ninth day begins with a little lecture by the queen for the day: her theme is the ancient traditional theme of masculine "wisdom," "Good wife and bad wife both need the stick."

able than the present. And if, as I said above, it was necessary, to bring out the power [*virtù*] of Moses, that the children of Israel should be slaves in Egypt; and if, to know the magnanimity of Cyrus, it was necessary that the Persians be oppressed by the Medes; and for Theseus's merit to be known, that the Athenians should be scattered; then, at the present time, if the power [*virtù*] of an Italian spirit is to be manifested, it was necessary that Italy be reduced to her present state; and that she be more enslaved than the Hebrews, more abject than the Persians, more widely dispersed than the Athenians; headless, orderless, beaten, stripped, scarred, overrun, and plagued by every sort of disaster.⁵

And though one man recently showed certain gleams, such as made us think he was ordained by God for our salvation, still we saw how, at the very zenith of his career, he was deserted by Fortune.⁶ Thus Italy, left almost lifeless, waits for a leader who will heal her wounds, stop the ravaging of Lombardy, end the looting of the Kingdom and of Tuscany, and minister to those sores of hers that have been festering so long. Behold how she implores God to send someone to free her from the cruel insolence of the barbarians; see how ready and eager she is to follow a banner joyously, if only someone will raise it up. There is no figure presently in sight in whom she can better place her trust than your illustrious house, which, with its fortune and its merits [*virtù*], favored by God and the Church of which it is now the head, can take the lead in this process of redemption.

The task will not too hard if you keep your eye on the actions and lives of those leaders described above. Men of this sort are rare and wonderful, indeed, but they were nothing more than men, and each of them faced circumstances less promising than those of the present. Their cause was no more just than the present one, nor any easier, and God was no more favorable to them than to you. Your cause *is* just: "for war is justified when it is necessary, and arms are pious when without them there would be no hope at all."⁷ Everyone is eager, and where there is such eagerness there can be no great difficulty, if you imitate the methods of those I have proposed as examples. Apart from this, we have experienced extraordinary, unexampled leadings from God in this matter; the sea has divided, a cloud has shown the way, a stone has yielded water, manna has rained from heaven.⁸ All things point toward your greatness. The

5. The reference is back to chapter VI.
6. The extraordinary bad luck of Cesare Borgia is detailed in chapter VII. It should be added that Machiavelli, though not without a romantic side, was not soft or eccentric in thinking that Cesare really did aspire to unify Italy: it was the common view of the time. "The Kingdom," below, is the kingdom of Na-

ples.
7. Livy uses these expressions in reporting a speech of Gaius Pontius to the Samnites (IX, I).
8. The Mosaic miracles are familiar enough; it is not clear by any means what recent prodigies Machiavelli would have cited if pressed for a modern parallel.

rest is up to you. God will not do everything, lest he deprive us of our free will and a part of that glory which belongs to us.

There is nothing surprising in the fact that none of the Italians whom I have named was able to do what we hope for from your illustrious house; no reason even for wonder if, after so many revolutions in Italy and so many military campaigns, it seems as if military manhood [*virtù*] is quite extinct. The reason is simply that the old methods of warfare were not good, and no one has been able to find new ones. Nothing does so much honor to a man newly risen to power, as the new laws and rules that he discovers. When they are well-grounded and have in them the seeds of greatness, these institutions make him the object of awe and admiration. In Italy there is no lack of material to be given new forms; the limbs of the nation have great strength [*virtù*], so long as the heads are not deficient. Only look at the duels and tourneys where a few men are involved, and you will find that the Italians excel in strength, in dexterity, in mental agility;[9] but when it is matter of armies, they don't stand the comparison. This all comes from the weakness of the heads; because those who know what they are doing cannot enforce obedience. Each one thinks he knows best, and there has not been anyone hitherto who has raised himself, by strength [*virtù*] or fortune to a point where the others would yield to him. This is the reason why for a long time, in all the wars waged over the last twenty years, whenever an army composed of Italians took the field, it showed up badly. Among the examples of this are, first, the Taro, then Alexandria, Capua, Genoa, Vailà Bologna, and Mestri.[1]

If, then, your illustrious house is to follow the example of those excellent men who redeemed their native lands, you must first of all, before anything else, provide yourself with your own armies; that is the foundation stone of any enterprise, and you cannot possibly have more faithful, more reliable, or better soldiers than your own. And though each may be a good man individually, they will be even better as a group, when they see themselves united behind a prince of their own, who will support and reward them. It is necessary to build up an army of this sort, if you are to defend yourself with Italian valor [*virtù*] against foreigners. Doubtless the

9. In a famous · hand-to-hand fight on February 13, 1503, eleven Italian champions soundly defeated eleven French champions, to the immense delight of the Italian public. These were the days of Bayard and Gaston de la Foix—of a half-nostalgic, still animate chivalry. See J. S. Bridge, *History of France* (Oxford, 1929), III, 165–67.

1. Machiavelli's mournful roll call of Italian disasters is arranged in strict chronological order, from the battle of Taro (July 5, 1495) when the French armies of Charles VIII first invaded Italy, to the devastation of Mestre near Venice by German and papal troops just before the battle of Vicenza (October 7, 1513). It's an impressionistic list, designed with skillful rhetorical intent to stir memories of Italian shame and disgrace in the mind of Lorenzo de' Medici, for whose special benefit (it seems likely) Machiavelli composed this final chapter.

Swiss and Spanish infantry have fearful reputations, yet they are both deficient in ways that will allow a third force not only to withstand them, but to feel confident of overcoming them. The Spaniards cannot stand up against horsemen; and the Swiss are bound to crumble when they they meet in battle enemies who are as stubborn as they are. We have seen this, and know by experience that the Spaniards could not hold up against French cavalrymen, and the Swiss were cut up by Spanish infantry. This last theory has not been completely tested, but we had a sample at the battle of Ravenna,[2] where the Spanish infantry came up against battalions of Germans, who are organized in the same way as the Swiss. The agile Spaniards, with the help of their spiked shields, got under the pikes of the Germans, or between them, and were able to stab at them without being in any danger themselves. If it had not been for the cavalry that charged them, the Spaniards would have eaten them all up. When you know the faults of these two infantries, you can set up a third sort, which will stand up to cavalry and not be afraid of infantry; this can be done by raising new armies and changing their formations. Such new inventions as these give a new prince the reputation of a great man.

The occasion must not be allowed to slip away; Italy has been waiting too long for a glimpse of her redeemer. I cannot describe the joy with which he will be greeted in all those districts which have suffered from the flood of foreigners; nor the thirst for vengeance, the deep devotion, the dedication, the tears, that will greet him. What doors would be closed to him? what people would deny him obedience? what envy could oppose him? what Italian would refuse allegiance? This barbarian occupation stinks in all our nostrils![3] Let your illustrious house, then, take up this task with that courage and with that hope which suit a just enterprise; so that, under your banner, our country may become noble again, and the verses of Petrarch may come true:

> Then virtue boldly shall engage
> And swiftly vanquish barbarous rage,
> Proving that ancient and heroic pride
> In true Italian hearts has never died.[4]

2. On the battle of Ravenna, one of the most desperately fought and technically innovative of the Italian wars, see chapter XIII, note 1, p. 39. A frequent opinion of modern historians is that the battle was decided by the artillery—a factor Machiavelli does not mention.
3. Machiavelli deliberately imitates the war cry of Julius II: "Fuori i barbari!" ("Out with the barbarians!") But one should not attribute to him the conception of a "nation" as it developed after the French Revolution. He wanted the Germans out, and to get them out he was even willing to call himself an Italian; but at heart he was a Florentine—and that's something else entirely.
4. Petrarch, canzone 128, "Italia mia, ben che'l parlar sia indarno," lines 93–96. The canzone is directed against "la tedesca rabbia," the German fury.

Backgrounds

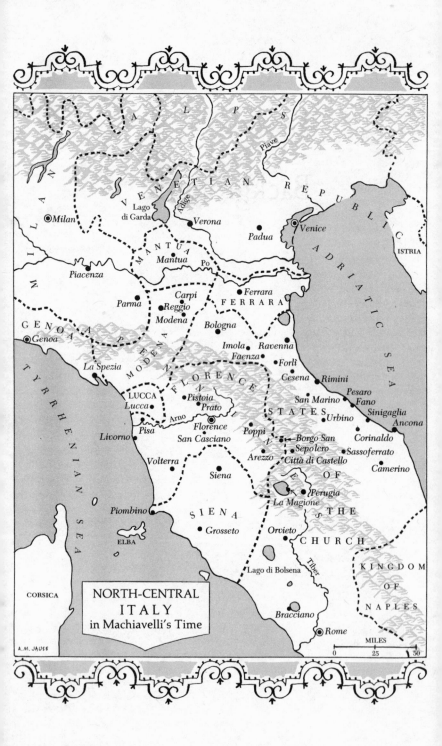

NORTH-CENTRAL
ITALY
in Machiavelli's Time

A.M. JAUSS

MILAN

ALPS

Piave

VENETIAN REPUBLIC

Lago
di Garda
Adige

Milan

Verona

MANTUA

Padua

Venice

ISTRIA

ADRIATIC SEA

Piacenza

Mantua

Po

Parma

Carpi

Reggio

Ferrara

FERRARA

GENOA

Modena

Bologna

Genoa

MODENA

Imola

Ravenna

La Spezia

Faenza

Forlì

APENNINES

Cesena

Rimini

FLORENCE

Pesaro

LUCCA

Pistoia

San Marino

Fano

Lucca

Prato

STATES

Sinigaglia

Arno

Urbino

Ancona

Livorno

Pisa

Florence

Poppi

Borgo San
Sepolcro

Corinaldo

San Casciano

OF

Sassoferrato

Volterra

Arezzo

Città di Castello

Camerino

Siena

La Magione

Perugia

TYRRHENIAN SEA

Piombino

SIENA

THE

ELBA

Grosseto

Orvieto

CHURCH

Lago di Bolsena

Tiber

KINGDOM

OF

CORSICA

NAPLES

Bracciano

Rome

MILES
0   25   50

Machiavelli the Working Diplomat

NICCOLÒ MACHIAVELLI

[The Legation to Cesare Borgia]†

Diplomacy in Renaissance Italy was no business for a man with weak nerves. Personal relations counted for a great deal, and decisions involving the life or death of a city had to be made, sometimes, on the basis of nothing more than a smile or an innuendo. Communications were abominable. Even though he was only a few hundred miles from home, the ambassador could not ask a question and get an answer (during the winter, particularly, when the Apennine passes were sometimes closed and always perilous) in much less than a week. There was no systematic reporting of news throughout Italy, far less throughout Europe. News spread by word of mouth, with casual couriers, travelers, and merchants as its carriers, and often its garblers. Dealing with a man like Cesare Borgia, who was impatient of temper and quick to act, an ambassador had to be bold, decisive, and independent, yet careful to avoid overstepping the bounds of his commission.

For back in Florence Machiavelli had to deal not just with one commander in chief, but with a committee, the Dieci di Balia, or as we would say, the Council of Ten, though the Italian means the "Ten of Council." Under this neutral title they were in fact the Ministry of War. They commissioned numerous Florentine citizens, among them Machiavelli, to serve as their agents at the courts of various princes in Italy and abroad; and from these agents they received reports, more or less detailed, as circumstances required. Among these agents, Machiavelli, a a simple civil servant, a secretary, occupied a position of no great eminence. He was not, for example, a nobleman like his contemporary Count Baldassare Castiglione, who served several different princes; he was not a prelate or dignitary of the Church. During his first days in the service, he was generally associated with another ambassador, to whom he was junior if not directly subordinate. But as his talents became known, he was sent on more and more important missions, and assumed more authority over their conduct. In June of 1502, he was sent, with Francesco Soderini, bishop of Volterra and brother of Piero Soderini, the chief magistrate of Florence, to deal with Cesare Borgia, then in his ascendant. For a sketch of Cesare's circumstances and intentions, see the Historical Introduction, pp. vii–xvi. Machiavelli and Francesco Soderini were much impressed with Cesare Borgia when they

†Translated by R.M.A. from Niccolò Machiavelli, *Legazione e commissarie*, ed. Sergio Bertelli (Milano: Feltrinelli, 1964), volume I (volume III of the Machiavelli *Opere*), pp. 335–45, 502–10.

first saw him, as he was just setting out on his conquests. In a letter from Urbino, dated June 26, 1502, they summarized his character:

> This Lord is very splendid and magnificent, and so fierce in battle that there's no great enterprise that he won't take lightly; in the pursuit of glory and reputation he never rests, and recognizes neither weariness nor danger; he has arrived at a new position before anyone understands that he has left the old one. He is well liked by his soldiers, and he has enrolled the best men in Italy. These qualities make him both victorious and dangerous for the future; added to which, he is always lucky.

The Florentines should, technically, have been natural allies of Cesare, since they were both allied to the king of France; but the connection was not one on which anybody could count. Cesare wanted the king's soldiers only until he could get together an army of his own; the Florentines, if they could only get back Pisa, wanted desperately to be left alone, so they could make their way by trading and manufacturing. But they were too fat a prize to live comfortably in the sea of sharks that was northern Italy. One of the fiercest and hungriest of these sharks was Cesare Borgia. Machiavelli's dealings with this up-and-coming tyrant (of which we can represent here only a small sample, culled from a second mission to Cesare in October-December, 1502) show him hard at work on the daily business of diplomacy —playing for time, persuading, promising, calculating, observing, serving the best interests of his city in whatever way he could, under extremely difficult and trying circumstances. It was his long experience in this sort of work that tempered the mind of Machiavelli toward the writing of *The Prince*, after Cesare Borgia was dead and after the republic for which Machiavelli worked so faithfully had gone down the drain.

The translation of these documents has been made from Machiavelli's *Legazione e commissarie* Volume III of his *Opere*). The translation aims at bald authenticity. Machiavelli's employers write committee-room prose at its worst; in Machiavelli's reports, the trivial rubs shoulders with the crucial; the spelling of names is very casual, and allusive formulas are everywhere. We are, as it were, in the workshop of sixteenth-century city-state diplomacy.

1

Deliberations of the Signoria

October 5, 1502

The Magnificent Lords, etc., by special decree, have sent to the same illustrious Duke Valentino as their envoy Nicholas Malclavellus,[1] with a salary which is stipulated elsewhere and with these instructions which are written below.

Departed, October 6.
Returned, January 23, 1503.

1. "Malclavellus" is a Latin secretary's instinctive effort to Latinize "Machiavelli" but it is etymologically correct; the name derives from the Latin for "bad keys," *mali clavelli*.

2

The Commission

Commission given to Niccolò Machiavelli, formulated by our esteemed masters on the fifth of October, 1502.

Niccolò, we send you to Imola[2] to find His Excellency the Duke Valentino with credentials to him; you will proceed there on horse as fast as you can, and in your first conference with him you will explain that, in recent days, since his return into the Romagna, we've learned of the estrangement and departure of the Orsini from His Excellency, and the gathering and conclave of them and their adherents near La Magione in the neighborhood of Perugia, and the story has gone round that the duke of Urbino and Signor Bartolommeo d'Alviano will be there too, in order to plan and plot actions against His Excellency, actions which we consider to be directed against the Most Christian King;[3] and we too have been slyly requested to send our man to that meeting, and talk with them; but we continue to be of our old opinion, desirous of being good friends of Our Master and His Excellency, firmly committed against separating ourselves or abandoning our devotion to the king of France;[4] because, living in friendship with him, and under his protection, our city cannot fail to recall, when it's a question of the king's interests, and His Excellency's friends and dependents, everything which has been done and promised in our interests, and so reciprocate with all the good offices of good friends; and it's for this reason that we've sent you posthaste to His Excellency, since we think the importance of the business requires it; and you should tell him again that in these movements of our neighbors, we intend to preserve the greatest respect for his interests, and maintain the same esteem for him that we have always had, in view of the fact that we consider all the friends of France to be our friends, and where it's a question of their interests, there it's also a question of ours. And this, it seems to us, ought to be enough for your first encounter, in which you will make it as clear as possible that we have great confidence and hope in His Excellency: and on this theme you can enlarge as much as you think proper, spelling out in your conversa-

2. Lying across the Apennines in the broad plain fronting the Adriatic Sea, Imola was only about fifty miles from Florence as the crow flies; but the actual distance was twice as much. As we learn below, one particularly urgent courier made the trip in about seventeen hours; most took longer. See the map of the area, p. 78.

3. The assembly at La Magione near Perugia, which did not actually convene till October 9 but was much talked of in advance, brought together local lords, sol-

diers, bravos, and family heads of the Romagna. Signor Bartolommeo d' Alviano was a Venetian soldier; his presence would greatly have strengthened the conspiracy. The plot was directed against Cesare, as captain of the Church, but also against his two chief supporters: his father, Pope Alexander VI, and the "Most Christian King," Louis XII of France.

4. "Our Master" is Louis XII, then with his army; "His Excellency" is Cesare.

tion all the details and circumstances of which the material allows, none of which need be expanded on here, as you're perfectly well acquainted with them: nor do we want you to talk of anything outside of this material, nor deal with it in any other way; and whenever His Excellency tries to push you further, we want you to tell us of it, and wait for our reply. And after this first opening statement, either in this first audience or later, will you thank His Excellency as warmly as you can for his good services to our merchants, which is a benefit we consider to be conferred on us, and a public benefaction; reminding him of the liberation of those goods which had been held up for some months past at Urbino, and about which we've just heard today from those merchants that they've been forwarded according to their instructions; with a great show of friendship, which will make clear that you have particular instructions to look into the matter; and then afterwards, when you think the occasion right, you can request of His Excellency in our name security and safe conduct through his states and territories for the goods of our merchants coming and going from the East; and this is a matter of considerable import, which you could call the very stomach of our city, and you must pay particular attention to it, and exercise all your diligence so that the outcome may be according to our desires.

3

Credentials Given to the Ambassador

October 5, 1502

To Duke Valentino.

Most Illustrious Lord, etc. We send to Your Excellency Niccolò Machiavelli, a citizen and our secretary, in order to acquaint you with various matters of great significance both to our friendship and present circumstances. We beg Your Lordship by our love to give this man the same trust that you would to ourselves.

4

Safe Conduct for Machiavelli

The Priors in the name of freedom and the Gonfalonier in the name of justice of the Florentine people, to all and sundry whom these letters may reach, greetings. We are sending Niccolò, son of Messer Bernardo Machiavelli, a very noble citizen and our secretary, to the most illustrious duke of Romagna, etc., on some of our business; and so we command all rectors, officials, subjects, and employees of ours, and we beg all you our friends and allies, to let pass the aforesaid Niccolò with all his goods and properties, without payment of any impost or excise; and if he should need any help or favor in order to arrive safely before the aforesaid lord, let him have it; and we will always be very ready to return a similar or greater favor, should need arise. Farewell.

From our palace, October 4, 1502.

Marcellus[5]

5

Machiavelli to the Ten

Magnificent and Distinguished Lords, my very particular masters. Since I found myself ill provided with horses at my departure, and it seemed to me that my duties required haste, I took post[6] at Scarperia and came to this place without any loss of time, where I arrived today around six o'clock; and because I had left behind my own horses and my servants, I presented myself immediately in traveling dress before His Excellency, who greeted me warmly; and as I presented my credentials, I explained to him the reason for my coming, and began to thank him for the restitution of our merchants' goods. Then I turned to the falling away of the Orsini and to the counsel they were holding with their adherents, and how Your Lordships had been secretly invited, and I reminded him of the views you hold regarding friendship with the king of France and your devotion to the Church; and I amplified on these topics with all the words that occurred to me, explaining that you felt bound to hold friendship with king and Church while avoiding complicity with their enemies. And I explained that in every action, Your Lordships are concerned to safeguard his particular interests, as befits the friendship you maintain with the king of France and the devotion you have always felt for his own power, since you consider all friends of France to be most faithful friends and allies of your own. His Excellency, on the matter of the restitutions, gave no answer at all; but, turning to the other particulars, he thanked Your Lordships for this kind and welcome demonstration: and then he said that he had always desired friendly relations with Your Lordships, and that any lapse in them should be laid to the malignity of others, not to his account; and he said he wanted to explain to me in particular what he had never told anyone else, regarding his

5. Marcello Virgilio di Adriano Berti, secretary of the Florentine chancellery.
6. Instead of riding his own horse all the way, he rented successive horses from the post service. As each beast covered only a short stage of the journey, a man could travel faster by post than on his own animal. Scarperia is a little village about fifteen miles northnortheast of Florence on the road to Imola.

coming with an army to Florence.[7] And he said that when Faenza had fallen and an attempt had been made on Bologna, the Orsini and Vitelli were on his back to get him to return to Rome by way of Florence; and when he said no, because the pope had ordered him to go another way, Vitellozzo threw himself at his feet in tears, begging him to go this way, and promising that he would do no harm either to the city or to the countryside. And he didn't want to grant even this much, until others came with similar requests that they be allowed to go there, but always with the proviso that the countryside should not be harmed and there should be no talk of the Medici. But since he was now going to Florence, he thought to profit by the occasion and reach a friendly agreement with Your Lordships: which shows that he had never in a business way talked at all or to any effect about the Medici, as the commissioners who treated with him know very well; nor did he ever want to have Pietro with him in his camp.[8] When they were at Campi, he says the Orsini and Vitelli often asked his permission to make a show of force before Florence or Pistoia, to show that those were feasible enterprises; but he never gave his consent, instead he gave them to understand, with a thousand protests, that he would fight them. The agreement then followed,[9] but it seemed to the Orsini and Vitelli that he had had his will, and they hadn't had theirs, since the event had turned out to his advantage and their loss, so that they began secretly to sabotage it, and did all they could to make trouble for Your Lordships and upset the agreement. And he couldn't properly set things right, partly because he couldn't be everywhere at once, and partly because Your Lordships hadn't come through with the advance which had been agreed on, and which once seemed about to be paid. Things standing thus about the end of last June, the rebellion of Arezzo broke out at that time:[1] concerning which, he said, he had never had any foreknowledge, as he had already assured the bishop of Volterra; but he certainly welcomed it, supposing it offered him a chance to achieve recognition. Yet even then nothing was done, either through bad luck on both

7. During the summer of 1501 Cesare Borgia, with his ragtag international army, had paid an ambiguous call on the Florentines. Cesare was much feared himself, and a chief captain in his army was Vitellozzo Vitelli, who bore a grudge against the Florentines because they had executed his brother Paolo. After some rather tense negotiations, Cesare was appointed "protector" of Florence, with an annual salary of 36,000 ducats. Always a threat to the republic under such circumstances was the possibility that someone might try to reinstate the Medici, who had been driven from Florence in 1494.
8. Pietro de' Medici, deposed and dis-

agreeable son of the Magnificent Lorenzo, who was always hanging around armies in the hope of being restored by them.
9. I.e., Cesare's agreement to "protect" Florence from enemies—including, in the first instance, himself. Technically, he took the city under his "condotta."
1. This was in June, 1502. Arezzo, a city dependent on Florence, tried to break away; and Vitellozzo Vitelli, a neighbor who was always itching to get at the Florentines, came to the aid of the rebels. The "bishop of Volterra" was Francesco Soderini, brother of the Florentine gonfalonier, Piero Soderini, and a political associate of Machiavelli's in an earlier mission to Cesare.

sides, or because your city was not then in a position to discuss and
decide matters which would have been of great advantage to both;
and yet he said that gave him no particular trouble, and being still
disposed to do you good, in view of the king's good will, he wrote
and sent men directly to Vitellozzo, telling him to clear out of
Arezzo: and not content with this, he went off with his men toward
Città di Castello, and could have taken Vitelli's own state from
him, because the chief men of the countryside came forward to
offer their help; and this, he said, was the prime source of Vitellozzo's discontent and ill humor. As for the Orsini, he said he didn't
know what made them discontented in the French court, and
couldn't tell without papal permission. But they perhaps resented
that the French king had treated him more honorably than Cardinal Orsini, and given him special privileges;[2] and then rumor had
said he was going to take their state away; so on that they broke
away, and now found themselves in this convocation of bankrupts.
And though he had received various messages from Signor Giulio
Orsini, declaring that he was not going to oppose him, etc., and it
wasn't reasonable to expect them to declare themselves openly,
because they had taken his money:[3] still, when they did declare
themselves, he expected they would prove crazier than people had
thought, since they weren't even able to pick the right time to
attack him—the king of France was in Italy, and His Holiness the
pope was still living, and those two things lit such a fire under him
that putting it out would require a different water than theirs. He
didn't worry about the loss of Urbino, because he hadn't forgotten
the way to get it back when he lost it.[4] And then he suggested that
now was the time, if Your Lordships wanted to be his friends, to
prove it; because he could now make friends with you without
having to placate the Orsini, as he had always had to do before. But
if Your Lordships delayed, and he meanwhile was reconciled with
the Orsini, who are still dealing with him, then the same old problems would come back; and as the Orsini could scarcely be satisfied
with any deal unless it replaced the Medici,[5] then Your Lordships
would be back in the same old jealousies and troubles. Thus he
thinks Your Lordships should declare yourselves at once to be his
friends or theirs, one way or the other, because if you put it off,

2. This would have been four years before, in 1498, when Cesare was sent as
papal legate to the court of France,
bearing the order which annulled Louis's
marriage with Jeanne of France and so
enabled him to marry Anne of Brittany.
Whatever the consequences for his domestic bliss, the shift of wives was a
great political coup for Louis.
3. Cesare had made it his business to
seem placatory and even generous toward the Orsini and Vitelli; it was by
means of these soft words and lavish
presents that he lured them into the trap
at Sinigaglia; see below.
4. Only two days before (October 5)
Urbino had revolted against Cesare as
part of the general rising of the Romagna, which was coming to a head with
the meeting at La Magione.
5. In Florence.

either the two parties will reach an agreement at your expense, or else one of them will be victorious, which in the hour of victory will be either hostile or else under no obligation to Your Lordships. And when you come to make your decision, he thinks you will see the necessity of it; he doesn't see how Your Lordships can take sides against the majesty of the king and the sanctity of the pope; and he adds that it would ease things for him if, when he moves Vitellozzo or others into one or another of his states, you would make a show with what forces you have in the direction of Borgo or those boundaries, in order to lend color to his actions.[6]

I listened very carefully as His Excellency went over the points given above: what he said was not just to the general effect that I report but in exactly the same words, which I have transcribed at length so that Your Lordships may better judge of the whole: I don't transcribe my own answers, as that isn't necessary: I tried very hard not to go beyond my commission, and in the matter of using your forces, I made no answer whatever; I simply said that I would write to Your Lordships, declaring his exact thoughts, in which I declared you would take extraordinary pleasure. And although His Excellency, as you see, showed a great desire to reach immediate agreement with you, still even when I pressed closely to draw him into some particulars, he always talked in large generalities, and I couldn't get anything out of him beyond what I've written. And since I'd mentioned in my opening remarks that there had been a certain turnaround in the state of Urbino, and His Excellency had said in his reply that he didn't much care what had happened in that dukedom, it occurred to me to ask in my reply how these things came about. To which His Excellency replied: My being too gentle, and taking too little care over the details, is what did me harm: I took that dukedom, as you know, in three days, and didn't ruffle a hair on anyone's head, except for Messer Dolce and two others, who had taken actions against His Holiness the pope; indeed, I went further, and appointed several of those leading citizens to offices in the state, one of them in charge of certain walls that I was having erected in the fort of San Leo. Two days ago, he conspired with some people of the countryside who made a show of bringing up a big beam for the work, and so they forced the gate, and the fortress was lost. Some say the cry that went up was Marco,[7] others Vitelli, others Orsini; but up to this point nobody has declared himself. Personally, I consider the dukedom was lost because it was a weak and sluggish state; the men were malcontents, whom I had overbur-

6. The suggestion is that the Florentines should mime an act of aggression so that Cesare could order Vitellozzo Vitelli, still technically in his service, into some disadvantageous position. "Borgo" is Borgo San Sepolcro.

7. "Marco" is San Marco, patron saint of Venice. "Overburdened with soldiery" means simply that there had been too many armies camped around Urbino, foraging off the countryside.

dened with soldiery; but I expect to take care of it all. And you write to your lords that they should look to their own affairs here; because if the duke returns to Urbino and he comes from Venice,[8] it's not by any means our loss and your gain; which is one more reason why we should trust one another.

This is, in effect, all that I can write to Your Lordships at this time; and though it's part of my assignment to write you how many visitors are at this nobleman's court, where they are staying, and many other local particulars, still, since I just arrived today, I can't be sure of the truth of it, and thus I'll save it for another occasion: and I commend myself to Your Lordships.

Your servant, Nicolaus Machiavellus. At Imola.

October 7, 1502
E.V.D.[9]

Held over to the next day at four P.M., the horse supplier being completely out, and I haven't been able to find an animal up to now. And I can add that yesterday His Excellency in his talk with me said that the day before Pandolfo Petrucci[1] had sent a secret message, pledging that he would give no favors to anyone who opposed His Excellency, and went on to give more general pledges to this effect.

On my way here I encountered Messer Agapito some two miles out of town, with seven or eight horses; and when he recognized me, I told him where I was going and who sent me. He made me very welcome, and went forward only a little distance before turning back. This morning, I realized that the said Messer Agapito was on his way to Your Lordships as the emissary of this duke, and because of my coming he turned back.[2] Farewell again.

October 8, 1502

I have given the present horseman two ducats on the understanding that he will be there tomorrow morning before daybreak, which should be around nine A.M. Will you be good enough to reimburse Ser Agostino Vespucci.[3]

* * *

8. The Florentines had good reason to fear the Venetians, who as their commercial rivals had lent troops to the Pisans in their struggle against Florence.
9. E.V.D. stands for Excellentissimae Vestrae Dominationis (Servitor), ("[Servant of] Your Most Excellent Lordship").
1. Pandolfo Petrucci was prince and tyrant of Siena.
2. The point being made is that Cesare had greater need of Florentine support than he let on; if the Florentines hadn't sent Machiavelli to him, he was on the point of sending Messer Agapito as an envoy to them.
3. Machiavelli asks that reimbursements for his expenses be paid to various of his friends, who would find ways to get the money to him.

77

Machiavelli to the Ten

Magnificent Lords, etc. By way of Bagno I wrote my latest to Your Lordships on the twenty-third, and since I wrote at length there of the departure of the French and the various opinions about it, there's no need for me now to say anything more of it, since there's nothing important to add.

The day before yesterday the boy of Ardingo, the courier, arrived, with two letters of Your Lordships' dated the twentieth and twenty-second, and though I made every effort after receiving them to talk with the duke, I could not do so, because my only chance was yesterday, and yesterday His Excellency was busy reviewing the infantry and in his other holiday pleasures, so I could not get to him; and this morning he rose early, and went off with the whole army to Santo Arcangelo, some fifteen miles from here and five miles from Rimini; so tomorrow I'll get up early and go to Rimini, since I can't lodge any closer because of the shortage of housing—it's very scant—even though people say we aren't to stop in this district for any time at all; but next day the army will move on to near Pesaro; nobody knows what's up; some think an attempt will be made on Sinigaglia, others say Ancona.[4] As for soldiers, he has those troops that I mentioned in my latest list, and in addition around thirty newly enrolled Albanian auxiliaries, in addition to 2,500 infantry from beyond the Alps, and about the same number of Italians, some of whom put on the show yesterday and the day before. You can figure that for every thousand infantry there are fifty horsemen capable of serving as cavalry; the artillery have moved at the same pace as the army's leader, with the necessary powder and shot. What sort of power the Orsini and the Vitegli have, nobody knows; we'll know better on the day when the armies get closer to one another; as I've often told Your Lordships, this duke is extremely secretive, and I don't think anyone but himself knows what he's about to do: even his chief secretaries have often told me that he never explains what he's going to do till he's already begun it, and he begins it when circumstances constrain him, and the situation is ripe, not otherwise; so I beg Your Lordships to excuse me, and don't think I'm negligent when I can't give Your Lordships exact information, since most of the time I can't even satisfy myself as to what is happening. Concerning San Leo and the deal he is making

4. Pesaro, Sinigaglia, and Ancona are stretched out along the Adriatic coast at intervals of about twenty to twenty-five miles; Cesare's interest wasn't in any of them, particularly, but in rounding up the conspirators of La Magione, who at the moment were desperately trying to pretend they were his best friends. When caught, they had taken Sinigaglia and proposed to present it to him as a peace offering. He took both it and them.

with Duke Guido there's no further news.[5] As for Camerino I wrote on another occasion what the duke told me, who had been there on official duties, and afterwards I wrote as much as I had been able to get out of that secretary to Cardinal Farnese, who told me that there was little hope for it, and that mostly on the part of the French: yesterday I heard from the bishop of Euna that things were practically settled, but I'd better wait for the last word, in order not to be mistaken again.

This morning Messer Remirro was found in two pieces on the public square, where he still is: the whole city has been to see him: nobody is sure of the reason for his death, except that it was the will of the prince, who shows himself capable of making men and breaking them as he pleases, according to their merits.[6]

The courier I mentioned above brought me twenty-five golden ducats and sixteen yards of black damask. I thank Your Lordships for the one thing as well as the other.

Because the court is on the move, no man has been assigned to me to go and pick up the three horses that Your Lordships say are at Poppi; let me beg of Your Lordships to ensure that they are properly cared for till I can arrange for them to come here.

Messer Bartolommeo Marcelli of Bagno, for whom the baron of Bierra lately wrote to our exalted masters, asks nothing but that a little time be granted before his appearance, so that he can get there; he's writing on this point to Piero di Braccio Martelli, who is acting as his lawyer in the case; and I again recommend his request to Your Lordships' consideration; may all your affairs go well.

Your servant, Nicolaus Machiavellus, Secretary

From Cesena, December 26, 1502, at ten P.M.
E.V.D.

* * *

79

Machiavelli to the Ten

Magnificent Lords, etc. Day before yesterday I wrote from Pesaro to Your Lordships describing what I understood of Sinigaglia: yesterday I went to Fano, and this morning early the duke with his whole army came here to Sinigaglia where were assembled all the Orsini and Vitellozzo, who as I wrote before had taken possession of this area. They went into the city, he went in with them and as soon as he was near the center, he turned to his guard and took

5. This deal clearly involved the fate of Urbino: "Duke Guido" is Guidobaldo da Montefeltro. Camerino, also captured by Cesare, was another city whose fate was up in the air.
6. See *The Prince*, chapter VII.

them all prisoner: and thus he has captured them all, and the district will be sacked everywhere; and it is now eleven P.M. I'm overwhelmed with business; I don't know if I'll be able to send this letter, for lack of anyone going that way. I'll write at length on another occasion; in my opinion, there won't be one of them alive tomorrow morning.

In Sinigaglia, the last day of December 1502.

All their people are in fact taken, and the papers which are being drawn up about them say that the traitors have been captured, etc.

I have given the present bearer three ducats, and Your Lordships will give him another three; for my share you will reimburse Biagio.[7]

Your servant, Nicolaus Machiavellus

80

Machiavelli to the Ten

Magnificent Lords, etc. Yesterday I wrote two letters to Your Lordships about everything that happened after the arrival of His Excellence the Duke in Sinigaglia, and of how he captured Paolo Orsini, the duke of Gravina, Vitellozzo, and Oliverotto; in the first I simply gave you notice of the event, and in the second I described things in more detail, adding all the things that His Excellency told me, and an account of public opinion regarding this lord and his doings. I would repeat these letters in detail if I thought they had not reached you safely. But as I sent the first with all the force of six ducats and the second with the force of three, by picked men, one Florentine, the other from Urbino, I'm in good hopes. Still, I will summarize everything yet again for Your Lordships, out of an excess of caution, just in case my first letters don't reach you. This lord left Fano yesterday morning, and with his whole army came up to Sinigaglia, which had been occupied, except for the fortress, by the Orsini and Messer Liverotto da Fermo. The day before, Vitellozzo had arrived in the district from Castello; they went one after the other to meet with the duke, and then accompanied him into the town and into a house; and then when they were all together in one room, my lord had them made prisoner; then he had all their troops disarmed, who were in the suburbs around the city, and sent half his own army to disarm some other retainers, who had been placed in different castles six or seven miles around Sinigaglia. Afterwards he called me into his presence about two in the morning, and with the most cheerful expression in the world joked with

---

7. Biagio Buonaccorsi, Machiavelli's oldest and most intimate friend.

me about these events, saying that he had spoken to me before about them, but hadn't explained his whole plan, which was true; then he added some wise and unusually affectionate words about our city, explaining all the reasons which made him eager for your friendship, as long as you aren't found wanting. Indeed, he left me in a state of astonishment, but I won't expand on this further, since I described it at length in last night's letter. He concluded that I should write three things to Your Lordships on his behalf. The first, that I was delighted with his success in having destroyed those men who were most bitterly hostile to the king, to himself, and to you; and in taking away every seed of scandal and discord that could have disturbed Italy; for all of which Your Lordships are much obliged to him. Next, that I should earnestly request and beseech Your Lordships in his name, that in order to make clear to the whole world that you have been his friends in this matter, you should send some cavalry to Borgo, and assemble some troops, so that you can move with him against Castello or Perugia, which are the next orders of business. And he said he wanted to move swiftly in this matter, and would have marched last night, if he hadn't been afraid that when he left town Sinigaglia would be put to the sack. And again he asked me to write that you should make every demonstration possible of being friendly to him, adding that for the present there was no reason to fear or suspect anything, since he was well armed and all your enemies were captured. *Finally*, he asked me to write Your Lordships, in connection with the capture of Vitellozzo, that if Duke Guido,[8] who is at Castello, should take refuge in your districts, he would appreciate your holding him a prisoner. I said that giving up political refugees didn't suit with the dignity of our city, and that you would never do it; he answered that I talked very well, but it would be quite adequate if Your Lordships simply held him in custody, and didn't let him go without prior approval. I agreed to write everything; and he will expect your answer.

I also wrote in my letter of yesterday that many men, well disposed and friendly to our city, have suggested to me that this was a great occasion for Your Lordships to place your city to advantage in the new order of things. Everyone thinks that with regard to France, Your Lordships can safely trust them; and the feeling here is that you should send one of your chief citizens to be ambassador there, particularly because of this turn of events, and not postpone this action, because a man of position who comes there with specific proposals to make, will find a good response. This point has been made to me time and again by people who wish well to our city; and I write it to Your Lordships with the same sincerity that I have

8. Guidobaldo da Montefeltro, duke of Urbino, currently out of a job.

always observed toward you. And this is in substance what I wrote in my second letter yesterday, perhaps even spelled out in more detail.

As for recent developments, last night about ten o'clock this lord had Vitellozzo and Oliverotto da Fermo put to death; the other two are still alive; it's thought they are waiting to see if the pope has his hands on the cardinal and the others at Rome. If he has, as they think, then they'll dispose of the whole parcel at once.

This morning early the fortress of Sinigaglia surrendered to the duke, and is now in his power; His Lordship left the same morning, and came here with his army; from here they will be heading toward Perugia or Castello for certain, and perhaps toward Siena; then they'll move down toward Rome, taking over all those strongholds of the Orsini, and the plan is to capture Bracciano, after which the others will go like a bonfire of straw. All this however is just popular conjecture. I'll remain here all day tomorrow, and the next day stay at Sassoferrato. You can imagine what sort of weather this is for making war, indeed you wouldn't believe it if I told you the hardships these troops are undergoing, as well as anyone who accompanies them, because it's a lucky man who has a roof over his head.

Messer Goro da Pistoia, an enemy of our city and rebel against it,[9] was with Vitellozzo, and is now being held here by certain Spaniards; I think for two hundred ducats, if Your Lordships wanted to spend that much, you could arrange for one of his present keepers to turn him over to one of your officials. Let Your Lordships consider this matter, and let me know what you think of it: I commend myself to Your Lordships; May all things go well with you.

Your servant, Nicholaus Machiavellus, Secretary

From Corinaldo, the first day of January, 1503.
E.V.D.

* * *

9. Goro da Pistoia was an active agent of the Medici in their efforts to overthrow the republic, and so a declared enemy of Machiavelli's party.

Machiavelli the Democrat

NICCOLÒ MACHIAVELLI

From *Discourses on the First Ten Books of Titus Livius*†

In chapter II of *The Prince* Machiavelli says that he will not discuss republics in this present treatise "because I've talked of them at length on
another occasion." It is accepted that he is referring here to the *Discourses
on Titus Livius*, or at least some of them—how much is still under
earnest scholarly debate. Since we can be sure *The Prince* was written in
1513, it is clear that some of the *Discourses* were written before that date.
But it is clear also that after that date many of them were read to—and
perhaps revised for—a group of intellectuals who made it a custom to meet
from time to time informally in the Rucellai gardens known as the Orti
Oricellari, off present via della Scala in Florence. Such clubs, academies,
and informal gatherings were frequent in Renaissance Italy; not even the
fact that the Medici were in power and many members of the group were
known to share republican sentiments, limited the freedom of discussion. In
the presence of people who shared his own interests, background, and
social standing, Machiavelli was clearly free to speak at more liberty than in
The Prince, and at greater length. Princes have short attention spans, and
must be fed wisdom in capsule doses; people who live by ideas are more
willing to hear them discussed fully. Without implying that Machiavelli
was a hypocrite in *The Prince*, one can nevertheless sense that he must
have expressed his mind more broadly in the *Discourses*.

The form of the book calls for some explanation. Titus Livius was a
native of Padua and a contemporary of Augustus, who wrote his gigantic
history of Rome from the first founding of the city; its customary title is
just that: *Ab urbe condita* ("From the founding of the city"). It must
have been an enormous book; what survives is only 35 books out of an original 142, and this makes a substantial volume which we in English custom-
arily refer to simply as "Livy." Machiavelli had a special feeling for Livy in
the first place became the historian, though he had lived under the empire
and had to deal with emperors, was a vigorous admirer of the Roman
republic. In addition, Machiavelli's father had contributed an index to one
of the very early printed editions of Livy and had been rewarded with a
copy of the book; Machiavelli grew up with the volume, and imbibed from
his early youth its strong assurance that practical lessons about human
behavior could be learned by studying the historic past. Livy is the most

---

†The text is taken from *The Prince and
the Discourses* (Modern Library, 1940);
the translation, by Christian Edward
Detmold, was originally published in
Boston, in 1882. Footnotes are by the
editor of this Norton Critical Edition,
who has also made a few silent cor-
rections in the Detmold translation.

warmly didactic of the Roman historians—more of the patrician than of the plebeian party, but above all an outspoken patriot, intent on learning from the glorious past what will help imperial Romans to deal with their dark present and even darker future.

[Book I]

INTRODUCTION

Although the envious nature of men, so prompt to blame and so slow to praise, makes the discovery and introduction of any new principles and systems as dangerous almost as the exploration of unknown seas and continents, yet, animated by that natural desire which impels me to do what may prove for the common benefit of all, I have resolved to open a new route, which has not yet been followed by any one, and may prove difficult and troublesome, but may also bring me some reward in the approbation of those who will kindly consider the aim of my efforts.

And if my poor talents, my little experience of the present and insufficient study of the past, should make the result of my labors defective and of little utility, I shall at least have shown the way to others, who will carry out my views with greater ability, eloquence, and judgment, so that if I do not merit praise, I ought at least not to incur censure.

When we consider the general respect for antiquity, and how often—to say nothing of other examples—a great price is paid for some fragments of an antique statue, which we are anxious to possess to ornament our houses with, or to set before artists who strive to imitate them in their own works; and when we see, on the other hand, the wonderful examples which the history of ancient kingdoms and republics presents to us, the prodigies of virtue and of wisdom displayed by the kings, captains, citizens, and legislators who have sacrificed themselves for their country—when we see these, I say, more admired than imitated, or so much neglected that not the least trace of this ancient virtue remains, we cannot but be at the same time as much surprised as afflicted. The more so as in the differences which arise between citizens, or in the maladies to which they are subjected, we see these same people have recourse to the judgments and the remedies prescribed by the ancients. The civil laws are in fact nothing but decisions given by their jurisconsults, and which, reduced to a system, direct our modern jurists in their decisions. And what is the science of medicine, but the experience of ancient physicians, which their successors have taken for their guide? And yet to found a republic, maintain states, to govern a kingdom, organize an army, conduct a war, dispense justice, and extend empires, you will find neither prince, nor republic, nor captain, nor citizen, who has recourse to the examples of antiquity! This neglect, I am persuaded, is due less to the weakness to which the vices of our religion have reduced the world, than to the evils caused by the proud indolence which prevails in most of the Christian states, and to the lack of real knowledge of history, the true sense of which is not known, or the spirit of which they do not comprehend. Thus the majority of those who read it take pleasure only in the variety of the events which history relates, without ever thinking of imitating the noble actions, deeming that not only difficult, but impossible; as though heaven, the sun, the elements, and men had changed the order of their motions and power, and were different from what they were in ancient times.

Wishing, therefore, so far as in me lies, to draw mankind from this error, I have thought it proper to write upon those books of Titus Livius that have come to us entire despite the malice of time; touching upon all those matters which, after a comparison between the ancient and modern events, may seem to me necessary to facilitate their proper understanding. In this way those who read my remarks may derive those advantages which should be the aim of all study of history; and although the undertaking is difficult, yet, aided by those who have encouraged me in this attempt, I hope to carry it sufficiently far, so that but little may remain for others to carry it to its destined end.

* * *

[Book I, Chapter 2]

OF THE DIFFERENT KINDS OF REPUBLICS, AND OF WHAT KIND THE
ROMAN REPUBLIC WAS

I will leave aside what might be said of cities which from their very birth have been subject to a foreign power, and will speak only of those whose origin has been independent, and which from the first governed themselves by their own laws, whether as republics or as principalities, and whose constitution and laws have differed as their origin. Some have had at the very beginning, or soon after, a legislator, who, like Lycurgus with the Lacedæmonians,[1] gave them by a single act all the laws they needed. Others have owed theirs to chance and to events, and have received their laws at different times, as Rome did. It is a great good fortune for a republic to have a legislator sufficiently wise to give her laws so regulated that, without the necessity of correcting them, they afford security to those who live under them. Sparta observed her laws for more than eight

1. Lycurgus, a semi-mythical figure whose "life" was written by Plutarch, is said to have given the Spartans (Lacedaemoni- ans) a complete code of laws at a single stroke.

hundred years without altering them and without experiencing a single dangerous disturbance. Unhappy, on the contrary, is that republic which, not having at the beginning fallen into the hands of a sagacious and skillful legislator, is herself obliged to reform her laws. More unhappy still is that republic which from the first has diverged from a good constitution. And that republic is furthest from it whose vicious institutions impede her progress, and make her leave the right path that leads to a good end; for those who are in that condition can hardly ever be brought into the right road. Those republics, on the other hand, that started without having a perfect constitution, but made a fair beginning, and are capable of improvement,—such republics, I say, may perfect themselves by the aid of events. It is very true, however, that such reforms are never effected without danger, for the majority of men never willingly adopt any new law tending to change the constitution of the state, unless the necessity of the change is clearly demonstrated; and as such a necessity cannot make itself felt without being accompanied with danger, the republic may easily be destroyed before having perfected its constitution. That of Florence is a complete proof of this: reorganized after the revolt of Arezzo, in 1502, it was overthrown after the taking of Prato, in 1512.[2]

Having proposed to myself to treat of the kind of government established at Rome, and of the events that led to its perfection, I must at the beginning observe that some of the writers on politics distinguished three kinds of government, viz. the monarchical, the artistocratic, and the democratic; and maintain that the legislators of a people must choose from these three the one that seems to them most suitable. Other authors, wiser according to the opinion of many, count six kinds of governments, three of which are very bad, and three good in themselves, but so liable to be corrupted that they become absolutely bad. The three good ones are those which we have just named; the three bad ones result from the degradation of the other three, and each of them resembles its corresponding original, so that the transition from the one to the other is very easy. Thus monarchy becomes tyranny; aristocracy degenerates into oligarchy; and the popular government lapses readily into licentiousness. So that a legislator who gives to a state which he founds, either of these three forms of government, constitutes it but for a brief time; for no precautions can prevent either one of the three that are reputed good, from degenerating into its opposite kind; so great are in these the attractions and resemblances between the good and the evil.

Chance has given birth to these different kinds of governments

---

2. Machiavelli speaks coolly and impassively of a failed experiment to which he had devoted his entire political life.

amongst men; for at the beginning of the world the inhabitants were few in number, and lived for a time dispersed, like beasts. As the human race increased, the necessity for uniting themselves for defence made itself felt; the better to attain this object, they chose the strongest and most courageous from amongst themselves and placed him at their head, promising to obey him. Thence they began to know the good and the honest, and to distinguish them from the bad and vicious; for seeing a man injure his benefactor aroused at once two sentiments in every heart, hatred against the ingrate and love for the benefactor. They blamed the first, and on the contrary honored those the more who showed themselves grateful, for each felt that he in turn might be subject to a like wrong; and to prevent similar evils, they set to work to make laws, and to institute punishments for those who contravened them. Such was the origin of justice. This caused them, when they had afterwards to choose a prince, neither to look to the strongest nor bravest, but to the wisest and most just. But when they began to make sovereignty hereditary and non-elective, the children quickly degenerated from their fathers; and, so far from trying to equal their virtues, they considered that a prince had nothing else to do than to excel all the rest in luxury, indulgence, and every other variety of pleasure. The prince consequently soon drew upon himself the general hatred. An object of hatred, he naturally felt fear; fear in turn dictated to him precautions and wrongs, and thus tyranny quickly developed itself. Such were the beginning and causes of disorders, conspiracies, and plots against the sovereigns, set on foot, not by the feeble and timid, but by those citizens who, surpassing the others in grandeur of soul, in wealth, and in courage, could not submit to the outrages and excesses of their princes.

Under such powerful leaders the masses armed themselves against the tyrant, and, after having rid themselves of him, submitted to these chiefs as their liberators. These, abhorring the very name of prince, constituted themselves a new government; and at first, bearing in mind the past tyranny, they governed in strict accordance with the laws which they had established themselves; preferring public interests to their own, and to administer and protect with greatest care both public and private affairs. The children succeeded their fathers, and ignorant of the changes of fortune, having never experienced its reverses, and indisposed to remain content with this civil equality, they in turn gave themselves up to cupidity, ambition, libertinage, and violence, and soon caused the aristocratic government to degenerate into an oligarchic tyranny, regardless of all civil rights. They soon, however, experienced the same fate as the first tyrant; the people, disgusted with their government, placed themselves at the command of whoever was willing to attack them, and this disposition soon produced an avenger, who was sufficiently well seconded to destroy them. The memory of the prince and the wrongs committed by him being still fresh in their minds, and having overthrown the oligarchy, the people were not willing to return to the government of a prince. A popular government was therefore resolved upon, and it was so organized that the authority should not again fall into the hands of a prince or a small number of nobles. And as all governments are at first looked up to with some degree of reverence, the popular state also maintained itself for a time, but not for long, lasting generally for about the lifetime of the generation that had established it; for it soon ran into that kind of license which inflicts injury upon public as well as private interests. Each individual only consulted his own passions, and a thousand acts of injustice were daily committed, so that, constrained by necessity, or directed by the counsels of some good man, or for the purpose of escaping from this anarchy, they returned anew to the government of a prince, and from this they generally lapsed again into anarchy, step by step, in the same manner and from the same causes as we have indicated.

Such is the circle which all republics are destined to run through. Seldom, however, do they come back to the original form of government, which results from the fact that their duration is not sufficiently long to be able to undergo these repeated changes and preserve their existence. But it may well happen that a republic lacking strength and good counsel in its difficulties becomes subject after a while to some neighboring state, that is better organized than itself; and if such is not the case, then they will be apt to revolve indefinitely in the circle of revolutions. I say, then, that all kinds of government are defective; those three which we have qualified as good because they are too short-lived, and the three bad ones because of their inherent viciousness. Thus sagacious legislators, knowing the vices of each of these systems of government by themselves, have chosen one that should partake of all of them, judging that to be the most stable and solid. In fact, when there is combined under the same constitution a prince, a nobility, and the power of the people, then these three powers will watch and keep each other reciprocally in check.

* * *

[Book I, Chapter 6]

WHETHER IT WAS POSSIBLE TO ESTABLISH IN ROME A GOVERNMENT CAPABLE OF PUTTING AN END TO THE ENMITIES EXISTING BETWEEN THE NOBLES AND THE PEOPLE

We have discussed above the effects of the quarrels between the people and the senate. These same differences having continued to the time of the Gracchi,[3] when they became the cause of the loss of liberty, one might wish that Rome had done the great things we have admired, without bearing within her bosom such cause of discords. It seems to me therefore important to examine whether it was possible to establish a government in Rome that could prevent all these misunderstandings; and to do this well, we must necessarily recur to those republics that have maintained their liberties without such enmities and disturbances; we must examine what the form of their government was, and whether that could have been introduced in Rome.

In Sparta we have an example amongst the ancients, and in Venice amongst the moderns; to both these states I have already referred above. Sparta had a king and a senate, few in number, to govern her; Venice did not admit these distinctions, and gave the name of gentlemen to all who were entitled to have a part in the administration of the government. It was chance rather than fore-sight which gave to the latter this form of government; for having taken refuge on those shallows where the city now is, for the reasons mentioned above, the inhabitants soon became sufficiently numerous to require a regular system of laws. They consequently established a government, and assembled frequently in council to discuss the interests of the city. When it seemed to them that they were sufficiently numerous to govern themselves, they barred the way to a share in the government to the newly arrived who came to live amongst them; and finding in the course of time that the number of the latter increased sufficiently to give reputation to those who held the government in their hands, they designated the latter by the title of "gentlemen," and the others were called the popular class. This form of government had no difficulty in establishing and maintaining itself without disturbances; for at the moment of its origin all those who inhabited Venice had the right to participate in the government, so that no one had cause to complain. Those who afterwards came to live there, finding the government firmly established, had neither a pretext for, nor the means of, creating disturbances. They had no cause, for the reason that they had not been deprived of anything; and they lacked the means, because they were kept in check by those who held the government, and who did not employ them in any affairs that might tempt them to seize authority. Besides, the new-comers in Venice were not sufficiently numerous to have produced a disproportion between the governing and the governed, for the number of nobles equalled or exceeded that of the others; and thus for these reasons Venice could establish and preserve that form of government.

Sparta, as I have said, being governed by a king and a limited

3. The Gracchi were popular Roman re- *The Prince*, chapter IX and note 3, page
formers of the second century B.C. See 30.

senate, could maintain itself also for a long time, because there were but few inhabitants, and strangers were not permitted to come in; besides, the laws of Lycurgus had obtained such influence that their observance prevented even the slightest pretext for trouble. It was also the easier for the citizens to live in union, as Lycurgus had established equality in fortunes and inequality in conditions; for an equal poverty prevailed there, and the people were the less ambitious, as the offices of the government were given but to a few citizens, the people being excluded from them; and the nobles in the exercise of their functions did not treat the people sufficiently ill to excite in them the desire of exercising them themselves. This last advantage was due to the kings of Sparta; for being placed in this government, as it were, between the two orders, and living in the midst of the nobility, they had no better means of maintaining their authority than to protect the people against all injustice; whence these neither feared nor desired authority, and consequently there was no motive for any differences between them and the nobles, nor any cause for disturbances; and thus they could live for a long time united. Two principal causes, however, cemented this union: first, the inhabitants of Sparta were few in number, and therefore could be governed by a few; and the other was, that, by not permitting strangers to establish themselves in the republic, they had neither opportunity of becoming corrupt, nor of increasing their population to such a degree that the burden of government became difficult to the few who were charged with it.

In examining now all these circumstances, we see that the legislators of Rome had to do one of two things to assure to their republic the same quiet as that enjoyed by the two republics of which we have spoken; namely, either not to employ the people in the armies, like the Venetians, or not to open the doors to strangers, as had been the case in Sparta. But the Romans in both took just the opposite course, which gave to the people greater power and infinite occasion for disturbances. But if the republic had been more tranquil, it would necessarily have resulted that she would have been more feeble, and that she would have lost with her energy also the ability of achieving that high degree of greatness to which she attained; so that to have removed the cause of trouble from Rome would have been to deprive her of her power of expansion. And thus it is seen in all human affairs, upon careful examination, that you cannot avoid one inconvenience without incurring another. If therefore you wish to make a people numerous and warlike, so as to create a great empire, you will have to constitute it in such manner as will cause you more difficulty in managing it; and if you keep it either small or unarmed, and you acquire other dominions, you will not be able to hold them, or you will become so feeble that you will fall a prey to whoever attacks you. And therefore in all our decisions we must consider well what presents the least inconveniences, and take that for the best, for we shall never find any course entirely free from objections. Rome then might, like Sparta, have created a king for life, and established a limited senate; but with her desire to become a great empire, she could not, like Sparta, limit the number of her citizens; and therefore a king for life and a limited senate would have been of no benefit to her so far as union was concerned. If any one therefore wishes to establish an entirely new republic, he will have to consider whether he wishes to have her expand in power and dominion like Rome, or whether he intends to confine her within narrow limits. In the first case, it will be necessary to organize her as Rome was, and submit to dissensions and troubles as best he may; for without a great number of men, and these well armed, no republic can ever increase or hold its new possessions. In the second case, he may organize her like Sparta and Venice; but as expansion is the poison of such republics, he must prevent her from making conquests, for such acquisitions by a feeble republic lead to ruin, as happened to both Sparta and Venice; the first of which, having subjected to her rule nearly all Greece, exposed its feeble foundations at the slightest accident, for when the rebellion of Thebes occurred, which was led by Pelopidas,[4] the other cities of Greece also rose up and almost ruined Sparta.

In like manner, Venice, having obtained possession of a great part of Italy, and the most of it not by war, but by means of money and fraud, when occasion came for her to give proof of her strength, she lost everything in a single battle.[5] I think, then, that to found a republic which should endure a long time it would be best to organize her internally like Sparta, or to locate her, like Venice, in some strong place; and to make her sufficiently powerful, so that no one could hope to overcome her readily, and yet on the other hand not so powerful as to make her formidable to her neighbors. In this wise she might long enjoy her independence. For there are but two motives for making war against a republic: one, the desire to subjugate her; the other, the apprehension of being subjugated by her. The two means which we have indicated remove, as it were, both these pretexts for war; for if the republic is difficult to be conquered, her defences being well organized, as I presuppose, then it will seldom or never happen that any one will venture upon the project of conquering her. If she remains quiet within her limits, and experience shows that she entertains no ambitious projects, the fear of her power will never prompt any one to attack her; and this would even be more certainly the case if her constituion and laws

4. In 379 B.C. Pelopidas of Thebes led a successful revolt against the Spartans, who had conquered and occupied his city.

5. The battle of Vailà. See *The Prince,* chapter XII, note 7, page 38.

prohibited all aggrandizement. And I certainly think that if she could be kept in this equilibrium it would be the best political existence, and would insure to any state real tranquillity. But as all human things are kept in a perpetual movement, and can never remain stable, states naturally either rise or decline, and necessity compels them to many acts to which reason will not influence them; so that, having organized a republic competent to maintain herself without expanding, still, if forced by necessity to extend her territory, in such case we shall see her foundations give way and herself quickly brought to ruin. And thus, on the other hand, if Heaven favors her so as never to be involved in war, the continued tranquillity would enervate her, or provoke internal dissensions, which together, or either of them separately, will be apt to prove her ruin. Seeing then the impossibility of establishing in this respect a perfect equilibrium, and that a precise middle course cannot be maintained, it is proper in the organization of a republic to select the most honorable course, and to constitute her so that, even if necessity should oblige her to expand, she may yet be able to preserve her acquisitions. To return now to our first argument, I believe it therefore necessary to take the constitution of Rome as a model rather than that of any other republic, (for I do not believe that a middle course between the two can be found,) and to tolerate the differences that will arise between the Senate and the people as an unavoidable inconvenience in achieving greatness like that of Rome.

* * *

[Book I, Chapter 12]

THE IMPORTANCE OF GIVING RELIGION A PROMINENT INFLUENCE IN
A STATE, AND HOW ITALY WAS RUINED BECAUSE SHE FAILED IN
THIS RESPECT THROUGH THE CONDUCT OF THE CHURCH OF ROME.

Princes and republics who wish to maintain themselves free from corruption must above all things preserve the purity of all religious observances, and treat them with proper reverence; for there is no greater indication of the ruin of a country than to see religion contemned. And this is easily understood, when we know upon what the religion of a country is founded; for the essence of every religion is based upon some one main principle. The religion of the Gentiles had for its foundation the responses of the oracles, and the tenets of the augurs and aruspices; upon these alone depended all their ceremonies, rites, and sacrifices. For they readily believed that the Deity which could predict their future good or ill was also able to bestow it upon them. Thence arose their temples, their sacrifices, their supplications, and all the other ceremonies; for the oracle of Delos, the temple of Jupiter Ammon, and other celebrated oracles, kept the world in admiration and devoutness. But when these afterwards began to speak only in accordance with the wishes of the princes, and their falsity was discovered by the people, then men became incredulous, and disposed to disturb all good institutions. It is therefore the duty of princes and heads of republics to uphold the foundations of the religion of their countries, for then it is easy to keep their people religious, and consequently well conducted and united. And therefore everything that tends to favor religion (even though it were believed to be false) should be received and availed of to strengthen it; and this should be done the more, the wiser the rulers are, and the better they understand the natural course of things. Such was, in fact, the practice observed by sagacious men; which has given rise to the belief in the miracles that are celebrated in religions, however false they may be. For the sagacious rulers have given these miracles increased importance, no matter whence or how they originated; and their authority afterwards gave them credence with the people. Rome had many such miracles; and one of the most remarkable was that which occurred when the Roman soldiers sacked the city of Veii; some of them entered the temple of Juno, and, placing themselves in front of her statue, said to her, "Will you come to Rome?" Some imagined that they observed the statue make a sign of assent, and others pretended to have heard her reply, "Yes." Now these men, being very religious, as reported by Titus Livius, and having entered the temple quietly, they were filled with devotion and reverence, and might really have believed that they had heard a reply to their question, such as perhaps they could have presupposed. But this opinion and belief was favored and magnified by Camillus and the other Roman chiefs.[6]

And certainly, if the Christian religion had from the beginning been maintained according to the principles of its founder, the Christian states and republics would be much more united and happy than in fact they are. Nor can there be a greater proof of its decadence than to witness the fact that the nearer people are to the Church of Rome, which is the head of our religion, the less religious are they. And whoever examines the principles upon which that religion is founded, and sees how widely different from those principles its present practice and application are, will judge that her ruin or chastisement is near at hand. But as there are some of the opinion that the well-being of Italian affairs depends upon the Church of Rome, I will present such arguments against that opinion as occur to me; two of which are most important, and cannot according to my judgment be controverted. The first is, that the evil example of the court of Rome has destroyed all piety and religion in Italy, which brings in its train infinite improprieties and disorders; for as we may presuppose all good where religion prevails, so where

6. Livy, V, 22.

it is wanting we have the right to suppose the very opposite. We Italians then owe to the Church of Rome and to her priests our having become irreligious and bad; but we owe her a still greater debt, and one that will be the cause of our ruin, namely, that the Church has kept and still keeps our country divided. And certainly a country can never be united and happy, except when it obeys wholly one government, whether a republic or a monarchy, as is the case in France and in Spain; and the sole cause why Italy is not in the same condition, and is not governed by either one republic or one sovereign, is the Church; for having acquired and holding a temporal dominion, yet she has never had sufficient power or courage to enable her to seize the rest of the country and make herself sole sovereign of all Italy. And on the other hand she has not been so feeble that the fear of losing her temporal power prevented her from calling in the aid of a foreign power to defend her against such others as had become too powerful in Italy; as was seen in former days by many sad experiences, when through the intervention of Charlemagne she drove out the Lombards, who were masters of nearly all Italy; and when in our times she crushed the power of the Venetians by the aid of France, and afterwards with the assistance of the Swiss drove out in turn the French.[7] The Church, then, not having been powerful enough to be able to master all Italy, nor having permitted any other power to do so, has been the cause why Italy has never been able to unite under one head, but has always remained under a number of princes and lords, which occasioned her so many dissensions and so much weakness that she became a prey not only to the powerful barbarians, but of whoever chose to assail her. This we other Italians owe to the Church of Rome, and to none other. And any one, to be promptly convinced by experiment of the truth of all this, should have the power to transport the court of Rome to reside, with all the power it has in Italy, in the midst of the Swiss, who of all peoples nowadays live most according to their ancient customs so far as religion and their military system are concerned; and he would see in a very little while that the evil habits of that court would create more confusion in that country than anything else that could ever happen there.

* * *

[Book I, Chapter 27]

SHOWING THAT MEN ARE VERY RARELY EITHER ENTIRELY GOOD OR ENTIRELY BAD

When Pope Julius II went, in the year 1505, to Bologna to expel the Bentivogli from that state, the government of which they had held for a hundred years, he wanted also to remove Giovanpaolo

7. In capsule form, these are the events of 1509–12.

Baglioni from Perugia, who had made himself the absolute master of that city; for it was the intention of Pope Julius to destroy all the petty tyrants that occupied the possessions of the Church. Having arrived at Perugia with that purpose, which was well known to everybody, he did not wait to enter the city with his army for his protection, but went in almost alone, although Giovanpaolo had collected a large force within the city for his defence. And thus, with the customary impetuosity which characterized all his acts, Julius placed himself with only a small guard in the hands of his enemy Baglioni, whom he nevertheless carried off with him, leaving a governor in his stead to administer the state in the name of the Church. Sagacious men who were with the pope observed his temerity and the cowardice of Baglioni, and could not understand why the latter had not by a single blow rid himself of his enemy, whereby he would have secured for himself eternal fame and rich booty, for the Pope was accompanied by all the cardinals with their valuables. Nor could they believe that he had refrained from doing this either from goodness or conscientious scruples; for no sentiment of piety or respect could enter the heart of a man of such vile character as Giovanpaolo, who had dishonored his sister and murdered his nephews and cousins for the sake of obtaining possession of the state; but they concluded that mankind were neither utterly wicked nor perfectly good, and that when a crime has in itself some grandeur or magnanimity they will not know how to attempt it. Thus Giovanpaolo Baglioni, who did not mind open incest and parricide, knew not how to, or, more correctly speaking, dared not, attempt an act (although having a justifiable opportunity) for which every one would have admired his courage, and which would have secured him eternal fame, as being the first to show these prelates how little esteem men merit who live and govern as they do. And he would have done an act the greatness of which would have overshadowed all the infamy and danger that could possibly result from it.

[Book I, Chapter 28]

WHY ROME WAS LESS UNGRATEFUL TO HER CITIZENS THAN ATHENS

In reading the history of republics we find in all of them a degree of ingratitude to their citizens; this, however, seems to have been the case to a less extent in Rome than in Athens, and perhaps less even than in any other republic. In seeking for the reason of this difference, so far as Rome and Athens are concerned, I believe it was because Rome had less cause for mistrusting her citizens than Athens. In fact, from the time of the expulsion of the kings until Sulla and Marius,[8] no Roman citizen ever attempted to deprive his

8. From the sixth to the first century B.C.

country of her liberty; so that, there being no occasion to suspect her citizens, there was consequently no cause for offending them unnecessarily. The very contrary happened in Athens, for Pisistratus had by fraud robbed her of her liberty at the very time of her highest prosperity; so soon as she afterwards recovered her freedom, remembering the injuries received and her past servitude, she resented with the utmost harshness, not only all faults, but the mere semblance of faults, on the part of her citizens. It was this that gave rise to the exile and death of so many of her illustrious men, and thence came the practice of ostracism and every other violence which that city exercised at various times against some of her noblest citizens. It is a very true saying of political writers, that those states which have recovered their liberty treat their citizens with greater severity than such as have never lost it. A careful consideration of what has been said on this subject will show that Athens is neither to be blamed, nor Rome to be praised, for their respective conduct, and that it necessarily resulted entirely from the difference of the events that occurred in those cities; for a penetrating observer will not fail to see that, if Rome had been deprived of her liberty in the manner Athens was, she would not have been more indulgent to her citizens than the latter. We may judge very correctly of this by her treatment of Collatinus and Publius Valerius after the expulsion of the kings; the first was exiled for no other reason than that he bore the name of the Tarquins, and the other was likewise sent into exile because he had excited suspicion by building a house on Mount Cœlius.[9] Seeing then how suspicious and severe Rome showed herself in these two cases, we may fairly judge that she would have been liable to the charge of ingratitude, the same as Athens, if she had been offended by her citizens in the beginning of her existence, before she had grown powerful. And so as not to be obliged to return to this subject of ingratitude, I shall continue what I have to say in relation to it in the next chapter.

[Book I, Chapter 29]

WHICH OF THE TWO IS MOST UNGRATEFUL, A PEOPLE OR A PRINCE

It seems to me proper here, in connection with the above subject, to examine whether the people or a prince is more liable to the charge of ingratitude; and by way of illustrating this question the better, I set out by saying that the vice of ingratitude springs either from avarice or fear. For when a people or a prince has sent a general on some important expedition where by his success he acquires great glory, the prince or people is in turn bound to reward him.

9. Livy, II, 2, 6–8.

But if instead of such reward they dishonor and wrong him, influenced thereto by avarice, then they are guilty of an inexcusable wrong, which will involve them in eternal infamy. And yet there are many princes who commit this wrong, for which fact Tacitus assigns the reason in the following sentence: "Men are more ready to repay an injury than a benefit, because gratitude is a burden and revenge a pleasure."[1] But when they fail to reward, or rather when they offend, not from avarice, but from suspicion and fear, then the people or the prince have some excuse for their ingratitude. We read of many instances of this kind; for the general who by his valor has conquered a state for his master, and won great glory for himself by his victory over the enemy, and has loaded his soldiers with rich booty, acquires necessarily with his own soldiers, as well as with those of the enemy and with the subjects of the prince, so high a reputation, that his very victory may become distasteful and a cause for apprehension to his prince. For as the nature of men is ambitious as well as suspicious, and puts no limits to one's good fortune, it is not impossible that the suspicion that may suddenly be aroused in the mind of the prince by the victory of the general may have been aggravated by some haughty expressions or insolent acts on his part; so that the prince will naturally be made to think of securing himself against the ambition of his general. And to do this, the means that suggest themselves to him are either to have the general killed, or to deprive him of that reputation which he has acquired with the prince's army and the people, by using every means to prove that the general's victory was not due to his skill and courage, but to chance and the cowardice of the enemy, or to the sagacity of the other captains who were with him in that action.

After Vespasian, while in Judæa, had been declared Emperor by his army, Antonius Primus, who was at the head of another army in Illyria, took sides with him, and marched straight into Italy against Vitellius, then Emperor in Rome, and in the most gallant manner routed two Vitellian armies, and made himself master of Rome; so that Mutianus, who had been sent there by Vespasian, found everything achieved and all difficulties overcome. The reward which Antonius received for this service was that Mutianus deprived him of the command of the army, and gradually reduced his authority in Rome to nothing; so that Antonius, indignant, went to see Vespasian, who was still in Asia, who received him in such manner that, being soon after deprived of all rank, he died almost in despair. History is full of similar examples.[2]

We have seen in our own day with how much courage and perseverance Gonsalvo de Cordoba conducted the war in Naples for King Ferdinand of Aragon against the French; how he defeated

1. Tacitus, *History*, IV, 3.   2. Tacitus, *History*, III, IV.

them, and conquered the kingdom for Ferdinand; and how he was rewarded by his king, who left Spain and came to Naples, and first deprived Gonsalvo of his command of the army, and then took the control of the strong places from him, and finally carried him off with him to Spain, where Gonsalvo soon after died in obscurity.[3]

Fear and suspicion are so natural to princes that they cannot defend themselves against them, and thus it is impossible for them to show gratitude to those who, by victories achieved under their banners, have made important conquests for them. If then a prince cannot prevent himself from committing such wrongs, it is surely no wonder, nor matter worthy of more consideration, if a people acts in a similar manner. For as a free city is generally influenced by two principal objects, the one to aggrandize herself, and the other to preserve her liberties, it is natural that she should occasionally be betrayed into faults by excessive eagerness in the pursuit of either of these objects. As to the faults that result from the desire for aggrandizement, we shall speak in another place; and those resulting from the desire to preserve her liberty are amongst others the following, namely, to injure those citizens whom she should reward, and to suspect those in whom she should place most confidence. And although the effects of such conduct occasion great evils in a republic that is already corrupt, and which often lead to despotism,—as was seen under Cæsar in Rome, who took for himself by force what ingratitude had refused him,—still, in a republic not yet entirely corrupt, they may be productive of great good in preserving her freedom for a greater length of time; as the dread of punishment will keep men better, and less ambitious.

It is true that, of all the people that ever possessed a great empire, the Romans were the least ungrateful; for it may be said that no other instance of their ingratitude can be cited than that of Scipio; for Coriolanus and Camillus were both exiled on account of the outrages which they had committed upon the people. The one was never pardoned, because he always preserved an implacable hatred against the people; but the other was not only recalled from exile, but was for the entire remainder of his life honored like a prince. The ingratitude to Scipio arose from jealousy such as never before had been felt towards any one else, and which resulted from the greatness of the enemy whom Scipio had conquered, from the great reputation which his victory after so long and perilous a war had given him, from the rapidity of his actions and the popular favor which his youth, his prudence, and other remarkable virtues had won for him. All of these were so great that everybody in

3. Gonsalvo de Cordoba (1453–1515) was known, because of his extraordinary record of victories, as the "Gran Capitan." A full account of his military triumphs, and of the pointed neglect that was their reward, can be collected from W. H. Prescott's creaky but vital *Ferdinand and Isabella* (1837).

Rome, even the magistrates, feared his influence and authority, which offended the intelligent men of Rome as an unheard of thing. And his manner of life was such that Cato the elder, who was reputed a man of the purest character, was the first to complain of him, saying that no city could call herself free where a citizen was feared by the magistrates. So that if in this case the people of Rome followed the opinion of Cato, they are entitled to that excuse which, as I have said above, those peoples and princes may claim who are ungrateful from suspicion and fear. In concluding, then, this discourse, I say that, as the vice of ingratitude is usually the consequence of either avarice or fear, it will be seen that the peoples never fall into this error from avarice, and that fear also makes them less liable to it than princes, inasmuch as they have less reason for fear, as we shall show further on.

* * *

[Book I, Chapter 37]

WHAT TROUBLES RESULTED IN ROME FROM THE ENACTMENT OF THE
AGRARIAN LAW, AND HOW VERY WRONG IT IS TO MAKE LAWS THAT
ARE RETROSPECTIVE AND CONTRARY TO OLD ESTABLISHED CUSTOMS

It was a saying of ancient writers, that men afflict themselves in evil, and become weary of the good, and that both these dispositions produce the same effects. For when men are no longer obliged to fight from necessity, they fight from ambition, which passion is so powerful in the hearts of men that it never leaves them, no matter to what height they may rise. The reason of this is that nature has created men so that they desire everything, but are unable to attain it; desire being thus always greater than the faculty of acquiring, discontent with what they have and dissatisfaction with themselves result from it. This causes the changes in their fortunes; for as some men desire to have more, whilst others fear to lose what they have, enmities and war are the consequences; and this brings about the ruin of one province and the elevation of another. I have made these remarks because the Roman people were not content with having secured themselves against the nobles by the creation of the Tribunes, to which they had been driven by necessity. Having obtained this, they soon began to fight from ambition, and wanted to divide with the nobles their honors and possessions, being those things which men value most. Thence the frenzy that occasioned the contentions about the agrarian law, which finally caused the destruction of the Roman republic. Now, as in well-regulated republics the state ought to be rich and the citizens poor, it was evident that the agrarian law was in some respects defective; it was either in the beginning so made that it required constant modifications; or the changes in it had been so long deferred that it became most obnoxious because it was retrospective in its action; or perhaps it had been good in the beginning and had afterwards become corrupted in its application. But whichever it may have been, this law could never be discussed in Rome without causing the most violent excitement in the city. There were two principal points in this law; one provided that no citizen could possess more than a certain number of acres of land, and the other that all the lands taken from their enemies should be divided amongst the Roman people. This affected the nobles disadvantageously in two ways; for those who had more land than the law allowed (which was the case with the greater part of the nobles) had to be deprived of it; and by dividing amongst the people the lands taken from the enemy, it took from the nobles the chance of enriching themselves thereby, as they had previously done. Now, as it was a powerful class that had been thus affected, and who considered resistance to this law as a defence of the public good, whenever the subject was brought up, it occasioned, as we have said, the most violent disturbances. The nobles used all patience and every means in their power to gain time and delay action upon the subject, either by calling out an army, or by getting one Tribune to oppose another who had proposed the law, or sometimes by yielding in part, or even by sending a colony to any place where lands were to be divided. This was done with the country of Antium, respecting which this law had caused a dispute; and therefore a colony drawn from amongst the citizens of Rome was sent there, to whom that country was assigned. In reference to this, Titus Livius makes the notable remark, that "it was difficult to find any one in Rome willing to inscribe his name to go to that colony; so much more ready were the people to desire possessions in Rome than to go and have them in Antium."

The troubles about this agrarian law continued to disturb Rome for some time, so that the Romans began to send their armies to the extreme ends of Italy, or even beyond; after which matters were seemingly calmed down, owing to the fact that the lands taken from the enemy were at a great distance from Rome, and remote from the eyes of the people, and were situated where it was not easy to cultivate them, and consequently they were less desirable. Besides this, the Romans became less disposed to deprive their vanquished enemies of their lands, as they had done before; and when they did so deprive any of them of their possessions, they sent colonies to occupy them; so that from these several causes the agrarian law lay, as it were, dormant until the time of the Gracchi, who, after having revived it, wholly destroyed the Roman republic. For the power of the adversaries of the law had increased twofold in the mean time, and its revival excited such feelings of hatred between the people and the Senate, that it led to violence and bloodshed beyond all bounds or precedent. So that, the magistrates being unable to check these disturbances, and neither party having any confidence in the public authorities, they both resorted to private expedients, and each of the factions began to look for a chief capable of defending them against the other. In these extreme troubles and disorders the people began to cast their eyes upon Marius, on account of his reputation, which was so great that they had made him Consul four times in succession, and with such short intervals between these several consulates that he was enabled to nominate himself three times more for that office. The nobility, seeing no other remedy against these abuses, gave their favor to Sulla, and made him chief of their party. Thus civil war was provoked, and after much bloodshed and varied fortunes the nobility retained the upper hand. In the time of Cæsar and Pompey these troubles were revived, Cæsar placing himself at the head of the party of Marius, and Pompey upholding that of Sulla; conflicts of arms ensued, and Cæsar remained master and became the first tyrant of Rome, so that that city never afterwards recovered her liberty.

Such was the beginning and the end of the agrarian law. And as I have demonstrated elsewhere that the differences between the Senate and the people had been instrumental in preserving liberty in Rome, because they had given rise to the enactment of laws favorable to liberty, therefore the results of this agrarian law may seem in contradiction with that previous conclusion. But I do not on that account change my opinion, for the ambition of the nobles is so great, that, if it is not repressed by various ways and means in any city, it will quickly bring that city to ruin. So that if the contentions about the agrarian law needed three hundred years to bring Rome to a state of servitude, she would have been brought there much quicker if the people, by these laws and other means, had not for so great a length of time kept the ambition of the nobles in check. This shows us also how much more people value riches than honors; for the Roman nobility always yielded to the people without serious difficulties in the matter of honors, but when it came to a question of property, then they resisted with so much pertinacity that the people, to satisfy their thirst for riches, resorted to the above-described extraordinary proceedings. The chief promoters of these disorders were the Gracchi, whose intentions in this matter were more praiseworthy than their prudence. For to attempt to eradicate an abuse that has grown up in a republic by the enactment of retrospective laws, is a most inconsiderate proceeding, and (as we have amply discussed above) only serves to accelerate the fatal results which the abuse tends to bring about; but by temporizing, the end will either be delayed, or the evil will exhaust itself before it attains that end.

* * *

THE PEOPLE ARE WISER AND MORE CONSTANT THAN PRINCES

Titus Livius as well as all other historians affirm that nothing is more uncertain and inconstant than the multitude; for it appears from what he relates of the actions of men, that in many instances the multitude, after having condemned a man to death, bitterly lamented it, and most earnestly wished him back. This was the case with the Roman people and Manlius Capitolinus, whom they had condemned to death and afterwards most earnestly desired him back, as our author says in the following words: "No sooner had they found out that they had nothing to fear from him, than they began to regret and to wish him back." And elsewhere, when he relates the events that occurred in Syracuse after the death of Hieronymus, nephew of Hiero, he says: "It is the nature of the multitude either humbly to serve or insolently to dominate."[4] I know not whether, in undertaking to defend a cause against the accusations of all writers, I do not assume a task so hard and so beset with difficulties as to oblige me to abandon it with shame, or to go on with it at the risk of being weighted down by it. Be that as it may, however, I think, and ever shall think, that it cannot be wrong to defend one's opinions with arguments founded upon reason, without employing force or authority.

I say, then, that individual men, and especially princes, may be charged with the same defects of which writers accuse the people; for whoever is not controlled by laws will commit the same errors as an unbridled multitude. This may easily be verified, for there have been and still are plenty of princes, and a few good and wise ones, such, I mean, as needed not the curb that controlled them. Amongst these, however, are not to be counted either the kings that lived in Egypt at that ancient period when that country was governed by laws, or those that arose in Sparta; neither such as are born in our day in France, for that country is more thoroughly regulated by laws than any other of which we have any knowledge in modern times. And those kings that arise under such constitutions are not to be classed amongst the number of those whose individual nature we have to consider, and see whether it resembles that of the people; but they should be compared with a people equally controlled by law as those kings were, and then we shall find in that

---

4. Livy, VI, 20, and XXIV, 25.

multitude the same good qualitites as in those kings, and we shall see that such a people neither obey with servility nor command with insolence. Such were the people of Rome, who, so long as that republic remained uncorrupted, neither obeyed basely nor ruled insolently, but rather held its rank honorably, supporting the laws and their magistrates. And when the unrighteous ambition of some noble made it necessary for them to rise up in self-defence, they did so, as in the case of Manlius, the Decemvirs, and others who attempted to oppress them; and so when the public good required them to obey the dictators and consuls, they promptly yielded obedience. And if the Roman people regretted Manlius Capitolinus after his death, it is not to be wondered at; for they regretted his virtues, which had been such that the remembrance of them filled every one with pity, and would have had the power to produce the same effect upon any prince; for all writers agree that virtue is to be admired and praised, even in one's enemies. And if intense desire could have restored Manlius to life, the Roman people would nevertheless have pronounced the same judgment against him as they did the first time, when they took him from prison and condemned him to death. And so we have seen princes that were esteemed wise, who have caused persons to be put to death and afterwards regretted it deeply; such as Alexander the Great with regard to Clitus and other friends, and Herod with his wife Mariamne.[5] But what our historian says of the character of the multitude does not apply to a people regulated by laws, as the Romans were, but to an unbridled multitude, such as the Syracusans; who committed all the excesses to which infuriated and unbridled men abandon themselves, as did Alexander the Great and Herod in the above-mentioned cases.

Therefore, the character of the people is not to be blamed any more than that of princes, for both alike are liable to err when they are without any control. Besides the examples already given, I could adduce numerous others from amongst the Roman emperors and other tyrants and princes, who have displayed as much inconstancy and recklessness as any populace ever did. Contrary to the general opinion, then, which maintains that the people, when they govern, are inconsistent, unstable, and ungrateful, I conclude and affirm that these defects are not more natural to the people than they are to princes. To charge the people and princes equally with them may be the truth, but to except princes from them would be a great mistake. For a people that governs and is well regulated by laws will be stable, prudent, and grateful, as much so, and even more, according to my opinion, than a prince, although he be esteemed wise; and, on the other hand, a prince, freed from the restraints of the law, will be more ungrateful, inconstant, and imprudent than a people simi-

5. "Life of Alexander" by Plutarch, LII; Josephus, *Antiquities* XV, vii, 4–7.

larly situated. The difference in their conduct is not due to any difference in their nature (for that is the same, and if there be any difference for good, it is on the side of the people); but to the greater
or less respect they have for the laws under which they respectively
live. And whoever studies the Roman people will see that for four
hundred years they have been haters of royalty, and lovers of the
glory and common good of their country; and he will find any
number of examples that will prove both the one and the other.
And should any one allege the ingratitude which the Roman people
displayed towards Scipio, I shall reply the same as I have said in
another place on this subject, where I have demonstrated that the
people are less ungrateful than princes. But as regards prudence and
stability, I say that the people are more prudent and stable, and
have better judgment than a prince; and it is not without good
reason that it is said, "The voice of the people is the voice of God";
for we see popular opinion prognosticate events in such a wonderful
manner that it would almost seem as if the people had some occult
virtue, which enables them to foresee the good and the evil. As to
the people's capacity of judging of things, it is exceedingly rare that,
when they hear two orators of equal talents advocate different measures, they do not decide in favor of the best of the two; which
proves their ability to discern the truth of what they hear. And if
occasionally they are misled in matters involving questions of courage or seeming utility, (as has been said above), so is a prince also
many times misled by his own passions, which are much greater
than those of the people. We also see that in the election of their
magistrates they make far better choice than princes; and no people
will ever be persuaded to elect a man of infamous character and corrupt habits to any post of dignity, to which a prince is easily influenced in a thousand different ways. When we see a people take an
aversion to anything, they persist in it for many centuries, which we
never find to be the case with princes. Upon both these points the
Roman people shall serve me as a proof, who in the many elections
of consuls and tribunes had to regret only four times the choice
they had made. The Roman people held the name of king in such
detestation, as we have said, that no extent of services rendered by
any of its citizens who attempted to usurp that title could save him
from his merited punishment. We furthermore see the cities where
the people are masters make the greatest progress in the least possible time, and much greater than such as have always been governed
by princes; as was the case with Rome after the expulsion of the
kings, and with Athens after they rid themselves of Pisistratus; and
this can be attributed to no other cause than that the governments
of the people are better than those of princes.[6]

6. Machiavelli's enthusiasm for popular
government was very exceptional in his
day, and contributed to his bad reputation almost down to the present, when it
suddenly became an article to his credit.

It would be useless to object to my opinion by referring to what our historian has said in the passages quoted above, and elsewhere; for if we compare the faults of a people with those of princes, as well as their respective good qualities, we shall find the people vastly superior in all that is good and glorious. And if princes show themselves superior in the making of laws, and in the forming of civil institutions and new statutes and ordinances, the people are superior in maintaining those institutions, laws, and ordinances, which certainly places them on a par with those who established them.

And finally to sum up this matter, I say that both governments of princes and of the people have lasted a long time, but both required to be regulated by laws. For a prince who knows no other control but his own will is like a madman, and a people that can do as it pleases will hardly be wise. If now we compare a prince who is controlled by laws, and a people that is untrammelled by them, we shall find more virtue in the people than in the prince; and if we compare them when both are freed from such control, we shall see that the people are guilty of fewer excesses than the prince, and that the errors of the people are of less importance, and therefore more easily remedied. For a licentious and mutinous people may easily be brought back to good conduct by the influence and persuasion of a good man, but an evil-minded prince is not amenable to such influences, and therefore there is no other remedy against him but cold steel. We may judge then from this of the relative defects of the one and the other; if words suffice to correct those of the people, whilst those of the prince can only be remedied by violence, no one can fail to see that where the greater remedy is required, there also the defects must be greater. The follies which a people commits at the moment of its greatest license are not what is most to be feared; it is not the immediate evil that may result from them that inspires apprehension, but the fact that such general confusion might afford the opportunity for a tyrant to seize the government. But with evil-disposed princes the contrary is the case; it is the immediate present that causes fear, and there is hope only in the future; for men will persuade themselves that the termination of his wicked life may give them a chance of liberty. Thus we see the difference between the one and the other to be, that the one touches the present and the other the future. The excesses of the people are directed against those whom they suspect of interfering with the public good; whilst those of princes are against apprehended interference with their individual interests. The general prejudice against the people results from the fact that everybody can freely and fearlessly speak ill of them in mass, even whilst they are at the height of their power; but a prince can only be spoken of with the greatest circumspection and apprehension. And as the subject leads me to it, I deem it not amiss to examine in the following chapter whether alliances with a republic or with a prince are most to be trusted.

[*Book I, Chapter 59*]

LEAGUES AND ALLIANCES WITH REPUBLICS ARE MORE TO BE TRUSTED THAN THOSE WITH PRINCES

As it is of daily occurrence that princes or republics contract leagues or friendships with each other, or that in like manner treaties and alliances are formed between a republic and a prince, it seems to me proper to examine whose faith is most constant and most to be relied upon, that of a republic or that of a prince. In examining the whole subject I believe that in many instances they are equal, but that in others there is a difference; and I believe, moreover, that agreements which are the result of force will no more be observed by a prince than by a republic, and, where either the one or the other is apprehensive of losing their state, that to save it both will break their faith and be guilty of ingratitude. Demetrius, called the Conqueror of Cities, had conferred infinite benefits upon the Athenians. It happened that, having been defeated by his enemies, he took refuge in Athens as a city that was friendly to him, and which he had laid under obligations; but the Athenians refused to receive him, which gave Demetrius more pain than the loss of his men and the destruction of his army.[7] Pompey, after his defeat by Cæsar in Thessaly, took refuge in Egypt with Ptolemy, whom on a former occasion he had reinstated in his kingdom, but was treacherously put to death by him.[8] Both these instances are attributable to the same reasons; yet we see that the republic acted with more humanity and inflicted less injury than the prince. Wherever fear dominates, there we shall find equal want of faith in both, although the same influence may cause either a prince or a republic to keep faith at the risk of ruin. For it may well happen that the prince is the ally of some powerful potentate, who for the moment may not be able to assist him, but who, the prince may hope, will be able to reinstate him in his possessions; or he may believe that, having acted as his partisan, his powerful ally will make no treaties or alliances with his enemies. Such was the fate of those princes of the kingdom of Naples who adhered to the French party. And with regard to republics this occurred with Saguntum in Spain, which hazarded her own safety for the sake of adhering to the Roman party; and with Florence when in the year 1512 she followed the fortune of the French. Taking all things together now, I

7. "Life of Demetrius" by Plutarch, XXX.

8. "Life of Pompey" by Plutarch, especially LXXVII.

believe that in such cases which involve imminent peril there will be found somewhat more of stability in republics than in princes.

* * *

[Book II, Chapter 13]

CUNNING AND DECEIT WILL SERVE A MAN BETTER THAN FORCE TO RISE FROM A BASE CONDITION TO GREAT FORTUNE

I believe it to be most true that it seldom happens that men rise from low condition to high rank without employing either force or fraud, unless that rank should be attained either by gift or inheritance. Nor do I believe that force alone will ever be found to suffice, whilst it will often be the case that cunning alone serves the purpose; as is clearly seen by whoever reads the life of Philip of Macedon, or that of Agathocles the Sicilian, and many others, who from the lowest or most moderate condition have achieved thrones and great empires. Xenophon shows in his Life of Cyrus the necessity of deception to success: the first expedition of Cyrus against the king of Armenia is replete with fraud, and it was deceit alone, and not force, that enabled him to seize that kingdom. And Xenophon draws no other conclusion from it than that a prince who wishes to achieve great things must learn to deceive. Cyrus also practised a variety of deceptions upon Cyaxares,[9] king of the Medes, his maternal uncle; and Xenophon shows that without these frauds Cyrus would never have achieved the greatness which he did attain. Nor do I believe that there was ever a man who from obscure condition arrived at great power by merely employing open force; but there are many who have succeeded by fraud alone, as, for instance, Giovanni Galeazzo Visconti in taking the state and sovereignty of Lombardy from his uncle, Messer Bernabò.[1] And that which princes are obliged to do in the beginning of their rise, republics are equally obliged to practise until they have become powerful enough so that force alone suffices them. And as Rome employed every means, by chance or choice, to promote her aggrandizement, so she also did not hesitate to employ fraud; nor could she have practised a greater fraud than by taking the course we have explained above of making other peoples her allies and associates, and under that title making them slaves, as she did with the Latins and other neighboring nations. For first she availed of their arms to subdue their mutual neighbors, and thus to increase her state and reputation; and after

9. Xenophon's *Cyropaedia*, a kind of moralizing romance, was translated into Latin by Poggio Bracciolini early in the fifteenth century. Machiavelli and his age still considered it historical.
1. Giangaleazzo Visconti deceived and then murdered his uncle, Messer Bernabò, in 1385; for a general account of the manners of the Italian despots, consult Burckhardt, *The Civilization of the Renaissance in Italy*, part I.

having subdued these, her power increased to that degree that she could subjugate each people separately in turn. The Latins never became aware that they were wholly slaves until they had witnessed two defeats of the Samnites, and saw them obliged to accept the terms of peace dictated to them. As this victory greatly increased the reputation of the Romans with the more distant princes, who felt the weight of their name before experiencing that of their arms, so it excited envy and apprehension in those who had seen and felt their arms, amongst whom were the Latins. And this jealousy and fear were so powerful that not only the Latins, but also the colonies which the Romans had established in Latium, together with the Campanians, whose defence the Romans had but a short time previously undertaken, conspired together against the Romans. The Latins began the war in the way we have shown that most wars are begun, not by attacking the Romans, but by defending the Sidicini from the Samnites, against whom the latter were making war with the permission of the Romans. And that it is true that the Latins began the war because they had at last become aware of the bad faith of the Romans is demonstrated by Titus Livius, when at an assembly of the Latin people he puts the following words into the mouth of Annius Setinus, a Latin Prætor: "For if now we can bear servitude under the specious name of equal confederates," &c.[2]

We see therefore that the Romans in the early beginning of their power already employed fraud, which it has ever been necessary for those to practise who from small beginnings wish to rise to the highest degree of power; and then it is the less censurable the more it is concealed, as was that practised by the Romans.

* * *

[Book III, Chapter 8]

WHOEVER WISHES TO CHANGE THE GOVERNMENT OF A REPUBLIC SHOULD FIRST CONSIDER WELL ITS EXISTING CONDITION

We have already shown that an evil-disposed citizen cannot effect any changes for the worse in a republic, unless it be already corrupt. Besides the reasons elsewhere given, this conclusion is confirmed by the examples of Spurius Cassius and Manlius Capitolinus.[3] This Spurius, being an ambitious man and wishing to obtain the supreme power in Rome, endeavored to gain the favor of the people by numerous benefits, such as selling to them the lands taken from the Hernici. This opened the eyes of the senate to his ambitious projects, and he became suspected, even by the people, to that point that when he offered them the proceeds of the sale of the

2. Livy, VIII, 4.
3. For the story of Spurius Cassius, see Livy II, 33, 41, and for that of Manlius Capitolinus, VI, 14–20.

grain which the government had caused to be brought from Sicily, the people refused it altogether; for it seemed to them as though Spurius offered it as the price of their liberty. But if this people had been corrupt, they would, so far from refusing this offer, have accepted it, and thus have opened the way for Spurius to the tyranny which now they closed against him.

The example of Manlius is even more forcible, and proves how this evil ambition to rule cancels the noblest qualities of mind and body, and the most important services rendered to a state. We see that this ambition had its origin with Manlius in his jealousy of the honors bestowed upon Camillus; and so blinded was he by it, that, regardless of the manners and customs of Rome, and without examining the condition of the state, which was not yet prepared to accept a vicious form of government, he set to work to stir up disturbances in Rome against the senate and the institutions of his country. Here we recognize the perfection of the constitution of Rome, and the excellent character of its population; for on the occasion of the fall of Manlius, not one of the nobility (so ardent generally in their mutual support and defence) made the slightest effort in his favor; nor did any of his relatives make any attempt to support him. And whilst the families of others accused were in the habit of showing themselves near them, all covered with dust and in deep mourning and sadness, for the purpose of exciting the commiseration of the people for the accused, not one of the family of Manlius appeared near him. The tribunes of the people, so accustomed always to favor every measure that seemed for the advantage of the people, and the more so in proportion as it was adverse to the interests of the nobility, in this instance united with the nobles for the purpose of suppressing a common enemy. And finally the people of Rome, ever most jealous of its own interests, and eagerly in favor of everything that was adverse to the nobles, had at first shown themselves well disposed towards Manlius; but the moment the tribunes summoned him and brought his case before them, the same people, having now from defenders become judges, condemned him, without regard to his former services, to suffer the death penalty. I therefore think that there is no fact in history that more effectually shows the excellence of the Roman constitution than this example, where not a single person of the whole city stirred to defend a citizen gifted with the best qualities, and who had rendered the most signal services to the public, as well as to private individuals. For the love of country had more power over them than any other sentiment; and they thought so much more of its present dangers, to which the ambition of Manlius exposed them, than of his past services, that they saw no other way of relieving themselves of those dangers than by his death. And Titus Livius says: "Thus ended the career of this man, who would have been memorable had he not been born in a free community."

This brings us to two important considerations: the first, that the means of attaining glory are different in a republic that is corrupt from what they are in a republic that still preserves its institutions pure; and the second (which is in a measure comprised in the first), that men in their conduct, and especially in their most prominent actions, should well consider and conform to the times in which they live. And those who, from an evil choice or from natural inclination, do not conform to the times in which they live, will in most instances live unhappily, and their undertakings will come to a bad end; whilst, on the contrary, success attends those who conform to the times. And doubtless we may conclude from the words of our historian that, if Manlius had been born in the times of Marius and Sulla, when the people were already corrupt, and when he could have moulded them according to his ambition, he would have achieved the same results and successes as Marius and Sulla, and the others who after them aspired to the tyranny. And in the same way, if Sulla and Marius had lived in the times of Manlius, they would have been crushed in their first attempt. For a man may well by his conduct and evil ways begin to corrupt a people, but it is impossible for him to live long enough to enjoy the fruits of it. And even if it were possible that by length of time he should succeed, the natural impatience of the people, which cannot brook delay in the indulgence of their passion, would prove an obstacle to his success, so that by too much haste, or from error he would be led to engage in his attempt at the wrong time, and thus end in failure.

To usurp supreme and absolute authority, then, in a free state, and subject it to tyranny, the people must have already become corrupt by gradual steps from generation to generation. And all states necessarily come to this, unless (as we have shown above) they are frequently reinvigorated by good examples, and brought back by good laws to their first principles. Manlius thus would have been regarded as a rare and memorable man if he had lived in a corrupt republic. And therefore all such as desire to make a change in the government of a republic, whether in favor of liberty or in favor of tyranny, must well examine the condition of things, and from that judge of the difficulties of their undertaking. For it is as difficult to make a people free that is resolved to live in servitude, as it is to subject a people to servitude that is determined to be free. Having argued above that in any such attempts men should well consider the state of the times and govern themselves accordingly, I will develop this subject more fully in the next chapter.

* * *

[*Book III, Chapter 9*]

WHOEVER DESIRES CONSTANT SUCCESS MUST CHANGE HIS CONDUCT WITH THE TIMES

I have often reflected that the causes of the success or failure of men depend upon their manner of suiting their conduct to the times. We see one man proceed in his actions with passion, another warily; and as in both the one and the other case men are apt to exceed the proper limits, not being able always to observe the just middle course, they are apt to err in both. But he errs least and will be most favored by fortune who suits his proceedings to the times, as I have said above, and always follows the impulses of his nature. Every one knows how Fabius Maximus conducted the war against Hannibal with extreme caution and circumspection, and with an utter absence of all impetuosity or Roman audacity.[4] It was his good fortune that this mode of proceeding accorded perfectly with the times and circumstances. For Hannibal had arrived in Rome whilst still young and with his fortunes fresh; he had already twice routed the Romans, so that the republic was as it were deprived of her best troops, and greatly discouraged by her reverses. Rome could not therefore have been more favored by fortune, than to have a commander who by his extreme caution and the slowness of his movements kept the enemy at bay. At the same time, Fabius could not have found circumstances more favorable for his character and genius, to which fact he was indebted for his success and glory. And that this mode of proceeding was the result of his character and nature, and not a matter of choice, was shown on the occasion when Scipio wanted to take the same troops to Africa for the purpose of promptly terminating the war. Fabius most earnestly opposed this, like a man incapable of breaking from his accustomed ways and habits; so that, if he had been master, Hannibal would have remained in Italy, because Fabius failed to perceive that the times were changed, and strategies would have to change as well. And if Fabius had been king of Rome, he might easily have lost the war, because he would never have been able to change his methods to suit the changing times. But Rome was a republic that produced citizens of various characters and dispositions, such as Fabius, who was excellent at the time when it was desirable to protract the war, and Scipio, when it became necessary to terminate it. It is this which assures to republics greater vitality and more enduring success than monarchies have; for the diversity of the genius of her citizens enables the republic better to accommodate herself to the changes

4. The tale of Fabius Cunctator and his part in the Second Punic War occupies   Livy through much of books XX–XXX.

of the times than can be done by a prince. For any man accustomed to a certain mode of proceeding will never change it, as we have said, and consequently when time and circumstances change, so that his ways are no longer in harmony with them, he must of necessity succumb. Piero Soderini, whom we have mentioned several times already, was in all his actions governed by humanity and patience. He and his country prospered so long as the times favored this mode of proceeding; but when afterwards circumstances arose that demanded a course of conduct the opposite to that of patience and humanity, he was unfit for the occasion, and his own and his country's ruin were the consequence. Pope Julius II. acted throughout the whole period of his pontificate with the impetuosity and passion natural to his character; and as the times and circumstances well accorded with this, he was successful in all his undertakings. But if the times had changed so that different counsels would have been required, he would unquestionably have been ruined, for he could not have changed his character or mode of action.

That we cannot thus change at will is due to two causes; the one is the impossibility of resisting the natural bent of our characters; and the other is the difficulty of persuading ourselves, after having been accustomed to success by a certain mode of proceeding, that any other can succeed as well. It is this that causes the varying success of a man; for the times change, but he does not change his mode of proceeding. The ruin of states is caused in like manner, as we have fully shown above, because they do not modify their institutions to suit the changes of the times. And such changes are more difficult and tardy in republics; for necessarily circumstances will occur that will unsettle the whole state, and when the change of proceeding of one man will not suffice for the occasion.

* * *

Machiavelli the Moralist

NICCOLÒ MACHIAVELLI

The Exhortation to Penitence†

There is no way to date the composition of "The Exhortation to Penitence," which survives in a single manuscript of Machiavelli's own hand-
writing. Florence had, and still has, a great many social and religious societies, before which their own members appear from time to time to deliver
addresses. As early as 1495, Machiavelli became a member of the Company
of Piety, but he need not have been restricted to preaching before it. Per-
formances of this character did not necessarily imply an unusual measure of
religious devotion in the speaker; they were part of the complex and long-
continued initiation rituals by which a society in which money, family, and
seniority counted overwhelmingly, prepared young men for formal positions
of leadership and decision. Thus there is no reason to scan this discourse
narrowly (as has often been done) for signs of irony or mental reservation.
No such signs are to be found. Machiavelli, we may be sure, made the
sermon that was expected of him, received the commendations that were
normal, and was set down as a serious and sensible young man, a thoroughly competent, reliable civil servant of middle rank. Florentine society
expected and wanted nothing more.

*De profundis clamavi ad te, Domine; Domine, exaudi vocem
meam.*[1] With your good will, honorable fathers and superior brothers, I am to talk to you this evening on the topic of penitence; and
it seemed best to begin my talk with the words of that reader in the
Holy Spirit, David the prophet, so that those who have sinned like
him may gain from his words the hope of receiving at last, at the
hands of the highest and most generous God, mercy; and never to
despair of obtaining it, since this man obtained it, and there cannot
possibly be united in any one person greater faults or greater penitence than in him, nor can there be conceived greater liberality on
the part of God than was shown in pardoning him. And thus in the
very words of the prophet let us say, "O Lord, I have called on you
out of the depths of my sin, in a voice humbled and choked with
tears. Mercy, O Lord; I beg it of you, and implore you, in your
infinite goodness, to bestow it on me." Nor should anyone despair
of obtaining it, if only, with tears in his eyes, with an afflicted heart,

†The text has been translated by the editor from Niccolò Machiavelli, *Opere letterarie*, ed. Luigi Blasucci (Milano:
Adelphi, 1964), pp. 207–11.
1. Psalm 130.

and in a melancholy voice, he requests it. Oh, the immense pity of God! His infinite goodness! God in his highest heavens knew how easy it was for man to fall into sin; he saw that if he stood strictly on his justice, it would be impossible for any man to gain salvation; nor could he provide a better remedy for human frailty than to warn the human race that it is not sin, but perseverance in sin, that will render him implacable. And thus he opened before mankind the pathway of penitence, by which, even after losing the other way, we may still get to heaven.

Penitence, then, is the only remedy that wipes out all the evils and errors of men, who, though they are very numerous and go about their business in many different ways, can still be divided very roughly into two sorts: those who are ungrateful to God, and those who are hateful to their neighbors.

But to understand our full ingratitude, it is necessary to consider what are the great benefits we have received from God. Think, then, how all things made and created were made and created for the benefit of man. You observe in the first place the immense expanse of the earth which, to make it habitable for man, he kept from being flooded everywhere with water, but left part of it uncovered for human use. And on it he caused to spring up all these many plants, animals, and grasses, and everything which grows from the earth, all for man's benefit; and not only did he order the earth to provide for man's existence, he ordered the oceans also to breed an infinity of creatures, to serve for man's nourishment. But, passing by these earthly thoughts, let us raise our eyes to heaven and consider the beauty of the things we see there; part of which he made for our service, and the other part so that, from knowing the splendor and marvelous workmanship of it, we might feel a deep and thirsty desire to know those other things which are hidden even further beyond. Don't you see how much trouble the sun takes to share his light with you, to generate by his power both ourselves and all the different things created by God for our use? Thus everything is created for the honor and benefit of man, and man is created only for the benefit and honor of God. To man he gave the power of speech, to praise him; he gave him features, not turned to earth like the other beasts, but raised to the heavens, so that he might continually contemplate him; he gave him hands so that he might raise temples and make sacrifices in his honor; he gave him reason and intellect so that he might reflect and know the grandeur of God. You see then with what ingratitude man presumes to rise against so great a benefactor! and how great is the punishment he deserves when he perverts the use of these things, and turns them to evil purposes! The tongue, which was made to honor God, is turned to blaspheming him; the mouth, formed to nourish us,

becomes a sewer, and a way to satisfy the gut with fancy, superfluous foods; the eyes, which should be turned up to God, turn
down to this earth; and the instinct to perpetuate the human race is
turned to lust and other lascivious pastimes; and thus, through all
these ugly actions, man transforms himself from a rational creature
to a brute beast. And when he shows this ingratitude to God, man
also changes himself from angel to devil, from master to slave, and
from human being to animal.

Those who are ungrateful to God can hardly fail to be hateful to
their neighbors. A man is an enemy to his neighbor when he lacks
charity. This it is, my fathers and brothers, only this is what raises
our souls to heaven; this and this alone is worth all the other virtues
of which men are capable; of this the Church speaks so broadly that
she declares, The man who has no charity has nothing. Saint Paul
speaks of this when he says, "Though I speak with the tongue of
men and of angels, and have not charity, I am become as sounding
brass."[2] On this one virtue is founded the faith of Christ. No man
can be full of charity who is not also full of religion, because charity
is patient and benign, without envy or perversity; it is never proud
or contemptuous, it repents its misdeeds instead of rejoicing in
them, it takes no pleasure in vanity, it endures all, believes all,
hopes always. O divine virtue, happy are those who possess you!
This is the celestial robe in which we must be dressed if we want to
be admitted to the heavenly marriage of our ruler Jesus Christ in
the kingdoms of heaven! and he who is not dressed in this robe will
be driven from the marriage feast, and cast into perpetual fires!
Anyone who lacks this virtue, it is obvious, must be an enemy to his
neighbor: he does not help his neighbor, or comfort him in his
weakness, or console him in his troubles; he neither teaches the
ignorant nor counsels the erring; he neither helps the good, nor
punishes the bad. These offenses against one's neighbor are serious,
but ingratitude against God is the most serious of all; and because
we often fall into these two vices, God the kindly creator has shown
us the road of redemption, which is penitence. And he has made
clear its power both by word and by deed: with words, when he
told Peter to forgive his brother, not seven times, but seventy times
seven.[3] And in deeds when he pardoned David for his adultery and
homicide, and pardoned Saint Peter for having denied him, not just
once but three times. For what crime will not God grant pardon,
my brethren, if he pardoned these men for these crimes? For not
only did he pardon them, he honored them among the elect and
lofty spirits of Heaven. But only because David, prostrate on the
earth, dissolved in tears and affliction, cried out: *Lord, have mercy
on me*; only because Saint Peter *wept bitterly*; he bitterly bewailed

2. I Corinthians 13:1.   3. Matthew 18:21.

his own fault, and David repented; both men deserved their pardon.

But because it's not enough to repent and bewail our faults, because we must prepare ourselves to work against sin, in order not to do evil again and to take away the very occasion of evil, it behooves us to imitate Saint Francis and Saint Jerome who undertook to mortify the flesh and so to prevent it from forcing them into evildoing. And so the first of them scarified himself with thorns, and the other beat his breast with a rock. But with what rock or what thorns shall we repress our itch for usury, or for shameful pleasures, or for the tricks we delight in playing on our neighbors? The only way is with gifts of charity, by doing honor to our neighbor, by doing good to him. But we are tricked ourselves by lust, tangled in error, caught in the snares of sin; and so we find ourselves in the gripe of the devil. To escape, we must have recourse to penitence, we must cry with David, *Lord, have mercy on me!* and with Saint Peter we must weep bitterly, and repent of all the faults we have committed—

> Repent and tune ourselves to this one theme,
> That worldly pleasure is a short-lived dream.[4]

4. Petrarch, *Canzoniere*, I, 13–14.

Machiavelli the Correspondent

NICCOLÒ MACHIAVELLI

From His Private Letters†

Machiavelli was one of the great letter writers. He should have been; it was his business. What is remarkable, given his unpopularity and the chaos of Italy at the time, is that many of his letters were preserved. Originally there must have been thousands; several hundred survive. As a letter writer, Machiavelli is notable for his extraordinary mobility and variety. With every different correspondent, and sometimes within the same letter, he shifts character and changes tone. Now he is jocose, now ironic, now severely practical, now self-mocking, occasionally conspiratorial. Out of these riches we have selected just three letters. The first, written to his old boss Piero Soderini after the collapse of the Florentine republic, condenses even further the already condensed political lessons of *The Prince*. A second letter is addressed to Francesco Vettori, the closest friend of Machiavelli's later years. Vettori was a cautious, cynical Florentine functionary at the papal court in Rome; with this wise, tough old bird, Machiavelli felt free to joke, complain, talk international politics, or compare wenching experiences. His letter describing the circumstances under which *The Prince* was composed is surely the most famous letter in Italian literature. Finally, a letter to Francesco Guicciardini, the famous historian of Florence, was written from a monastery to which Machiavelli (then in his fifties and long since removed from major public office) had been sent to select a special preacher for an upcoming religious festival in Florence. With Guicciardini, who fancied himself a joker and a cynic, Machiavelli is even more earthy than with Vettori. The scene that results is worthy of one of Machiavelli's stage comedies—*La Clizia* or *La Mandragola*—from which, alas, the present volume has no room even to excerpt.

1

January 1512 (1513), Florence
To Piero Soderini, in Ragusa[1]

A letter of yours came to me in a hood,[2] yet after ten words I recognized it. I am sure the crowds at Piombino will recognize you,

---

†The text of the letters is from Allan Gilbert, trans. and ed., *Machiavelli, the Chief Works and Others* (Durham, N.C.: Duke University Press, 1965), volume II. Unless otherwise noted, the foot-notes are by Gilbert.
1. This letter is apparently a rough draft, with notes (bracketed and itali-cized by Gilbert) for possible expan-sions. Piero Soderini, gonfalonier of the

and of your hindrances and Filippo's I am certain, because I know one is harmed by a little light, the other by too much. January does not trouble me, if only February supports me with his hands. I am sorry about Filippo's suspicion, and in suspense wait for its end. [*He who does not know how to fence overcomes him who knows fencing.*]

Your letter was short but I by rereading it made it long. It was pleasing to me because it gave me a chance to do what I feared to do and what you remind me that I should not do; and this part alone I have observed in it as without application. At this I would wonder, if my fate had not shown me so many and such varied things that I am obliged to wonder but little, or to confess that I have not comprehended while reading and experiencing the actions of men and their methods of procedure.

I understand you and the compass by which you navigate; and if it could be condemned, which it cannot, I would not condemn it, seeing to what port it has taken you and with what hope it can feed you. Consequently, I see, not with your mirror, where nothing is seen but prudence, but with that of the many, which is obliged in political affairs to judge the result when they are finished, and not the management while they are going on. Each man according to his own imagination guides himself. And I see various kinds of conduct bringing about the same thing, as by various roads one comes to the same place, and many who work differently attaining the same end. The actions of this pontiff[3] and their results have furnished anything needed to confirm this opinion.

Hannibal and Scipio were equally excellent in their military attainments; one of them with cruelty, treachery and lack of religion kept his armies united in Italy and made himself admired by the people, who to follow him rebelled against the Romans; the other, with mercy, loyalty and religion, in Spain got from those people the same effect; both of them won countless victories. But because it is not usual to bring up the Romans, Lorenzo de'Medici disarmed the people to hold Florence; Messer Giovanni Bentivoglio in order to hold Bologna armed them; the Vitelli in Città di Castello and the present duke of Urbino in his territory destroyed the fortresses in order to retain those states; Count Francesco Sforza and many others built them in their states to make themselves sure

---

Florentine Republic, had been driven into exile by the return of the Medici. The letter, addressed to him at Ragusa, would have to go to the southernmost tip of Sicily to find him. The "crowds at Piombino" are therefore, like "January," "February," and almost certainly "Filippo," part of a secret code. [*Editor.*]

2. In a hood: as an enclosure within another letter, mailed from a different address.

3. Julius II, who was always surprising Machiavelli by coming to unexpected ends by unexpected paths. He added one more surprise to the list about a month after this letter was written by dying unexpectedly, February 20, 1513. [*Editor.*]

of those states. [*To test Fortune, who is the friend of young men, and to change according to what you find. But it is not possible to have fortresses and not to have them, to be cruel and compassionate.*] Titus the Emperor believed he would lose his position on any day when he did not benefit somebody; some others might believe they would lose theirs on the day when they did anybody a favor. To many, weighing and measuring everything, success comes in their undertakings. [*As Fortune gets tired, anything is ruined. The family, the city, every man has his Fortune founded on his way of proceeding, and each Fortune gets tired, and when she is tired, she must be got back in another way. Comparison of the horse and the bridle about fortress.*] This Pope Julius, who hasn't a pair of scales or a yardstick in his house, gains through chance—although unarmed—what through organization and arms he scarcely could attain.

We have seen and see every day those I have mentioned, and countless others who could be used as instances, gaining kingdoms and sovereignties or falling, according to circumstances; and a man who was praised while he was gaining is reviled when he is losing; and frequently after long prosperity a man who finally loses does not in any way blame himself but accuses the heavens and the action of the Fates. But the reason why different ways of working are sometimes equally effective and equally damaging I do not know, but I should much like to know. So in order to get your opinion I shall be so presuming as to give mine.

I believe that as Nature has given each man an individual face, so she has given him an individual disposition and an individual imagination. From this it results that each man conducts himself according to his disposition and his imagination. On the other hand, because times vary and affairs are of varied types, one man's desires come out as he had prayed they would; he is fortunate who harmonizes his procedure with his time, but on the contrary he is not fortunate who in his actions is out of harmony with his time and with the type of its affairs. Hence it can well happen that two men working differently come to the same end, because each of them adapts himself to what he encounters, for affairs are of as many types as there are provinces and states. Thus, because times and affairs in general and individually change often, and men do not change their imaginings and their procedures, it happens that a man at one time has good fortune and at another time bad.

And certainly anybody wise enough to understand the times and the types of affairs and to adapt himself to them would have always good fortune, or he would protect himself always from bad, and it would come to be true that the wise man would rule the stars and the Fates. But because there never are such wise men, since men in the first place are shortsighted and in the second place cannot command their natures, it follows that Fortune varies and commands men and holds them under her yoke. And to verify this opinion, I think the instances given above, on which I have based it, are enough, and so I expect one to support the other.

To give reputation to a new ruler, cruelty, treachery and irreligion are enough in a province where humanity, loyalty and religion have for a long time been common. Yet in the same way humanity, loyalty and religion are sufficient where cruelty, treachery and irreligion have dominated for a time, because, as bitter things disturb the taste and sweet ones cloy it, so men get bored with good and complain of ill. These causes, among others, opened Italy to Hannibal and Spain to Scipio; thus both of them found times and things suited to their way of proceeding. At that very time a man like Scipio would not have been so successful in Italy, or one like Hannibal so successful in Spain, as they both were in the provinces where they acted.

Niccolò Machiavelli

2

10 December 1513, Florence
To Francesco Vettori, his benefactor, in Rome

Magnificent Ambassador:

"Never late were favors divine."[4] I say this because I seemed to have lost—no, rather mislaid—your good will; you had not written to me for a long time, and I was wondering what the reason could be. And of all those that came into my mind I took little account, except of one only when I feared that you had stopped writing because somebody had written to you that I was not a good guardian of your letters, and I knew that, except Filippo and Pagolo,[5] nobody by my doing had seen them. I have found it again through your last one of the twenty-third of the past month, from which I learn with pleasure how regularly and quietly you carry on this public office, and I encourage you to continue so, because he who gives up his own convenience for the convenience of others, only loses his own and from them gets no gratitude. And since Fortune wants to do everything, she wishes us to let her do it, to be quiet, and not to give her trouble, and to wait for a time when she will allow something to be done by men; and then will be the time for you to work harder, to stir things up more, and for me to leave my farm and say: "Here I am." I cannot however, wishing to return

---

4. Petrarch, *Triumph of Eternity* 13.
5. Filippo Casavecchia and Pagolo Vet- tori, brother of the recipient of the letter.

equal favors, tell you in this lettter anything else than what my life is; and if you judge it is to be swapped for yours, I shall be glad to change it.

I am living on my farm, and since I had my last bad luck, I have not spent twenty days, putting them all together, in Florence. I have until now been snaring thrushes with my own hands. I got up before day, prepared birdlime, went out with a bundle of cages on my back, so that I looked like Geta when he was returning from the harbor with Amphitryo's books.[6] I caught at least two thrushes and at most six. And so I did all September. Later this pastime, pitiful and strange as it is, gave out, to my displeasure. And of what sort my life is, I shall tell you.

I get up in the morning with the sun and go into a grove I am having cut down, where I remain two hours to look over the work of the past day and kill some time with the cutters, who have always some bad-luck story ready, about either themselves or their neighbors. And as to this grove I could tell you a thousand fine things that have happened to me, in dealing with Frosino da Panzano and others who wanted some of this firewood. And Frosino especially sent for a number of cords without saying a thing to me, and on payment he wanted to keep back from me ten lire, which he says he should have had from me four years ago, when he beat me at *cricca* at Antonio Guicciardini's. I raised the devil, and was going to prosecute as a thief the waggoner who came for the wood, but Giovanni Machiavelli came between us and got us to agree. Battista Guicciardini, Filippo Ginori, Tommaso del Bene and some other citizens, when that north wind was blowing, each ordered a cord from me. I made promises to all and sent one to Tommaso, which at Florence changed to half a cord, because it was piled up again by himself, his wife, his servant, his children, so that he looked like Gabburra when on Thursday with all his servants he cudgels an ox.[7] Hence, having seen for whom there was profit, I told the others I had no more wood, and all of them were angry about it, and especially Battista, who counts this along with his misfortunes at Prato.[8]

Leaving the grove, I go to a spring, and thence to my aviary. I have a book in my pocket, either Dante or Petrarch, or one of the lesser poets, such as Tibullus, Ovid, and the like. I read of their tender passions and their loves, remember mine, enjoy myself a while in that sort of dreaming. Then I move along the road to the inn; I speak with those who pass, ask news of their villages, learn

6. A reference to a story founded on the *Amphitryo* of Plautus.
7. Gabburra, apparently a butcher, is unknown.
8. Battista Guicciardini was podestà (mayor) of Prato when it was taken by the Spanish forces in 1512; as an immediate result the Medici were restored to Florence. It is remarkable that Machiavelli could use the fall of Prato in a jest.

various things, and note the various tastes and different fancies of men. In the course of these things comes the hour for dinner, where with my family I eat such food as this poor farm of mine and my tiny property allow. Having eaten, I go back to the inn; there is the host, usually a butcher, a miller, two furnace tenders. With these I sink into vulgarity for the whole day, playing at *cricca* and at trich-trach, and then these games bring on a thousand disputes and countless insults with offensive words, and usually we are fighting over a penny, and nevertheless we are heard shouting as far as San Casciano. So, mixed up with these lice, I keep my brain from growing mouldy, and satisfy the malice of this fate of mine, being glad to have her drive me along this road, to see if she will be ashamed of it.

On the coming of evening, I return to my house and enter my study; and at the door I take off the day's clothing, covered with mud and dust, and put on garments regal and courtly; and reclothed appropriately, I enter the ancient courts of ancient men, where, received by them with affection, I feed on that food which only is mine and which I was born for, where I am not ashamed to speak with them and to ask them the reason for their actions; and they in their kindness answer me; and for four hours of time I do not feel boredom, I forget every trouble, I do not dread poverty, I am not frightened by death; entirely I give myself over to them.

And because Dante says it does not produce knowledge when we hear but do not remember, I have noted everything in their conversation which has profited me,[9] and have composed a little work *On Princedoms*, where I go as deeply as I can into considerations on this subject, debating what a princedom is, of what kinds they are, how they are gained, how they are kept, why they are lost. If ever you can find any of my fantasies pleasing, this one should not displease you; and by a prince, and especially by a new prince, it ought to be welcomed. Hence I am dedicating it to His Magnificence Giuliano.[1] Filippo Casavecchia has seen it; he can give you some account in part of the thing in itself and of the discussions I have had with him, though I am still enlarging and revising it.

You wish, Magnificent Ambassador, that I leave this life and come to enjoy yours with you. I shall do it in any case, but what tempts me now are certain affairs that within six weeks I shall finish. What makes me doubtful is that the Soderini we know so well are in the city, whom I should be obliged, on coming there, to visit and talk with. I should fear that on my return I could not hope to dismount at my house but should dismount at the Bargello, because though this government has mighty foundations and great

9. This seems to be Machiavelli making notes on Livy's *History* for his own *Discourses*, out of which rose *The Prince*.
1. Giuliano de' Medici, later duke of Nemours, son of Lorenzo the Magnificent. He resided in Florence after the restoration of the Medici in 1512, but in 1513 withdrew to Rome.

security, yet it is new and therefore suspicious, and there is no lack of wiseacres who, to make a figure, like Pagolo Bertini, would place others at the dinner table and leave the reckoning to me.[2] I beg you to rid me of this fear, and then I shall come within the time mentioned to visit you in any case.

I have talked with Filippo about this little work of mine that I have spoken of, whether it is good to give it or not to give it; and if it is good to give it, whether it would be good to take it myself, or whether I should send it there.[3] Not giving it would make me fear that at the least Giuliano will not read it and that this rascal Ardinghelli will get himself honor from this latest work of mine.[4] The giving of it is forced on me by the necessity that drives me, because I am using up my money, and I cannot remain as I am a long time without becoming despised through poverty. In addition, there is my wish that our present Medici lords will make use of me, even if they begin by making me roll a stone; because then if I could not gain their favor, I should complain of myself; and through this thing, if it were read, they would see that for the fifteen years while I have been studying the art of the state, I have not slept or been playing, and well may anybody be glad to get the services of one who at the expense of others has become full of experience. Of my honesty there should be no doubt, because having always preserved my honesty, I shall hardly now learn to break it; he who has been honest and good for forty-three years, as I have, cannot change his nature; and as a witness to my honesty and goodness I have my poverty.

I should like, then, to have you also write me what you think best on this matter, and I give you my regards. Be happy.

Niccolò Machiavelli, in Florence.

3

17 May 1521, Carpi
To his Magnificent Master Francesco Guicciardini, J.U.D.,[5] Governor of Modena and Reggio, most worthy and especially to be most honored * * *

Magnificent Sir, Ruler to be Most Respected:
I was on the privy seat when your messenger came, and just then

---

2. Pagolo Bertini is unknown and the meaning of the sentence is uncertain. [But "dismounting at the Bargello" is very clear; it means being called before the central police authority on suspicion of conspiring with Soderini against the Medici.—*Editor*.]
3. There is a story that Machiavelli did give Giuliano the book, but that someone else at the same time gave him a brace of fine greyhounds, so the book

was set aside. [*Editor*.]
4. Piero Ardinghelli was secretary to Pope Leo X. Machiavelli seems to have feared that [if] Giuliano had not read *The Prince*, Ardinghelli would steal ideas from it and offer them as his own.
5. J.U.D. means "Juris Utriusque Doctor," i.e., "Doctor of Both Laws" (canon and civil). All these formalities are burlesque, as is the letter. [*Editor*.]

I was thinking of the absurdities of this world, and I was giving all my attention to imagining for myself a preacher after my mind for the place at Florence, and he would be just what would please me, because in this I intend to be as obstinate as in my other opinions. And because I never failed that city by not benefiting her when I could—if not with deeds, with words, if not with words, with gestures—I do not intend to fail her this time either. It is true that I know I am opposed, as in many other things, to the opinion of the citizens there: they would like a preacher who would show them the road to Paradise, and I should like to find one who would teach them the way to go to the house of the Devil; they would like, besides, that he should be a man prudent, blameless and true; and I should like to find one crazier than Ponzo, more crafty than Fra Girolamo, more of a hypocrite than Frate Alberto,[6] because it would seem to me a fine thing, worthy of the goodness of these times, that all we have experienced in many friars should be experienced in one, because I believe the true way of going to Paradise would be to learn the road to Hell in order to avoid it. Seeing, besides this, how much credit a bad man has who conceals himself under the cloak of religion, I can easily conjecture how much of it a good man would have who in truth and not in pretense continued to tread muddy places like St. Francis. So since my fancy seemed to me good, I have planned to take Rovaio,[7] and I believe that if he is like his brothers and sisters, he will be just right. I should be glad if, next time you write, you will give me your opinion.

I continue in idleness here because I cannot carry out my commission until the general and the assessors are chosen, and I keep ruminating on how I can sow so much discord among them that either here or elsewhere they may go to hitting each other with their sandals; and if I do not lose my wits, I believe I am going to succeed; and I believe that the advice and help of Your Lordship would assist greatly. So if you would come as far as this with the excuse of a pleasure jaunt, it would not be a bad thing, or at least by writing give me some master strokes. If you once every day would send me a servant just for this purpose, as you have today, you would do several good things: for one, you would give me light on some things quite to my purpose; for another, you would make me more esteemed by those in the house, seeing the messages come thick. And I can tell you that on the arrival of this arbalester with the letter, making a bow down to the earth, and with his saying that he was sent specially and in haste, everybody rose up with so many signs of respect and such a noise that everything was turned

6. Ponzo is obscure; Fra Girolamo is Savonarola; Frate Alberto is from the *Decameron* 4. 2.

7. Giovan Gualberto, a Florentine, and a Franciscan.

upside down, and I was asked by several about the news. I, that its reputation might grow, said that the emperor was expected at Trent, and that the Swiss had summoned new diets, and that the king of France wanted to go in person to speak with that king, but that his councilors advised him against it; so that they all stood with open mouths and with their caps in their hands; and while I write I have a circle of them around me, and seeing me write at length they are astonished, and look on me as inspired; and I, to make them wonder more, sometimes hold my pen still and swell up, and then they slaver at the mouth, but if they could see what I am writing, they would marvel at it more. Your Lordship knows that these friars say that when one is confirmed in grace, the Devil has no more power to tempt him. So I have no more fear that these friars will make me a hypocrite, because I believe I am very well confirmed.

As to the lies of the Carpigiani, I should like a contest in that matter with all of them, because quite a while ago I trained myself in such a way that I do not need Francesco Martelli[8] for a servant, because for a long time I have not said what I believed, nor do I ever believe what I say, and if indeed sometimes I do happen to tell the truth, I hide it among so many lies that it is hard to find.

To that governor I did not speak, because having found lodgings, I thought speaking to him useless. It is true that this morning in church I stared at him a bit while he was standing to look at some paintings. He did seem to me well set up, and I can believe that the whole corresponds to the part, and that he is what he seems, and that his crooked back is not a liar;[9] hence that if I had your letter with me, I should have made an attempt at drawing a bucketful out of him. At any rate, no damage has been done, and I expect tomorrow some advice from you on my affairs and that you will send one of the same arbalesters and that he will hurry and get here all sweaty, so that the household will be amazed; for by so doing you will bring me honor, and at the same time your arbalester will get a little exercise, which for the horses on these spring days is very wholesome.

I might write to you also some other things, if I were willing to weary my fancy, but I wish for tomorrow to keep it as fresh as I can. I send my regards to Your Lordship, and may you ever prosper as you desire.

> Your faithful Niccolò Machiavelli,
> Ambassador to the Minor Friars.

8. Unknown.
9. The original of this sentence is not clear. [But the general implication is plain that the man's crooked back is a good index to his crooked mind.—*Editor.*]

Machiavelli the Poet[†]

NICCOLÒ MACHIAVELLI

From *Carnival Songs*

Carnival songs were a special phenomenon of the Florentine Renaissance; they were part of that rich ceremonial life so eloquently celebrated by Burckhardt in his *Civilization of the Renaissance in Italy*. The biggest carnival fiestas used to be held in Rome, the next most elaborate in Venice, but the Florentines made most of the songs. *Canti Carnaschialesci* were written by poets and princes (including the Magnificent Lorenzo), by monks and tailors and tosspots, by the artisan in his shop and the tripe seller on the street corner. Because carnival is a time of license and misrule, frankly related to the old pagan festival of Saturnalia, many of these songs (which can be read in the still classic edition of Professor Singleton) were comic or bawdy or both. All the more surprising is a sequence of songs from the pen of Machiavelli, probably composed for some sort of pageant or masquerade. Groups of costumed performers evidently came onto a stage or into a cleared space, and explained in song their plight or their desires. Ladies debated with their lovers the consequences of kindness or severity; hermits chorused the praises of the contemplative life; and a choir of blessed spirits appeared, to sing in passionate accents the praises of peace. And in this particular poem, just as in *The Prince*, when Machiavelli wishes to express the highest reach of his patriotic enthusiasm, he begins to echo unmistakably the poetry of Petrarch, especially the great patriotic *canzone*, "Italia mia" (*Rime*, CXXVIII).

HYMN OF THE BLESSED SPIRITS[†]

Blessed spirits are we,
Who from those seats on high
Have come down here to earth's low floor
Because indeed we see
In what distress the peoples lie,
And what slight reasons stir men up to war;
We want to show
To him who strays from Truth's bright star,
That nothing here below
Brings to Our Lord such heartfelt ease
As when men lay down arms and live in peace.
    The life on earth of humankind

[†]Translated by the editor from Machiavelli, *Opere letterarie*, ed. Luigi Blasucci (Milano: Adelphi, 1964), pp. 331–333.

Is martyrdom, bitter and cruel and long;
Hateful their pains, and no cure can they find
For their disease; and so their constant song
Is but of endless grief and pain,
Of which all day and night they must complain,
Lamenting, wailing every wrong,
Sobbing aloud and calling out their grief,
And each man asking mercy and relief.

    This is for God a bitter pain,
As it must be for any living heart
Where traces of humanity remain;
And so he told us to impart,
And to you people here below explain,
How fierce his anger is and his disdain
At seeing how his kingdom disappears.
His flock grows ever fewer with the years—
Unless new ways come in with the new swain.[1]

    So deep is the fierce thirst to lay
This ancient country waste
Which once gave laws to all of humankind,
That you are wholly blind
And don't see how your quarrels pave the way
For enemies who press you thick and fast.
The Turkish sultan, day by day,
Sharpens his sword, and rubs his bloody hands,
Ready to burst upon your peaceful lands.[2]

    Raise, then, your weapons high
Against a cruel foe;
But to your own, bring healing remedy.
Lay down that old hostility
Fostered between you since long, long ago.
Turn on the real foe your common strength,
Else heaven will at length
Deny to you the right to any force,
Seeing that pious zeal in you has run its course.

    Dismiss, then, all fears,
All hatreds and rancorous jeers,
All cruelty, avarice, pride:
Bring back honor and trust,
The love of the true and the just,
And turn back the world to the ages of gold:
The heavenly gates will then open wide
To let the blessed people inside,
And the fire of virtue [*virtù*] will never grow cold.

1. The "new swain" is Leo X, elected to the papacy early in 1513; the allusion thus places composition of this song very close indeed to the period when *The Prince* was being written.
2. The Turkish sultan is Selim I, who ruled from 1512 to 1521. He was in fact a voracious conqueror, who is said to have complained at one point that the whole world was not big enough to satisfy his imperial ambitions. Whether he ever actually contemplated a descent on Italy is doubtful; but his constant thrashing about upset the entire Mediterranean.

NICCOLÒ MACHIAVELLI

On Occasion†

Machiavelli's little poem on "Occasion"—or, perhaps, we should say "Opportunity"—is not really Machiavelli's poem; it is a not-very-faithful translation of the twelfth epigram of Ausonius, a grammarian of the fourth century A.D., who lived near Bordeaux, and wrote a number of poems, including a description of the Moselle River and a Cento Nuptialis, consisting of verses and half-verses of Virgil, rearranged with incredible virtuosity to produce a poem of incredible obscenity.

Whatever he thought of Ausonius, Machiavelli was always interested in Opportunity; and he revealed some of his thoughts by dedicating this translation to Filippo de' Nerli, whom there is reason to think he knew through the *conversazione* at the Orti Oricellari, where Machiavelli read many parts, if not all, of the *Discorsi*. Filippo was sixteen years younger than Machiavelli; in 1512—when the Republic fell, the Medici returned to Florence, and Machiavelli's active political career lay in ruins—Filippo was barely twenty-seven years old, and he was a partisan of the Medici. Opportunity was advancing to meet him, just as she was turning her back on Machiavelli. In addressing his young friend on the topic of Lady Luck, Machiavelli's basic advice was, "Don't let her get away!" and it's not beyond thinking that he hoped some of his friend's timely fortune might rub off on himself. He was always a hopeful man.

> —Who are you, lady of no mortal mien,
> Endowed by heaven with such a lofty air?
> Why wingéd feet? Why are you never seen
> At rest?—I am Occasion: sparse and rare
> Are my acquaintance, and I'm ill at ease
> From standing with one foot upon a sphere.
> My flight is swift as any fitful breeze;
> Wings on my feet sustain me in the air,
> So when I pass, nobody really sees.
>   Low on my brow before me spreads my hair,
> So that it covers all my breast and face;
> Thus, no one knows me, coming, till I'm there.
> Of hair behind my head there's not a trace,
> Hence, one I've turned against, or hurried by,
> Can never catch me: it's no good to try.
>
> —Tell me, then: who's this person by your side?
> —She's Penitence; and this you'd better note,
> Who misses me, gets her to be his bride.
>   And you who stand here talking, you who dote
> On idle chatter, while the hour lingers,
> Wise up a bit, you klutz, you've missed the boat,
> And I've already slipped between your fingers!

†Translated by the editor from Machia- velli, *Opere letterarie*, ed. Luigi Blasuc- ci (Milano: Adelphi, 1964), p. 325.

Interpretations

J. R. HALE

The Setting of *The Prince*: 1513–1514[†]

Life at Sant' Andrea[1] had its own mild distractions. Machiavelli's house was beside the inn, and he owned a little woodland, some olives, and vines. He took pleasure in rural occupations, like bird-snaring, and in passing the afternoons in gossip and cards over a glass of wine, but these occupations could give pleasure only when part of a daily routine that was ballasted with something more weighty and absorbing. When in August he began to spend the evenings working at a treatise *De principatibus*[2] they fell into place, but in the spring and early summer the burnt countryside must have seemed to him the *Stinche*[3] where men were punished for being unemployed. From a career of often hectic industry, long journeys, and meetings with men whose levers moved the world, his horizon had shrunk to idleness and the chatter of a rural hamlet. Before leaving for Sant' Andrea he had told Vettori in a letter of 9 April that "fortune has decreed that, knowing nothing of silk manufacture nor the wool business, nor of profit or loss, I must talk politics, and unless I take a vow of silence I must discuss them." And the politics he wished to talk was present politics. Dead politics, history, was to satisfy him later, as it had intrigued him before, but his instinct now was to discuss the political struggles of which he was himself a casualty—an instinct he determined to resist.

During the weeks after his release from prison there had been puzzling and threatening moves among the great powers. On 23 March Louis[4] had arranged a truce with Venice and on 1 April with Spain, which left him free to repair his fortunes in Italy. In Italy this gave rise to widespread bewilderment. Why had Ferdinand[5] given his enemy a free hand? "If this truce between France and Spain is true," Vettori wrote to Machiavelli on 19 April,

> either the Catholic King is not the astute and prudent man he is thought to be, or some mischief is brewing, and what has often been mooted has got into these princes' heads, and Spain, France, and the Emperor[6] intend to divide up our poor Italy.

And returning to the subject two days later, he wrote: "Since this truce is assured, I wish we could walk together from the Ponte Vecchio along via de' Bardi and on to Castello, and discuss what fancy

---

†From J. R. Hale, *Machiavelli and Renaissance Italy* (London, 1961, 1972), chapter 7. Footnotes are by the editor of this Norton Critical Edition.
1. Machiavelli's country house, at Sant' Andrea in Percussina, near San Casciano.
2. "On princely governments."

3. Dungeons.
4. Louis XII of France.
5. Ferdinand, V of Castile, and Leon, II of Aragon, best known as "The Catholic."
6. Maximilian, the Holy Roman emperor.

has got into Spain's head." And he ended: "I would be glad of your opinion, because to tell you the truth without flattery, I have found you to be sounder in these matters than any other man I have spoken to."

This was an invitation that Machiavelli could not resist. It broke his resolve to forget current affairs and held him from finding solace in books. He replied from Sant' Andrea with a commentary on the political scene which ran to between two and three thousand words. "While I read your letter," he wrote on 29 April,

> which I have read many times, I quite forgot my miserable state, and thought myself back in those activities which cost me—all for nothing—so much fatigue and time. And although I have sworn neither to think of nor discuss politics—my coming to stay in the country bears witness to that—all the same, to reply to your request, I am forced to break my vow.

The next shift in the pattern of international relations was given by the battle of Novara on 6 June. Louis and the Venetians had attempted to take the Milanese[7] from its duke, Massimiliano Sforza, but at this battle the French were completely routed by the Swiss, who, in their own interest, had constituted themselves the duke's somewhat proprietary guardians. On 20 June Machiavelli gave his opinion in a letter dated from Florence, for he did not take his self-exile too literally, and escaped from time to time from the dullness of Sant' Andrea to the news, the women, and the drinking companions of the city. Though he was no longer concerned with political affairs, he said, he could not resist discussing them. Novara had been a great victory for the papal, anti-French party, and when Machiavelli referred to it as one of the events "among the other great good fortunes, which have befallen His Holiness the pope and that illustrious family," he was probably hoping that matters were more auspicious for his obtaining some favor from Leo,[8] if Vettori should take up his suit again. He went on to survey the situation especially from Leo's point of view: what moves should the pope take next?

The correspondence continued through July and into August as a sort of political game. Each proposed a settlement that would bring peace to Italy and invited the other to criticize it. Their letters were full of reference to "my peace" and "your peace." Machiavelli was prepared to make great concessions. France should have Milan and thus be satisfied; Spain should have Naples; the pope the States of the Church; Venice should keep the bulk of her mainland possessions. The parties aggrieved by this arrangement would be the duke of Milan (but he was an unimportant cipher) and Germany and the Swiss—but France would keep them in check. This "peace"

---

7. I.e., the city of Milan.   8. Leo X, the Medici pope.

correspondence began from a suggestion from Vettori, but it was Machiavelli to whom it meant most. For Vettori it was largely a recreation, and, seeking a solution less passionately than Machiavelli, he was, in an off-hand way, less doctrinaire and more realistic, hoping less for a panacea than a stop-gap. For Machiavelli, with nothing else to do, the correspondence was a central preoccupation and, besides, there was always the hope that what he wrote would find its way to the eyes of the Medici.

In a letter of 12 July Vettori had said that Leo wanted to maintain the Church in all the possessions he found her endowed with "unless to make over some to his relations Giuliano [his younger brother] or Lorenzo [his nephew], to whom he is eager to give states." It seemed that there would soon be new jobs for men of experience who could commend themselves to the Medici. Machiavelli did not represent himself as a man of glibly encouraging counsels. Vettori had seen Milan, Venice, and Ferrara as uniting to contain France and the Swiss. Machiavelli's answer was downright. Milan would always be a danger spot, with its weak duke and Swiss tutelage, he pointed out on 10 August.

> As for the union of the other Italians—you make me laugh. First, because there never will be any union that will do any good, and even if the leaders were united it would not be enough, for they have no arms worth a halfpenny. . . . In the second place, because the tails are not united to the heads—if this generation takes a step to further any cause, they fall to squabbling amongst themselves.

Vettori, on the 20th, attempted to defend the morale of Italian armies, pointing out that even the French were not uniformly effective. In 1494 they had promenaded through the peninsula, but Novara had seen them defeated, and now they were frightened by —of all countries—England, who had hardly known how to tell one end of a sword from another for twenty-five years.[9]

Machiavelli replied on the 26th in a letter dated from Florence. The Italians, as at present organized in mercenary bands, would never change and become good soldiers. The best armies are those composed of native troops—it was so amongst the Romans and is true today of the Swiss. If the French could be victors one day and be vanquished another, can the Italians become victors in their turn? No. The French won against divided and mixed armies, and when they lost it was to national forces, like those of the Swiss (at Novara) and English (at the battle of the Spurs).[1] He reviews the international situation, starting with a scathing description of the

9. Henry VIII of England and Francis I of France were truculent antagonists, and Henry was especially aggressive.

1. The battle of Guinegatte (1513), in which Henry VIII, with the Emperor Maximilian, defeated the French.

heads of states. Significantly, the only one who is flatteringly described is the pope.

> We have a pope who is wise, prudent and respected; an unstable and fickle emperor, a haughty and timid king of France; a king of Spain who is miserly and close-fisted; a king of England who is rich, wrathful and thirsty for glory; the Swiss—brutal, victorious, and insolent, and we Italians—poor, ambitious, and craven.

With this mixture any peace—either "yours" or "mine"—is difficult, and none likely. Nor can one be framed by reason alone. Monarchs behave so irrationally—as the emperor with the Swiss, whom he should fear but does not—"that I hesitate to judge anything." He confessed himself terrified by the situation. If France does not protect Italy (once given Lombardy, a condition of Machiavelli's "peace") he sombrely concludes his letter, "then I see no other remedy, and will now begin to mourn with you our ruin and slavery, which, if it does not happen today, or tomorrow, will come in our time." This was the last letter he wrote to Vettori before telling him, on 10 December, that he had almost finished a short treatise *De principatibus*.

The Prince, as this work came to be known, is a natural outcome of Machiavelli's interest in external affairs, and in a sense is a continuation of the "peace" correspondence in treatise form. He had not yet shown (as he was to show later in the *Discourses*) much interest in internal, constitutional affairs. His work for the Ten had led him to think primarily of Florence's impact on other states. He was concerned with Italian resistance to France and Spain, not with the balance of classes within his own city. He accepted the fact of Medicean domination. The Florentines had shown in their welcome of Giovanni and their rapture over his being made Pope that they endorsed the family's return. Machiavelli was still hopeful of employment. The Medici had as yet done nothing within Florence so threatening to the republican constitution as to divert his attention from the enthralling and tragic scenes in Italy and Europe as a whole. When he ceased to write to Vettori in August he continued to think about how to give strength to states which had no armies and little desire to unite against their common enemies. His diplomatic career had shown him some of the factors that led to power in the modern world, in Cesare Borgia he had seen an enthralling attempt to knock a new state together. Preoccupied with the need for drastic action in external affairs, it was natural for Machiavelli, though a republican in sympathy—was not the state which canalized the energies of all sections of the community potentially the strongest?—to think in terms of princes. To reason *de principatibus* was, besides, the most dynamic way of relieving his own nostalgia for action in diplomacy and war.

The work was a release, too, from personal distress. Writing to his nephew Giovanni Vernaccia on 4 August, Machiavelli tells him of the death of a three-day-old daughter, and says towards the end of the letter: "I am well in body—but ill in every other way. And I see no hope save from God." The letter of 10 December, perhaps the most famous letter ever written by an Italian, shows how the hours spent each day in his study helped to bring a measure of balance and even exhilaration into his life as a whole.[2]

At this important moment, then, the documents do not fail us. In the spring and summer the "peace" correspondence showed his all-consuming interest in the international political scene. In the autumn, as this letter proves, he drew on his experience and his reading to add—though in a profoundly personal way—to the popular class of books *de regimine principum*, "On Princely Rule." And when it was drafted he began to see it as a possible means of getting employment and to think of dedicating it to the pope's older brother, who was rumored to be on the point of obtaining a principality of his own from the territories of the Church. How far *De principatibus* resembled the final *Il Principe* at this unplumbed and unpolished stage is not known, but probably the only major change was the addition some time afterwards of the dedication and the last chapter, the exhortation to the dedicatee to liberate Italy from the barbarians.

The book was a discussion of princedoms, with special emphasis on new ones—the result of recent conquest, the products of change and themselves liable to change—and on how to render them stable through the exercise of special qualities by the prince himself, by his choice of agents and his use of a national army. Finally, Machiavelli justifies the book by showing that politics is a science from which men can learn, not just a learned recreation to be indulged in while Fortune dictates what is done; Fortune, he emphasizes, can, and must, be made to serve the deft and resolute prince. It was written to satisfy a need, but the impulse was a personal rather than a specific political one; the energy with which it was written imposed a unity of mood rather than of content. So far as is known, it was never subjected to final revision nor actually presented to Giuliano or his nephew Lorenzo, to whom Machiavelli dedicated it when Giuliano died in 1516.

The Prince reflects Machiavelli's fifteen years' experience in the chancery service. They had been years of war or of an uneasy peace that was scarcely distinct from war. The consistent good faith he vaunted in himself as an employee could be folly or treachery if

2. See the full letter, pages 130–33.

practiced by statesmen, under cover of whose purely pragmatic use of truth and falsehood ordinary citizens could indulge their own harmless rectitude. "Everyone realizes how praiseworthy it is for a prince to honor his word and to be straightforward rather than crafty in his dealings; nonetheless contemporary experience shows that princes who have achieved great things have been those who have given their word lightly." Machiavelli does not simply endorse the use of bad faith in case of necessity—the lie that diverts the killer from his victim—but as a natural part of statecraft. He had seen and admired the success of princes like Louis XII, Ferdinand, Cesare Borgia, Alexander VI and Julius II, and seen that all had depended at times on deception. As an amateur of war he was familiar with the need for stratagem and deceit, and had read the praise of these devices in ancient writers on military matters. As a diplomatist he had combated men who were professionally committed to outwit and deceive him; as Soderini's *mannerino*[3] he had been the victim of malice and intrigue. He had, besides, a relish for cleverness, whatever form it took. All these factors, together with the dramatic form in which he couched his arguments, help to push his observations on good faith and bad faith to an extreme. If men were good, then one should be good in return, "but because men are wretched creatures, who would not keep their word to you, you need not keep your word to them." Machiavelli could not observe without exhorting. It is the "go thou and do likewise" tone that has caused offense, not the evidence from which this advice is deduced. His impatience of observation for its own sake, without it being stripped, as it were, for action, led him to omit saving clauses which might otherwise humanize his statements. "Men will always be false to you unless they are compelled by necessity to be true" is not a statement to be literally maintained by a man in the circle of his family and friends, but in the form "A statesman in time of crisis should act as though men will always be false," it is less open to criticism. Moreover, his assumption that craft and cruelty are necessary is accompanied by an acceptance that they stain a prince's noblest attribute—his glory.

There is hardly a year from Machiavelli's career in the chancery that cannot be shown to have provided some evidence, or reflection on events, that helped to shape *The Prince*. A clear reference to his French experience that justice and reason are but subsidiary weapons—that the unarmed man is "Ser Nihilo"[4]—is to be found in Chapter 14, which is about the need for a national army. "Among other evils caused by being disarmed, it renders you contemptible." *The Prince* contains three chapters on soldiers. The worst sort are

3. "Little man."   4. "Mr. Nothing."

mercenary—and he instances Vitelli. Only slightly better are friendlies, auxiliaries—and he describes the perils that threatened Florence owing to her use of French troops against Pisa. Then, "I shall never hesitate to cite Cesare Borgia and his conduct as an example," Machiavelli wrote, and went on to describe how, after experimenting with mercenary and auxiliary troops, Cesare came to rely upon his own subjects. The lessons of the mission to Cesare and the advice of the tract *Remarks on the raising of money* recur here in extended form: negotiation must be based on strength; neutrality is fatal. And the warning he gives there that the Florentines have a baneful optimism which sees a day's sunshine as lasting for ever is echoed in a warning to princes not to be taken unawares by war "as it is a common fault of men not to reckon on storms during fair weather." The judicial murder of Ramiro Lorqua, brusquely reported in the dispatch of 26 December 1502, now becomes a symbol of wisely resolute political action. In Chapter 12 when Machiavelli states that "the main foundations of every state, new states as well as ancient or composite ones, are good laws and good arms," we hear an echo from the infantry ordinance, and his reflections in Chapter 6 on the problems facing a reformer, whose own side only supports him halfheartedly while his opponents fight *à l'outrance*,[5] reflect his own teething troubles with the militia. The chapter "How much human affairs are governed by fortune, and how fortune may be opposed" is almost all extended from passages in the letter to Soderini in Ragusa; so, too, the musing on the phenomenon of different means producing identical ends, the conclusion that "the successful man is he whose mode of procedure accords with the needs of the times." In Chapter 3 of *The Prince*, about states that absorb new territories, the tone of the argument —concise, intense, and personal—and the matter itself (the problem is illustrated by the recent behavior of the French in Italy) make it seem like a continuation of the "peace" correspondence. This chapter epitomizes the way in which Machiavelli called on his past experience. The point that "men must be either pampered or crushed" was made in 1503 in the pamphlet on the Val di Chiana rebellion. His scorn of those who play for time instead of taking active precautions was confirmed, as we have seen, by his earliest diplomatic encounters. He goes on to elaborate the argument he had had with d'Amboise in 1500 about the errors of French policy in Italy. D'Amboise had defended French support of the Borgia by referring to promises made by Louis to Alexander VI. Machiavelli's comment in *The Prince* is fortified by the behavior of Julius II in cancelling papal promises to the Bolognese. "A prudent ruler," he

5. "To the bitter end."

says, "cannot, and should not, honor his word when it places him at a disadvantage, and when the reasons for which he made his promise no longer exist."

This dour conclusion was the result of his own observation, and this is true of all the conclusions in *The Prince*. Conversations with the illustrious shades of antiquity play a much smaller part than the letter of 10 December might have led Vettori to believe, and he illustrates all his important points by quoting contemporary instances. He repeats his double indebtedness in the dedication.

> I have not found among my belongings anything as dear to me or that I value as much as my understanding of the deeds of great men, won for me from a long acquaintance with contemporary affairs and a continual study of the ancient world.

But this statement, though it increased the fashionableness and respectability of the work, conceals the dependence on raw contemporary experience.

His use of historical illustrations was rhetorical and arbitrary. In the last years of his life, when writing the *History of Florence*, he arranged his evidence, and sometimes warped it, to drive home general principles. He does this even more in the earlier work, where he was not concerned with the past, even the immediate past, as such. He cuts the film to obtain significant stills: Cesare Borgia's shoddy decline becomes irrelevant; "I know of no better precepts to give a new prince than ones derived from Cesare's actions," he writes in Chapter 7. He is not concerned to re-create. His aim is to expose in history the nerve of resolute actions. He is not concerned to qualify his conclusions. The hesitations, the exceptions, the safeguards could be shaded in when they were applied to particular situations. When he comes to a subject which cannot be reduced to black and white, he moves aside. "There are many ways in which a prince can win [the people] over. These vary according to circumstances, so no definite rule can be given and I shall not deal with them here." The style he uses shows a similar scorn of sinuosities. There are few literary flowers: a handful of metaphors and analogies, most of these being pithy, familiar, and racy, and one parable in which David is shown refusing Saul's arms when he goes out against Goliath: "arms belonging to someone else either fall from your back [mercenaries], or weigh you down [auxiliaries], or impede your movements [a mixture of both]."

Machiavelli was not seeking in *The Prince* to give specific advice for the present situation, but the book is vibrant, nevertheless, with the conviction that advice is needed and that he is the one to give it. "The wish to acquire more," he remarks in Chapter 3, "is admittedly a very natural and common thing." It followed that change and flux should be taken as a norm, and that rulers should never relax their vigilance. There was a danger, especially when disasters were coming thick and fast, that men would throw up their hands and declare themselves the playthings, not the masters, of events. The book stresses man's responsibility to act; fortune—the pattern of events—can be directed by the self-reliant man. It is true that, in one sense, Cesare's own downfall "was not his fault but arose from the extraordinary and inordinate malice of fortune," but in another sense he fell because, at a moment of crisis, he wavered; though ill at the time of Pius III's election, on that pope's death he should not have supported Giuliano della Rovere, who, as Julius II, remembered all too clearly the injuries that Cesare had formerly done him. "So the duke's choice was a mistaken one, and it was the cause of his ultimate ruin." Men should never blame fate for their disasters; "the only sound, sure, and durable methods of defence are those based on your own actions and prowess."

The importance of his work, and its novelty, Machiavelli claimed, resided in the fact that he was concerned only with *il vero*,[6] the true picture of what actually happened, and that he only talked about politics in terms directly deduced from the way in which men had behaved and did behave. To have a private morality up one's sleeve and put it to one's nose when the stench of political morality became too great was sheer hypocrisy. Referring to the extreme cruelty of Hannibal, he noted that "the historians, having given little thought to this, on the one hand admire what Hannibal achieved, and on the other condemn what made his achievements possible." But you cannot have it both ways—admire the end and deplore the means. Machiavelli emphasized that his approach (familiar enough in discussion and dispatch) was something new in a work of political theory. Writing for statesmen, he will do them the service of writing in terms that they can apply directly to the problems of the real world. "Since my intention is to say something that will prove of practical use to the inquirer," he emphasized in Chapter 15,

> I have thought it proper to represent things as they are in real truth, rather than as they are imagined . . . the gulf between how one should live and how one does live is so wide that a man who neglects what is actually done for what should be done learns the way to self-destruction rather than self-preservation. The fact is that a man who wants to act virtuously in every way necessarily comes to grief among so many who are not virtuous. . . . If a person wants to maintain his rule he must learn how not to be virtuous, and to make use of this or not according to need.

6. "The truth."

Quixotry, in fact, is one of the worst foibles a statesman can indulge in.

There was naturally an embarrassment in talking so frankly even in a manuscript not intended, so far as we know, for the press, but this insistence on a double standard of morality, a sense of private right and wrong from which the responsible ruler must diverge as necessity dictates, is made to play a surprisingly emphatic role in *The Prince*. One more example will suffice to show how Machiavelli labored the point. "You have to understand this, that a prince, and especially a new prince," he wrote in Chapter 18, "cannot observe all those things which give men a reputation for virtue, because, in order to maintain his state, he is often compelled to act in defiance of good faith, of charity, of human courtesy, of religion." The point about this remark is not that it is shocking but that it is obvious. The lessons of *The Prince* do not require the anxious moral glosses with which Machiavelli surrounds them. Statesmen had been functioning efficiently on Machiavellian lines for centuries, and by begging them to be self-conscious about the motives for their actions, Machiavelli was not aiding but embarrassing their freedom of action.

If Machiavelli had been born to the ruling class, he would not have been concerned to defend its acceptance of expediency. As it was, he could not identify himself with the prince without bringing with him the conscience of a subject. For all its dogmatic force there is a tentative, apologetic note in *The Prince*. This is what I would do, Machiavelli seems to be saying, and this is why it would be allowable for me to do it. The streak of republican high-mindedness, which was never far beneath the surface in Florence, forced Machiavelli to make those explanations which blackened his reputation with posterity. There were complex motives which helped him identify himself with the interests of his Prince: confidence in his own powers, frustration at the bungling of others, a sense of urgency, the glamor of power; but none of these lifted him clear of the standards of his family and his class. Princes, especially new princes, must use cruelty and fraud to secure themselves, he wrote, and princes all over Europe would have greeted this dictum with an acquiescent and unalarmed nod. But Machiavelli could not leave the matter there. He elaborated, saying of cruelties: "We can say that cruelty is used well (if it is permissible to talk in this way of what is evil) when it is employed once for all, and one's safety depends on it, and then it is not persisted in." It is as though Machiavelli's Prince had started life as an honest bourgeois, and needed constant reassurance that he need act no longer as a private citizen. The assumption that political action would be based on expediency was part of Machiavelli's novel approach to his subject; the laboring of this assumption a reminder that he brought to it a not altogether unconventional state of mind.

[After writing *The Prince*, Machiavelli sent the manuscript to Vettori, in the hope that Vettori, through his connections at the papal court, might be able to arrange a post of some sort. But Vettori either couldn't or wouldn't help his old friend, so their correspondence turned to other topics, mostly girl chasing. Toward the end of 1514, however, politics came up again, and events turned Machiavelli back to a reconsideration of his manuscript.]

It is possible that it was at this point that Machiavelli took up *The Prince* and on rereading it gained the impetus to crown it with the "Exhortation to Liberate Italy from the Barbarians." Here at last, through Paolo's patronage,[7] was the longed-for chance of employment with the Medici. Here was a concrete proposal which would call for talents such as his, and a situation to which much of the subject-matter of *The Prince* was directly relevant. Italy now stood in even greater peril of invasion than at the end of 1513. He began by dwelling on the urgency of the situation. In his letter of 10 December 1514, he had urged a French alliance; now, in this last chapter, with an optimism of which there had been no trace in his correspondence in 1513, he urged that the opposing Swiss and Spanish armies were not invincible. He referred again, as he had in the recent letter of 31 January, to Duke Valentino—"a gleam of hope has appeared before now which gave hope that some individual might be appointed by God for her redemption, yet at the highest summit of his career he was thrown aside by fortune." Now there was a second chance to save Italy. But salvation must come from strength—and Machiavelli, the creator of the militia, and identified with it as with no other aspect of his career, spent more than a third of his space stressing the need for an indigenous army trained on lines superior to the recently reconstituted militia forces, damaging the literary shape of the chapter for the sake of an emphasis that would direct attention to his own qualifications for employment.

This personal plea, and the note of passionate faith that Italy's salvation could be at hand which occurs in two paragraphs of this exhortation, were vain. Cardinal dei Medici, who had known of Machiavelli's ideas through Francesco Vettori, had not been softened by them. On hearing of Paolo's interest in Machiavelli he wrote to Giuliano to forbid his employment. Once more Machiavelli had to turn from thoughts of an active life to one of reflection; from an absorption with external relations and the actions of princes to a growing concern with internal relations and constitu-

7. Vettori's brother Paolo was in the service of Giuliano de' Medici.

tional expedients. He was not to write to Vettori again for twelve years. Modern events had no place for him. He turned instead to the study of the past.

FELIX GILBERT

The Humanist Concept of the Prince and *The Prince* of Machiavelli†

The attention of one who studies the development of political thought, particularly of that gravitation toward political realism which was accomplished at the beginning of the modern era and is associated with the name of Machiavelli, is constantly arrested by that passage in the fifteenth chapter of *The prince* in which Machiavelli himself speaks of the guiding principles underlying the whole of his observations.

> It now remains for us to consider what ought to be the con- duct and bearing of a Prince in relation to his subjects and friends. And since I know that many have written on this subject, I fear it may be thought presumptuous in me to write of it also; the more so, because in my treatment of it I depart from the views that others have taken. But since it is my object to write what shall be useful to whosoever understands it, it seems to me better to follow the real truth of things than an imaginary view of them. For many Republics and Princedoms have been imag- ined that were never seen or known to exist in reality. And the manner in which we live, and that in which we ought to live, are things so wide asunder that he who quits the one to betake him- self to the other is more likely to destroy than to save himself.

In this passage Machiavelli succinctly summarizes the methodo- logical principles underlying the argument of *The prince* and later of the *Discorsi*, and draws a firm and definite line of demarcation between himself and his "idealist" predecessors, who sought to adapt and subordinate political theory to a theological or metaphysi- cal pattern. Machiavelli took his stand on observation and experi- ences derived from political practice; without a purely empirical foundation all insight into the true nature of politics, all compre- hension of the laws behind political phenomena, seemed to him impossible. A sense of pride seems to emerge from his repudiation of the standpoint of his predecessors and from his statement and

†From *The Journal of Modern History*, XI, 4 (December 1939), pp. 449–83. Footnotes are by the editor of this Nor- ton Critical Edition; Professor Gilbert's copious and informative notes are not included here.

defense of the revolutionary position which he had adopted; it is as if he himself foresaw the far-reaching consequences implicit in the application of the methods of realism to the realm of political thought.

It may perhaps be legitimate to draw yet another conclusion from the passage quoted. Machiavelli's attack on the political theorists of the last hundred years shows that he was perfectly well aware that with *The prince* he was plunging into a highly controversial subject; therefore a comparison of Machiavelli's work with the literature he attacked may give us a clue to the origins of *The prince* and the reorientation of political theory that it implied. For it is common experience that the real substance of an intellectual discussion is not at the time fully recognized by the disputants themselves. Differences of opinion that later only seem to be differences of a "technical" kind appear at first to be profound and insuperable, and the fundamental principles common to both sides in the discussion are overlooked. And even when the cleavage is really as profound as the disputants themselves suppose, concentration on the same question creates a certain connection between the opposite sides; in a new theory there is often to be traced the influence of an old one which it has combated and superseded. For this reason it may not be without interest to devote some attention to those writers whom Machiavelli subjected to such trenchant criticism in *The prince*.

When Machiavelli wrote *The prince*, humanism was the ruling intellectual force of the day. It had exercised its influence on political theory and produced its own political literature, which, particularly the writings of the humanists on the subject of the prince, Machiavelli must have had in mind. The political ideas of the humanist writers of the *quattrocento*[1] are, however, so largely overshadowed by the systematic social philosophy of the middle ages which preceded them and the "realist" political science that immediately followed them, that they have never so far been thoroughly examined. Since an investigation of the *quattrocento* literature on the subject of the prince may perhaps throw Machiavelli's book into sharper relief, we seem to be justified in devoting our attention to this neglected sphere and in attempting a comprehensive survey of the conception of the prince as it had developed in the humanistic literature of the *quattrocento*.

[In his first section, Gilbert shows that the rise of independent city-states and military autocrats (condottiere) who took charge of them forced fifteenth-century humanists to undertake a thorough review of classical theories of royal and princely government.]

1. Fifteenth century.

II

In an account of the political trends in the Italy of the *quat-trocento*, the necessary basis for our main task, the description and analysis of the prince-literature of the humanists, is to be found. Yet, by affording this description of the political situation and by showing the connection between the political events and the reawakening of the interest in princes and princeship, we seem already to have arrived at an opinion on this subject contrary to that usually held. For Machiavelli's censorious verdict, quoted above, has been often reiterated; and it has been generally accepted that the political writings of the humanists lacked the urge of politi-cal conviction and were remote from, and alien to, reality; whereas we, by drawing attention to the political developments which led the humanists to take up the question of the prince, seem, on the contrary, to demonstrate a direct connection between the literature of this genre and the political conditions under which it was writ-ten. Yet such a statement is not intended to imply more than that the original impulse sprang from reality. Beyond that, the question as to what extent the humanists were influenced by reality, and what rudiments of realism there were in their writings before Machiavelli set up the realistic principle as the basis of his political thought, can be determined only by a detailed consideration of their writings; it can be determined only by finding out whether these writings represent more than a resuscitation of known and tra-ditional ideas or whether they deviate from the traditional mode and contain new and original thought. Our task, therefore, of exam-ining the prince-literature of the humanists distinctly falls into two parts: first, to investigate these writings in relation to their literary models and try to distinguish between what is new and original and what is traditional in them; after this to more closely examine the respects in which these writings deviate from tradition with special regard to their connection with the political situation of their time. Thus we shall try to find out whether they form a link in the chain that led to Machiavelli's realism.

There can be no doubt that these writings are, in the main, of abstract nature. As has already been hinted at, two intellectual cur-rents met in the humanist literature on the subject of the prince. In the first place, as products of humanism, these writings were based on antiquity and were chiefly intended to be a reproduction of ancient ideas. In the second place, they were part of the centuries-old stream of the mirror-of-princes literature. Unlike the problem of the "good citizen" or "the best state," antiquity provided no authoritative literary pattern for the problem of the "good prince." There was scope for ancient influence to show itself in the treat-ment and handling of individual aspects of the problem. But the medieval "mirror of the accomplished prince" was the sole available pattern for its treatment as a whole.

The medieval picture of the prince had not been static and unchanged. Beginning in a limited way, by emphasizing the religious significance of the prince's function, it had enlarged its scope by adopting the concept of the prince as the governing member of a living body. Then, at the end of the thirteenth century, it had undergone a fundamental transformation, mainly as a result of the impact of the political doctrine of Aristotle, and had tried to embrace the whole field of political institution, especially in its military and judiciary aspects. It was in this highly developed form, in which the influence of antiquity was already apparent, that it exercised an influence on later times. The best and fullest example of this development is the work of Egidio Colonna.

Egidio's book has an enormous scope, which was probably the main reason for its popularity. Egidio aimed at completeness in dealing with his subject. He intended to leave no aspect of it untouched. He dealt alike with the prince as a personality and with princedom as an institution; he dealt as well with the prince's character and the ordering of his court and household as with the object of the state and its administration and with the art of war. Yet, in spite of the handbook character of his work, Egidio's rigidly dogmatic attitude is essentially that of the middle ages. The medieval character of the book is demonstrated, in the first place, by its method. Egidio argues purely deductively from general propositions and assumptions regarding the nature of the universe. In the second place, his work is infused with the concepts of medieval Christianity. In his eyes the whole of man's worldly, social existence is coordinated with the life beyond. From this assumption he deduces the prince's place in the world. The prince is the intermediary between God and man. Most of the attributes Egidio demands of kings and kingships he deduces from this proposition. He states, for instance, that the prince's goal should not be the acquisition of power, honor, or wealth, but that he must aim rather at developing those qualities in himself that fit him to fulfil his religious functions. Egidio proceeds to build up a system of Christian princely ethics. The prince, he says, must set an example to his subjects, both in the conduct of his private life and the ordering of his court and household. Thus, when Egidio describes the ordering of the prince's household, he merely draws a picture of how a model household ought to be managed according to the precepts of religion. He deduces the prince's political duties from those principles of natural justice by which the prince himself was bound and which it was his duty to see applied.

On comparing Egidio's treatment of the subject with that of the humanists, one is at first struck by the apparent absence of any common feature. The writings of the latter are characterized, above all, by those elements which distinguish the political thought of humanism from that of the middle ages. The religious orientation of political life has lost its former predominance. Thus, while for Egidio the good ruler's reward was an outstanding position in the hierarchy of the next world, for the humanists his reward was fame. That is but one example of how the humanists abandoned religious motives in their political theory. Further, the humanists introduced a new basis for discussion. They founded their arguments on historical example instead of abstract theoretical deduction. The historical examples that they used were, of course, taken exclusively from the ancient world, particularly the Roman world; and all their political theorizing was patterned on antiquity. Beyond these characteristically humanist features, however, a careful study of these writings on the prince will reveal a number of traits which they have in common with the medieval conception. Like the medieval authors, the humanists attempted to discover a norm and to describe the ideal prince. In both cases the qualities of this ideal prince were determined by a political conception which is fundamentally peaceful and unrealistic: the tasks of the *quattrocento* prince were exclusively confined—like those of his medieval predecessor—to the administration of justice and the maintenance of peace. In accordance with this basic principle, the just and mild king, surrounded by wise councilors and keeping within the confines of the law, remained the ideal of the *quattrocento*. Even apart from this common basic attitude, however, it is possible to trace the direct influence of Egidio in the *quattrocento* literature on the prince and especially in the works of the two writers who dealt most fully with the subject: Platina's (1421–81) *De vero principe* and Francesco Patrizi's (1412–94) *De regno*. These authors, like Egidio, dealt both with the personal side of princeship and with princeship as an institution, and thus a certain resemblance between their works and his was created. Egidio had set up a kind of standard of completeness to which any subsequent treatise on the subject was expected to conform. Nevertheless, Patrizi's and Platina's books both exhibit certain characteristic deviations. Patrizi expanded the boundaries of his subject by a section devoted to the prince's education, in which he classified the art of warfare as a necessary part of the prince's training. With Platina the problems of state administration are considered in relation to ethics, to a certain extent as practical examples of the application of virtues. This shows that more importance was attached to the personal than to the institutional side of the problem. The shorter writings, such as those of Majo, Poggio, Pontano, and Beroaldus, are confined to dealing with the personality of the prince and consist of no more than catalogues of virtues.

Thus, besides the introduction of a new method of approach and the omission of the religious motivation, the emphasis on the catalogue of virtues is the main feature by which these humanist writings are distinguished from their medieval predecessors. It is not hard to explain why the humanists focused on and developed the subject of princely virtues as formulated in the medieval mirror of princes. The explanation lies in the influence of the classical world. By confining themselves to the composition of catalogues of virtues, the writers could pattern themselves closely on ancient models and adopt the schemes provided by Aristotle in the *Nicomachean ethics* or by Cicero in *De officiis*. Under this influence the humanist catalogue of virtues took on a new aspect and came to differ from those of the middle ages. Purely worldly virtues took their place beside the religious ones and even superseded them in the degree of interest they aroused; moreover, those worldly virtues were considered purely from the point of view of their effect, their advantages and disadvantages being exactly weighed. This is particularly true of the virtue of *liberalitas*, which was now regarded as a means of consolidating the position of the ruler. The question whether a prince should strive to make himself feared or loved was discussed as a serious, practical problem; and though it was invariably answered in the traditional idealist manner, opportunities for realistic observations were necessarily provided in the course of the discussion. With Pontano (1426—1503) this literary form ceased to be merely an enumeration of individual virtues and emerged as a compact and comprehensive psychological sketch. The specific contribution of the humanist writers to the development of the mirror-of-princes literature can thus be characterized as an amplification and a more searching discussion of the problems raised in the earlier catalogues of virtues. Starting from this approach, they succeeded in presenting a new problem: Was it permissible, they asked, to apply to the specific case of the prince the ethical norm postulated quite generally for every human being? Must not the prince practice virtues differing essentially from those of his subjects or of the ordinary citizen?

At this point we have found a connecting link between the humanists and Machiavelli—this despite the fact that, at the first sight, an abyss seems to separate the idealist conception of the prince from the realistic conception of power-politics which dominated Machiavelli's writings. The *quattrocento*, by concentrating attention on the ethical problems of princeship and thus on the personal characteristics of the prince, started a tendency which reached its culmination in Machiavelli's proposition that the vital, the determining, factor in politics was the prince's personality. And one can say that the famous chapters of *The prince*, in which Machiavelli investigates the qualities that make the successful prince and in which he falls most foul of conventional morality, were but a consequence of pushing to its logical conclusion the argument that first appeared in the writings of the humanists: whether the virtues and characteristics of the prince ought not to be different from those of the private citizen.

III

While indicating that there is some connection between the humanists and Machiavelli, we have already broached the important question whether the humanist writings were touched by the politics of their time and can be considered as having presaged the realism of Machiavelli. This question cannot be answered in the affirmative simply on the strength of this one point—that the humanists were already aware of the problem as to the difference between prince and private citizen—since this problem did not present itself to them in the light of its true importance but rather as a by-product, an unexpected result reached almost automatically in the course of the inquiry. On the contrary, in general we have seen that the humanist writings invariably started by accepting the traditional identity between the ideal prince and the ideal human being; and, because of this fact, their contents and form were, to a large extent, predetermined by the medieval tradition of the mirror of princes. And even those elements which they added—the more comprehensive catalogue of virtues and the stronger emphasis on the personality of the prince—were endorsed by a literary authority, that of antiquity.

Yet these innovations, though facilitated by a literary authority, cannot be said to have originated there. With regard to the enlargement of the catalogue of virtues, the manner in which it was transformed and the choice of the secular virtues selected for particular emphasis clearly reveal the influence of contemporary reality. One result of this influence is that the external signs of princely power and display now receive particular attention. Egidio had considered the possession of power and worldly honors as of no significance. He even regarded with a certain amount of distrust all bodily games and exercises which provided opportunities of princely display. But in the writings of the *quattrocento*, hunts, tourneys, and games counted as the essential constituents of the princely life and were described in great detail. They belonged to *magnificentia*, which now made its appearance as one of the most characteristic virtues of the prince. And in company with *magnificentia* there was introduced the pregnant idea of *majestas*, a heading which included everything which contributed to making an outward impression of princely power. How completely Majo (d. 1493) identified this conception with the very idea of the prince is shown by the fact that he

entitled his book "*De majestate*." Pontano attached no less importance to the new conception of *majestas*. A great part of his work—
and he himself regarded it as a particularly important and original
part—is devoted to the question of princely deportment. Pontano
maintains that the prince's gestures, his way of speaking, the sound
of his voice, and even his dress and table manners—the whole of his
life, in fact—must be subject to exact rules which are stated in
minute detail; Pontano's view amounts to the claim that the respect
accorded to the prince is determined by his outer bearing and
deportment. He must rise above his subjects by the strict observance of an elaborate ceremonial. This is a superficial answer to the
question concerning the essence of princely power, but it is an attitude that wholly corresponds to the excessive regard for form which
characterizes the Renaissance and is reflected in the ceremonial prescriptions of the lists of court precedence which originated in Italy
at that time.

But it is the declining interest in the institutional aspect of the
problem and the concentration of the writers' attention on the personality of the prince which most clearly reveals the influence of
political reality. For this change in emphasis was wholly appropriate
to the ruthless character of *quattrocento* princeship with its dependence on the personal qualities of the ruler. The purely personal
approach to the subject is apparent in Majo's book, more perhaps
than in any other. At the same time it is a good illustration of a
work intimately associated with a specific political situation. It is
distinguished from the remaining prince-literature by the fact that
its primary purpose was to prove that a contemporary ruler, Ferrante of Naples, was to be regarded as an embodiment of the ideal
prince. Majo planned the book with that object in view. He starts
each chapter with a brief description of a special virtue; he then
goes on to demonstrate with the aid of quotations from ancient
authors how necessary that virtue is for a ruling prince, and ends
the chapter by quoting some deed or incident from the life of Ferrante as an illustration of that particular virtue having been realized
in practice. There is, of course, a large dose of humanist flattery in
this method of treatment. This is made abundantly plain when
Majo's idealized portrait is compared with the character of the real
Ferrante, which was certainly not ideal. But Majo's work does not
consist entirely of empty eulogy. He makes a serious attempt to
survey and appreciate with some completeness the historical events
of Ferrante's reign. The attempt, of course, led him into making
some remarkably false judgments and ascribing some remarkably
unreal motives to Ferrante. Nevertheless, Majo had a certain feeling
for the historical significance of individual events. For example, in
his section on "Justice" he deals very thoroughly with the overthrow

of the powers of feudalism in Naples and the establishment of a
strong, central government and quite rightly emphasizes it as the
most important event of Ferrante's reign. Majo regards every historical event as being purely and simply the consequence of the
prince's personality. History had ceased to be conceived of as being
controlled by the intervention of God or supernatural powers; the
only decisive factor was now the personality of the prince. Majo's
attitude illustrates a conception of history generally accepted at the
time. It shows that the tendency of the *quattrocento* princeship literature to accentuate the personal aspects of the problem was
rooted in the historical individualism of the age.

In spite, however, of these traits by which contemporary politics
have left their stamp on the humanist writings, in the main, as we
said, the idealistic conception remained unchanged; and, although
there are instances where practical problems crept in and are clearly
recognizable, there is no manifestation of a thoroughgoing realism,
no appreciation of the power-factor and the egoistic purposes which
dominate the political life. That is the more strange since a definite
trend of realism did exist in the *quattrocento*, and since writers,
having practical aims in view, knew and used the vocabulary of
unqualified realism. An example of this in the prince-literature is
Diomede Carafa (1406–87), *De regis et boni principis officio*.[2]
That Carafa's interests were entirely concentrated on practical questions is shown by the very chapter headings of his book: "De
tuendo imperio, de jure dicendo et justitia servando, de re familiari
et vectigalibus administrandis, de subditorum civitatisque commodis
preservandis."[3] Certainly, Carafa, like his contemporaries, was fond
of quoting maxims from ancient authors and apophthegms from traditional controversies; but he is basically concerned only with the
practical lessons to be drawn from these generalizations, and the
conclusions at which he arrives are often surprisingly similar to
Machiavelli's. The best illustration of this is the sentence in which
he announces that the guiding principle of politics is self-interest:
"Kings and peoples of the whole world, deliberating concerning the
government of their affairs, pursue their own advantages and are
wont to put their interests before the ties of relationship and friendship." But Carafa's work derives its exceptional character simply
from the fact that it does not belong to the scheme of humanist
prince-literature: it was a political memorandum, written by the
leading Neapolitan minister for the use of a Neapolitan princess
who had just been married to the Duke of Ferrara; it was not
intended for publication. As soon as an author had literary ambi-

2. "On the office of a king and a good
prince."
3. "On protecting one's rule, on declaring the law and preserving justice, on
family life and managing one's money,
on preserving the property of subjects
and the city."

tions, he felt it necessary to set an ideal standard and write of an imaginary political world.

Thus, the humanist prince-writings only reflect contemporary reality to that extent of embodying the historical individualism of their age; they do not go so far as to adopt a thoroughgoing realism. Yet even their inability to go beyond a purely literary and idealistic attitude to politics has a factual cause and should be explained in terms of the author's general intellectual background. Political consciousness in general, no less than the specific historical individualism embodied in the works we are discussing, was decisively influenced by the fact that Italy of the *quattrocento* was politically isolated from the rest of Europe. It was an epoch of mutually balancing powers striving after an equilibrium. The Italian political situation in the *quattrocento* consisted of a number of known and calculable forces, and success was in the hands of him who knew how to calculate and give due weight to each. All the factors of the political situation were within the perspective of the intelligent observer. This ceased to be the case after the French invasion of 1494, which put an end to Italy's isolation and brought her once more within the orbit of the inexorable dynamics of world-historical events. History, in other words, once more appeared as the manifestation of an incomprehensible and uncontrollable power. Underlying the political rationalism of Machiavelli and the *cinquecento* was a passionate concern to discover the hidden laws of history's involutions. The principle of political realism was born on men's striving to learn the laws of politics by penetrating to their very essence. By the application of those laws, once they have been discovered, Machiavelli's prince would have it within his power to be the master of politics. Thus, all trace of the idealized human personality as such vanished from Machiavelli's portrait of the prince, and its place was taken by the superpersonal conception of reasons of state. Prior to the upheaval of the French invasion an optimistic faith in man's power to have the whole of politics within his purview, and understand it, could still be preserved. In concentrating attention on the personal factor in politics, the *quattrocento* writers prepared the way to a "realistic" psychological approach to politics, such as exists now; but, inasmuch as the limits of man's control over history had not yet been discovered, there was, as yet, no need to abandon the ideal standard of the middle ages, and it was still possible to regard the setting-up of the notion of an ideal human being, with all the pedagogic appeal that such a notion possessed, as a serious contribution to political thought.

[In his fourth section, Gilbert shows that new justifications of princely authority were required by new challenges from republics and by the diminished prestige of the Holy Roman Empire. Two responses were the "democratic" concept of the prince espoused by Alberti, which held that the prince was essentially the servant of his people; and the absolutist ideal, which represented the prince as the vessel of divine inspiration, the creative political man in his own right. Both theories drew strength from the revived interest of the fifteenth century in Plato; both influenced Machiavelli in positive as well as reactive ways.]

v

The humanist prince-literature both influenced the later mirror-of-princes writings and contributed to the classical political theories of the Renaissance which developed in the *cinquecento*. That is to say, it lived on in the two literary trends from which it was chiefly composed. Yet it is not these trends that we wish to follow now. It was some passages from Machiavelli's *The prince* that afforded a starting-point for this study by suggesting that there was some connection between Machiavelli's *The prince* and the humanist prince-literature. Has this proved to be the case? At various points we have found definite links between Machiavelli and the humanists: when they raised the problem as to the difference between prince and private citizen, when they envisaged the prince as a creative political force—these are tendencies which clear the way for Machiavelli and which he took up. Thus it can be said that, although in the decisive factor of political realism, this literature did not, in any sense, pave the way for Machiavelli. Machiavelli nevertheless incorporated in his book certain intellectual trends which had already been developed by the humanists.

Yet it is not these general trends alone that associate Machiavelli with the humanist prince-literature. Machiavelli was aware that he dealt, though from a new point of view, with matters that had been treated before; we now maintain that he was consciously refuting his predecessors and that this intention has left its mark on the structure of the *The prince*. That, then, is the thesis which we hope that this study will enable us to prove. First, there is reason to believe that Machiavelli endeavored to adapt the form of his book to the conventional literary form of this genre. There are especially two facts which render this supposition probable. In the first place, like the works of Machiavelli's predecessors, all the earliest manuscripts of *The prince* have Latin chapter headings. Secondly, however, the dedication of *The prince* to Lorenzo Medici is an imitation of Isocrates' *Address to Nicocles*; and, as already stated, it is this address that was considered as the best-known ancient example of a "mirror of princes." Since for that reason the humanists frequently referred to this speech, it is clear that Machiavelli followed an established tradition when he adopted Isocrates as his model.

But the connection is a far more specific one. We have already drawn attention to the fact that certain sections of *The prince* relate to the discussion raised by the humanist catalogue of virtues, and it is my contention that Machiavelli deliberately undertook these chapters as a refutation.

I refer to chapters XV–XIX of *The prince*. They constitute a coherent section, distinct from the remainder of the work; for in chapter XV Machiavelli states that he is about to examine the qualities necessary for a prince, and, after enumerating them one by one, he writes in chapter XIX, "Having now spoken of the chief of the qualities above referred to, the rest I shall dispose of briefly with these general remarks," and indicates that, having discussed the more important qualities in detail, he will deal summarily with the remainder. This summary forms the substance of the nineteenth chapter. Thus, the subject taken up in chapter XV is concluded with the termination of chapter XIX. The contention that these chapters form a whole is further supported by the opening sentence of chapter XV: "It now remains for us to consider what ought to be the conduct and bearing of a prince in relation to his subjects and friends . . . ," in which Machiavelli himself indicates that he is commencing a new theme with this chapter. This sentence indicates, moreover, that the chapters were written with the deliberate intention of providing an up-to-date rendering of the subject matter contained in the humanist catalogues of virtue, for it was the habit of the humanists to deal with general questions, such as that of a prince's relations with his subjects and friends by introducing them into the conventional literary framework of the princely qualities, which, in its turn, was presented as a catalogue of virtues. And this is precisely what Machiavelli sets out to do, only from a new and realistic point of view. It is this chapter, moreover, which contains Machiavelli's criticism of his predecessors' approach to politics quoted at the beginning of this paper—the passage, that is to say, in which he expressly states that he is about to treat of matters that have often been dealt with before. A passage in chapter XVI affords further support to this theory. When Machiavelli starts discussing whether a prince should strive to be loved or feared, he characterizes the question as a *disputà* and thus shows that he was well aware of previous discussions of the subject. His chapter headings make the link we are trying to establish even plainer. The headings of chapters XVI, XVII, and XVIII, respectively, are: "De liberalitate et parsimonia";[4] "De crudelitate et pietate; et an sit melius amari quam timeri, vel e contra";[5] "Quomodo fides a principibus sit deservanda";[6] "De contemptu et odio fugiendo."[7] Practically the

---

4. "Of liberality and parsimony."
5. "Of cruelty and clemency, and whether it is better to be loved than feared, or vice versa."
6. "How princes should keep their word."
7. "On avoiding contempt and hatred."

same chapter headings might have been used by the humanists in their catalogues of virtues; and, although the latter discuss the subject in far greater detail, Machiavelli has emphasized precisely those qualities which, in the works of the humanists, it appears important for the prince to possess. There appears to be no doubt that Machiavelli did not merely refute the idealist interpretation of politics in general but that he wrote with the conscious aim of discrediting the idealized conception of the prince as contained in the catalogues of the virtues. The "realistic" thesis of chapter XV was intended to replace that false conception. It is possibly another instance of the fact, often to be observed, that in proclaiming certain aspects of his thesis Machiavelli was motivated by a spirit of contradiction—perhaps even by a certain exuberant pleasure in paradox. Such an idea is thoroughly consistent with the view of those of Machiavelli's contemporaries whose opinions we have reason to value and who stress this trait as a characteristic feature of his work. They were fully aware of the polemical character of Machiavelli's writings, concealed for us by the originality of his principles and the positive value of his contribution to political thought.

Let us now inquire whether our conclusion that chapters XV–XIX form a compact, independent whole, written by Machiavelli for the express purpose of adding a sequel and a refutation to the humanist's catalogues of virtues, tallies with what we know of the composition of *The prince*.

The most recent comprehensive discussion of the composition of *The prince* is to be found in Friedrich Meinecke's introduction to a German translation of *The prince*. Meinecke bases his conclusions on Machiavelli's letter to Vettori of December 10, 1513, the only document in which Machiavelli himself refers to his own work. He writes:

> I have composed a treatise *De principatibus* in which I enter as deeply as I can into the science of the subject, with reasonings on the nature of principality, its several species, and how they are acquired, how maintained, how lost. . . . [Philippo] will be able to inform you about it, and about the discussions I have had with him on the subject, although I am still amplifying and pruning the work.

Meinecke claims that Machiavelli's remarks in this letter must apply not to the whole of *The prince* but only to the first eleven chapters of it, and he also states that there are certain signs that chapter XI was originally intended to be the final chapter. He therefore infers that the work originated in sections and that the chapters following chapter XI did not form part of Machiavelli's original conception but represented a subsequent addition. In in the second part of *The prince*, which he states begins with chapter XII, Meinecke also distinguishes various subsections. Thus, chapters XII–XIV belong together, because they deal with military affairs; and chapters XV–XVIII seem to him "a small special treatise on the relations of politics to the ethical values and feelings of the prince's subjects."

All this fits admirably into our own thesis. Meinecke mentions in support of his theory that Machiavelli changed the title of the work from *De principatibus* to *Il principe*, thereby indicating that a change of emphasis had occurred in the course of writing it and that a new theme had forced its way into the foreground. We may perhaps add that *De principe* was the title used by the humanists and that the alteration of title thus confirms our theory of a close connection between the train of thought of the second half of *The prince* and the humanist writings on the subject. So far, our views correspond exactly with those of Meinecke. But in other respects the acceptance of our thesis involves parting from him. Although, as we mentioned above, Meinecke distinguishes various subsections in the second half of *The prince*, beginning with chapter XII, he believes that the second half of the book was conceived as a whole. This view is not, however, compatible with the thesis we are advocating, for it is an essential implication of our thesis that chapters XV–XIX did not originate as an elaboration of a trend of thought suggested by the general scheme of *The prince* but rather in response to an external literary stimulus. It follows that chapter XV begins an entirely new section and that no link whatever bridges the gap between it and the three preceding chapters. We must rather assume that the second part of *The prince*, commencing with chapter XII, consists of several distinct complexes of ideas loosely grouped together. We therefore suggest the following sequence in the composition of *The prince*. Having completed working out his original idea in the first eleven chapters, Machiavelli proceeded to revise and amplify his work. In the course of this revision he added a more detailed account of his favorite subject, the art of war. He then felt impelled to examine his work from the point of view of the problems dealt with in the writings of his humanist predecessors, and was thus induced to write a polemical reply to the traditional catalogues of virtues. In the remaining chapters he discussed at length certain additional problems raised in the literature of his time.

The structure of *The prince* has always been examined in the hope of finding a solution to the much debated question whether the Italian nationalism of the last chapter formed an integral part of Machiavelli's political outlook or whether it was merely a decorative conclusion—a rhetorical, humanist ornament. If we are right in our theory that from chapter XV onward Machiavelli was inspired

by opposition to the humanists who preceded him and that, consequently, the second part of *The prince* is very loosely composed and
forms no connected unity, I believe we have to accept, as a further
result, that also the last chapter, which is not prepared for by any
hint in the preceding sections of the book, stands by itself, mainly
intended as a concluding rhetorical flourish. This conclusion must
not be interpreted as a denial of national feeling in Machiavelli, but
it does show that nationalism had no definite and prescribed place
in his system. It indicates that nationalism and realism, the appearance of which revolutionized political consciousness and political
thought, were only gradually conceived as interdependent forces.

ERNST CASSIRER

Implications of the New Theory of the State†

The Isolation of the State and Its Dangers

The whole argument of Machiavelli is clear and coherent. His
logic is impeccable. If we accept his premises we cannot avoid his
conclusions. With Machiavelli we stand at the gateway of the
modern world. The desired end is attained; the state has won its
full autonomy. Yet his result has had to be bought dearly. The state
is entirely independent; but at the same time it is completely isolated. The sharp knife of Machiavelli's thought has cut off all the
threads by which in former generations the state was fastened to
the organic whole of human existence. The political world has lost
its connection not only with religion or metaphysics but also with
all the other forms of man's ethical and cultural life. It stands alone
—in an empty space.

That this complete isolation was pregnant with the most dangerous consequences should not be denied. There is no point in over-
looking or minimizing these consequences. We must see them face
to face. I do not mean to say that Machiavelli was fully aware of all
the implications of his political theory. In the history of ideas it is
by no means unusual that a thinker develops a theory, the full purport and significance of which is still hidden to himself. In this
regard we must, indeed, make a sharp distinction between Machiavelli and Machiavellism. There are many things in the latter that
could not be foreseen by Machiavelli. He spoke and judged from his
own personal experience, the experience of a secretary of the state

†From Ernst Cassirer, *The Myth of the State* (New Haven, Connecticut: Yale University Press, 1973), chapter XII. Professor Cassirer's notes have been trimmed a little here and augmented a bit there, in view of the special circumstances of this edition.

of Florence. He had studied with the keenest interest the rise and fall of the "new principalities." But what were the small Italian tyrannies of the Cinquecento when compared to the absolute monarchies of the seventeenth century and with our modern forms of dictatorship? Machiavelli highly admired the methods used by Cesare Borgia to liquidate his adversaries. Yet in comparison with the later much more developed technique of political crimes these methods appear to be only child's play. Machiavellism showed its true face and its real danger when its principles were later applied to a larger scene and to entirely new political conditions. In this sense we may say that the consequences of Machiavelli's theory were not brought to light until our own age. Now we can, as it were, study Machiavellism in a magnifying glass.

There was still another circumstance that prevented Machiavellism from coming to its full maturity. In the centuries that followed, in the seventeenth and eighteenth centuries, his doctrine played an important role in practical political life; but, theoretically speaking, there were still great intellectual and ethical forces which counterbalanced its influence. The political thinkers of this period, with the single exception of Hobbes, were all partisans of the "Natural Right theory of the state." Grotius, Pufendorf,[1] Rousseau, Locke looked upon the state as a means, not as an end in itself. The concept of a "totalitarian" state was unknown to these thinkers. There was always a certain sphere of individual life and individual freedom which remained inaccessible to the state. The state and the sovereign in general were *legibus solutus*. But this meant only that they were free from legal coercion; it did not mean that they were exempt from moral obligations. After the beginning of the nineteenth century, however, all this was suddenly called in question. Romanticism launched a violent attack against the theory of natural rights. The romantic writers and philosophers spoke as resolute "spiritualists." But it was precisely this metaphysical spiritualism that paved the way for the most uncouth and uncompromising materialism in political life. In this regard it is a highly interesting and remarkable fact that the "idealistic" thinkers of the nineteenth century, Fichte and Hegel, became the advocates of Machiavelli and the defenders of Machiavellism. After the collapse of the theory of natural rights the last barrier to its triumph was removed. There was no longer any great intellectual or moral power to check and counterbalance Machiavellism; its victory was complete and seemed to be beyond challenge.

That Machiavelli's *Prince* contains the most immoral things and that Machiavelli has no scruples about recommending to the ruler

1. Hugo Grotius and Samuel Pufendorf were distinguished jurists of the seventeenth century—the first Dutch, the second German. [*Editor.*]

all sorts of deception, of perfidy, and cruelty is incontestable. There are, however, not a few modern writers who deliberately shut their eyes to this obvious fact. Instead of explaining it they make the greatest efforts to deny it. They tell us that the measures recommended by Machiavelli, however objectionable in themselves, are only meant for the "common good." The ruler has to respect this common good. But where do we find this mental reservation? *The Prince* speaks in quite a different, in an entirely uncompromising way. The book describes, with complete indifference, the ways and means by which political power is to be acquired and to be maintained. About the *right use* of this power it does not say a word. It does not restrict this use to any consideration for the commonwealth. It was only centuries later that the Italian patriots began to read into Machiavelli's book all their own political and national idealism. In any word of Machiavelli, declared Alfieri, we find the same spirit, a spirit of justice, of passionate love for freedom, of magnanimity and truth. He who understands Machiavelli's work in the right way must become an ardent enthusiast for liberty and an enlightened lover of all political virtues.

This is, however, only a rhetorical answer to our question, not a theoretical one. To regard Machiavelli's *Prince* as a sort of ethical treatise or a manual of political virtues is impossible. We need not enter here into a discussion of the vexed problem whether the last chapter of *The Prince*, the famous exhortation to deliver Italy out of the bonds of barbarians, is an integral part of the book or a later addition. Many modern students of Machiavelli have spoken of *The Prince* as if the whole book were nothing but a preparation for this closing chapter, as if this chapter were not only the climax but also the quintessence of Machiavelli's political thought. I think this view to be erroneous, and, as far as I see, the *onus probandi*[2] rests in this case with the advocates of the thesis. For there are obvious differences between the book taken as a whole and the last chapter, differences of thought and differences of style. In the book itself Machiavelli speaks with an entirely detached mind. Everyone may hear him and make what use he will of his advice which is available not only to the Italians but also to the most dangerous enemies of Italy. In the third chapter Machiavelli discusses at great length all the errors committed by Louis XII in his invasion of Italy. Without these errors, he declares, Louis XII would have had no difficulty in attaining his end, which was to subjugate the whole of Italy. In his analysis of political actions Machiavelli never gives vent to any personal feeling of sympathy or antipathy. To put it in the words of Spinoza he speaks of these things as if they were lines, planes, or solids. He did not attack the principles of morality; but he could

2. "Burden of proof." [*Editor.*]

find no use for these principles when engrossed in problems of political life. Machiavelli looked at political combats as if they were a
game of chess. He had studied the rules of the game very thoroughly. But he had not the slightest intention of changing or criti-
cizing these rules. His political experience had taught him that the
political game never had been played without fraud, deception,
treachery, and felony. He neither blamed nor recommended these
things. His only concern was to find the best move—the move that
wins the game. When a chess champion engages in a bold combination, or when he tries to deceive his partner by all sorts of ruses and
stratagems, we are delighted and admire his skill. That was exactly
Machiavelli's attitude when he looked upon the shifting scenes of
the great political drama that was played before his eyes. He was
not only deeply interested; he was fascinated. He could not help
giving his opinion. Sometimes he shook his head at a bad move;
sometimes he burst out with admiration and applause. It never
occurred to him to ask by whom the game was played. The players
may be aristocrats or republicans, barbarians or Italians, legitimate
princes or usurpers. Obviously that makes no difference for the man
who is interested in the game itself—and in nothing but the game.
In his theory Machiavelli is apt to forget that the political game is
not played with chessmen, but with real men, with human beings
of flesh and blood; and that the weal and woe of these beings is at
stake.

It is true that in the last chapter his cool and detached attitude
gives way to an entirely new note. Machiavelli suddenly shakes off
the burden of his logical method. His style is no longer analytical
but rhetorical. Not without reason has that last chapter been compared to Isocrates' exhortation to Philip.[3] Personally we may prefer
the emotional note of the last chapter to the cold and indifferent
note of the rest of the book. Yet it would be wrong to assume that
in the book Machiavelli has concealed his thoughts; that what is
said there was only a sham. Machiavelli's book was sincere and
honest; but it was dictated by his conception of the meaning and
task of a *theory* of politics. Such a theory must describe and ana-
lyze; it cannot blame or praise.

No one has ever doubted the patriotism of Machiavelli. But we
should not confuse the philosopher with the patriot. *The Prince*
was the work of a political thinker—and of a very radical thinker.
Many modern scholars are liable to forget or, at least, to underrate
this radicalism of Machiavelli's theory. In their efforts to purge his
name from all blame they have obscured his work. They have portrayed a harmless and innocuous but at the same time a rather triv-

3. See L. A. Burd's notes in his edition of "*Il Principe*," p. 366.

ial Machiavelli. The real Machiavelli was much more dangerous—
dangerous in his thoughts, not in his character. To mitigate his
theory means to falsify it. The picture of a mild or lukewarm
Machiavelli is not a true historical portrait. It is a "fable
convenue"[4] just as much opposed to the historical truth as the conception of the "diabolic" Machiavelli. The man himself was loath
to compromise. In his judgments about political actions he warned
over and over again against irresolution and hesitation. It was the
greatness and the glory of Rome that in Roman political life all half
measures were avoided.[5] Only weak states are always dubious in their
resolves, and tardy resolves are always hateful.[6] It is true that men,
in general, seldom know how to be wholly good or wholly bad. Yet
it is precisely this point in which the real politician, the great statesman, differs from the average man. He will not shrink from such
crimes as are stamped with an inherent greatness. He may perform
many good actions, but when circumstances require a different course
he will be "splendidly wicked."[7] Here we hear the voice of the real
Machiavelli, not of the conventional one. And even if it were true
that all the advice of Machiavelli was destined only for the "common good," who is the judge of this common good? Obviously no
one but the prince himself. And he will always be likely to identify
it with his private interest: he will act according to the maxim: *L'état
c'est moi*.[8] Moreover, if the common good could justify all those
things that are recommended in Machiavelli's book, if it could be
used as an excuse for fraud and deception, felony, and cruelty, it
would hardly be distinguishable from the common evil.

It remains, however, one of the great puzzles in the history of
human civilization how a man like Machiavelli, a great and noble
mind, could become the advocate of "splendid wickedness." And
this puzzle becomes the more bewildering if we compare *The
Prince* with Machiavelli's other writings. There are many things in
these other writings that seem to be in flagrant contradiction with
the views exposed in *The Prince*. In his *Discourses* Machiavelli
speaks as a resolute republican. In the struggles between the Roman
aristocracy and the plebeians his sympathy is clearly on the side of
the people. He defends the people against the reproach of inconstancy and fickleness;[9] he declares that the guardianship of public
freedom is safer in the hands of the commons than in those of the
patricians.[1] He speaks in a very disparaging tone of the *gentiluom-
ini*, of those men who live in opulence and idleness on the revenues
of their estates. Such persons, he declares, are very mischievous in
every republic or country. But even more mischievous are those who

4. A "made-up story." [*Editor*.]
5. *Discourses*, Book II, chap. 23.
6. Idem, Book II, chap. 15; Book I,
chap. 38.
7. Idem, Book I, chap. 27. [See pp.
104–5 of this Norton Critical Edition

—*Editor*.]
8. "The state is me." [*Editor*.]
9. Idem, Book I, chap. 58. [See pp.
112–16 of this Norton Critical Edition
—*Editor*.]
1. Idem, Book I, chaps. 4, 5.

are lords of strongholds and castles besides their estates, and who have vassals and retainers who render them obedience. Of these two classes of men the Kingdom of Naples, the Romagna and Lombardy were full; and hence it happened that in these provinces no commonwealth or free form of government ever existed; because men of this sort are the sworn foes to all free institutions.[2] Taking everything into consideration, declares Machiavelli, the people are wiser and more constant than a prince.[3]

In *The Prince* we hear very little of these convictions. Here the fascination of Cesare Borgia is so strong that it seems completely to eclipse all republican ideals. The methods of Cesare Borgia become the hidden center of Machiavelli's political reflections. His thought is irresistibly attracted to this center. "Upon a thorough review of the duke's conduct and actions," says Machiavelli,

> I see nothing worthy of reprehension in them; on the contrary, I have proposed them and here propose them again as a pattern for the imitation of all such as arrive at dominion by the arms or fortune of others. For as he had a great spirit and vast designs, he could not well have acted otherwise in his circumstances: and if he miscarried in them, it was entirely owing to the sudden death of his father, and the desperate condition in which he happened to lie himself at that critical juncture.[4]

If Machiavelli reprehends anything in Cesare it is not his character; it is not his ruthlessness, his cruelty, his treachery and rapacity. For all this he has no word of blame. What he blames in him is the only grave error in his political career: the fact that he allowed Julius II, his sworn enemy, to be elected pope after the death of Alexander VI.

There is a story according to which Talleyrand,[5] after the execution of the Duke of Enghien by Napoleon Bonaparte, exclaimed: "C'est plus qu'un crime, c'est une faute!"[6] If this anecdote be true then we must say that Talleyrand spoke as a true disciple of Machiavelli's *Prince*. All judgments of Machiavelli are political and moral judgments. What he thinks to be objectionable and unpardonable in a politician are not his crimes but his mistakes.

That a republican could make the Duca Valentino his hero and model seems to be very strange: for what would have become of the Italian Republics and all their free institutions under a ruler like Cesare Borgia? There are however two reasons that account for this seeming discrepancy in Machiavelli's thought: a general and a par-

2. Idem, Book I, chap. 55.
3. Idem, Book I, chap. 58. [See pp. 112–16 of this Norton Critical Edition —*Editor.*]
4. *The Prince*, chap. 7.
5. Charles Maurice de Talleyrand-

Périgord (1754–1838), the subtlest and most devious diplomat of his day. [*Editor.*]
6. "It is more than a crime, it is a mistake." [*Editor.*]

172 · *Ernst Cassirer*

ticular one. Machiavelli was convinced that all his political thoughts were entirely realistic. Yet when studying his republicanism we find very little of this political realism. His republicanism is much more "academic" than practical; more contemplative than active. Machiavelli had served, sincerely and faithfully, the cause of the city-state of Florence. As a secretary of the state he had combated the Medici. But when the power of the Medici was restored he hoped to retain his post; he made the greatest efforts to make his peace with the new rulers. That is easily understandable. Machiavelli did not swear by the words of any political program. His was not a stern unyielding and uncompromising republicanism. He could readily accept an aristocratic government; for he had never recommended an ochlocracy, a dominion of the populace. It is not without reason, he declares, that the voice of the people has been likened to the voice of God.[7] But on the other hand he is convinced that to give new institutions to a commonwealth, or to reconstruct old institutions on an entirely new basis, must be the work of one man.[8] The multitude is helpless without a head.[9]

Yet if Machiavelli admired the Roman plebs, he had not the same belief in the power of the citizens of a modern state to rule themselves. Unlike many other thinkers of the Renaissance he did not cherish the hope of restoring the life of the ancients. The Roman Republic was founded upon the Roman virtù—and this virtù is lost, once for all. The attempts to resuscitate ancient political life appeared to Machiavelli as idle dreams. His was a sharp, clear, and cool mind; not the mind of a fanatic and enthusiast like Cola di Rienzi. In Italian life of the fifteenth century Machiavelli saw nothing to encourage his republican ideals. As a patriot he felt the strongest sympathies for his fellow citizens, but as a philosopher he judged them very severely; his feeling bordered on contempt. Only in the North he was still able to find some traces of love of freedom and the ancient virtù. The nations of the North, he says, have to a certain degree been saved because they did not learn the manners of the French, the Italians, or the Spaniards—this corruption of the world.[1] This judgment about his own times was irrevocable. Machiavelli did not even admit that it could be questioned by anyone. "I know not," he says,

> whether I may not deserve to be reckoned in the number of those who deceive themselves, if, in these discourses of mine, I render excessive praise to the ancient times of the Romans while I censure our own. And, indeed, were not the excellence which then

7. *Discourses*, Book I, chap. 58. [See pp. 112–16 of this Norton Critical Edition—*Editor*.]
8. Idem, Book I, chap. 9.
9. Idem, Book I, chap. 44.
1. Idem, Book I, chap. 55. "Perchè non

hanno possuto pigliare i costumi, nè franciosi, nè spagnuoli, nè italiani; le quali nazioni tutte insieme sono la corruttela del mondo." [Translated loosely in the text.—*Editor*.]

prevailed and the corruption which prevails now clearer than the sun, I should proceed more guardedly in what I have to say . . . . But since the thing is so plain that everyone sees it, I shall be bold to speak freely all I think, both of old times and of new, in order that the minds of the young who happen to read these my writings may be led to shun modern examples, and be prepared to follow those set by antiquity whenever chance affords the opportunity.[2]

Machiavelli was by no means especially fond of the *principati nuovi*, of the modern tyrannies. He could not fail to see all their defects and evils. Yet under the circumstances and conditions of modern life these evils seemed to him to be unavoidable. There is no doubt that Machiavelli personally would have abhorred most of the measures he recommended to the rulers of the new states. He tells us in so many words that these measures are most cruel expedients, repugnant not merely to every Christian, but to every civilized rule of conduct and such as every man should shun, choosing rather to lead a private life than to be a king on terms so hurtful to mankind. But, as he adds very characteristically, whoever will not keep to the fair path of virtue, must, to maintain himself, enter the path of evil.[3] *Aut Caesar aut nihil*[4]—either to lead a private, harmless and innocuous life, or to enter the political arena, struggle for power, and maintain it by the most ruthless and radical means. There is no choice between these two alternatives.

When speaking of Machiavelli's "immoralism" we must, however, not understand this term in our modern sense. Machiavelli did not judge human actions from a standpoint "beyond good and evil." He had no contempt for morality; but he had very little esteem for men. If he was a skeptic, his skepticism was a human rather than a philosophical skepticism. The best proof of this ineradicable skepticism, of this deep mistrust of human nature, is to be found in his comedy *Mandragola*. This masterpiece of comic literature reveals perhaps more of Machiavelli's judgment about his contemporaries than all his political and historical writings. For his own generation and his own country he saw no hope. And in his *Prince* he tried to inculcate the same conviction of the deep moral perversion of men upon the minds of the rulers of states. This was an integral part of his political wisdom. The first condition for ruling men is to understand man. And we shall never understand him as long as we are suffering from the illusion of his "original goodness." Such a conception may be very humane and benevolent; but in political life it proves to be an absurdity. Those that have written upon civil government lay it down as first principle, says

2. Idem, Book II, Preface.
3. Idem, Book I, chap. 26.
4. "Either Caesar or nothing." [*Editor.*]

Machiavelli, and all historians demonstrate the same, that whoever would found a state, and make proper laws for the government of it, must presuppose that all men are bad by nature, and that they will not fail to show that natural depravity of heart, whenever they have a fair opportunity.[5]

This depravity cannot be cured by laws; it must be cured by force. Laws are, indeed, indispensable for every commonwealth—but a ruler should use other and more convincing arguments. The best foundations of all states, whether new, old, or mixed, says Machiavelli, are good laws and good arms. But since good laws are ineffective without arms, and since, on the other hand, good arms will always give due weight to such laws, I shall here no longer argue about laws but speak about arms.[6] Even the "saints," the religious prophets have always acted according to this principle as soon as they became rulers of states. Without this they were lost from the very beginning. Savonarola failed to attain his end, because he had neither power to keep those steady in their persuasion who acknowledged his mission nor to make others believe who denied it. Hence it comes that all the prophets who were supported by an armed force succeeded in their undertakings, whereas those that had not such a force to rely on were defeated and destroyed.[7]

Of course Machiavelli prefers by far the good, the wise, and noble rulers to the bad and cruel ones; he prefers a Marcus Aurelius to a Nero. Yet if you write a book that is destined solely for these good and just rulers, the book itself may be excellent but it will not find many readers. Princes of this kind are the exception, not the rule. Everyone admits how praiseworthy it is in a prince to keep faith, and to live with integrity. Nevertheless, as matters stand, a prince has also to learn the opposite art: the art of craft and treachery.

A prince ought to know how to resemble a beast as well as a man, upon occasion: and this is obscurely hinted to us by ancient writers who relate that Achilles and several other princes in former times were sent to be educated by Chiron the Centaur; that as their preceptor was half-man and half-beast, they might be taught to imitate both natures since one cannot long support itself without the other. Now, because it is so necessary for a prince to learn how to act the part of a beast sometimes, he should make the lion and the fox his patterns: for the lion has not cunning enough of himself to keep out of snares and toils; nor the fox sufficient strength to cope with a wolf: so that he must be a fox to enable him to find out the snares, and a lion in order to terrify the wolves.[8]

5. Idem, Book I, chap. 3.
6. *The Prince*, chap. 12.

7. Idem, chap. 6.
8. Idem, chap. 18.

This famous simile is highly characteristic and illuminating. Machiavelli did not mean to say that a teacher of princes should be a brute. Yet he has to do with brutal things and must not recoil from seeing them eye to eye and from calling them by their right names. Humanity alone will never do in politics. Even at its best politics still remains an intermediary between humanity and bestiality. The teacher of politics must therefore understand both things: he must be half man, half beast.

No political writer before Machiavelli had ever spoken in this way. Here we find the clear, the unmistakable and ineffaceable difference between his theory and that of all his precursors—the classical as well as the medieval authors. Pascal says that there are certain words which, suddenly and unexpectedly, make clear the sense of a whole book. Once we meet with these words we no longer can have any doubt about the character of the book: all ambiguity is removed. Machiavelli's saying that a teacher of princes must be *un mezzo bestia e mezzo uomo*[9] is of such a kind: it reveals, as in a sudden flash, the nature and purpose of his political theory. No one had ever doubted that political *life*, as matters stand, is full of crimes, treacheries, and felonies. But no thinker before Machiavelli had undertaken to teach the *art* of these crimes. These things were done, but they were not taught. That Machiavelli promised to become a teacher in the art of craft, perfidy, and cruelty was a thing unheard of. And he was very thorough in his teaching. He did not hesitate or compromise. He tells the ruler that since cruelties are necessary they should be done quickly and mercilessly. In this case, and in this case alone, they will have the desired effect: they will prove to be *crudeltà bene usate*.[1] It is no use postponing or mitigating a cruel measure; it must be done at one blow and regardless of all human feelings. A usurper who has won the throne must not allow any other man or woman to stand in his way; he must extirpate the whole family of the legitimate ruler.[2] All these things may be called shameful; but in political life we cannot draw a sharp line between "virtue" and "vice." The two things often change places: if everything is considered we shall find that some things that seem to be very virtuous, if they are turned into actions, will be ruinous to the prince, whereas others that are regarded as vicious are beneficial.[3] In politics all things change their place: fair is foul, and foul is fair.

It is true that there are some modern students of Machiavelli

9. "Half beast, half man." [*Editor.*]
1. "Cruelties well used." [*Editor.*]
2. *Discourses*, Bk. III, chaps. 4, 30; cf. *The Prince*, chap. 3: "a possederli sicuramente basta avere spenta la linea del principe che li dominava." ["To hold them securely it suffices to have wiped out the line of the prince who used to rule them."—*Editor.*]
3. *The Prince*, chap. 15.

who see his work in quite a different light. They tell us that this work was by no means a radical innovation. It was, after all, a rather commonplace thing; it belonged to a familiar literary type. *The Prince*, these writers assure us, is only one of the innumerable books that, under various titles, had been written for the instruction of kings. Medieval and Renaissance literatures were full of these treatises. Between the years 800 and 1700 there were accessible some thousand books telling the king how to conduct himself so that he may be "clear in his great office." Everyone knew and read these works: *De officio regis, De institutione principum, De regimine principum.* Machiavelli simply added a new link to this long list. His book is by no means *sui generis;*[4] it was rather a typical book. There is no real novelty in *The Prince*—neither a novelty of thought nor a novelty of style.[5]

Against this judgment we can, however, appeal to two witnesses: to the witness of Machiavelli himself and to that of his readers. Machiavelli was deeply convinced of the originality of his political views. "Prompted by that desire which nature has implanted in me fearlessly to undertake whatsoever I think offers a common benefit to all," he wrote in the Preface to his *Discourses*, "I enter on a path which, being untrodden by any though it involve me in trouble, may yet win me thanks from those who judge my efforts in a friendly spirit."[6] This hope was not disappointed: Machiavelli's readers judged likewise. His work was read not only by scholars or by students of politics. It had a much wider circulation. There is hardly one of the great modern politicians who did not know Machiavelli's book and who was not fascinated by it. Among its readers and admirers we find the names of Catarina de' Medici, Charles V, Richelieu, Queen Christina of Sweden, Napoleon Bonaparte. To those readers the book was much more than a book; it was a guide and lodestar in their political actions. Such a deep and permanent influence of *The Prince* would hardly be understandable if the book were only a specimen of a well-known literary type. Napoleon Bonaparte declared that of all political works those of Machiavelli were the only ones worth reading. Can we think of a Richelieu, a Catarina de' Medici, a Napoleon Bonaparte as enthusiastic students of works such as Thomas Aquinas' *De regimine principum*, Erasmus' *Institutio principis Christiani* or Fénélon's *Télémaque*?

In order to show the striking contrast between *The Prince* and all the other works *De regimine principum* we need, however, not rely

4. "Unique." [*Editor.*]
5. See Allan H. Gilbert, *Machiavelli's "Prince" and Its Forerunners. "The Prince" as a Typical Book "de Regimine Principum"* (Duke University Press, 1938).
6. See above, p. 94. [*Editor.*]

on personal judgments. There are other and better reasons to prove that there is a real gulf between Machiavelli's views and those of all previous political writers. Of course *The Prince* had its forerunners; what book has not? We may find in it many parallels to other writers. In Burd's edition most of these parallels have been carefully collected and annotated. But literary parallels do not necessarily prove parallels of thought. *The Prince* belongs to a "climate of opinion" quite different from that of previous writers on the subject. The difference may be described in two words. The traditional treatises *De rege et regimine, De institutione regis, De regno et regis institutione* were *pedagogical* treatises. They were destined for the education of princes. Machiavelli had neither the ambition nor the hope of being equal to this task. His book was concerned with quite different problems. It only tells the prince how to acquire his power and how, under difficult circumstances, to maintain it. Machiavelli was not naïve enough to assume that the rulers of the *principati nuovi,* that men like Cesare Borgia, were apt subjects for "education." In earlier and later books that called themselves *The King's Mirror* the monarch was supposed to see, as in a mirror, his fundamental duties and obligations. But where do we find such a thing in Machiavelli's *Prince?* The very term "duty" seems to be missing in his book.

The Technique of Politics

Yet if *The Prince* is anything but a moral or pedagogical treatise, it does not follow that, for this reason, it is an immoral book. Both judgments are equally wrong. *The Prince* is neither a moral nor an immoral book: it is simply a technical book. In a technical book we do not seek for rules of ethical conduct, of good and evil. It is enough if we are told what is useful or useless. Every word in *The Prince* must be read and interpreted in this way. The book contains no moral prescripts for the ruler nor does it invite him to commit crimes and villainies. It is especially concerned with and destined for the "new principalities." It tries to give them all the advice necessary for protecting themselves from all danger. These dangers are obviously much greater than those which threaten the ordinary states—the ecclesiastic principalities or the hereditary monarchies. In order to avoid them the ruler must take recourse to extraordinary means. But it is too late to seek for remedies after the evil has already attacked the body politic. Machiavelli likes to compare the art of the politician with that of a skilled physician. Medical art contains three parts: diagnosis, prognosis, and therapy. Of these a sound diagnosis is the most important task. The principal thing is to recognize the illness at the right moment in order to be able to make provision against its consequences. If this attempt fails the case becomes hopeless. "The physicians," says Machiavelli,

> say of hectic fevers, that it is no hard task to get the better of them in their beginning, but difficult to discover them: yet in course of time, when they have not been properly treated and distinguished, they are easily discovered, but difficult to be subdued. So it happens in political bodies; for when the evils and disturbances that may probably arise in any government are foreseen, which yet can only be done by a sagacious and provident man, it is easy to ward them off; but if they are suffered to sprout up and grow to such a height that their malignity is obvious to every one, there is seldom any remedy to be found of sufficient efficacy to repress them.[7]

All the advice of Machiavelli is to be interpreted in this spirit. He foresees the possible dangers that threaten the different forms of government and provides for them. He tells the ruler what he has to do in order to establish and to maintain his power, to avoid inner discords, to foresee and prevent conspiracies. All these counsels are "hypothetical imperatives," or to put it in the words of Kant, "imperatives of skill." "Here," says Kant, "there is no question whether the end is rational and good, but only what one must do in order to attain it. The precepts for the physician to make his patient thoroughly healthy, and for a poisoner to ensure certain death, are of equal value in this respect, that each serves to effect its purpose perfectly."[8] These words describe exactly the attitude and method of Machiavelli. He never blames or praises political actions; he simply gives a descriptive analysis of them—in the same way in which a physician describes the symptoms of a certain illness. In such an analysis we are only concerned with the truth of the description not with the things spoken of. Even of the worst things a correct and excellent description can be given. Machiavelli studied political actions in the same way as a chemist studies chemical reactions. Assuredly a chemist who prepares in his laboratory a strong poison is not responsible for its effects. In the hands of a skilled physician the poison may save the life of man—in the hands of a murderer it may kill. In both cases we cannot praise or blame the chemist. He has done enough if he has taught us all the processes that are required for preparing the poison and if he has given us its chemical formula. Machiavelli's *Prince* contains many dangerous and poisonous things, but he looks at them with the coolness and indifference of a scientist. He gives his political prescriptions. By

7. *The Prince*, chap. 3.
8. See Kant, *Fundamental Principles of the Metaphysics of Morals.* English trans. by T. K. Abbott, *Kant's Critique of Practical Reason and Other Works on the Theory of Ethics* (6th ed. New York and London, Longmans, Green & Co., 1927), p. 32.

whom these prescriptions will be used and whether they will be used for a good or evil purpose is no concern of his.

What Machiavelli wished to introduce was not only a new science but a new *art* of politics. He was the first modern author who spoke of the "art of the state." It is true that the idea of such an art was very old. But Machiavelli gave to this old idea an entirely new interpretation. From the times of Plato all great political thinkers had emphasized that politics cannot be regarded as mere routine work. There must be definite rules to guide our political actions; there must be an art (*technē*) of politics. In his dialogue *Gorgias* Plato opposed his own theory of the state to the views of the sophists—of Protagoras, Prodikos, Gorgias. These men, he declared, have given us many rules for our political conduct. But all these rules have no philosophical purport and value because they fail to see the principal point. They are abstracted from special cases and concerned with particular purposes. They lack the essential character of a technē—the character of universality. Here we grasp the essential and ineradicable difference between Plato's technē and Machiavelli's *arte dello Stato*.[9] Plato's technē is not "art" in Machiavelli's sense; it is knowledge (*epistēmē*) based on universal principles. These principles are not only theoretical but practical, not only logical but ethical. Without an insight into these principles no one can be a true statesman. A man may think himself to be an expert in all problems of political life, because he has, by long experience, formed right opinions about political things. But this does not make him a real ruler; and it does not enable him to give a firm judgment, because he has no "understanding of the cause."[1]

Plato and his followers had tried to give a theory of the *Legal* State; Machiavelli was the first to introduce a theory that suppressed or minimized this specific feature. His art of politics was destined and equally fit for the illegal and for the legal state. The sun of his political wisdom shines upon both legitimate princes and usurpers or tyrants, on just and unjust rulers. He gave his counsel in affairs of state to all of them, liberally and profusely. We need not blame him for this attitude. If we wish to compress *The Prince* into a short formula we could perhaps do no better than to point to the words of a great historian of the nineteenth century. In the introduction to his *History of English Literature* Hippolyte Taine declares that the historian should speak of human actions in the same way as a chemist speaks of different chemical compounds. Vice and virtue are products like vitriol or sugar and we should deal with them in the same cool and detached scientific spirit. That was exactly the method of Machiavelli. To be sure he had his personal

9. "Art of the State." [*Editor.*]   1. See Plato, *Republic*, 533B.

feelings, his political ideals, his national aspirations. But he did not allow these things to affect his political judgment. His judgment was that of a scientist and a technician of political life. If we read *The Prince* otherwise, if we regard it as the work of a political propagandist, we lose the gist of the whole matter.

LEO STRAUSS

[Machiavelli the Immoralist] †

We shall not shock anyone, we shall merely expose ourselves to good-natured or at any rate harmless ridicule, if we profess ourselves inclined to the old-fashioned and simple opinion according to which Machiavelli was a teacher of evil. Indeed, what other description would fit a man who teaches lessons like these: princes ought to exterminate the families of rulers whose territory they wish to possess securely; princes ought to murder their opponents rather than to confiscate their property since those who have been robbed, but not those who are dead, can think of revenge; men forget the murder of their fathers sooner than the loss of their patrimony; true liberality consists in being stingy with one's own property and in being generous with what belongs to others; not virtue but the prudent use of virtue and vice leads to happiness; injuries ought all to be done together so that, being tasted less, they will hurt less, while benefits ought to be conferred little by little, so that they will be felt more strongly; a victorious general who fears that his prince might not reward him properly, may punish him for his anticipated ingratitude by raising the flag of rebellion; if one has to choose between inflicting severe injuries and inflicting light injuries, one ought to inflict severe injuries; one ought not to say to someone whom one wants to kill "Give me your gun, I want to kill you with it," but merely, "Give me your gun," for once you have the gun in your hand, you can satisfy your desire. If it is true that only an evil man will stoop to teach maxims of public and private gangsterism, we are forced to say that Machiavelli was an evil man.

Machiavelli was indeed not the first man to express opinions like those mentioned. Such opinions belong to a way of political thinking and political acting which is as old as political society itself. But Machiavelli is the only philosopher who has lent the weight of his name to any way of political thinking and political acting which is as old as political society itself, so much so that his name is commonly used for designating such a way. He is notorious as the clas-

†This is the introduction to Professor Strauss's *Thoughts on Machiavelli* (Glen- coe, Ill.: The Free Press, 1958).

sic of the evil way of political thinking and political acting. Callicles and Thrasymachus, who set forth the evil doctrine behind closed doors, are Platonic characters, and the Athenian ambassadors, who state the same doctrine on the island of Melos in the absence of the common people, are Thucydidean characters. Machiavelli proclaims openly and triumphantly a corrupting doctrine which ancient writers had taught covertly or with all signs of repugnance. He says in his own name shocking things which ancient writers had said through the mouths of their characters.[1] Machiavelli alone has dared to utter the evil doctrine in a book and in his own name.

Yet however true the old-fashioned and simple verdict may be, it is not exhaustive. Its deficiency justifies to some extent the more sophisticated views which are set forth by the learned of our age. Machiavelli, we are told, was so far from being an evil teacher of evil that he was a passionate patriot or a scientific student of society or both. But one may wonder whether the up-to-date scholars do not err much more grievously than the old-fashioned and simple, or whether what escapes the up-to-date scholars is not much more important than what escapes the simple and the old-fashioned, although it may be true that the one thing needful which is ignored by the sophisticated is inadequately articulated and therefore misinterpreted by the men of noble simplicity. It would not be the only case in which "a little philosophy"[2] generates prodigious errors to which the unphilosophic multitude is immune.

It is misleading to describe the thinker Machiavelli as a patriot. He is a patriot of a particular kind: he is more concerned with the salvation of his fatherland than with the salvation of his soul. His patriotism therefore presupposes a comprehensive reflection regarding the status of the fatherland on the one hand and of the soul on the other. This comprehensive reflection, and not patriotism, is the core of Machiavelli's thought. This comprehensive reflection, and not his patriotism, established his fame and made him the teacher of many men in all countries. The substance of his thought is not Florentine, or even Italian, but universal. It concerns, and it is meant to concern, all thinking men regardless of time and place. To speak of Machiavelli as a scientist is at least as misleading as to speak of him as a patriot. The scientific student of society is unwilling or unable to pass "value-judgments," but Machiavelli's works abound with "value-judgments." His study of society is normative.

But even if we were forced to grant that Machiavelli was essentially a patriot or a scientist, we would not be forced to deny that he was a teacher of evil. Patriotism as Machiavelli understood it is collective selfishness. The indifference to the distinction between

1. *Prince*, chaps. 17 (Dido) and 18   2. Bacon, *Essays* ("Of Atheism").
(Chiron).

right and wrong which springs from devotion to one's country is less repulsive than the indifference to that distinction which springs from exclusive preoccupation with one's own ease or glory. But precisely for this reason it is more seductive and therefore more dangerous. Patriotism is a kind of love of one's own. Love of one's own is inferior to love of what is both one's own and good. Love of one's own tends therefore to become concerned with one's own being good or complying with the demands of right. To justify Machiavelli's terrible counsels by having recourse to his patriotism, means to see the virtues of that patriotism while being blind to that which is higher than patriotism, or to that which both hallows and limits patriotism. In referring to Machiavelli's patriotism one does not dispose of a mere semblance of evil; one merely obscures something truly evil.

As regards the "scientific" approach to society which many of its adherents trace to Machiavelli, it emerges through the abstraction from the moral distinctions by which we take our bearings as citizens and as men. The indispensable condition of "scientific" analysis is then moral obtuseness. That obtuseness is not identical with depravity, but it is bound to strengthen the forces of depravity. In the case of lesser men, one can safely trace such obtuseness to the absence of certain intellectual virtues. This charitable explanation could not be tolerated in the case of Machiavelli, who was too thoughtful not to know what he was doing and too generous not to admit it to his reasonable friends.

We do not hesitate to assert, as very many have asserted before us, and we shall later on try to prove, that Machiavelli's teaching is immoral and irreligious. We are familiar with the evidence which scholars adduce in support of the contrary assertion; but we question their interpretation of the evidence. To say nothing of certain other considerations, it seems to us that the scholars in question are too easily satisfied. They are satisfied that Machiavelli was a friend of religion because he stressed the useful and the indispensable character of religion. They do not pay any attention to the fact that his praise of religion is only the reverse side of what one might provisionally call his complete indifference to the truth of religion. This is not surprising since they themselves are likely to understand by religion nothing other than a significant sector of society, if not an attractive or at any rate innocuous piece of folklore, to say nothing of those sincerely religious people who are gratified by any apparent benefit conferred upon religion. They misinterpret Machiavelli's judgment concerning religion, and likewise his judgment concerning morality, because they are pupils of Machiavelli. Their seemingly open-minded study of Machiavelli's thought is based on the dogmatic acceptance of his principles. They do not see the evil character of his thought because they are the heirs of the Machiavellian tradition; because they, or the forgotten teachers of their teachers, have been corrupted by Machiavelli.

One cannot see the true character of Machiavelli's thought unless one frees himself from Machiavelli's influence. For all practical purposes this means that one cannot see the true character of Machiavelli's thought unless one recovers for himself and in himself the pre-modern heritage of the western world, both Biblical and classical. To do justice to Machiavelli requires one to look forward from a pre-modern point of view toward an altogether unexpected and surprising Machiavelli who is new and strange, rather than to look backward from today toward a Machiavelli who has become old and our own, and therewith almost good. This procedure is required even for a purely historical understanding. Machiavelli did know pre-modern thought: it was before him. He could not have known the thought of the present time, which emerged as it were behind his back.

We thus regard the simple opinion about Machiavelli as indeed decisively superior to the prevailing sophisticated views, though still insufficient. Even if, and precisely if we are forced to grant that his teaching is diabolical and he himself a devil, we are forced to remember the profound theological truth that the devil is a fallen angel. To recognize the diabolical character of Machiavelli's thought would mean to recognize in it a perverted nobility of a very high order. That nobility was discerned by Marlowe, as he ascribed to Machiavelli the words "I hold there is no sin but ignorance." Marlowe's judgment is borne out by what Machiavelli himself, in the Epistles Dedicatory to his two great books, indicates regarding his most precious possession. We are in sympathy with the simple opinion about Machiavelli, not only because it is wholesome, but above all because a failure to take that opinion seriously prevents one from doing justice to what is truly admirable in Machiavelli: the intrepidity of his thought, the grandeur of his vision, and the graceful subtlety of his speech. Not the contempt for the simple opinion, nor the disregard of it, but the considerate ascent from it leads to the core of Machiavelli's thought. There is no surer protection against the understanding of anything than taking for granted or otherwise despising the obvious and the surface. The problem inherent in the surface of things, and only in the surface of things, is the heart of things.

There are good reasons for dealing with Machiavelli in a series of Walgreen lectures. The United States of America may be said to be the only country in the world which was founded in explicit opposition to Machiavellian principles. According to Machiavelli, the founder of the most renowned commonwealth of the world was a fratricide: the foundation of political greatness is necessarily laid in crime. If we can believe Thomas Paine, all governments of the Old World have an origin of this description; their origin was conquest and tyranny. But "the Independence of America [was] accompanied by a Revolution in the principles and practice of Governments": the foundation of the United States was laid in freedom and justice. "Government founded on a moral theory, on a system of universal peace, on the indefeasible hereditary Rights of Man, is now revolving from west to east by a stronger impulse than the Government of the sword revolved from east to west."[3] This judgment is far from being obsolete. While freedom is no longer a preserve of the United States, the United States is now the bulwark of freedom. And contemporary tyranny has its roots in Machiavelli's thought, in the Machiavellian principle that the good end justifies every means. At least to the extent that the American reality is inseparable from the American aspiration, one cannot understand Americanism without understanding Machiavellianism which is its opposite.

But we cannot conceal from ourselves the fact that the problem is more complex than it appears in the presentation by Paine and his followers. Machiavelli would argue that America owes her greatness not only to her habitual adherence to the principles of freedom and justice, but also to her occasional deviation from them. He would not hesitate to suggest a mischievous interpretation of the Louisiana Purchase[4] and of the fate of the Red Indians. He would conclude that facts like these are an additional proof for his contention that there cannot be a great and glorious society without the equivalent of the murder of Remus by his brother Romulus. This complication makes it all the more necessary that we should try to reach an adequate understanding of the fundamental issue raised by Machiavelli.

We may seem to have assumed that Machiavelli is the classic exponent of one of the two fundamental alternatives of political thought. We did assume that there are fundamental alternatives, alternatives which are permanent or coeval with man. This assumption is frequently denied today. Many of our contemporaries are of the opinion that there are no permanent problems and hence no permanent alternatives. They would argue that precisely Machiavelli's teaching offers ample proof for their denial of the existence of permanent problems: Machiavelli's problem is a novel problem; it is fundamentally different from the problem with which earlier political philosophy was concerned. This argument, properly elaborated, has some weight. But stated baldly, it proves merely that the perma-

3. *Rights of Man*, Part the Second, Introduction.
4. Cf. Henry Adams, *The First Adminis-* *tration of Thomas Jefferson* (New York, 1898) II, 56, 71–73, 254.

nent problems are not as easily accessible as some people believe, or that not all political philosophers face the permanent problems. Our critical study of Machiavelli's teaching can ultimately have no other purpose than to contribute towards the recovery of the permanent problems.

SHELDON S. WOLIN

[The Economy of Violence]†

While there had been few political theorists before Machiavelli who would have contested the elementary proposition that "security for man is impossible unless it be conjoined with power,"[1] there had been still fewer prepared to declare power the dominant mark of the state. Indeed, it has been and remains one of the abiding concerns of the Western political theorist to weave ingenious veils of euphemism to conceal the ugly fact of violence. At times he has talked too sonorously of "authority," "justice," and "law," as though these honorific expressions alone could transform coercion into simple restraint. True, the psychological impact of power is softened and depersonalized if it is made to appear the agent of an objective good. True, too, there are numerous and subtle forms of coercion that shade off from the extreme of violence. That the application of violence is regarded as abnormal represents a significant achievement of the Western political tradition, yet if it is accepted too casually it may lead to neglect of the primordial fact that the hard core of power is violence and to exercise power is often to bring violence to bear on someone else's person or possessions. Writers before Machiavelli cannot be accused of having ignored power. The classical and mediaeval theorists had spoken long and eloquently of its brutalizing and corrupting effects on those who were called to exercise it. They rarely faced up, however, to the problem of the cumulative effect on society of the consistent application of coercion and the not infrequent use of violence. This evasion had come about largely because attention to power had arisen primarily in connection with the establishment or reform of a political system. It had been assumed that once affairs were set in motion along the prescribed paths, once proper education, the spread of knowledge or of faith, the improvement of social morality, and all of the other pressures flowing from a rightly ordered envi-

†From *The Politics of Vision* (Boston: Little, Brown, 1960), pp. 220–35. Some of Professor Wolin's copious and informative notes have been omitted or curtailed.

1. *Discourses*, I, 1; *History*, II, 2. [Throughout Professor Wolin's notes, "*History*" refers to Machiavelli's *Florentine History.—Editor*.]

ronment had begun to operate, there would be progressively less need for the systematic application of force. Nor is it easy to see in what ways the modern political theorist has illumined the problem by the focal concepts of "decision-making," "the political process," and "who gets what, when, and how." All that can be said with confidence is that euphemisms for power and violence have not been dispelled by positivism.

With Machiavelli the euphemisms were cast aside and the state was directly confronted as an aggregate of power. Its profile was that of violence. Machiavelli believed that the vitalities of politics could not be controlled and directed without the application of force and the threat at least of violence. This conclusion was sustained partly by a certain scepticism about what Yeats once called "the profane perfection of mankind." It was also the outcome of a conviction about the inherent instability of the political world which could be combated, and then only partially, by resolute action. Equally important, however, in making power and violence urgent matters was the nature of the context in which power was exerted: the tightly-packed condition of political space which mocked any merely verbal attempt at translating power into simple direction or supervision of the affairs of society. Inevitably the role of the political actor was to dispense violence. This was most sharply defined in the case of the ruler who, after seizing power, was compelled "to organize everything in that state afresh."[2] "The new prince, above all other princes, cannot possibly avoid the name of cruel."[3] Even when the political actor was not faced with the task of creating a *tabula rasa*, he could not avoid inflicting injuries on some one. He must act while hemmed in by vested interests and expectations, privileges and rights, ambitions and hopes, all demanding preferential access to a limited number of goods.

If this were the nature of political action, what has been called an obsession with power on Machiavelli's part might be better described as his conviction that the "new way" could make no greater contribution than to create an economy of violence, a science of the controlled application of force. The task of such a science would be to preserve the distinguishing line between political creativity and destruction. "For it is the man who uses violence to spoil things, not the man who uses it to mend them, that is blameworthy."[4] The control of violence was dependent upon the new science's being able to administer the precise dosage appropriate to specific situations. In corrupt societies, for example, violence represented the only means of arresting decadence, a brief but severe shock treatment to restore the civic consciousness of the

2. *Discourses*, I, 26.
3. *Prince*, XVII.

4. *Discourses*, I, 9.

citizenry.[5] In other situations there might well be a diminishing need for extreme actions; men could be managed by playing on their fears, by using the threat rather than the actuality of coercion. But every application had to be considered judiciously, because the indiscriminate exercise of force and the constant revival of fear could provoke the greatest of all dangers for any government, the kind of widespread apprehension and hatred which drove men to desperation. The true test of whether violence had been rightly used was whether cruelties increased or decreased over time.[6]

This preoccupation with economy was manifest also in Machiavelli's discussion of the external forms of violence—war, imperialism, and colonialism. One of the basic aims of the *Art of War* was to demonstrate that, while military action remained an unavoidable fact of the political condition, its costliness could be reduced by proper attention to strategy, discipline, and organization. *The Prince* and *The Discourses* followed the same theme of economy with counsels like these: a prince ought carefully to consider his resources, because, while a war may be started out of whim, it could not be as easily stopped; an unreliable army was an inefficient instrument of violence because it multiplied devastation without any of the compensations of victory; to avoid a necessary war was costly, but to prolong it was equally prodigal; a prince who found his position weakened by a victory had overestimated his power resources.[7]

In the matter of imperialism Machiavelli adverted to the example of Rome for the significant reason that Roman imperial policy had sought to preserve the wealth of the subject populations and their native institutions, thereby limiting the cost in devastation for both conqueror and conquered. If imperialism were handled efficiently the destructive consequences could be minimized, and the whole transaction reduced to a mere change in power.[8] In contrast to Rome's controlled use of violence were those destructive wars which had been compelled by necessities, such as hunger, plague, or overpopulation.[9] Necessity was the enemy of calculated violence.

While Machiavelli's economy of violence subsumed both domestic and external actions, it never seriously entertained the proposition that the incidence of force could be appreciably lessened in international politics. The effects of violence might be controlled, but the resort to it would not diminish. He saw quite clearly that

5. Ibid., III, 22. Yet there were also societies which had become so corrupt as to be beyond redemption. Here power was unavailing. *Discourses*, I, 16.
6. *Prince*, VIII; *Discourses*, I, 45; III, 6. In *Prince* XIX there was a significant contrast drawn between the degree and kind of violence needed to establish a new state, as exemplified by Severus, with that needed to maintain a state, as in the case of Marcus. Only the latter is called truly glorious by Machiavelli.
7. *Discourses*, II, 10; III, 32; *History*, VI, I.
8. *Discourses*, II, 6, 21, 32.
9. Ibid., II, 7.

the absence of arbitrating arrangements, such as law and institutional procedure, left the international field more exposed than the domestic to conflicts of interest and the drives of ambition.[1] On the other hand, he believed that the internal politics of society could be structured by a variety of methods aimed at minimizing the need for extreme acts of repression. The importance of law, political institutions, and habits of civility was that in regularizing human behavior they helped to reduce the number of instances in which force and fear had to be applied.

Machiavelli's most important insight into the problem of internal power politics came when he began to explore the implications of a political system based on the active support of its members. He grasped the fact that popular consent represented a form of social power which, if properly exploited, reduced the amount of violence directed at society as a whole. One reason for the superiority of the republican system consisted in its being maintained by the force of the populace, rather than by force over the populace.[2] The economy of force which resulted from the people's feeling a sense of common involvement with the political order made it in the interests of the prince to cultivate their support. Lacking this, he would have to draw on his own fund of violence and the eventual result would be "abnormal measures" of repression. "The greater his cruelty, the weaker does his regime become."[3] Far from limiting his initiative, popular approval could be utilized to depreciate the great cost in violence of radical reforms. In a revolution by consent (*commune consenso*), only the few had to be harmed.[4]

In evaluating Machiavelli's economy of violence it is easy to criticize it as being the product of a technician's admiration for efficient means. A century like ours, which has witnessed the unparalleled efficiency displayed by totalitarian regimes in the use of terror and coercion, experiences difficulty in being tolerant on the subject. Yet to see Machiavelli as the philosopher of Himmlerism would be quite misleading; and the basic reason is not alone that Machiavelli regarded the science of violence as the means for reducing the amount of suffering in the political condition, but that he was clearly aware of the dangers of entrusting its use to the morally obtuse. What he hoped to further by his economy of violence was the "pure" use of power, undefiled by pride, ambition, or motives of petty revenge.[5] A more meaningful contrast to Machiavelli would be the great modern theoretician of violence, Georges Sorel. Here is a true example of the irresponsible political intellectual, fired by romantic notions of heroism, preaching the use of violence

1. See the working-paper of Machiavelli reproduced in Machiavel, *Toutes les lettres*, ed. E. Barincou, 2 vols., 6th ed. (Paris: Gallimard, 1955), Vol. I, p. 311.

2. *Discourses*, I, 9.
3. Ibid., I, 16.
4. Ibid., III, 7.
5. Ibid., II, 20; III, 8.

for ends which are deliberately and proudly clothed in the vague outline of the irrational "myth," contemptuous of the cost, blinded by a vision of virile proletarian barbarians who would revitalize the decadent West.[6] In contrast, there was no hint of child-like delight when Machiavelli contemplated the barbarous and savage destructiveness of the new prince, sweeping away the settled arrangements of society and "leaving nothing intact." There was, however, the laconic remark that it was better to be a private citizen than to embark on a career which involved the ruin of men.[7] This suggests that the theorist like Machiavelli, who was aware of the limited efficacy of force and who devoted himself to showing how its technique could be used more efficiently, was far more sensitive to the moral dilemmas of politics and far more committed to the preservation of man than those theorists who, saturated with moral indignation and eager for heroic regeneration, preach purification by the holy flame of violence.

* * * In most commentaries, Machiavelli's prince has emerged as the heroic ego incarnate, exhilarated by the challenges of political combat, unencumbered by moral scruples, and utterly devoid of any tragic sense of the impermanence of his own mission. In the preceding pages we have deliberately used the term "political actor" instead of "prince" or "ruler" to suggest that if the prince is looked upon as a kind of actor, playing many roles and wearing many masks, we may then better see that Machiavelli has given us something more than a single-dimensional portrait of a power-hungry figure. What we have is a portrait of modern political man drawn with dramatic intensity: if there was heroism, there was also anguish; if there was creativity, there was also loneliness and uncertainty.

These overtones were part of the new setting in which political action occurred. Machiavelli's actor was, to borrow a phrase from Merleau-Ponty, "*l'expression d'un monde disloqué.*"[8] He performed in a universe hushed in moral stillness: there were no prefigured meanings, no implicit teleology—"it looks as if the world were become effeminate and as if heaven were powerless"[9]—and no comforting backdrop of a political cosmos, ruled by a divine monarch and offering a pattern for earthly rulers. Yet by his vocation, political man was compelled to act, to affirm his existence as a thoroughly politicized creature. To be committed to political action meant surrendering the multiple dimensions of life, and concentrating exclusively on the single dimension of politics.

6. *Réflexions sur la violence*, 10th ed. (Paris, 1946), pp. 120–122, 168, 173–174, 202, 273.
7. *Discourses*, I, 26.
8. "The expression of a dislocated world." [*Editor.*] Maurice Merleau-Ponty, *Humanisme et terreur*, 8th ed. (Paris: Gallimard, 1947), p. 205.
9. *Discourses*, II, 2.

By the nature of his situation political man must be an actor, for he addresses himself not to a single political condition, but to a variety of political conditions. Circumstances change, the conjunction of political factors follows a shifting pattern, hence the successful political actor cannot afford a consistent and uniform character. He must constantly rediscover his identity in the role cast for him by the changing times.[1] The mercurial quality of Machiavelli's political actor stands in sharp contrast to the classical and mediaeval conception of the character of the good ruler. The older writers had viewed political knowledge as enabling men to establish stable situations, points of fixity within which ethical behavior became possible. Towards this end, they emphasized the importance of training men's characters so that virtue, for example, would be an habitual disposition towards the good.[2] For this reason classical and mediaeval writers tended to be suspicious of "prudence" and rarely ranked it among the supreme virtues.[3] Prudence implied a character which reacted too glibly to changing conditions.

Machiavelli's criticism of traditional moral theory was not, as has often been supposed, founded on cynicism or amorality. Nor is the more valid contention, that he was intent on divorcing the norms of political conduct from those governing private relationships, fully correct. Instead his concern was, first, to indicate the situations where political action ought to conform to the standards commonly applied to private conduct. Thus when a government operated within a stable, secure environment it ought to follow the accepted virtues such as compassion, good faith, honesty, humaneness and religion. Under these circumstances public and private ethics were identical.[4] But Machiavelli's second concern was to point out that, because most political situations were unstable and subject to to flux, "a commonwealth and a people is governed in a different way from a private individual."[5] To adopt the rules of accepted morality was to bind one's behavior by a set of consistent habits. But rigidities in behavior were not suited to the vagaries of an inconsistent world. Moreover, to act uniformly merely armed one's opponents with a foreknowledge of your probable reactions to a given situation.[6] There was the further difficulty that one must act in a world where the other actors did not follow the same code.[7] To be sure, a similar issue arose in private relationships when other men did not honor the same moral usages, yet the cases were different because the responsibilities were different: in the one the indi-

1. *Prince*, XV; XVIII; *Discourses*, III, 9; Letter to Soderini (1513 ?), *Toutes les lettres*, vol. II, 327.
2. Aristotle, *Politics*, 1332 b; 1337 a 11; see Aquinas: "Justice is a habit (*habitus*), whereby a man renders to each one his due with constant and perpetual will." *Summa Theologiae*, II, II, Q. 58, art. 1.
3. An important exception is the recognition by Aquinas of a distinctively political form of prudence.
4. *Prince*, XV; XVIII.
5. Cited in *Il Principe* by Burd, p. 290 fn.
6. *Prince*, XV.
7. Ibid., XVIII.

vidual suffered for being a moral man in an immoral society, while in the other a whole society might be injured because of the moral scruples of the ruler.[8]

But if politics posed issues for which common morality was inadequate, it did not follow that there was no connection between political action and traditional moral dictates. In the first place, it was difficult to govern a society and gain support if all of the ruler's actions violated the moral usages cherished by society. As a political actor, the ruler must be a "skilful pretender and dissembler," he must "seem" to have the virtues of good faith, charity, humanity, and religion. This was part of his mastery in the art of illusions. "Men are so simple and so subject to present needs that he who deceives in this way will always find those who will let themselves be deceived."[9]

The basic question, however, was whether Machiavelli believed morality to be nothing more than a useful factor in political manipulation. Did morality constitute a set of restraints or merely a datum for successful action? Machiavelli's own words are so crucial that they deserve to be quoted at length:

> I will even venture to say that [the virtues] damage a prince who *possesses them and always observes them*, but if he seems to have them they are useful. I mean that he should seem compassionate, trustworthy, humane, honest, and religious, and *actually be so*; but yet he should have his mind so trained that, when it is necessary not to practice these virtues, he can change to the opposite and do it skilfully. It is to be understood that a prince, especially a new prince, cannot observe all the things because of which men are considered good, because he is often obliged, if he wishes to maintain his government, to act contrary to faith, contrary to charity, contrary to humanity, contrary to religion. It is therefore necessary that he have a mind capable of turning in whatever direction the winds of Fortune and the variations of affairs require, and . . . that *he should not depart from what is morally right, if he can observe it*, but should know how to adopt what is bad, when he is obliged to.[1]

This passage suggests that instead of belaboring Machiavelli for pointing out the limitations of private ethics, attention ought to be directed instead at the dual role which is thus created for the political actor. He is made to perform in an atmosphere of tensions where accepted moral values limit his behavior in normal circumstances, while a distinctively political ethic, accompanied by the new knowledge, comes into play when circumstances of necessity appear. By itself each form of ethic is inadequate. The normally bad acts justified by the political ethic would, if unrestrained by the

8. *Discourses*, II, 12.　　　　　1. Ibid.
9. *Prince*, XVIII.

inhibiting pressure of common morality, encourage unlimited ambition and all of its destructive consequences. On the other hand, if common morality were to be extended to situations for which it had not been designed, the consequences would be destructive of the order and power which made private morality possible. It was the anguishing situation of the political actor that he must decide which form of ethic should govern, but while the new science could facilitate his choice it could not compensate for the fact that he must partially dwell outside the realm of what is usually considered goodness. This means, in effect, that Machiavelli broke with classical theory which had approached the problems of political action with the question of how men could develop their moral potentialities through a life devoted to political office. But for Machiavelli the problem became more acute, for the issue no longer involved the statesman's quest for a moral perfection which, by its very moral quality, would benefit the community; it involved instead the political actor who was driven to break the moral law in order to preserve his society.

There was still another reason why politics could not satisfy the aspiration towards moral fulfillment. Traditional ethical notions operated on the assumption that the result of ethical conduct would be the creation of a desirable or more desirable state of affairs; that, for example, to act honestly or in good faith would produce situations which would be characterized by honesty and good faith. But Machiavelli rejected this notion of the literal translation of ethical acts into ethical situations and substituted instead a notion of the irony of the political condition. "Some things seem to be virtuous, but if they are put into practice will be ruinous . . . other things seem to be vices, yet if put into practice will bring the prince security and well-being."[2] Thus there was a kind of alchemy in the political condition whereby good was transmuted into evil, and evil into good.[3] Take, for example, the classical virtue of liberality which prescribed that acts of generosity should be done in a restrained manner. For Machiavelli's political actor such advice would be absurd; he was not a private donor, but a public figure whose actions, to be significant, needed a well-publicized flourish, even a vulgar display. But even with this amendment, it was doubtful that liberality qualified as a political virtue at all. The political actor usually expended not his private resources but public revenues. In a political setting liberality was translated into taxes, and these, in turn, were certain to breed popular resentments. Hence the vice of niggardliness became a political virtue; it was transformed, in fact, into liberality because it gave the subject a greater share of his own property.[4] Again, take the case of the trusting ruler who

2. Ibid., XV.   4. *Prince*, XV-XVI.
3. Ibid., XV; *History*, V, I.

refused to believe that most men were vicious and ready to deceive at every turn. If a ruler of this type were to govern according to the virtue of clemency, he would soon be driven to adopt increasingly more severe and cruel measures in order to retain power. On the other hand, the contradictions of politics were such that a ruler who applied rational cruelty at the proper time would be more truly humane. Cruelty, when used economically, was more merciful than clemency, for where the first injured only the few and the rest were restrained by apprehension, the second bred disorders which injured the *una universalità intera*. Nevertheless, the justification of cruel measures was not meant to imply that any method of retaining power was equal in moral worth to any other method. Cruelty might be useful in attaining certain ends, such as security, but it could not bring true glory.[5]

Machiavelli's concern with the shortcomings of traditional ethics and his quest for a suitable political ethic stemmed from a profound belief in the discontinuities of human existence. This was expressed in his view of history. History was conceived not as a smoothly flowing continuum, but as a process which irrupted in destructive frenzy, obliterating the achievements and memory of the past and condemning man to a perpetual labor of recovery.[6] Equally important, there were discontinuities between the forms of existence at a particular time. Religion, art, economic activity, private life and public seemed to be carried on according to special logics of their own, unconnected by any overarching heteronomous principle.[7] Thus man dwelt in a fragmentized universe and his special anguish came from being condemned to live in several alien worlds at once. If political existence was to be lived in a world of its own, it was imperative that there be relevant criteria for ordering existence. Relevancy, in turn, was conceived by Machiavelli in terms of the conditions to which the criteria appertained; that is, to the particular world of politics. This was expressed in his frequent use of the word *necessità* in describing political situations. By *necessità* he did not mean a form of determinism, but rather a set of factors challenging man's political creativity, manageable only if man treated them as strictly political, excluding all else from his span of attention.[8]

In terms of ethics this did not mean that politics was to be conducted without ethical criteria, but that the criteria could not be imported from the "outside." The failure to appreciate this has led many modern critics of Machiavelli into false dilemmas. It does not follow, as one modern writer would have it, that because politics demands an ethic different from private life that "moral imperatives

5. *Prince*, VIII.
6. *Discourses*, II, 5.
7. Ibid., II, Preface; II, 5.
8. Ibid., I, 1; 3; 28; II, 12; III, 12.

do not have absolute value."[9] This is to put the issue badly, for the real questions are, what morals? what is meant by "absolute"? The whole point of Machiavelli's argument was to urge that precisely because of the unescapably autonomous nature of politics, it was all the more compelling that criteria for action be established and that appropriate means be fashioned for their implementation. In brief, the denial of heteronomy need not entail a denial of morality in politics, any more than the impossibility of ethical criteria follows from the denial of ethical absolutes.

J. H. WHITFIELD

Machiavelli's Use of *Ordini*†

Although at first he may look a little dense and formidable, especially to a student without Italian, Professor Whitfield is important, indeed essential, to a modern explorer of Machiavelli. There are two reasons for this: his method, and his conclusions. The method is linguistic analysis—a detailed, often statistical, account of what is called the constitutive vocabulary of Machiavelli. These are crucial words or groups of closely associated words, which, as they occur over and over again within various contexts in Machiavelli's writings, tend to define themselves and assert their importance in the structure of his thought. When traced out, they often reveal as much about the pattern of his thinking as do his explicit statements. Obviously, this sort of study, which has become very widespread of late, can be done only on the basis of the original text. Professor Whitfield did not originate the approach; that honor goes to Professor Fredi Chiappelli, whose important *Studi sul linguaggio di Machiavelli* was published at Florence in 1952. Professor Whitfield, like many later users of the method, has his differences with Chiappelli, but like all of them remains very much in his debt; and so far as recent discussion of Machiavelli goes, this is clearly one of the most vital and fruitful of approaches. We have tried to accommodate the reader who is without Italian by translating all extended passages, and by italicizing the key words, wherever possible, within the original passages quoted by Whitfield. We should also warn the reader that for quick allusion Whitfield uses the abbreviations D (*Discorsi*) and P (*Principe*), and jumps about with great agility from one of Machiavelli's writings to another. But for a student of vocabulary no other procedure is possible.

Professor Whitfield's conclusions are also noteworthy. He is the foremost modern exponent of a "white" rather than a "black" Machiavelli, seeing in him a democratically minded, humane republican, rather than a cynical, obsequious instigator of tyrants. Whether one agrees with his arguments or

9. Wilhelm Nestle, "Politik und Moral im Altertum," *Neue Jahrbücher für das Klassische Altertum, Geschichte und deutsche Litteratur und für Pädagogik* (1918), s. 225.
†From J. H. Whitfield, *Discourses on Machiavelli* (Oxford, 1969), chapter

VIII. The text of this chapter is based on the paper "Osservazioni sul Machiavelli," read to the International Congress of Italian Studies at Magdalene College, Cambridge, on August 18, 1953. Italics on certain words have been added by the editor of this Norton Critical Edition.

not, it is essential to know that they exist, and to take the measure of their often formidable strength.

Whitfield begins by observing that discussions of Machiavelli commonly concentrate on *The Prince* to the neglect of his other writings; and that this has led to an overemphasis on brutal and cruel concepts, even when not overtly expressed—at the expense of important political ideas, such as those clustering around the word *ordini*, meaning "orders," or "rules," or "laws," or "ordinances." To make the point that these uses of *ordini* and related words are significant, Whitfield must first exclude commonplace and apolitical uses of them, like "order one's dinner" or "by order of the pope."

* * *

In the political works of Machiavelli these banal uses have been burnt nearly out (and are excluded from my figures). Here the Florentine tradition of *ordini*, resolutely in the plural, and with the sense of constitutional arrangements or devices—closely linked to *leggi*, but differentiated—has become predominant. This is all the more obvious in that Machiavelli suffers little from that inhibition which drives Italian critics to vary their terms of reference (*il Leopardi, il nostro, il grande recanatese, il poeta del dolore mondiale, il poeta di Silvia*,[1] etc.). This is not to make him systematic, or unvarying. For his variants he has one or two synonyms (as *ordini, modi, instituti, statuti*), and one or two latinising terms, which are synonymous, but have a solemn value and a rarer use (as *ordini, constituzioni; civile, politico*). In the chapter of the *Discorsi* which we found quoted[2] he comes back, in three pages, twenty times to the series *ordini, ordinare*; and with these there are the allied terms, *leggi* (4), *constituire*—which we shall find the nobler variant for *ordinare* (1); and what these add up to, the *vivere civile* (2), which, as with Filippo de'Nerli,[3] here adds the significant adjective, and finds the specific opposite: 'il che testifica tutti gli ordini primi di quella citta essere stati piú conformi ad uno vivere civile e libero, che a uno assoluto e tirannico.'[4]

This is not only the vocabulary of those like Nerli, who may be following Machiavelli: it is in conformity with Giovanni Cavalcanti, as where he puts these words into the mouth of Rinaldo degli Albizzi: 'Non sapete voi che la lunga consuetudine si ritrova in tra le *leggi*? e chi dalla *legge* si parte rinunzia al ben vivere ed alla civile libertà.'[5] But it is still more strikingly in accord with Machiavelli's

---

1. "Leopardi, our man, the great man from Recanata, the poet of cosmic grief, the poet of Silvia." [*Editor.*]
2. *Discorsi*, I, 9. [*Editor.*]
3. Filippo de' Nerli was a sixteenth-century Florentine chronicler, who talked of "ordini" as the conditions of a free civil society. He's also the friend to whom Machiavelli dedicated the poem on "Occasion," p. 138 of this book. [*Editor.*]
4. *Discorsi*, I, 9.

"Which shows that all the first ordinances of that city were better suited to free civil society than to an absolutist tyranny." [*Editor.*]
5. Giovanni Cavalcanti, *Istorie Fiorentine*, III, ii.
"Don't you know that the long working of custom is found in the laws? and anyone who departs from the laws renounces all hope of proper living and civil liberty." [*Editor.*]

own vocabulary, particularly in *Discorsi* I. Here the figures are elo-quent. For the series *ordini*, etc., 326; for *leggi*, 126; for *costituire*, 9; for *constituzioni*, 6. Without taking into our account the slightly vaguer *modi*, often used in the same sense as *ordini*, the group totals 468 instances for 174 pages. The dominant interest and intention of Machiavelli in the first book of the *Discorsi* is to find, or rather, to recover, the *ordini* which are conducive to the mainte-nance of a *vivere civile e libero*. The second book concerns itself with Rome's expansion, and it is natural that the use should slacken. Even so, the totals are not insignificant: *ordini*, 116: *leggi*, 9; *constituzioni*, 2 for 126 pages. The third book, with its more float-ing subject-matter, and its concern with individual examples, does not return to the intensity of Bk. I, though it advances on Bk. II, and here the comparable figures are: 138, 26, 1 for 148 pages. For the whole work, and the whole series, the total is 761 instances for 448 pages. Is there any other significant element in Machiavelli's political vocabulary for which a similar result could be obtained?

* * *

In *Discorsi* I we have the power-house of Machiavelli's ideas, and it is natural that the vocabulary we have found dominant there should be re-echoed in the other works of his maturity. Thus in the *Discorso sopra il riformare lo stato di Firenze*, with its offer of glory for Leo X through the establishment of a stable republic in Flor-ence, the count for *ordini*, etc., is 36 for 18 pages. And with this is the clear echo of D. I, 10: 'Oltre di questo non è esaltato alcuno uomo tanto in alcuna sua azione, quanto sono quelli, che hanno con *leggi*, e con *istituti* riformato le republiche e i regni: questi sono, dopo quelli che sono stati Iddii, i primi laudati. . . .'[6] In this *Dis-corso* Machiavelli is offering his ideas as a programme, and it is nat-ural that his vocabulary should be at its most characteristic. In the *Istorie Fiorentine* he is following his authorities for a record where stability and *ordini* are often lacking. In consequence, the whole series, *ordini*, etc., *leggi*, totals only some 125 instances for 535 pages. But though the pattern is different, the impression of a single direction for Machiavelli is unchanged, and it is in the margins, at the beginning of the Books (especially Bks. IV and V) or when aroused by some particular episode (the tyranny of the Duke of Athens, or the Ciompi), that Machiavelli adds his own reflections to the history, and his characteristic vocabulary then comes tum-bling out.

* * *

6. *Discorso di M.N. sopra il riformare lo Stato di Firenze, ad finem.*
"Apart from this, no man is exalted in any one of his actions as much as those who with laws and institutions have re-formed republics and kingdoms; after those who have been deified, these have merited the highest praise." [*Editor.*]

The count for the works I have considered so far comes close to a thousand uses for this series, all subordinate to a *vivere civile*; and it is obvious that it could be swelled—apart from pronominal continuations, which I have never added—by other related words. But it is fitting that we should pause here with this emergence of the word *assoluto*, and with this firm statement that absolutism and *buoni ordini* are incompatibles. The Machiavelli we have been considering is clearly and incontrovertibly the supporter of a *vero vivere libero e civile*, and the unswerving antagonist of despotism. Despotism and *ordini* can only be reconciled in the person of a Romulus, whose role is to resolve the anarchy he finds, where violence is thrust upon him, and found a *vivere civile*. But this unanimity is for the Machiavelli of the 'other works', and for the general he is the author only of the *Prince*. It is the *Prince* which has given Machiavelli his reputation, and it is an opposite reputation to this. It is time for us to come back to the *Prince*.

If I were to put together all the passages which have asserted the absolutism that underlies the *Prince* this would be a book, and not an essay. I can not refrain, however, from quoting one of the older testimonies, for the downrightness of its terms:

> The political sentiment of Italian independence is felt clearly and powerfully in Machiavelli, and particularly in that book where the disillusioned republican evoked a monarchy, and what a monarchy! the most absolute, the most tyrannical, the most naked that has ever been imagined.[7]

That was Cesare Balbo a century ago,[8] and it is easy to see why I should wish to quote it as the antithesis of what has gone before. Nor, though fashions in Machiavelli scholarship have changed since then, have the authoritative judgments grown unrecognizably different. Thus I may limit my reference to two who still hold sway, to Toffanin and Chabod. The first of these maintained, in his book on *Machiavelli e il Tacitismo*, that the contradiction between the absolutist spirit of the Prince and the republican spirit of the *Discorsi* must not draw us into error about his true faith in the necessity of an absolute rule. And more recently, perhaps even more authoritatively, Professor Chabod prefaced his edition of the *Prince* with a portrait of its protagonist:

> By December the new man has been sketched out, and placed, all by himself, on the political stage; hard, thoughtful, impenetrable, a man to compress within himself the life of an entire state. Because, now, every other voice falls silent; the people have become a scattered mob who wait for the outcome of things.[9]

7. Editor's translation.
8. *Della Monarchia rappresentativa in*   *Italia*, I, 7.
9. Editor's translation.

And a page later Professor Chabod sees this, in terms that will be familiar to all readers of De Sanctis, as the culmination of a Renascence process, with the Renascence itself an artistic and literary phenomenon, taking place in the collapse of the social and political world. Only the Prince remains alive in this world of *letterati* and cynical indifference.[1]

This view of the Renascence is simplicity itself to grasp, and well entrenched in the popular imagination. But I cannot help thinking that Chabod, in giving strong voice to it, had forgotten a capital passage in the very text on which he based it, and which he was editing. For Machiavelli himself, in the last chapter of the *Prince*, and on page 124 of Professor Chabod's own edition, had put forward his view of what was living or was dead in the Italy of his time—that is, in the Renascence.

> Qui è virtù grande nelle membra, quando la non mancassi ne'capi. Specchiatevi ne'duelli e ne'congressi de'pochi, quanto li Italiani sieno superiori con le forze, con la destrezza, con lo ingegno. Ma come si viene alli eserciti, non compariscono. E tutto procede dalla debolezza de'capi.[2]

Here, indeed, we have a pretty pattern in counterpoint. For Chabod, it is obvious that the people are dead, the Prince only is alive; and for Machiavelli, the prince is dead, the people living.

> Because now every other voice falls silent; the prince is the only living figure,[3]

says Chabod. *E tutto procede dalla debolezza de' capi*,[4] retorts Machiavelli. As an explanation of the Renascence we may give ear to the one, or to the other. But as an explanation of the thought of Machiavelli Professor Chabod can not here be right. Thus one of the best-known of Machiavelli's utterances can raise a doubt on the validity of the critics' judgments on him. Is this an isolated case? and is the old opposition made by Taine a true one? It is the moment for us to look to the *Prince*, not in the light of the critics —who quote, and repeat, each other—but in the light of the vocabulary which we have seen established as central for the other works of Machiavelli.

Ordini, ordinare, bene ordinato, leggi, constituzioni, il vivere civile, il vivere politico, onore, vituperio, sicurtà: are these words, so indicative of a *forma mentis*, present in the *Prince*, or has he here a new vocabulary of absolutism, based, let us say, on *spegnere*? It is

1. Chabod, ed., *Il Principe*. 1944, 19, 20. [*Editor*.]
2. "The limbs of the nation have great strength, so long as the heads are not deficient. Only look at the duels and the tourneys where a few men are involved, and you will find that the Italians excel in strength, in dexterity, in mental agil- ity; but when it comes to armies they don't stand comparison at all. This all comes from the weakness of the heads." [*Editor*.]
3. Editor's translation.
4. "And the whole thing proceeds from the weakness of the heads." [*Editor*.]

now that we can turn to the index at the end of Professor Chiappel-li's study of Machiavelli's language.[5] Here, at least, the answer is unequivocal: not one of the series has struck Professor Chiappelli's eyes as he looked for the significant words of the *Prince*. But this is not a proof they are not there: it is instead, a proof that if you read the *Prince* in isolation, and base your reading on its reputation, you will see in it only what you came to find; and what you see will be a part, and a distortion. When we come to what is actually there it may seem, at first sight, of significance that neither *il vivere civile* or *politico* are represented in the *Prince*. This may be because Machia-velli puts republics on the one side at the start; but it may be acci-dental, for the formative elements of the *vivere civile*, which are the *ordini*, are there from the beginning to the end. In the twenty-six chapters of this short treatise, devoted, as we have seen asserted, to promotion of the most unbridled absolutism, Machiavelli returns sixty-five times to the theme of *ordini* and *ordinare*; and to this series we have to add the fourteen *leggi* and the three cases of *con-stituzioni, costituire*. Leaving on one side the cases where *ordinare* means to command, or *ordinario* has its ordinary sense, we have a total of over eighty cases, some of them, as we shall see, as full of emphasis as any we have found elsewhere.

Not only is that a body of evidence which we should not over-look, but the series provides, at the beginning and the end of the book, the sheet-anchors which keep Machiavelli's boat out of the rough sea of despotism. The first chapter of the *Prince* is so brief that we may take the second as the starting-point; and here from it is Machiavelli's judgment on the hereditary states which, for obvious reasons, he will leave mainly out of his argument.

> Dico, adunque, che negli stati ereditari e assuefatti al sangue del loro principe sono assai minori difficultà a mantenerli che ne'nuo-vi; perché basta solo non preterire *l'ordine* de'sua antenati, e di poi temporeggiare con li accidenti; in modo che, se tale principe è di ordinaria industria, sempre si manterrà nel suo stato, se non è una estraordinaria ed eccessiva forza che ne lo privi.[6]

This warning, put well in view upon the threshold of his treatise, is only in another guise what we have seen repeated, on the threshold of the treatment of conspiracies in *D*. III, 5, that princes start to lose their state when they begin to break its *ordini*. But, as we know, the Italy of 1513 was without valid *ordini*, a country without banks or shelter from the flood. In the absence of hereditary

5. Professor Fredi Chiappelli. *Studi sul linguaggio di Machiavelli* (1952) [*Editor.*]
6. "Let me say, then, that hereditary states which have grown used to the family of their ruler, are much less trou-ble to keep in hand than new ones are; it is simply a matter of not upsetting the customs of the old regime and adjusting them instead to meet new circumstances. Hence if a prince is just ordinarily in-dustrious, he can always keep his posi-tion, unless some unusual or excessive act of force deprives him of it." [*Editor.*]

princes, Machiavelli has to be concerned with the 'new prince.' And here, as the pendant to ch. ii, is Machiavelli's offer to Lorenzo in ch. XXVI:

> Questo nasce, che gli *ordini* antiqui di essa non erano buoni; e non ci è suto alcuno che abbia saputo trovare de'nuovi; e veruna cosa fa tanto onore a uno uomo che di nuovo surga, quanto fa le nuove *legge* e li nuovi *ordini* trovati da lui. Queste cose, quando sono bene fondate e abbino in loro grandezza, lo fanno reverendo e mirabile.[7]

Honor in the establishment of *ordini*: this which is the middle of ch. XXVI is also its beginning, where Machiavelli decided that these were times 'da onorare uno nuovo principe, e se ci era materia che dessi occasione a uno prudente e virtuoso di introdurvi forma che facessi onore a lui e bene alla università degli uomini di quella.'[8] The hereditary state runs on its *ordini*, and will only be overthrown by force from outside (*lo straordinario*); the new state can only be established permanently by *ordini*. Such are the alpha and the omega of this tyrants' alphabet. And this aim of general good, which is the beginning of the chapter, is its ending also, where there suddenly springs forth one of the rich and Machiavellian epithets: Let the House of Medici take on this just enterprise, 'acciò che, sotto la sua insegna, e questa patria ne sia nobilitata.'[9]

Honor for the Prince, *ordini* of his devising to give stability and security, ennoblement not of himself, but of his country, as the latter state: is it not, perhaps, because this has an idyllic ring about it that critics have been ready to lop off this chapter as unconnected with the rest? We must turn back the pages to chapters which none have thought of omitting from the canon. In ch. VI Machiavelli enumerates the four great prototypes, Moses, Cyrus, Romulus, Theseus. Through this chapter there resounds a word which we have met in ch. XXVI: *occasione*. Their opportunity lay in their country's unhappy plight. But did they use it for their own aggrandisement? 'Queste occasioni pertanto feciono questi uomini felici; e la eccellente virtù loro fece quella occasione esser conosciuta; donde la loro patria ne fu nobilitata e diventò felicissima.'[1] How did they do this? A reader of Professor Chiappelli will guess they did it by a liberal use of *spegnere*. But those who have followed my argument so

---

7. "The reason is simply that the old methods of warfare were not good, and no one has been able to find new ones. Nothing does so much honor to a man newly risen to power, as the new laws and rules that he discovers. When they are well grounded and have in them the seeds of greatness, these institutions make him the object of awe and admiration." [*Editor.*]

8. "to hail a new prince in Italy, [since] there is material here that a careful, able leader could mold into a new form which might bring honor to him and benefits to all men." [*Editor.*]

9. "so that, under your banner, our country may become noble again." [*Editor.*]

1. "Specific occasions brought these men to power, and their unusual abilities [*virtù*] enabled them to seize the occasion, and so to make their countries noble and very fortunate." [*Editor.*]

far will know already that they did it—is not the inclusion of
Romulus the proof?—by the creation of new *ordini*. And, in fact,
ten times in four pages comes the series *ordini*, etc. It is here that
there occurs a reference to Savonarola which I cannot help thinking
has been generally misunderstood. Moses, Cyrus, Theseus and
Romulus could not have established firmly 'le loro *constituzioni'*
had they remained unarmed; and for this deficiency Savonarola
'ruinò ne'sua *ordini* nuovi.' Unarmed Savonarola, the others armed:
all occupied in the foundation of new *ordini*. Surely, if among the
ordini nuovi of Savonarola there had been an *ordinanza*,[2] he might
have qualified like the other four, and ended as they did, in words
that are redolent of the spirit of *D.* I, 10, 'potenti, securi, onorati,
felici.'[3] We have seen there the respect which Machiavelli accords
to those who found, the odium he gives to those who destroy.
There is no case where he expresses contempt for an *ordinatore*, and
the company of Savonarola here, with Moses, Cyrus, Theseus and
Romulus, is proof enough that Machiavelli did not speak ironically,
though this has been the usual interpretation put on it by the critics, who have been always quick to see irony where Machiavelli
never thought of putting it.

We have seen how Machiavelli looked approvingly at France,
while his friend Francesco Vettori saw more sharply the flaws that
underlay appearances. What he repeated five times in the *Discorsi*
occurs in the same wording in the *Prince*.

> Intra'regni bene ordinati e governati, a'tempi nostri, è quello di
> Francia; e in esso si trovano infinite *constituzioni* buone, donde
> depende la libertà e sicurtà del re. Delle quali la prima è il parla-
> mento e la sua autorità: perché quello che *ordinò* quel regno,
> conoscendo l'ambizione de'potenti e la insolenzia loro . . . vol-
> endo assicurarli (= l'universale) . . . constituí uno iudice. . . .
> Né possé esser questo *ordine* migliore né più prudente, né che sia
> maggiore cagione della securtà del re e del regno.[4]

When Machiavelli repeats himself in identical terms there is no
compulsion for us to think that he has changed his mind. The aim
is liberty and security, and for France it was bound up, in the *Discorsi*, with that ordering which left arms and finance to the king's
discretion, but limited his actions in other matters as the laws
ordained. True, that is not repeated here; but then, it is not
repealed, and the certificate of these "infinite *constituzione* buone'

2. "Ordering of the orders" (a full idea
of discipline). [*Editor*.]
3. "Powerful, secure, honored, and
happy." [*Editor*.]
4. *P*. XIX.
  "Among the well-ordered and -gov-
erned kingdoms of our time is that of
France, where one can observe a great
many institutions making for the liberty
and security of the king. Outstanding
among these is the parliament, and its
authority. The founder of the kingdom,
clearly knowing the ambition of the nobility and their insolence . . . wishing to
reassure them (the people) . . . established a third judicial force. . . . There
could hardly be a better or more prudent arrangement than this, nor one
serving to promote better the security of
king and kingdom." [*Editor*.]

is an unlimited one. Would it not need a special statement to elimi-
nate it? And may it not link in Machiavelli's mind with the opening of P. XIV?

> Debbe, adunque, uno principe non avere altro obietto né altro
> pensiero, né prendere cosa alcuna per sua arte, fuora della guerra
> e ordini e disciplina di essa; perché quella è sola arte che si espetta
> a chi comanda.[5]

For what has this that needs be incompatible with that other firm
declaration in the *Art of War*, 'Perché i regni che hanno buoni
ordini, non danno l'imperio assoluto ai loro re, se non negli
eserciti?'[6]

It is perhaps unnecessary for me to dwell again here on the heavy
emphasis which Machiavelli gives to the need to avoid hatred and
contempt, and win benevolence; on the parallel between what he
says about princes in *D*. III, 22 (Valerius, not Manlius, as model;
the affability, humanity and piety of Cyrus in Xenophon) with the
closing paragraph of *P*. XIX (what you can of Marcus Aurelius,
what you are forced to of Severus); or on the relevance of Piero
Soderini, as assessed in *D*. III, 41, proceeding in all things with
humanity and patience, and so bringing his city to its fall, to the
famous words in *P*. XVIII on the need perchance to 'operare
contro alla fede, contro alla carità, contro alla umanità, contro alla
religione.'[7] But with regard to this same chapter, which has often
given offense, I may allege two glosses from the *Discorsi* which perhaps limit its scope. In *D*. III, 42, Machiavelli talks of faith
between princes, as opposed to faith between princes and their subjects (which we have seen dealt with in another way, in terms of
inviolable *ordini* and of benevolence), and he adds a specific reference backwards to the *Prince*, where this same theme 'largamente è
disputato.' And later in *P*. XVIII there are the words which have
seemed to many sufficient proof of cynicism: 'Facci dunque uno
principe di vincere e mantenere lo stato; e'mezzi sempre saranno
iudicati onorevoli e da ciascuno laudati. . . .'[8] But this again
attaches to the public theme, states against states, not princes
against subjects, and is to be read in the light of the parallel passage
of *D*. III, 41,

> perché, dove si delibera al tutto della salute della patria non vi
> debbe cadere alcuna considerazione né di giusto né d'ingiusto, né
> di piatoso né di crudele, né di laudabile né d'ignominioso; anzi,

---

5. "A prince, therefore, should have no
other object, no other thought, no other
subject of study, than war, its rules and
disciplines; this is the only art for a man
who commands." [*Editor*.]

6. *A.d.G.*, I, 203–4.
"In kingdoms which are well ordered,
they don't give the kings absolute sway,

except over the army." [*Editor*.]

7. "do things against his word, against
charity, against humanity, against religion." [*Editor*.]

8. "Let a prince, therefore, win victories
and uphold his state; his methods will
always be considered worthy, and everyone will praise him. . . ." [*Editor*.]

posposto ogni altro rispetto, seguire al tutto quel partito che le salvi la vita, e mantenghile la libertà.[9]

The desperate action envisaged by Machiavelli is to save, not to enslave. By that saving clause it will be seen that what he said was not intended as a chains-at-any-price encouragement to the Prince, but something still depending on the cruel dilemma which life offered to Piero Soderini, and where he achieved cruelty, by being kind.

Here, of course, is the case of Caesar Borgia, and it will be clear that this also must be illuminated from the *Discorsi*. The link is Romulus. Romulus was violent, not to spoil, but to mend, and thus, accused by facts, he was excused by the effect. In the one chapter he was put forward as the founder of a *vivere civile*; and in the next there came the contrast with Julius Caesar, and the possibility of greater glory—see Petrarch—for one who had at his command a city which should be corrupt. *Possedere una città corrotta, non per guastarla in tutto come Cesare, ma per riordinar la come Romolo.*[1] But Romulus, with Moses, Cyrus, Theseus, is avowedly one of the patterns of the *Prince*; and the word that Machiavelli used for Romulus in the *Discorsi* ('perché colui che è violento per guastare, non quello che è per *racconciare*, si debbe riprendere')[2] is the same word he uses for Caesar Borgia and Romagna in the *Prince*:

> Era tenuto Cesare Borgia crudele: nondimanco quella sua crudeltà aveva *racconcia* la Romagna, unitola, ridottola in pace e in fede.[3]

And this, of *P*. XVII, confirms the earlier statement of *P*. VII,

> aversi acquistata amica la Romagna e guadagnatosi tutti quelli populi, per avere cominciato a gustare el bene essere loro.[4]

This, with the subsequent remark on his 'intenzione alta,' makes it plain that Machiavelli does not propose Caesar Borgia as the pattern for a tyrant, but in the mould of Romulus. As with Romulus, the facts accuse, and the effect excuses. But if it were not good it could not then excuse. *P*. VII is the modern rendering of *D*, I, 9, and here again it may be right at least to refer to Guicciardini, who,

9. "For where the very safety of the country depends upon the resolution to be taken, no considerations of justice or injustice, humanity or cruelty, nor of glory or of shame, should be allowed to prevail. But putting all other considerations aside, the only question should be, What course will safe the life and liberty of the country?" [*Editor.*]

1. "To possess a corrupt city, not to ruin it wholly like Caesar, but to reorganize it like Romulus." [*Editor.*]

2. "For he is to be reprehended who commits violence for the purpose of destroying, and not he who employs it for beneficent purposes." [*Editor.*]

3. "People thought that Cesare Borgia was cruel, but that cruelty of his reorganized the Romagna, united it, and established it in peace and loyalty." [*Editor.*]

4. "not only controlled the Romagna, but controlled it as a friend, and won over the people of the district as soon as they began to savor the benefits of his rule." [*Editor.*]

though a sharp denouncer of Borgia iniquity, explains the loyalty of Romagna in a way that is flattering to Cesare.[5] For this is a testimonial from one who had especial cause to know conditions in Romagna.

We may come back finally to the one word in the series for which I have so far offered no parallel within the *Principe*: *vituperio*.[6] Echoing through all Machiavelli's works there is the conviction of the trough into which Italy has sunk, to be the *vituperio del mondo*. Since the *Prince* offers the remedy for this plight it would be strange were the exclamation missing from its pages. Instead it bursts out twice in ch. XII, the one where Machiavelli laments the uselessness of mercenary arms. 'E il fine della loro virtú è stato che Italià è stata corsa da Carlo, predata da Luigi, sforzata da Ferrando e *vituperata* da'Svizzeri.'[7] Then as a final valediction to the chapter: 'tanto che li hanno condotta Italia stiava e *vituperata*.'[8] This is the Machiavelli who added in *D. I*, 10 the *vituperio* of tyranny to the *vituperio* of defeat.

Ed è impossibile che quelli che in stato privato vivono in una republica, o che per fortuna o virtù ne diventono principi, se leggessono le istorie, e delle memorie delle antiche cose facessono capitale, che non volessero quelli tali privati vivere nella loro patria piú tosto Scipioni che Cesari; e quelli che sono principi, piú tosto Agesilai, Timoleoni, Dioni, che Nabidi, Falari, e Dionisii: perché vedrebbono questi essere sommamente *vituperati*, e quelli eccessivamente laudati.[9]

The ideal prototypes for Machiavelli's Prince are Moses (Dante's law-giver, *legista e obbediente*), Romulus (the *riordinatore* of a *vivere civile*), Cyrus (the affable), and Theseus (the slayer of monsters); and Phalaris and Dionysius are not recommended in its pages. Even more, in his dedication to Lorenzo de'Medici Machiavelli put himself forward as one who came equipped with 'una con-

5. *Storia d'Italia*, III, VI, 169: "ricordavansi ancora gli uomini, che per l'autorità e grandezza sua, e per l'amministrazione sincera della giustizia, era stato tranquillo quel paese dai tumulti delle parti, dai quali prima soleva essere vessato continuamente con spesse uccisioni di uomini; con le quali opere si aveva fatti benevoli gli animi dei popoli."

["Men still recalled that because of his authority and majesty, and the honest administration of justice, that region had remained free from the struggles of parties which had previously vexed it, with frequent murdering of men; and in this way he had gained the good will of the people."—*Editor*.]

6. "Disgrace." [*Editor*.]

7. "And the result of their prowess has been that Italy has been overrun by Charles, sacked by Louis, raped by Ferdinand, and disgraced by the Swiss." [*Editor*.]

8. "So that they have brought Italy to a state of slavery and contempt." [*Editor*.]

9. "And it is impossible that those who have lived as private citizens in a republic, or those who by fortune or courage have risen to be princes of the same, if they were to read history and take the records of antiquity for example, should not prefer Scipio to Caesar; and that those who were [originally] princes should not rather choose to be like Agesilaus, Timoleon, and Dion, than Nabis, Phalaris, and Dionysius; for they would then see how thoroughly the latter were despised, and how highly the former were appreciated." [*Editor*.]

tinua lezione delle cose antique.'[1] That is the equivalent of the phrase above from the *Discorsi*, which, in their turn, are this treasure from antiquity. He, more than most men, had made capital of ancient things; nor could he have forgotten either them, nor else this chapter of the *Discorsi*, on which the ink may scarcely then have been dry, with its eloquent contrast between *vituperio* and danger for the tyrant, and honor with security for the man who should 'ordinare un regno buono.' And as a proof that he had not forgotten, *ordini*, *onore* and *sicurtà* are his recipes in the pages of the *Prince*. It is only because his critics have persisted in seeking in the *Discorsi* (when they have troubled to look so far) the author of the *Prince*, instead of recognizing in the *Prince* the author of the *Discorsi*, that the vital elements of Machiavelli's political vocabulary —the only ones which have what Professor Chiappelli would call a technical nature—have not been recognized. But they find the same expression, and have the same validity in both of these two books.

I remember the dismay which a remark of mine upon the innocency of Machiavelli's intentions once caused in an Italian reviewer. It was as though I had stolen the best jewel in his crown; as if there was something derogatory in his greatness in anything so near to simplicity of mind as innocence of intentions. Is there not in one of Leopardi's *Pensieri* the sad reflection on the general tendency of civilized languages to make goodness and stupidity synonymous? In this investigation I shall only plead the evidence he has himself provided. Yet I know there will be some who will not forgive me for finding him forgiveable. To these I shall offer one last quotation, which has often lingered in my mind since I first wrote on Machiavelli in 1946:

> Io non so se io mi prenderò una provincia dura e piena di tanta difficultà, che mi convenga o abbandonarla con vergogna, o seguirla con carico; volendo difendere una cosa, la quale, come ho detto, da tutti gli scrittori è accusata. Ma, communque si sia, io non giudico, né giudicherò mai essere difetto difendere alcuna opinione con le ragioni, sanza volervi usare o l'autorità o la forza. Dico, adunque, come di quello difetto di che accusano gli scrittori la moltitudine, se ne possono accusare tutti gli uomini particolarmente, e massime i principi; perché ciascuno che non sia regolato dalle leggi, farebbe quelli medesimi errori che la moltitudine sciolta.[2]

1. "An extended study of antiquity." [*Editor*.]
2. "I know not whether, in undertaking to defend a cause against the accusations of all writers, I do not assume a task so hard and so beset with difficulties as to oblige me to abandon it with shame, or to go on with it at the risk of being weighed down by it. Be that as it may, however, I think, and ever shall think, that it cannot be wrong to defend one's opinions with arguments founded upon reason, without employing force or authority. I say, then, that individual men, and especially princes, may be charged with the same defects of which writers accuse the people; for whoever is not controlled by laws will commit the same errors as the unbridled multitude." *Discorsi*, I, 58. [*Editor*.]

The author of these sentiments was never a supporter of an absolute authority, not even in the pages of the *Prince*.

GENNARO SASSO†

[The Origins of Evil]

From whatever point of view one examines the problem of politics, one's attention is always abruptly recalled to the "cruelty," the "wickedness," the "evil" which seem to be the inevitable modes of its practical realization, and which—as we have seen—cannot be understood outside the general Machiavellian conception of man and of history. If (as Machiavelli really thought) man cannot overcome the boundary which separates him from things because of the obstacle that he encounters in his own nature; if, therefore, the reality surrounding him is nothing but a succession of events to the inner meaning of which he never penetrates; then it's perfectly comprehensible that to keep from being overwhelmed by this onslaught he should try to oppose it with every means that the historic situation allows him to find and use. The principle that rules his action does not coincide with the principle that rules the action of things, since one is tied up with the very nature of man and is inherent in his insuperable limits, and the other results simply from the casual sum of all the human actions running together to form a situation; and the mingling of these actions is too complex, the probability of man's being overwhelmed by them is too great, for him to avoid (in his desperate efforts to control a world of such variety and difficulty) the necessity to break faith, destroy his subjects or his enemies, and to strip himself, when the times require it, of every last feature of humanity.

From its first page to its last, *The Prince* is permeated with these observations about the necessity, the inevitability of evil in a world which knows no goodness but only cruel and perverse man ("any man who tries to be good all the time is bound to come to ruin among the great number of those who aren't good").[1] And from this vision it has seemed logical to conclude that this evil, the presence of which among men Machiavelli so often emphasizes, is simply the fundamental and immutable character of their nature, inclined from all eternity to evil rather than good, and hence wholly incapable of resisting its own impenetrable malice. Certainly Machiavelli speaks, in more than one passage of his works, and more particularly

---

†Translated by the editor from Gennaro Sasso, *Niccolò Machiavelli, storia del suo pensiero politico* (Napoli, 1958), pp. 290–303. The copious and erudite foot- notes of the original have been curtailed here.

1. *Prince*, chapter XV.

in *The Prince*, of men who are ungrateful, fickle, wicked, ready to forgive "sooner the death of their father than the loss of their patrimony;" and this pessimistic view of human nature—a radical pessimism, as we see, and without any softening extenuations—seems confirmed by that page of the eighteenth chapter in which he writes "that if all men were good," then his precepts would not apply. From this very bitterness of his toward a harsh, cruel world there seems to rise (as has been very finely observed)[2] a sigh of aspiration toward a different society of good men and pure. Generalizations of this sort, which check out so fully against the texts of Machiavelli himself, are not to be doubted; and the substantial critical consensus on this point would seem to confirm that we have reached a truth so clear it need no longer be put in discussion. Men are bad; they won't keep faith with you; therefore you need not keep faith with them. In this simple formula, which has behind it such a formidable force of textual evidence, the entire political thought of Machiavelli seems to be summarized.[3]

Except—and this is the essential point of the question—it suffices to push just a little further with the analysis, to become aware that even in such a simple assertion there lies hidden an equivocation, a subtle and insistent contradiction. In fact, if we try to answer the question "Where do political evil, wickedness, and cruelty come from?" by saying that they come from man's efforts to counter by these means the cruelty of others, not only do we leave completely vague the reason for this malice of the "others," but we've also wiped out our preceding explanation, according to which evil rises from the natural inclination of the human soul itself. If we want to hold to that explanation, we can't possibly say that the evil in us has its roots in the evil of others, or even in the suspicion that others may commit evil against us. Of the two alternatives, therefore, one clearly excludes the other, and thus we can't use both of them to explain the thought of Machiavelli. And on the other hand, if we press the question just a little further, it's not hard to see that, when we've shown that they are incompatible, one more look will exclude both of them from consideration altogether. We exclude the first—that which says evil is the consequence of man's natural inclination—because in such a case there would be no understanding why Machiavelli so often proposes evil, not simply as the natural condition of man, but as the end of his action, as a program that he should try to realize in every way for his own safety. (And if, in response, someone should say that even the evil that

2. Benedetto Croce, "Machiavelli e Vico" in *L'etica e la politica* (Bari, 1945), pp. 250–9.
3. On this point it suffices to cite Gerhard Ritter, *Die Dämonie der Macht* (München, 1948), pp. 33–34, 184 n. 17. [An English translation by F. W. Pick is titled *The Corrupting Influence of Power* (Hadleigh, England, 1952).—*Editor.*]

Machiavelli proposes as a program has its roots in the original evil of human nature, it would be easy to answer that if this evil is rooted simply in a response or a conscious program, then it can't be founded on instinct, and its reason must be sought somewhere else than in the nature of man.) The second alternative is excluded because if one cruelty is explained by another, one still has to explain the second cruelty, which was posed as a term of explanation; and even if we concede that men have become bad through suspicion of the badness of others, the real root of this timid psychology of theirs would still have to be found. But to do that, we would have to have recourse, not to the psychological inclination of man (which would be tautological), and not even to the presumed inclinations of his nature, but to his particular situation in history, the limit to which his power is confined, and which thus exposes him forever to the risk of being overcome by a course of events the nature of which he has never been able to grasp. Hence, man's inclination to evil is not necessary,[4] not constitutive (as if man as Machiavelli conceived him bore on his brow the indelible marks of that demonic *Lust for Power* that a German historian has tried to paint there)—it is the consequence of the limitation of human nature. And as for the cruelty of others (about which Machiavelli often speaks) that's a necessary hypothesis in men whose power to understand the interrelatedness of things is sharply limited, and who must therefore always strain in a desperate effort to achieve in some way the security of themselves or their state. In the third chapter of the first book of the *Discorsi*, Machiavelli will directly assert that "anyone who commands a republic and decrees laws within it, will have to suppose that all men are wicked, and that they will give rein to the malignity of their nature any time they are free to do so." The observation could not clarify better the point that human badness is not conceived by Machiavelli as an immutable fact of human nature, but as a hypothesis (a "supposition") which anyone who finds himself caught up in the living texture of a political action cannot fail to keep always in front of his eyes.

Evil, therefore, is not an immutable characteristic of the human soul, but a possible consequence of man's position in history, one of the techniques of which he may make use in his incessant struggle against the forces that threaten to undermine his security: and the direction pointed by Machiavelli's posing of the political problem is not toward the simple, indiscriminate admission that politics is evil and nothing but evil, the finished expression of an essentially demonic human nature, but toward the assertion that on the politi-

---

4. On the meaning of "necessity" see the observations of Meinecke, *Die Idee der Staatsräson*, pp. 46 ff. [Meinecke's essay, first published in 1924, has been translated into English by Douglas Scott as *Machiavellism* (London, 1947).—*Editor.*]

cal plane, the distinction between good and bad, between the useful and the honest (to use the venerable Ciceronian terms, dear to the Florentine humanists of the fifteenth century) should be understood not as an absolute set of alternate values, but as an opportunity to run before "the winds of fortune" or tack against them, as the weather and the time permit. Politics are thus the array of techniques that man may assume, as the times allow, in order to overcome the contradiction of his basic historical condition; hence it's perfectly understandable that, given this formulation of the problem, evil is justified from within by this initial situation which calls it forth (or can call it forth) as an instrument of liberation. In this sense one could say that, though it is born from a root of negation, from a limit and a contradiction, the art of politics rises to a lucid understanding of ends and means, and thus of its own genesis, the situation from which it sprang. But one should add at once that this knowledge of ends and means, and of the human limits by which politics justifies its crude and ruthless nature, implies a further awareness that this limit can never be wholly surpassed, that Fortune is a threatening and ever-present reality in the life of states, and that it would therefore be a grave and even fatal error if men should ever suddenly feel themselves released from the hard duty of following Fortune and controlling her motions. "It's a common defect of men, when the weather is good, never to think of the storms," so wrote Machiavelli at the end of the twenty-fourth chapter; and to this habit he assigns the cause of their defeats and their ruin—which is simply an imaginative and literary way of underlining this specific condition of human nature and all the political duties that derive from it. To confirm this view, it's enough to read a few pages of *The Prince*.

The seventh chapter, as is well known, describes the deeds of Cesare Borgia, and the techniques used by this exemplary prince to render solid and durable "those states which the arms and good fortune of other had granted to him." In these pages, striking for their sharpness of judgment and narrative vigor, Machiavelli passes in review, with unemotional precision, all the cruelty, trickery, and arts of the lion, as well as the fox, that the duke employed throughout his political life to achieve his ends and realize his "lofty" aspirations. And yet it would be hard to find in the whole chapter a single word that underlines a gratuitous cruelty; that implies political action is the consequence of a natural, and thus instinctive and irrational will to power; or that describes Duke Valentino's cruelty not as a political technique required by his situation as a "new prince" but as a necessary manifestation of the basic malice of human nature. Such a word would have been moralistic, it would have presupposed a set of political values based not on the concrete reality of things, but on a coarse and generic conception of human nature. There are no pages in any political writer that hold more closely than these to the bare essentials, to the nub of the matter, to the rigorous and unadorned logic of things. Cesare Borgia is portrayed not as a cruel prince, but as a prince who knows how to use cruel techniques when needed, and who is so far from being dominated by the cruelty and malice of his human nature that it is he who dominates them, and fixes with calculated coldness the moment and the circumstances in which their intervention is necessary, indispensable. Men, says Machiavelli, should be either flattered or destroyed; the head of a state should know how to use, now the arts of the fox, now the arts of the lion, because anyone who is "always a lion" shows that he "understands" very little of the complex problem of political action. A cruelty adopted when it's not called for—not justified, that is, by the superior "necessity of securing oneself"—is for Machiavelli an ill-used cruelty; a prince who doesn't know how to manage his mind, inclining it now towards cruelty and now towards goodness, is a dilettante, because neither good nor evil behavior will succeed unless it is adapted to particular times and circumstances. And if one reads carefully chapter eight, describing those who "came to be princes by crime," specifically the "criminal and nefarious" skills of Agathocles the Syracusan and Oliverotto da Fermo, it's easy to see that here too the cruelties in which these two persons freely indulged arose, not from any presumed innate malice on their part, but from the objective necessities of their political positions, which thus form the only criterion by which to distinguish cruelty used for good and used for evil. And this in connection with men whom Machiavelli does not hesitate to exclude from the number of the truly virtuous.

Certainly, our having denied that Machiavellian political thought derives its hateful nature from the evil implicit from eternity in the human mind, doesn't mean that we want soften the harshness of its theoretical formulation, nor try (which would be ridiculous) to "reconsecrate" its frank and open worldly nature. On the contrary, so sharp is the contrast between this and conventional formulations of the political problem, so deep is the break that Machiavelli makes with the traditional way of thinking, that even his mind does not always work at the highest tension of its theoretical formulations. He comes close on occasion to the limits of self-contradiction; as when, after observing that "you cannot call it virtue [*virtù*] to murder your fellow citizens, betray your friends, to be without faith, without pity, without religion; such proceedings may win you a crown, but not glory," he admits clearly that "if you consider the virtue [*virtù*] of Agathocles in confronting dangers and overcoming them, and the strength of his mind in sustaining adversity and overcoming it, no reason will appear why he should be thought inferior to any captain of the highest excellence,"[5] And yet suddenly he repeats that "nonetheless, his savage cruelty and inhumanity, with his infinite crimes, prevent him from being considered among men of great excellence." A page, this one, among the most tormented and dramatic of *The Prince*, and which raises a problem that cannot be resolved—as has been proposed[6]—by a distinction between actions directed to the common good (like those of Valentino) and actions directed at one's own personal benefit (like those of Oliverotto).[7] For if we do that, identifying Machiavelli's own position with the first of these two alternatives, we destroy the conflict which emerges clearly from the pages of chapter eight between his conception of politics and his vital moral conscience which feels a need to impose limits and place reservations on the boldest insights of that conception. Whether or not they're directed to the "service" of the subjects (and even those of Agathocles served the public good!), cruelties remain cruelties, they offend the moral conscience; and this is the tough problem that Machiavelli lived out in its bitterness, to its last consequences, without ever trying to soften it by means of imaginary and much too facile distinctions.

But on the other hand, the conflict does not imply uncertainty of thought or incoherence of attitude; at every moment the doctrine remains firm, as is evident to anyone who reads the other pages of *The Prince*, particularly the last section of chapter eight. For there, in perfect agreement with what Machiavelli will assert later, in the fifteenth, seventeenth, and above all in the eighteenth chapters, all these limitations and cautious distinctions are fused together into an explicit and concrete formulation which views good and evil entirely as instruments of political action. And in fact the chapter concludes with a discussion of the good and evil uses of cruelty, and with the explicit reduction of all forms of human behavior to the

5. *The Prince*, VIII; see also the important analogous words of *Discourses*, I, 26.

6. G. Pepe, *La politica dei Borgia* (Napoli, 1945), pp. 277–8.

7. Similarly, the observation (often repeated, according to which Machiavelli's "cruelties" would find their real justification in their end, which is clearly that of reconciling and not destroying (see, for example, *Discorsi* I, 9)—this observation suffers from both abstraction and imprecision. For the problem in Machiavelli is not that of justifying by the goodness of the end the cruelty of the means, not that of justifying by the well-being of the state or nation the immorality of the actions taken to sustain it, but the specific problem of cruelty, evil, slaughter, when one is led to it by the cold logic of politics. Pretending to justify by the goodness of the end the cruelty of the means amounts to nothing but an evasion of the problem that Machiavelli has dramatically posed and actually suffered with, down to its final consequences; and everything he wrote, from his youth down to *The Prince* and *The Discourses*, offers clear testimony of this. For, after all, cruelties don't cease to be such when they are "well used," and killing men is never anything but killing men, even if Machiavelli's prince is led to do it, not by personal cruelty, but by the necessity of his state. Machiavelli is a great and grievous moral conscience (to use the words of Croce) precisely because of the clarity and courage with which he has seen and formulated this dramatic problem. Taking the other alternative, one runs the risk of making him, not a great moral conscience, but a little seeker after pretexts and compromises.

simple measurement of the useful, and that which is useful to the state. Similarly, when discussing in chapter fifteen all the qualities that may be found in a head of state, Machiavelli certainly knows how to distinguish the good, the best, and the responsible; but, restricting himself to purely political considerations, the criterion according to which he classifies and evaluates actions is not at all their greater or lesser ethical excellence, but simply their usefulness, their concrete suitability to the times. Of course there are political means that can't fail to be considered cruel— "and I know," Machiavelli writes, "everyone will agree that among these many qualities a prince certainly ought to have all those that are considered good." And yet, "since he can't have and exercise them all, because the conditions of human life simply do not allow it, a prince must be shrewd enough to avoid the public disgrace of those vices that would lose him his state." Thus, Machiavelli concludes, "he should not be too worried about incurring blame for any vice without which he would find it hard to save his state. For if you look at matters carefully, you will see that something resembling virtue, if you follow it, may be your ruin, while something else resembling vice will lead, if you follow it, to your security and well-being." Thus, once again (and in one of the most powerful pages of the whole work), the necessity of doing evil, the necessity of incurring infamy, has its justification—not in a presumed original sin of human nature, but in the concrete reality of things which alone gives sense and significance to the political devices of men.

Another demonstration that politics is not the consequence of original sin, but a clear and distinct recognition that good and evil are significant terms only in relation to the circumstances under which they are asked to operate, is found in full within chapter eighteen. In fact, the problem of good faith and of treaties, which is the main topic of this chapter, is posed only in terms of this basic concept. Machiavelli certainly understands "how praiseworthy it is in a prince to keep his word and live with integrity rather than by craftiness," he knows perfectly well that between the two ways of fighting, one with laws and the other with force, the first is proper to men and the second to beasts. But Machiavelli knows also that "because the first method does not always suffice, you sometimes have to turn to the second," that "a prince has to know how to use one nature as well as the other," since "one without the other produces no lasting effect." And these precepts of his—about which he himself says that they would not be good rules, if men were not what they are—derive, not from a completely pessimistic intuition about the evil of human nature, but, when we look carefully, from a precise awareness of man's situation in history, of the necessity in which he finds himself, of having recourse to evil in order to protect his own security. "And this must be understood," Machiavelli in fact observes, "that a prince, and especially a new prince, cannot observe all those practices for which men are considered good, because he is often required, in order to maintain his state, to act against his word, against charity, against humanity, against religion. And thus he has to have a mind ready to turn itself according to the way the winds of fortune and the fluctuation of events command him; and, as was said above, he shouldn't abandon the good when he can cling to it, but be ready to enter upon evil when he has to." For the statesman, therefore, having "a mind ready to turn wherever the winds of fortune command him," means simply "being ready to enter on evil when he has to." And this, we think, is the very nucleus of the chapter, the key to Machiavelli's entire conception of politics. Taken in its simplest formulation, out of the context which binds it to all the rest of Machiavelli's thought, this notion of human wickedness can lead to arbitrary and misshapen conclusions. The "badness" of men, about which Machiavelli talks in the first part of the chapter with such impressive stylistic energy, is not in fact an original "sin," an immutable fact of human nature; rather, as we've just seen, it is a consequence of that necessity which constrains man at every moment of his life, which denies him all relaxation, and requires him to watch events continually, "so that when fortune shifts, he may be found ready to resist her." If man could command the stars and the fates, if his struggle against fortune had been decided forever in advance in his favor, politics would not be colored in such dark tonalities, and evil would no longer have any serious reason for existing in the structure of political action. In a universe peacefully or at least securely ruled by human virtue, the risk of being destroyed or killed would bear only on the weak and incompetent, and fortune in its constant threatening presence would not require us to confront unhesitatingly even the reputation of being evil and cruel. But fortune is nothing but the insurmountable boundary of human nature; it cannot be conquered once and for all, but only temporarily controlled by virtue [*virtù*]; the future of man is rendered uncertain, for Machiavelli, by the threat of the tempest always implicit in every human situation. And thus in that continual expectation of ruin which is, for Machiavelli, the life of states, anyone who tries to command destiny must have the courage to descend into the depths of even the most "criminal and nefarious" ways of life, in his efforts to keep from being overwhelmed by the gigantic forces of the times.

From the analysis of these pages, we may turn then to the core of the problem previously laid out, with this lesson learned: that politics is for Machiavelli the prime reality of human life, the only objective that man should always pursue, and to which he should be prepared to sacrifice every other activity, every other conviction, even his own soul. Politics is thus, beyond question, an autonomous reality, in the sense that nothing extraneous or contrary to its logic can pretend to control it; but in the strict sense of the word, it cannot even be called autonomous, since in the Machiavellian universe there is no value that can be set aside and withheld from use as its instrument—nothing with respect to which politics has any need to affirm its autonomy and independence. From this point of view the famous question whether or not Machiavelli "discovered" and affirmed "the category of politics"—of that politics which, as they say, is beyond or rather this side of moral good and evil[8]—reveals its basic historiographic abstractness. It's not that the politics of Machiavelli cannot be identified with the utilitarian or economic moment of human life, so much as that, outside that moment, there is no other which can serve with the same authority as the basis for a definition of good and evil. A distinction between utility and morality does not exist in the writings of Machiavelli, for the simple reason that being moral, being good, is for him a necessity which is qualitatively no different from the necessity that makes men immoral and bad. The useful is the only horizon of human life, because the position of man in history is always precarious; how then could it be presented as a distinct moment, when there's nothing in the world from which it has to be distinguished? The thesis sketched here should not be thought of as a proposal to find in Machiavelli the outlines of a theoretical defense of political activity; that's inconceivable, given his formulation of the problem. It simply emphasizes the absolute preeminence that politics assumes in Machiavelli's thought—and yet the very notion of preeminence carries with it a subtle logical inconsistency.

In fact one can't affirm the autonomy of politics without implying a nexus and relatedness between politics and ethics. But in Machiavelli, it has been stated (and very truly), ethics doesn't mingle with politics, and therefore remains a simple desire, a sentiment, a melancholy aspiration toward an unattainable society of men who are good and pure; by the same token that politics is something quite different, ethics finally defies reduction to the status of an autonomous category. In reality, Machiavelli's evident uncertainty in the face of the cruder formulations of his own doctrine (as in the pages previously described, on Agathocles of Syracuse and Oliverotto da Fermo) serves to underline the absolute and exclusive character of politics. It is a politics which declares itself decisively as the unique value of human life, the only activity for man to follow, to which he must be ready to sacrifice all his other ideals, and before which there is good reason for that mournful

8. This is the classic thesis of Croce, "Machiavelli e Vico." See above, note 2.

Machiavellian grief over a lost world or one which never existed, a world of goodness and purity, the loss of which can be sensed in the pages of *The Prince*.

This sense of loss and this uncertainty bring to the fore the limits of a politics so broadly founded in evil and cruelty, and wholly devoid, if not in its "intentions," of the great human values which make up the enduring strength of political institutions themselves. But this limit is the historic limit of Machiavelli's entire work: the limit, and at the same time the condition of his political will. That was the will of a man well aware of the seriousness of the situation he intended to transform, and determined to cling to the terms of concrete reality, who thereby was led to an intellectual idealization of the political techniques put at his disposal by that same decadent society. What really lies behind Machiavelli's pretense that the prince can enter into evil, and explore decisively and unashamedly the most wicked and "nefarious" of ways, if not the preservation on an idealized plane of the passive and unproductive political approach (compounded of intrigue, cruelty, and sterile trickery) practiced by those Italian princes on whom Machiavelli placed the blame for the ruin of Italy? The evil that he considers an essential part of political action (and of which his assumptions quietly destroy the negative ethical view) may look from one angle like an effort to overcome the objective political conditions of contemporary Italy; but from another aspect, it simply reproduces in itself the same limits and the same contradictions that Machiavelli denounced in the historical situation. And this is the source, both of the grandeur and of the narrowness of Machiavelli's accomplishment. There's nothing degenerate about it; it rises out of open, polemical opposition to the mean and pointless crimes of Italian politicians; but it is grounded, not simply in the generous sentiments of a man who wants to found a new politics because he is aware of the decay of an old society, but also in the limitations of a man who wants to operate effectively in a historic situation, and thus cannot help accepting its essential boundaries.

The limitation, the inner difficulty of this politics, broadly based on hateful and "beastly" techniques that Machiavelli describes in *The Prince*, coincides closely with his political will, and with the limit which that will imposed on his analysis. This limit, it must be repeated, certainly carries no implication that Machiavelli deluded himself over the ease with which his program could be put into effect. Anyone who thought that to be the case would understand nothing of his thought, of his ruthless reduction of all moral values to simple tools of political action, of that harsh program which is in effect justified and rendered necessary by Machiavelli's precise intuition of the contradictions in human nature: contradictions which

express in abstract form what Machiavelli had learned through concrete political experience in the affairs of Italy. In this sense—and
it's a point of fundamental importance—the difference between
The Prince and the *Discourses* is a very deep one; and it's interesting to note that it derives precisely from the differing breadth of
their historic conceptions. On the broad canvas of national life
which the *Discourses* treat with a depth that has no parallel in
Machiavelli's other works, the immediate crudeness of *The Prince's*
politics is softened. The cruelties which in *The Prince* still had a
quality of personal, immediate intention, lose that tone of excep-
tionality; they no longer seem, as it were, a challenge flung in a gesture of defiance at the misery of the world, but turn into one constitutive tonality within a larger and more fully articulated system.
From this point of view as well, the concept of politics rising from
the conceptions developed in the *Discourses* appears richer (even if
less sharply outlined and dramatic) because the historical understanding that sustains it is deeper and more fully thought out. To
repeat now the reasons for the differences between the two works,
to reexamine the relative shallowness of *The Prince* by comparison
with the *Discourses*, would involve repeating all that has been said
already about their origins, their motives, their specific problems;
here it was simply a matter of clarifying the origins and significance
of Machiavellian politics, clearing away all categorical discussions of
the morality or immorality of their maxims, and grasping the
connection of the system with the fundamental themes of his
thought and his experiences.

JOHN PLAMENATZ

In Search of Machiavellian Virtù†

Mr. Plamenatz begins his essay by contrasting three different writers on
Machiavelli (Meinecke, Whitfield, and Villari), who attribute to him three
different concepts of *virtù*, and assign to each a different order of importance. He then turns to an analysis of the way in which Machiavelli actually
uses the word in his text.

If we read only English translations of Machiavelli, we are hard
put to it to discover what he meant by *virtù*. For his translators,
more often than not, do not render *virtù* by "virtue." They have an
excellent excuse for not doing so; for *virtù*, as Machiavelli uses it,
often does not mean what "virtue" means in the English of our
day. So they render *virtù* by some other word, such as valor, ability,

†From *The Political Calculus*, ed. An-
thony Parel (Toronto: University of To-   ronto Press, 1972), pp. 157–78.

merit, courage, or genius, or by some combination of words. Take for example the nineteenth chapter of the first book of the *Discourses*, which in most editions, both Italian and English, is from two to three pages long. In it Machiavelli speaks of *virtù* ten times; Detmold, in one of the most widely used of English translations, renders *virtù* by "virtue" only twice, and on both occasions adds the word "valor," presumably in the hope of coming closer to the original; while Allan Gilbert, the most recent and perhaps the most accurate of Machiavelli's translators into English, abstains altogether from the word "virtue" in his version of this chapter.[1] On all ten occasions he renders *virtù* by "ability," leaving it to the reader to judge from the context what kind of ability is in question. Detmold renders *virtù* by "character," "virtue and valor," "vigor and ability," "genius and courage," "good qualities and courage," "great abilities and courage," "military ability," "merits." If we take only this chapter, Gilbert is the more prudent translator of the two, and also the more faithful to the original. Yet *virtù*, as Machiavelli uses the word, has not quite the same meaning, or range of meanings, as the broader and more colorless English word "ability." Which is not to suggest that Gilbert was wrong to prefer it to the more varied expressions to which Detmold resorted.

In the third chapter of *The Prince*, Machiavelli praises the Romans for their foresight. He says of them that "seeing their troubles far ahead, [they] always provided against them, and never let them continue in order to avoid war, because they knew that such a war is not averted but is deferred to the other's advantage. . . . Nor did they approve what all day is in the mouths of the wise men of our age: to profit from the help of time; but they did profit from that of their own vigor [*virtù*] and prudence."[2] Here *virtù* is associated with prudence. The Romans looked far ahead, taking resolute and timely action. What, according to Machiavelli, do the wise —the falsely-wise—mean by "the help of time"? They mean that we can see only a little way ahead, and that therefore difficult decisions are best left untaken. This is the excuse of the pusillanimous. True, we cannot be sure of the future, but we must look ahead as far as we can, seeing what is to be done for the best, and doing it in good time. With the old Romans, at least in the days of Machiavelli, foresight, energy, and courage went naturally together.

In the sixth chapter of *The Prince*, speaking of men who have become rulers, Machiavelli says: "they had from Fortune nothing more than opportunity, which gave them matter into which they

---

1. For Detmold's rendering see his translation of the *Discourses* in the Modern Library College edition of *The Prince* and the *Discourses*, 172–4; for Gilbert's see *Machiavelli: The Chief Works and Others*, tr. Allan H. Gilbert, I, 244–5.

2. Gilbert, *Chief Works*, I, 17. I shall quote only from Allan Gilbert's translation of Machiavelli, putting the word *virtù* or other Italian words or phrases in brackets next to Gilbert's renderings of them.

could introduce whatever form they chose; and without opportunity, their strength of will [*la virtù dello animo loro*] would have been wasted, and without such strength, the opportunity would have been useless";[3] and then, a little further on, he continues: "Their opportunities then made these men prosper, since their surpassing abilities [*la eccellente virtù loro*] enabled them to recognize their opportunities. As a result, their countries were exalted and became very prosperous."[4] Here *virtù* consists, in the first place, of strength of will or mind, and in the second, of insight. The possessor of *virtù* sees his chance to mould something to his own design, not some inert or physical thing, but something human, some community or some aspect of communal life; he has imagination and intelligence enough to see what can be done, to see what is invisible to others, and strength of purpose enough to do it. He is strong, bold, and of good judgment, to his own great advantage and to the advantage of his people or community.

This is not to say that, in the opinion of Machiavelli, these qualities fail to qualify as *virtù* unless their possessor actually gets what he wants for himself or his people. Courage, energy, and intelligence do not cease to be what they are when they fail of their purpose. Small men have small purposes and are often successful, but their success is no evidence of *virtù* in them, and great men—who are great because their courage, energy, and intelligence are out of the ordinary—sometimes fail. One of the meanings that Machiavelli gives to *virtù* is the capacity to form large and difficult purposes, and to act resourcefully and resolutely in pursuit of them. *Virtù*, in this (the heroic) sense, is imagination and resilience as well as courage and intelligence. There is no scope for it except where there are difficulties, where there are risks to be taken; and where risks are taken, there is a chance of failure. Machiavelli's feelings towards the most notorious, and (in some eyes) the most oddly chosen, of his heroes varied considerably. There was a time when he came close to despising Cesare Borgia—not because Borgia failed of his purpose but because he lost his nerve and his dignity when things went against him.

Villari is right when he says that Machiavellian *virtù* is "fruitful of glory." The actions it inspires are of the kind that bring fame or reputation: fame where *virtù* is heroic and reputation where it is civic. But it is a mistake to include, as Meinecke does, ambition among the qualities that make up *virtù*. I have found no example of Machiavelli using the word in such a way as to suggest that ambition is itself a part of *virtù*. True, he thought well of ambition, and was himself ambitious. The desire for glory promotes *virtù*; it is the strongest of the forces that move men to display it, especially the

3. Ibid., 25.   4. Ibid., 26.

heroic kind. And even the citizen who displays only civic *virtù* is concerned for his good name; and this concern, though it is not what is ordinarily called ambition, is akin to it. But to hold that ambition is a prime mover of *virtù* is still not to treat ambition as a part of *virtù*.

In some of the most discussed pages he wrote, in the eighth chapter of *The Prince*, Machiavelli denies that a really wicked man who achieves a great ambition can be said to be virtuous, even though he displays great strength of mind and courage. This denial has been called half-hearted, and is certainly ambiguous. Speaking of Agathocles, a potter's son who by ruthless means became tyrant of Syracuse, Machiavelli says: "It cannot, however, be called virtue [*virtù*] to kill one's fellow-citizens, to betray friends, to be without fidelity, without mercy, without religion; such proceedings enable one to gain sovereignty but not fame. If we consider Agathocles' ability [*se si considerassi la virtù di Agatocle*] in entering into and getting out of dangers, and his greatness of mind in enduring and overcoming adversities, we cannot see why he should be judged inferior to any of the most excellent generals [*a qualunque eccellentissimo capitano*]. Nevertheless, his outrageous cruelty and inhumanity . . . do not permit him to be honored among the noblest men [*che sia infra li eccellentissimi uomini celebrato*]."[5] The translator, in a footnote to the passage I have quoted, suggests that the first *virtù* means moral excellence, and the second, the kind attributed to Agathocles, courage and prudence. This, no doubt, is why he renders only the first as "virtue."

Now the other great "captains"—for example, Romulus or Cesare Borgia—to whom Machiavelli attributes *virtù* were not morally excellent. Or at least, he was not pointing to their moral excellence when he spoke of their *virtù*. He was pointing to much the same qualities in them as he found in Agathocles—to their courage, energy, fortitude, and ability to see and to seize opportunities. These qualities are, of course, compatible with moral excellence just as they are with cruelty, murder, and perfidy. They are qualities that men, wherever they recognize them for what they are, are disposed to admire. It is not peculiar to Machiavelli that he admired them. They are also, so Machiavelli tells us (and surely he is right?), qualities that men are the readier to recognize and to admire, the better they like, or the more they come to accept, their effects. That is why the crimes of the man of heroic *virtù* are so often excused when his achievement is recognized, and why he is admired in spite of them. He is not admired for being murderous, perfidious, and cruel. For the cowardly, the irresolute, and the stupid, and those who lose their heads in the face of danger or unexpected difficulties,

5. Ibid., 36.

may also kill, betray, and be cruel. He is admired for the largeness and boldness of his purpose, for his resolution, courage, and skill in carrying it out, for daring to do what has to be done to achieve it. Yet there are limits to this admiration; it is sometimes given grudgingly or even withheld from someone of whom it cannot be denied that he possesses these rare qualities. Not because he lacks moral excellence; for the others, the honored, the *celebrati*, may do so too. Borgia, as Machiavelli describes him, is not less selfish than Agathocles. But because his purpose, when achieved—no matter what his motives in pursuing it—is not accepted by others, is not found good by them or does not attract their sympathy, or else because, in pursuing it, he commits unnecessary crimes. If he is wantonly cruel or treacherous, or if his purpose or achievement is unintelligible to others or awakens no response in them, then his qualities are not admired or perhaps even recognized, or are so grudgingly, even though they are of a kind ordinarily much admired. *Virtù*, wherever it is recognized, is apt to be admired because it consists of qualities that most men understand and wish they had. Why then was it not admired in Agathocles? Why the reluctance to admit that he had it? Was it because he lacked moral excellence? Or because he was entirely selfish? I doubt whether Machiavelli had such reasons as these in mind when he wrote the eighth chapter of *The Prince*. Not that he cared nothing for moral excellence or unselfishness. But these things, I suggest, seemed irrelevant to him when he was asking how it came about that Agathocles was less admired than other men of no greater strength of purpose, resourcefulness and courage than himself.

The *virtù* that Machiavelli speaks of in *The Prince* is for the most part not civic but heroic. In the *Discourses* he has more to say about the *virtù* of the citizen, and what he says there allows us to draw some conclusions about how the two kinds of *virtù* are connected. In the eleventh chapter of book I he says: "Kingdoms depending on the vigor [*virtù*] of one man alone are not very lasting because that vigor departs with the life of that man . . . It is not, then, the salvation of a republic or kingdom to have a prince who will rule prudently while he lives but to have one who will so organize it that even after he dies it can be maintained."[6] And in the first chapter of the same book he says: "Those who read in what way the city of Rome began, and by what lawgivers and how she was organized, will not marvel that so much vigor was kept up in that city for so many centuries [*che tanta virtù si sia per più secoli mantenuta in quella città*] and that finally it made possible the dominant position to which that republic rose."[7]

The *virtù* "of one man alone" is the *virtù* of the ruler or of the

6. Ibid., 226.   7. Ibid., 192.

founder of a state or religion, whereas the *virtù* that survived in Rome for centuries was widespread among the citizens. Clearly, there are here two kinds of *virtù* in question; they may have something in common but they also differ. If a state is to be well organized or reformed, it must have a founder or restorer who has the first and rarer kind of *virtù*. But, unless it is well organized or reformed, its citizens are unlikely for long to have much of the second kind, the kind that many can share. So much is, I think, clearly implied by Machiavelli in these and other chapters of the *Discourses*, even though he never distinguishes between two kinds of *virtù*.

Speaking in the *Discourses* (book I, chapter 4) of the dissensions between patricians and plebeians in the Roman republic, he says that a republic cannot "in any way be called unregulated [*inordinata*] where there are so many instances of honorable conduct [*dove sieno tanti esempli di virtù*]; for these good instances have their origin in good education; good education in good laws; good laws in those dissensions that many thoughtlessly condemn. For anyone who will properly examine their outcome will not find that they produce any exile or violence damaging to the common good, but laws and institutions conducive to public liberty."[8] The examples of *virtù* are examples of devotion to the republic and respect for her laws, of civic virtue, and we are told that they abounded in Rome, not only in spite of dissensions, but indeed—though indirectly, no doubt—because of them. Dissension sometimes enhances respect for law, and therefore civic virtue, since this respect is part of that virtue; and sometimes has the opposite effect. In the *History of Florence* (book III, chapter 1), Machiavelli enquires why discord between the nobles and the people strengthened the republic in ancient Rome and weakened it in Florence. It was, he thinks, because the Roman people, unlike the Florentines, were moderate and content to share power with the nobles. Thus "through the people's victories the city of Rome became more excellent [*virtuosa*] . . . and . . . as she increased in excellence [*virtù*], increased in power." Whereas in Florence, the nobles, deprived of office by the people, when they tried to regain it "were forced in their conduct, their spirit, and their way of living not merely to be like the men of the people [*popolani*] but to seem so . . . [so much so that] the ability in arms [*virtù dell'armi*] and the boldness of spirit [*generosità di animo*] possessed by the nobility were destroyed, and these qualities could not be rekindled in the people, where they did not exist, so that Florence grew always weaker and more despicable."[9]

8. Ibid., 203—I do not know why Gilbert has translated *esempli* by *instances* rather than *examples*, for Machiavelli is speaking here of conduct which he think is exemplary.
9. Ibid., III, 1141.

It would seem, then, that even civic virtue is, or may be, aristocratic in origin, and later acquired by the people from the nobles,
provided that the people are moderate. The *virtù* of the citizen is
more than just respect for the laws and institutions, and more than
courage and devotion to the community; it is also a kind of wisdom
or self-restraint which it would be misleading to call *prudence*, as
that word is now used in English.

The *virtù* of the citizen does not consist of all the qualities in
him that help to make the state strong; it consists only of qualities
that he exhibits when he acts as a citizen. The Romans, at least in
the days of the republic, were (so thought Machiavelli) a religious
people, and Rome was the stronger for their being so. Yet being
religious is no part of *virtù*, as Machiavelli conceives of it. For religion sustains both goodness (*bontà*), or what might be called private morals, and civic virtue. We are told in the *Discourses* (I, 55)
that: "Where this goodness [*bontà*] does not exist, nothing good
can be expected, as nothing good can be expected in regions that in
our time are evidently corrupt, as is Italy above all, though in such
corruption France and Spain have their share. If in those countries
fewer disorders appear than we see daily in Italy, the cause is not so
much the goodness of the people—which for the most part no
longer exists—as that they have a king who keeps them united, not
merely through his ability [*virtù*] but also through the still
unruined organization of these kingdoms. In Germany this goodness
and this religion are still important among the people. These qualities enable many republics to exist there in freedom and to observe
their laws so well that nobody outside or inside the cities dares to
try to master them."[1] It is the *virtù* of its citizens that makes a
state formidable, and this *virtù* is sustained by religion and good
morals. It is sustained also by good laws and institutions, for if a
state were not well organized (*ordinata*) *virtù* could not survive for
long inside it. Thus good laws and civic virtue support one another,
and both are supported by religion and morals.

The well-ordered state is not—so Machiavelli implies—the slow
work of time, the undesigned effect of human endeavor that men
learn to value as they come to appreciate its benefits. It is the
achievement of one, or of at most a few, clear-sighted and bold men
who see further and dare more than other men do. These men, the
founders and restorers of states and religion, possess a *virtù* far rarer
than that of the ordinary citizen, even at his Roman best. They
have greater foresight and insight, more firmness of purpose, more
ruthlessness (*feròcia*), and a courage that most men—even the
brave—lack. They can set aside scruples to achieve some large aim.

1. Ibid., I, 307.

They may not be good men, but it is good that there should be such men; for if there were not, there would exist no well-ordered states, and therefore little scope for either the more ordinary virtue of the citizen or for the goodness that Machiavelli always praises except when it endangers the state. This goodness, which he attributes to the old Roman and to the German of his own day, is not quite goodness as the Christian understands it, or as many who are not Christians have understood it, whether in our times or in others. He says so little about it that we cannot be sure quite what it consists of. He says much less about it than about *virtù*—which does not in the least mean that he holds it of little account. On the contrary; for he tells us that no community can do without it—can for long have either internal security or be formidable to other communities. All this he tells us, though he also tells us that sometimes it takes a man willing to set this goodness aside to establish or to save a community.

If we do Machiavelli the simple justice of attributing to him only opinions that he expressed or clearly implied, we must not even say that he valued goodness, as distinct from *virtù*, merely for its political effects. We must say only that he had more to say about its political effects than about its nature—which is perhaps not surprising in a historian and a writer on politics.

[Plamenatz goes on to argue that Machiavelli did not believe *virtù* was an end in itself, or that there were two spheres for *virtù* to be exercised in, one of which was "higher" than the other. Neither did he believe that *virtù* was better, or more to be regarded than goodness; nor did he occupy himself with defining the limits of the individual's obligation to the state. All these formulas, says Plamenatz, represent answers to questions that Machiavelli never asked—because his essential concern was with politics as an art in itself.]

Chabod says that Machiavelli's absorbing passion is for politics, and that he takes little interest in anything else. This is substantially true; for Machiavelli, though he speaks of other things, especially in his plays and letters, speaks of them much as he does of politics. As, for example, when he speaks of love—or, rather, of the pursuit of women. Here too there is something definite to be attained, and the pursuer must be resourceful, skilful, and bold if he is to attain it. Love, as Machiavelli speaks of it, is an activity less absorbing, less admirable, less fruitful of glory, than government and war, but in several respects it is similar. It is a game, perhaps, a distraction, and yet is not unlike the serious business from which it distracts. I speak, of course, not of any theory about love to be found in Machiavelli's writings, nor of his treatment of women, but only of an attitude to love revealed in his two plays and some of his letters.

"The truth," says Chabod, "is that Machiavelli leaves the moral ideal intact and he does so because it does not concern him."[2] Perhaps it would be better to say that it does not concern him directly; for, as we have seen, he holds that a community cannot be well ordered for long, nor formidable to others, unless its members are honest and good—unless, like the old Romans and the Germans of his day, they have *bontà* and not merely *virtù*. And *bontà* has more of morality about it than has *virtù*. But Machiavelli has little to say about it, and has nowhere a word of sympathy for the troubled conscience. As Chabod puts it, "he is ignorant, not only of the eternal and the transcendent, but also of the moral doubt and the tormenting anxiety that beset a conscience turned in upon itself."[3]

Ridolfi expresses a different opinion, and speaks of "the intimate religious foundation of his conscience which breathes from all his works."[4] It seems to have breathed for few besides Ridolfi. By all means, let us take care how we speak of Machiavelli. Let us not say that he was without religion or that he was untroubled by conscience, or—as some have said—that his *Exhortation to Penitence* was not a moment of piety in his life but a "frivolous joke." Chabod, taken literally may well be wrong; Machiavelli was perhaps not "ignorant of the eternal and transcendent" and was almost certainly (being intelligent, sensitive, and self-critical) often a prey to moral doubt and anxiety. No man reveals all that is in him in the writings he leaves behind him. But the fact remains that Machiavelli has much to say about *virtù* and little about moral goodness, and that *virtù*, as he speaks of it, has nothing to do with conscience. Machiavelli was not entirely a political animal; no man ever is. Yet the spirit that "breathes from all his works" is political.

Not only because he writes mostly about politics and war but also —and above all—because the image of man that his writings project is, in a broad sense of the word, political. He seems to admire above all the man who knows what he wants and who acts resolutely and intelligently to get it. Such a man need not be engaged in politics or war; he need not be a ruler or a general, a citizen or a soldier. He can be anything, if only he has definite aims making large demands on him, and has strength of mind and ability enough to meet them. Machiavelli never said that the qualities he so much admired are displayed only in politics and war, and we are not to conclude that he thought so. Yet they are displayed largely in these two spheres, and they are the spheres in which he took the deepest interest. The man who knows what he wants and acts resolutely to get it must often, especially if he has some large and difficult aim,

2. Federico Chabod, *Machiavelli and the Renaissance*, tr. D. Moore (London 1958), 142.
3. Ibid., 93.
4. Roberto Ridolfi, *The Life of Niccolò Machiavelli*, tr. Cecil Grayson (London 1963), 253.

use others for his purposes. He need not always do so (he may be an artist) but often he must. He is a wielder of power and influence. So the sphere of *virtù*, though it is wider than just politics and war, is nevertheless in a broad sense political. It consists above all of activities in which men work together, or against one another, or make use of each other, in the pursuit of definite aims.

It consists of only a part of life. Now, in general, it is no criticism of a man to say that he is concerned with only a part of life. If he makes his theme clear to his readers and leaves nothing important out of account, they have no cause of complaint. The economist studies only a part of human behavior, and when he makes assumptions about the motives, aims, and capacities of men, presumably makes only such as he thinks are relevant to his purpose. Nobody is moved to say of Ricardo that he is ignorant of the eternal and the transcendent, or of moral doubt and anxiety. And if anyone did say it, we should think it beside the point. But when Chabod says it of Machiavelli, we think it a point worth making, whether we agree with him or not. We think this, not because Machiavelli's subject is politics and not economics, but because of the way he writes about it, the quality of his interest in it. He does not go about his business as Ricardo does about his; he does not attempt a systematic explanation of just one sphere of human activity, making only such assumptions about men's aims and capacities as he thinks necessary to his limited purpose. Unsystematic though he is, limited though his interests are, he makes large and bold statements about man, so that his readers get the impression that he claims to be taking the measure of their species. And the impression is not mistaken.

Machiavelli is a great writer whose moods and feelings infect his readers. What he admires is indeed admirable, and also rare. Firmness of purpose, presence of mind, resourcefulness, the ability to see more clearly and further than others, fortitude in adversity: these qualities and the others that make up *virtù* are everywhere exalted. It is through them, above all, that man makes his presence felt in the world, and in them that he takes pride. *Virtù* is opposed to *fortuna*, to chance, to the unforeseen, to the external and the hostile. Machiavelli appeals to sentiments that are strong in most men—to men without religion as much as those with it. To display *virtù* is not to do God's will, nor is it to behave morally; it is to make your will and your person count for something in the eyes of other men and your own. Which is not to say that *virtù* cannot be displayed in the service of God or in acting morally. Machiavelli, who in some moods despised Savonarola, in others admired him; he admired him for what he had of *virtù* (courage, a strong will, and fortitude) and despised him for what he lacked (understanding and foresight).

There is a perverse streak in Machiavelli. He likes to make himself out worse than he is. He likes at times to shock his contemporaries, and he has shocked posterity to the threshold of our own "unshockable" age. Yet his "philosophy" is not so much immoral as it is defective. For, unlike the "political scientist" of today, he does present us with something that deserves to be called a philosophy: with reflections upon what is essentially human about man. He has a philosophy in the sense that Montaigne—who is even less systematic than he is—has one.

If we conceive of man as Machiavelli describes him we miss a great deal that is distinctively human about him. We forget that he is a contemplative being and a problem to himself, that he is as much frustrated as inspired by his imagination, that many of his purposes—no matter how exalted and powerful he is—are half-formed and change imperceptibly. Above all, we forget that much that makes life seem valuable to him comes of his uncertainties and hesitations, his doubts and anxieties, his sense that there is more to him than he is aware of, his not quite knowing what he is moving towards even though he is to some extent self-propelled. Those who do not know what they want and are not resolute in trying to get it are not necessarily poor in spirit. Men are not always allies or enemies, masters or servants, in the pursuit of definite aims; they are also involved with one another, and with the groups and communities they belong to, in ways that are comforting or hurtful, exciting or depressing, and yet unrelated to such aims. These sides of life are just as much specifically human, setting man apart from the other animals, enriching his imagination, sharpening his intelligence, deepening his emotions, as the formation and pursuit of clear and realistic aims.

Machiavelli did not deny this; he merely took no account of it. If he had neglected it because it was not relevant to his purpose, there would be no objecting to him on that score. If he had been what we today call a political scientist, it would be absurd to complain that he had too political a conception of man. But he was not a political scientist in that sense; he did not aim at explaining systematically a limited but important sphere of human activity. True, he wrote very largely (though unsystematically) about politics; but in the course of doing so he indulged in reflections about man that suggest that man is pre-eminently political in the sense that what he values most in his own species are rare qualities finding their largest scope in politics and war, or in activities similar to them. It may be true that man admires these qualities as much as any, but it is not true that they, more than others, give savor to his life. Machiavelli did not say they do but he wrote as if he thought they did. He made altogether too much of *virtù*, especially the heroic kind.

ROBERT M. ADAMS

The Rise, Proliferation, and Degradation of Machiavellism: An Outline

The history of Machiavellism, it has been well said, is a history of misunderstandings. The word has stood, in its time, not only for trickery, equivocation, and unscrupulous cruelty, but also for utter honesty and surgical accuracy of thought. It has stood for audacious republicanism, craven support of tyranny, and unscrupulous tyrannicide; for fanatical Catholicism and for religious toleration; for national liberation and enslavement to the devil; for cynical opportunism and the highest of moral principles. Not all these interpretations can be right, and the current popular use of the word is less right than most. Still, at this late date, there's no use protesting; *Machiavellism* is set in the language to describe unscrupulous political behavior.

But to write an account of unscrupulous political behavior (ambition, greed, falsehood, cruelty) would take us far and wide, back into the mists of antiquity, around the globe, and down to the present day—in a reasonable assurance that the future won't be much different. With most of this wickedness the Florentine secretary had absolutely nothing to do, and we can therefore cheerfully discard it to the historians of infamy. The present outline is more modest; it aims to present in capsule form the elements of a chronology tracing some specific ways in which Machiavelli's reputation and influence developed and at the same time diffused across three centuries. A severely practical way to begin this story is with a bald summary of the publishing history of *The Prince*.

I. *Manuscripts, editions, translations*

1513: *The Prince* was written under circumstances described in Machiavelli's famous letter to Vettori. Some time between 1516 and 1519 he changed the dedication, but without trying very actively to press the book or his own fortunes with Lorenzo. Handwritten copies circulated for nearly twenty years, how widely we don't know. In 1523, nine years before *The Prince* was published and four years before Machiavelli's death, a rascal named Agostino Nifo cribbed wholesale from one of these manuscripts, and after translating his pickings into Latin, published a treatise on government that in substance was pure Machiavelli. Cardinal Reginald Pole said that in 1529 Thomas Cromwell, one of Henry VIII's most hardbitten agents, recommended to him a new Italian book on politics. It may or may not have been *The Prince*. Pole, writing ten years later (and in a spirit of bitter hostility to Cromwell, Henry, and the English Reformation) said that it was, and that Cromwell, by reading it, had become an agent of Satan. About this time the story became current that Niccolò Machiavelli gave the devil his popular title of "Old Nick." Though false, the association stuck; not only was Machiavelli regularly described as devilish, but the devil in time came to be described as Machiavellian.

1532: Antonio Blado, having obtained the necessary permission from Pope Clement VII (Giulio de' Medici), began to publish Machiavelli's writings. *The Prince* appeared in Rome on January 4, and on May 8 Bernardo di Giunta published an edition in Florence. He reprinted in 1537 and 1540; and the busy Venetian publishers picked up the text, issuing seven editions (1537, 1540, 1541, 1546, 1550, 1552, 1554) in less than twenty years.

1550: The first *Collected Works* of Machiavelli were published; from its engraved portrait, this is called the Testina edition.

1553: *The Prince* was first translated into a foreign language; a French version by Guillaume Capel appeared in Paris.

1560: *The Prince* was translated into Latin, the international language of scholarship, by Sylvester Telius (Tegli) Fulginatus and published at Basel.

1640: *The Prince* was published in English; Edward Dacres was the translator. There had been previous translations into English, and they survive in the odd manuscript, but none was published till the episcopal censorship broke down in 1640.

II. *The Index and the Bartholomew Massacre*

1559: The entire works of Machiavelli were placed on the Index of Prohibited Books, compiled by the Holy Inquisition in Rome. This act resulted from the decrees of the Council of Trent, which met from 1545 to 1563 in order to stiffen the discipline of the Roman Church against Protestantism. Pope Paul the Fourth, whose entire life had been spent as an inquisitor, and who was a mortal enemy of heresy in any form, urged on the compiling of the Index, and widened its scope, so that it dealt not just with heresy, but with morality

and manners in general. Since Machiavellism was sometimes associated in Protestant countries with the Jesuit
order, it is interesting to note that at Ingolstadt in
Bavaria, the Jesuit college held a book-burning in 1615,
at which Machiavelli's works were incinerated.

1572: Beginning on St. Bartholomew's night, and for several
weeks thereafter, the Catholic leaders of France made
a sudden, concerted effort to wipe out the entire
Huguenot (Protestant) population of France. They
succeeded, to the extent of approximately 50,000 murders. Charles IX was King of France at the time, but
he was young (twenty-two), weak, and flighty: the
power in the country lay with his mother, Catherine
de' Medici. She was hated as an Italian and a Medici,
as a favorer of Italian and particularly papal courtiers,
as a secretive and treacherous person, and finally as a
reader of Machiavelli. The Catholic treachery of the
Saint Bartholomew's Massacre thus came to be blamed
on Machiavelli by the Protestants—just at a time when
Catholics were being forbidden to read him, because
he was on the Index.

1576: Innocent Gentillet, a French Huguenot enraged by
the Massacre of Saint Bartholomew, wrote the book by
which Machiavelli was largely to be known for years
to come, the *Discours sur les moyens de bien gouverner
. . . contre Nicolas Machiavel, Florentin.* As translations into the languages of Protestant countries were
many years away, as the Huguenots were dispersed
across Europe and carried their hatred of Machiavelli
with them, and as Catholics themselves could not read
or even possess copies of Machiavelli's text, Gentillet
had a major influence. For instance, Antonio Possevino,
an Italian Jesuit, wrote in 1592 a Latin *Judgment of
Four Authors,* one of whom was Machiavelli. Because
Gentillet's book was divided into three parts, Possevino
took for granted that *The Prince* was, too—thereby
betraying the fact that he had never laid eyes on it, but
based his "judgment" on the opinion of one whom he
considered a heretic. Gentillet was translated into English thirty-eight years before Machiavelli himself.

III. *Ragion di Stato*

When Machiavelli went on the Index, he did not
disappear completely from the Catholic countries; any
devout Catholic could read him by getting a dispensation, and not everyone even bothered getting formal

permission. Lawyers especially could not help dealing with Machiavelli's central idea that the prince, being responsible for the survival of the state, is entitled to use extraordinary means (as we would say, "executive privilege") toward that end. How extraordinary these means could legitimately become was a typical lawyer's question: it involved qualifying, softening, and moralizing Machiavelli's basic insight, often without mentioning him at all. This was relatively easy to do because, as we must never forget, Machiavellism was but a minor current in the broad stream of political thought, the main body of which runs straight and clear, from Erasmus's *Institution of a Christian Prince* (1515) to Fénelon's *Télémaque* (1699), with indefinite extensions before and after. In this majority view, politics is properly an engine of morality and is entitled to depart from strict morality only in extreme emergencies.

1580s: Paolo Paruta, a Venetian lawyer and historian, wrote a set of *Political Discourses* (not published till 1599), in which he discussed, very much after Machiavelli's manner, a number of case histories. The question was whether the right policy had been followed, under the circumstances, and whether the practical advantages of certain actions did not outweigh their moral obliquity. But in the end Paruta was more a moralist than a politician.

1585: Alberico Gentili, a liberal Italian jurist who ended his career at Oxford, was bold enough to mention Machiavelli directly. In his big book *On Embassies* he declared (III, 9) that Machiavelli exposed the powers of the prince as a deliberate satiric warning against excesses in the use of a power healthy in itself.

1589: Giovanni Botero gave the name *Ragion di stato*, or reason of state, to the book he wrote watering down Machiavelli's doctrine of special princely authority, and the phrase became immensely popular. As Botero worked out his position, it combined faith in a strong central authority with the comfortable expectation that that authority would be used for strictly moral ends and without any undue excesses.

1621: Ludovico Zuccolo in his brief *Ragione di stato* honed Botero's rather unctuous Machiavellism back to something like its original sharpness.

1576: Jean Bodin enters the story of Machiavellism from a

special angle. Because Machiavelli was thought to be an atheist, who saw value in religion only as an engine of political influence, anyone in the sixteenth century who spoke for the toleration of several religious creeds was judged to be a Machiavellian. Bodin was a jurist and political theoretician, who espoused religious toleration (known to most true believers of the day as religious indifference) in his big book called *La République*. Thus, though he seems to mention Machiavelli only to refute him, and perhaps accepted the Huguenot story that he was responsible for the massacre of St. Bartholomew's Eve, Bodin was labelled a Machiavellian. As late as 1605, Ben Jonson brings onto the stage of *Volpone* Sir Politic Would-be, who airily explains how to get along abroad in matters of religion:

And then for your religion, professe none;
But wonder, at the diversitie of all;
And, for your part, protest, were there no other
But simply the lawes o'th'land, you could content you:
NIC: MACHIAVEL, and monsieur BODINE, both
Were of this minde.

Act IV, scene 1

IV. *Elizabethan Dramatists and Other Vilifiers*

1589: Elizabethan audiences were used to pretty strong stuff on the tragic stage, partly because one of the dramatists' favorite models was Seneca, partly because one of their favorite locales was Italy. Italians as the Elizabethans saw them were sophisticated, insincere, corrupt, and cruel; they stabbed with stilettos, poisoned with Borgia rings, betrayed their friends, slept with their sisters, and associated with papal agents, all of whom itched to murder and torture high-minded Protestant folk. In short, Italians were natural Machiavellians, and Christopher Marlowe hardly had to introduce Machiavelli at all when he brought the arch villain onstage as prologue to *The Jew of Malta*. Barabas, the hero-villain of that tragedy, is so fierce and unscrupulous that nobody else could possibly introduce him.

MACHIAVEL (*as Prologue*):
Albeit the world think Machiavel is dead,
Yet was his soul but flown beyond the Alps;
And, now the Guise is dead,[1] is come from France

---

1. Henry, the third duke of Guise, was a leader in the massacre of St. Bartholomew's Eve; he was murdered by Henry III in 1588.

> To view this land and frolic with his friends.
> To some perhaps my name is odious;
> But such as love me guard me from their tongues,
> And let them know that I am Machiavel,
> And weigh not men, and therefore not men's words.
> Admired I am of those that hate me most:
> Though some speak openly against my books,
> Yet will they read me, and thereby attain
> To Peter's chair; and when they cast me off,
> Are poisoned by my climbing followers.
> I count religion but a childish toy,
> And hold there is no sin but ignorance. . . .

1592: Robert Greene, in his autobiographical *Groatsworth of Wit*, compares Machiavelli in a single sentence to Cain, Judas, and Julian the Apostate.

1611: John Donne, in *Ignatius his Conclave*, introduces the founder of the Jesuits, Ignatius Loyola, disputing with Machiavelli before Lucifer himself, as to which of them is the more effective agent of evil. Machiavelli is overcome, but not before he has made a strong case for his own supreme villainy.

As these few instances indicate, the figure of Machiavelli and the word Machiavellian quickly became standard, multipurpose terms of abuse, without any more specific meaning than "bad." Edward Meyer, in *Machiavelli and the English Drama*, and Felix Raab, in *The English Face of Machiavelli*, illustrate the range of usage at length; summary views can be had from Mario Praz, "Machiavelli and the Elizabethans" in *The Flaming Heart*—or, for that matter, from half a page of the *Oxford English Dictionary*.

Finally, as usage became looser and looser, the habit spread of attaching Machiavelli's name to any sort of chicanery—as the following titles indicate:

1648: *The Machivilian Cromwellist and Hypocritical Perfidious New Statist*, by William Prynne.

1674: *Machiavellus Gallicus*. Argues that Machiavelli has been metamorphosed into Louis XIV. The author was German.

1679: *Rustic Machiavellism*, by Christian Weiss. A comedy.

1681: *Machiavil Redivivus. Being an exact discovery or narrative of the principles & politics of our bejesuited modern fanatics.*

1683: *Matchiavel Junior or the Secret Acts of the Jesuits.*

1711: *On Medical Machiavellism*, by Valentini.

1713: *On Literary Machiavellism*, by Michael Lilienthal. Apart from these specific titles, there are innumerable usages like *erotic machiavellism, marital machiavellism, commercial machiavellism, popular machiavellism*, and *social machiavellism*, not to mention outright forgeries, like *Napoleon's machiavellism*, which is supposed to consist of Napoleon's annotations on *The Prince*, and is in fact nothing but a flagrant fake.

V. *French Controversialists, English Republicans, and a King of Prussia*

a. In the intricate scrimmages between Catholic and Protestant factions, between Court and Fronde, which fill French history of the early seventeenth century with sectarian clamor, the name of Machiavelli is likely to turn up as a term of abuse, and his ideas as quiet, useful weapons, on any side of any controversy.

1638: Henri, Duc de Rohan, hard-bitten general and leader of the Huguenot cause, begins his treatise on *The Interest of Princes and States* with the ringing aphorism, "Nations are governed by princes and princes are governed by interest." The book, a tough, clear assessment of France's national interest vis à vis Spain, was addressed to Cardinal Richelieu; it is written in the spirit of Machiavelli, though it does not invoke his name.

1639: Gabriel Naudé, librarian to Cardinal Mazarin and a man of great and miscellaneous learning, wrote *Considerations politiques sur les coups d'état*, meaning by *coups d'état* "tricks or ruses of government." This book, which became very popular, drew on some of Machiavelli's arguments to defend the use of extraordinary measures, including the St. Bartholomew massacre— conditioning the use of these measures only on pious public purposes of manifest importance.

1640: Louis Machon wrote, at Richelieu's behest, an *Apologie pour Machiavel* which emphasized the power of the French monarchy, independent of moral or ecclesiastical sanctions, specifically those of the pope. It is a rare and odd instance of Machiavellism walking hand in hand with Gallicanism.

1652: Claude Joly, writing a sardonic *Catechism of the Court*, found in Machiavelli a handy stick with which to lash out at Italian-born Cardinal Mazarin, Richelieu's successor in building the structure of centralized French power for Louis XIV. "Maximes italiennes et machiavellistes" are those that Joly thinks Mazarin follows, and that he thinks decent folk will be revolted by. In a parody of the creed, he says that Mazarin was begotten by Machiavelli's ghost upon Cardinal Richelieu.

b. Though Machiavelli was a bogeyman on the English stage, and his name a word of popular abuse, a number of radical English puritans who had taken the trouble to read the *Discourses* and the *Florentine History* found a good deal to admire in him. At first they shrank from saying so openly, but as the decades passed, they became more and more explicit.

1651: Andrew Marvell, paying tribute to Cromwell in the "Horatian Ode," praised him in the cool, measured tones appropriate to a Machiavellian prince, who, for the good of his cause and the benefit of his people, will violate religious, political, and moral taboos. It's been argued that because Marvell never mentions Machiavelli, the influence is hypothetical. So it is, but the hypothesis is a strong one, because Marvell was a notably close man. If, like Milton, he had left a commonplace book, it would surely have showed, like Milton's, knowledge of Machiavelli's republicanism and sympathy with it.

1656: James Harrington in his imaginary commonwealth of *Oceana*, though he sometimes criticized Machiavelli for not seeing deeply enough into the principle of economic and social balance, was generally ecstatic in his praise. Machiavelli is "the learned disciple of the ancients," "the only politician of later ages," and "the incomparable patron of the people."

1675: Henry Nevile translated Machiavelli's complete works, accurately and sympathetically, and in his political dialogue *Plato Redivivus* (1681) spoke glowingly of "the divine Machiavelli."

1682: Algernon Sidney, an ardent republican executed for treason in 1683 after a long and stormy career, wrote some *Discourses concerning Government*, first published in 1698; he sees Machiavelli as a premature Sidney, a pure, idealistic republican.

c. As everyone has seen almost from the beginning, the first step to be taken by anyone who expects to behave like the popular version of a Machiavellian villain is to distance himself as far as possible from Machiavelli. Nobody illustrated this procedure better than Frederick, King of Prussia, later to be known as Frederick the Great.

1740: The young king, who after a liberal and even rebellious young manhood had just succeeded to the throne, joined with M. de Voltaire to write a book explicitly against Machiavelli. Frederick had literary and musical aspirations—he wrote pretty good French and played at the flute; Voltaire was his cultural adviser, who hoped to steer him toward peaceful and humane pursuits. The book they wrote together was called simply *Anti-Machiavel*. Voltaire's part in it was largely confined to polishing the style and making arrangements for publication. Frederick's reactions to *The Prince* were his own, and they consisted of horrified disapproval. What he disliked was very much what had distressed English royalists in the political thought of Hobbes: both writers emphasized the authority of the sovereign, but seemed to admit that anyone who could get the sovereignty was entitled to keep and defend it, even against the old sovereign. In *The Prince* Frederick saw a clear blueprint for successful regicide: a reader of Machiavelli's book couldn't help learning how to depose Frederick and wipe out his line. Naturally displeased with this thought, he vigorously denounced Machiavelli as cruel, treacherous, faithless, irreligious, and so forth. Even as he was writing the book, however, he was meditating a treacherous, unannounced attack on his neighbor, Maria Theresa, Queen of Hungary, from whom he wrested Silesia as ruthlessly as if he had been Cesare Borgia himself. Thus began Frederick's long and bloody career of conquest. Voltaire, who had hoped to make his pupil an enlightened and humane ruler, was not pleased; but he was careful not to say anything too explicit about a ruler as powerful as Frederick.

VI. *Before, During, and After the French Revolution*

In the history of Machiavellism, as in almost every other aspect of human life, the French Revolution marks a watershed. For a quarter of a millennium, the major terms in which Machiavelli could be discussed had appeared set; and there seemed little one could do with him except ring changes on the old alternatives. Was he a wicked man, a good man, or a scientifically neutral man? Was he a supporter of tyrants (who could be represented as law and order), or of republican government (which could be represented as regicide)? One could choose among these alternatives or try to combine them, as did the first two figures who follow;

but with the second pair, who have fully absorbed the meaning of the Revolution, we're in another world.

1762: Jean Jacques Rousseau, in the *Social Contract*, returned to Gentili's old point, by saying that in *The Prince* Machiavelli professed to teach kings, but it was the people he really taught. *The Prince* was a book for republicans, and by not seeing this fact, previous readers had shown themselves either superficial or corrupt.

1799: Citizen Toussaint Guiraudet, writing at the very crest of the Revolution, brought out an edition of Machiavelli's *Works* in French translation, for which he wrote an uneasy preface. He praised Machiavelli for all the virtues appropriate to the exact moment—as a patriot, a religious neutral, and an authoritarian who, knowing the limits of freedom, would certainly have approved the severe restrictive measures with which Napoleon was in process of putting an end to the Revolution. He actually intimated that Machiavelli would have welcomed the French invasion of Italy. In short, being absorbed in current events himself, Guiraudet submerged Machiavelli in them. Understanding the temper of the early sixteenth century was obviously the last and least of his considerations.

1801-1802: In these years, G.W.F. Hegel was delivering to a handful of students at Jena the lectures that later became *The Philosophy of History*. Hitherto, Machiavellism had always meant a readiness to violate, in the interests of a real, immediate state, the general and permanent laws of reason and nature, often identified with those of Christianity. Hegel, by turning this static and uniform law of reason/nature/Christianity into the continually progressing and reconciling dialectic, converted the actual state into an ideal state. Literally, every actual state was the ultimate achievement so far of the world-spirit in the process of working itself out. Thus Hegel could and did acclaim Machiavelli as one who, even in proposing the lower forms of evil, worked effectively toward the higher form of good.

1808: Goethe published *Faust, Part I*. Practically from the first minute of his appearance, Mephisto announces himself as a Hegelian Machiavelli-figure. He is "part of that Power that in always willing evil always procures good." Whether on these terms God is himself the dialectic, or simply a super-Machiavelli manipulating the dialectic and Mephisto within it, may be argued; but it doesn't matter, for the whole premise of Machiavellism—that evil is different from good as politics is different from morality—has evaporated. In the unified vision of the dialectic, antithesis contributes as much as thesis to the ongoing, always provisional synthesis.

VII. *Conclusion*

A number of formulas have been invoked to account for the declining influence of Machiavellism in the nineteenth and twentieth centuries. The simplest and most capacious is simply that the world has been Machiavellianized. When moral principles ceased to be independent, unchanging public rules controlling the behavior of those who professed them—when principles were replaced by ideas of interest, progress, or class solidarity—then Machiavellism lost most of its point. The modern political liar isn't Machiavellian; he doesn't even want to deceive; he's simply telling his constituency what it wants to hear: that's his business. Machiavellism is possible only in an age of public morality, or at least of moral expectations—and that's not our own. The decisive change has to be dated some time around the French Revolution.

In his own time, for example, Napoleon, that giant Janus-figure of modernity, was rarely discussed in Machiavellian terms, or else only clumsily abused. Some analogies with *The Prince* might have seemed appropriate, but overall the comparison was wrong because the dynamics of the Napoleonic situation were entirely different from those of the Renaissance. Though in the end he betrayed the Revolution, Napoleon was a revolutionary leader; his strength depended on the skill with which he evoked and manipulated the passions of oppressed and frustrated classes. Not so *Il Principe*, not so at all. Machiavelli spoke to the very special conditions of his own youth. Italy prior to the death of Lorenzo was a closed system of fixed entities, much smaller, much less stable than the states of eighteenth-century Europe, but similarly organized and having in common the same essential beliefs. Jockeying, balancing, trading for power within a little group of established dynastic states was the true business of Machiavelli's prince, and equally of princes and diplomats of the European family during the eighteenth century. Napoleon inaugurated that age of mixed ideological and imperialist wars through which we are still trying to live. Mass societies, organized into nations, or rallied behind political dogmas, or identified with particular races, would have seemed strange and wonderful to Machiavelli. Indeed, the later sixteenth century, with its hideous wars of religion unleashed by the Reformation, is somewhat analogous to the twentieth century, with its wars of ideology unleashed primarily by the French and Russian Revolutions. One can perhaps see the elements of a recurring cycle in this alternation. In any case, of all the modern dictators from Franco to Hitler, Dzhugashvili, and Papa Doc, only Mussolini has ever so much as paid lip service to Machiavelli, and as usual with that brutal windbag, it was all bluff. Mussolini neither knew nor cared anything about Machiavelli except as intellectual salad dressing for his own bitter herbs. Wars of ideology, the outcome of deep politics, tend to create fanatics and demagogues in about equal quantities; and neither class really has much use for Machiavelli.

As an active political influence, Machiavellism has thus been effectively dead and buried for two centuries. That may be one major influence contributing to the new and better understanding of Machiavelli as a figure in his own right—to the growth of reasoned factual scholarship based on acquaintance with all the surviving texts, not just the misunderstanding of one.

ROBERT M. ADAMS

The Interior Prince, or Machiavelli Mythologized†

For hundreds of years after *The Prince* made its first public, posthumous debut, Niccolò Machiavelli was considered a man who deliberately advocated evil and unscrupulous methods in order to deal with political realities that could readily be handled by more enlightened and humane techniques. In painting this picture of the man and his teachings, it was of course advantageous to consider as little as possible the situation in which Machiavelli actually wrote, the princely family to whom he addressed his major book, and the other writings he composed. Commentators like Innocent Gentillet, who held Machiavelli directly responsible for the Saint Bartholomew's Eve massacre, and Frederick the Great, who saw in Machia-

†The first pages of this essay, in slightly altered form, appeared in *American Scholar* (Summer 1975), as preface to a rather different body of reflections. I am grateful to the editor of *American Scholar* for permission to reprint.—R.M.A.

velli a diabolic tutor of regicides and usurpers, established a tradition which still has its representatives in Professors Butterfield, Prezzolini, and Leo Strauss.[1] Professor Strauss, who in this company is no extremist, declares in particular that Machiavelli, when he taught the deliberate enacting of evil, represented an entire wicked, authoritarian way of thinking, against which the basic premises of American democracy stand, not only as a protest, but as a shining exception. Neither in word nor deed are Americans Machiavellian, and this is a very good thing precisely because Machiavelli was such a very bad man. Though we should indeed study Machiavelli, according to Professor Strauss, it will be only to take measure of the various enormities from which we have escaped, and against which we must still be on guard.

But of recent years this idea has turned almost 180 degrees around. Starting as far back as Alfieri but growing steadily in assurance and volume, another tradition has emphasized the idealistic, enthusiastic, patriotic, and democratically minded Machiavelli. This figure is the author of the twenty-sixth chapter of *The Prince*, understood not as fine-sounding palaver atop a book of cynical opportunism, but as the sincere expression of Machiavelli's ultimate political objectives. The ardent declaration of chapter twenty-six is supported by evidence from the *Discourses on Titus Livius*, letters, poems, histories, and biographies; what seems to contradict it, in the earlier chapters of *The Prince*, is explained as the result of special historical circumstances in 1513. Thus of recent years we have acquired an altogether new Machiavelli. No doubt there are faults to be found with this new figure. He is unrealistic in maintaining his attachment to a citizen army long after professionals had fully proved their superiority; he verges on the pedantic in his fondness for Roman precedents; and his passionate hatred of the barbarians harrying Italy sometimes obscures his sense of practicality. If a prince promises to drive out the hateful foreigner, Machiavelli is a little prone to think he can do it without the vast human energies, painfully molded into a unity, that we now know were required. But these are naïve and generous faults, diametrically opposed to those of cynicism and selfish brutality, which used to be laid to Machiavelli's account. If anything, the new Machiavelli is a little too good, after the strong, bad, brown Machiavelli that we were used to; he's been complained of, as almost insipid.

Simultaneously, though by no sort of logical consequence, the other half of the picture has also altered violently. It's by no means as clear as it used to be thought fifty years ago that enlightened and

---

1. Authors, respectively, of *The Statecraft of Machiavelli* (London, 1940) *Machiavelli anticristo* (Roma, 1954), and *Thoughts on Machiavelli* (Glencoe, Ill., 1958). Jacques Maritain and a host of lesser figures also have some claim to membership in this society.

civilized methods (persuasion, leadership, bargaining) are capable of leading mass populations or of directing international relations toward ideal aims of peace and justice. In fact, it's pretty clear that without some curious helps they're not; and so we are less inclined to blame Machiavelli—even accepting that he was as "Machiavellian" as his popular reputation used to imply—for being tarred with a brush which seems to have left its sticky touches on our hands and on practically everyone else's. It doesn't take much ingenuity, even accepting Professor Strauss's premises, to draw from them entirely contrary conclusions. Suppose America was founded on non- or anti-Machiavellian principles: well, on the evidence, this experiment in idealism and virtue worked satisfactorily under a particular set of favorable conditions (a rapidly expanding economy, the isolation provided by two major oceans, the comforting presence of the British Empire as a force consciously balancing the big powers against one another, if not always keeping peace among them). But now, as we can see simply by looking around, things are different. Faced with new and complex international responsibilities, sapped by malignant ulcers at home and abroad, a cumbersome giant afraid of its own strength, American democracy can no longer draw inspiration from its old idealisms. High time, then, a devil's advocate might say, to change in the direction of Machiavelli —still taking his name to stand for something like that Elizabethan stage-villain who is all that Professor Strauss seems to recognize in our Niccolò.

Machiavelli himself often thought in bilateral alternatives, he had a strikingly either-or style (especially in *The Prince*), and his influence has been in the same direction. He tends to polarize people into thinking in terms of opposed extremes. This is certainly what has happened—to the detriment of good sense—when we start positing any modern nation, particularly the United States of America, as either virtuous and inept or wicked and efficient. A number of potent practical circumstances exist to prevent this set of two-way alternatives from ever being posed in real life. For one thing, modern rulers—not only in America, but almost everywhere—are more deeply involved in history, society, and ongoing social processes, than any prince of whom Machiavelli could have conceived. Except, perhaps, for the Shah of Iran, no modern ruler exists who has anything like the Italian-Renaissance prince's individual freedom of untrammeled decision. Even if they should want to, modern rulers can't be very good or very bad under most circumstances, because they are tied to a constituency or bound by an ideology, or simply don't have the resources for large-scale, long-range, high-powered vice or virtue in a tough, expensive, and crowded modern world.

In fact the whole concept of war as a prudent commercial enterprise grounded in self-interest, which Machiavelli took largely for granted, seems to be obsolete these days. In the early sixteenth century, armies were small, armaments were relatively inexpensive, most campaigns were short, and so there was a genuine possibility of getting enough booty to pay for the work and danger of grabbing it. Nowadays, on the other hand, most forms of warfare are not prudent at all—they are simply tests of how much of the fabric of existing society the competing parties are willing to see destroyed. This is most obvious in the instance of high-technology (i.e., atomic) warfare, which almost automatically wipes out both participants along with all differences between winner and loser and any conceivable bystander who might try to discriminate the two. But it is also true of partisan or guerilla warfare, where the "popular" cause draws its strength from the readiness of the fighters to destroy everything, themselves included, down to the scorched earth, because they are not only confident their cause can start anew, but eager to see it do so. The various guises of such a war include terror, assassination, sabotage, and the random murder of irrelevant innocents; its techniques, familiar to the point of being obvious, are surprise, diffusion, and the sort of unquestioning faith in the cause which makes of every revolutionary a self-guided bomb. Traditionally, guerilla warfare of this sort used to be thought efficacious only for defensive actions, as in the defense of a homeland against invaders; but recent bloody experience suggests that it can be exported as well, and given an offensive character. Thus both current brands of warfare are in some sense absolute: to make its point, one destroys everything, the other anything, but both are wars of extermination. Liquidating the class enemy by gun, torture, or labor camp may take a little longer than exploding megatonnage, but social engineering by holocaust is the name of both games (making a desert and calling it peace is the phrase of Tacitus), and neither activity represents prudential violence of the sort commended by Machiavelli.

Old-fashioned "Machiavellian toughness" was simply a particular symbolic language for conveying in capsule form the same lessons as common discourse or persuasion. In the seventh chapter of *The Prince* we learn of the fate of Remirro de Lorca, once Cesare Borgia's feared, efficient lieutenant in the Romagna, who (having outlived his usefulness to his employer) was found on Christmas morning, 1502, lying on the public square in Cesena "in two pieces with a stick and a bloody knife beside him." It was a graphic and memorable way of saying, "The stick may hurt, but the knife can cut the stick," or alternatively, "There is a power behind the power you think you hate, that you don't know whether to love or hate, but that you'd certainly better fear." However one defines the message (as with Christian parables, its vagueness is part of its enduring fascination), the point that Cesare's action was emblematic instruction acted out on the body of his own ex-lieutenant is very clear. And in fact Machiavelli says again and again, in *The Prince* and elsewhere, that Cesare was strict with individuals only as a way of avoiding the greater cruelty that would have been involved in mass levies, factional murders, communal rioting, burning, and looting. The historians tell us that is not idle talk; Cesare ran a clean administration in the Romagna, where such a thing had not been heard of for centuries. His violence was exemplary, his regime stood on popular support gained by giving the people good government. This is one sort of violence, Machiavelli's sort; pointedly pedagogic, severely economical. But when random hostages are picked up and butchered, populations deported, or bombs left to go off in crowded restaurants, killing whom they will, no political point is being made to which a practical response can be framed. Neither is there any response to one atomic bomb except another.

Machiavellian calculation in the modern world is thus an extremely various thing, depending primarily on where one stands, who one is. A thoroughly convinced revolutionary will want by whatever means to render the present arrangement of things unworkable at the earliest possible moment, so the world can get on with building a better one; and to build a better one he will blithely liquidate the class enemy in any necessary numbers. ("You can't make an omelet without breaking eggs," said Lenin; and it is nice to think of the many executioners whose hearts have been lifted, as they went about their necessarily messy chores, by this homely domestic metaphor.) The possessor of privileges who wants to hold onto them and thinks he can do so will pursue the classic tactics of his position, to bribe, divide, confuse by subterfuge, or directly brutalize those who seem about to undermine his position. Both parties, if pushed to the limit, are capable of destroying, not only one another, but an ancient institution so intangible yet so familiar to us that we are sometimes in danger of forgetting its very existence. For lack of a better term, I will call it the marketplace—meaning by that vague metaphor not only the area where goods are bought and sold according to each dealer's estimate of their value to him, but also the area of persuasion and prudential judgment, where ideas, tastes, values, styles, and inevitably follies are in competition with one another. The idea of buying and selling is really adventitious to the marketplace under this definition; not so the idea of accepting and rejecting. What is essential is a range of options and alternatives upon which individual judgment is exercised.

As so loosely defined, it is of course clear that the marketplace can never be altogether abolished. But it can be radically narrowed, as we are vividly reminded when we see pictures of Russian troopers with water-cannon advancing on an exhibit of abstract art in a Moscow park, or when we think, less dramatically, of the quiet, deadly tyranny of small-town conformity in midland America, outback Australia, darkest Africa, or a thousand different areas of the world. The marketplace is a fragile, because ordinarily an intangible, phenomenon: its traditional enemies have been the church militant and the parochial moralist, the army, the policeman, and the political commissar; the spread-eagle patriot and the fanatical factionary. These are all people who thrive on fear of the unknown and the uncertain. They attack the marketplace as a breeding ground for unfamiliar ideas and practices, which they reject or value only as they seem to serve one immediate partisan purpose or another. Particularly nowadays, when the world is a pretty fearful place, they have succeeded remarkably in narrowing the sphere of intellectual competition and free individual judgment throughout the world. In the climatic struggle between entrenched privilege and organized insurrection—if such a struggle ever comes about or is allowed to form up—they will doubtless combine between them, professing utter hostility and acting in instinctive concert, to squeeze the marketplace as small as they can. In the vulgar mind, such suppression may well be tagged, however absurdly, with the name of Machiavelli. But for people to whom preservation of the marketplace is important, there is also a position—not a very easy one, to be sure—and for holders of this position there are words of Machiavellian wisdom, though they reach us from a distance, and like all words of wisdom must be applied shrewdly to particulars.

In nutshell form, the most general Machiavellian precept is, Do good when you can, do evil when you must; do both unhesitatingly, and don't lie to yourself about which is which. About ultimate goals, Machiavelli has virtually nothing to tell us; a *vivere civile, buono, e libero* is nothing but a nondescript, all-purpose container into which practically any substance can be packed. If we want such a society, he says, as with anything else of value in this world, we must be prepared to sacrifice to get it. Sacrifice means doing unpleasant things to get pleasant ones. Like good international relations, good government does not consist of imagining the best possible things that can be done and then doing them. In large measure, it consists of doing minimum actual evil in order to achieve maximum potential good. There is no way this cannot be a gamble. For instance, a ruler may start by doing evil in order to do good, but enjoy the evil so much that he continues in it for its own sake. Trying to correct him is a gamble imposed on a gamble. That a measure worked once is no reason at all to think it will work again; when running rapids, you're better off dodging rocks than studying

244 · *Robert M. Adams*

charts. Guicciardini stands ready to remind us that the dream of absolute security may be the most dangerous thing in the world:

> Anyone who looks into treaties will notice that nothing ruins them more than the desire to keep oneself too safe: this is why the parties write in restrictions of time, implicate third parties, and mix in extraneous matters, which give rise to further trickery. There's even reason to think that fortune, who controls these things, scorns the man who tries to free himself from her power by being too safe; thus I conclude that it is safer to execute treaties with a bit of danger than with an eye to ultimate safety.[2]

To accept such hazardous conditions as the best that can be had requires some *sang-froid*; one has to be prepared to lose without panic and to win without overconfidence, in the recognition that there is no foolproof system for beating the horses of history, any more than there is a way to keep out of the game entirely.

Given an attachment to the *vivere civile, buono, e libero* which is possible around a marketplace and hardly without it, what are the necessities of the present day? Certainly not to engage in an all-out defense of the system of international privilege as it currently exists —exists too flagrantly and shamelessly to need description. Such a course, if it does not lead to atomic holocaust, leads to "police actions" here, there, and everywhere, a long string of struggles which we may confidently expect to take place only where the self-appointed and very unreliable policeman is at maximum disadvantage, and his antagonist has every natural advantage. No safer—indeed, a good deal more dangerous in the short run—would be an effort to set up everywhere the worker's paradise, with its attendant slave-labor camps, secret police, blinded press, and barbed-wire fences. The more sweeping the contrast is made, the more widely the lines are drawn, the clearer it becomes that either extreme position, for a man who cares about the mental marketplace, is folly.

The first major corollary of the great Machiavellian precept is, Discriminate. The world is not divided into two tightly organized camps but into hundreds of loosely organized or largely unorganized units. The United States used to be a great capitalist nation, and it still is; but the actual life going on within that formulaic identity has changed enormously, incredibly, over the past hundred years. Sweden is commonly reckoned a capitalist country also, but it is more socialist than capitalist, and yet seems to suffer from no particular crisis of identity. Governments like those of Indonesia, Turkey, and Mexico have made curious compromises of their own; they are not quite democracies nor yet altogether dictatorships, neither instances of classic capitalism nor of working socialism. And so it

2. *Ricordi*, ed. Palmarocchi, 277.

goes, through a whole spectrum of alternatives. On the "other side," so-called, we find a similar range of peculiar institutions, from the half-open society of Yugoslavia, the still emerging shape of the new China, the blighted experiment that went down (not without a shove or two from outside) in Chile, an Algerian phenomenon of which we have very indistinct news. As soon as one starts discriminating, it becomes plain that the "worldwide revolution" of our time, though it often calls itself "socialist" or "communist," is commonly nationalist in some degree, and to that extent neither unified, resistable, nor deserving of resistance. Nationalism is generally a vehicle for sentiments of local autonomy, indigenous freedoms, social variety, group pride. These are very close indeed to the sentiments that led the United States of America to separate themselves violently from the British Empire; what we are seeing now throughout the world are further waves of a tide in which we were ourselves one of the early ripples. Perhaps in some parts of the world we can hold this tide back for a while (it's the traditional role of those who make a revolution first to be jealous and resentful of followers)—but only at the cost of brutalizing both ourselves and our opponents, at the cost of terrible suffering and hideous poverty for our own generation and those to come. Discriminating among movements means accepting some which call themselves "communist" as inevitable and desirable, and working against others which seem to be neither. It means looking with more cynicism than the United States has yet mustered at the credentials of those self-appointed heroes who offer to "save their countries from communism," to make sure that they are not common swindlers and plunderers, complete with pre-established Swiss bank accounts.

The attempt to discriminate can hardly fail to involve error, because it involves an effort at foresight; it is an attempt to manage policy as a discreet driver controls his automobile, with at least half an eye to the situation a quarter of a mile down the road. In one real sense, the man who does not try to foresee things is never mistaken; he responds only to what has actually happened, never makes guesses about what might happen, and is 100 percent certain of his facts before he responds to them. He is also 100 percent dead whenever they move faster than he does. The stream of historical traffic is moving, in the twentieth century, faster than it ever did before, under pressure of populations, communications, the general fluidity of modern life. Of all movements that the world has ever known, modern nationalism is the most likely to change fundamentally over the relatively short haul and without outside interference. The longer the current wave of revolutions takes to break, the less it will look like a wave at all, because in many places it will be lost in the inevitable backwash. The Allies did not beat Napoleon in 1815;

they could not have beaten him while he remained the personifica-
tion of a nation in arms. He had to transform himself (as surely,
inevitably he did) into a reactionary, self-aggrandizing tyrant, before
his downfall was certain. Such transformations and reversals are not
everywhere inevitable in the twentieth century, but that the process
will take place somewhere is inevitable; and in these cracks and
crevices of a less than monolithic structure, it is possible that the
critical mind may grow.

If irregular development is the general nature of modern international society, then the second major corollary of the great Machiavellian precept is, Delay. This sounds more negative than it really is,
because, just as the search for absolute safety is the most dangerous
of delusions, so the effort to stop change altogether is the surest way
to bring it about, in its most violent and sudden form. The art of
strategic delay is obviously the art of yielding here in order to push
there—of taking the initiative under favorable circumstances, cutting one's losses decisively under impossible circumstances, and
managing in-between circumstances with a strict eye to one's actual
objectives—but never, never allowing oneself to suppose that historic movement can be stopped altogether. The recent left-wing
military regime in Portugal was clearly the consequence of the long
clerico-fascist dictatorship of Salazar, during which time stood still
for Portugal. So changes can and must take place, and they will not
always be minor or gradual. If it were a system of privilege that we
were engaged in defending, the cumulative effect of these changes
would inevitably be erosive. But for anyone who is concerned with
the free marketplace of ideas (as defined above), it is the way
change takes place, not the fact that it takes place, which matters.
Blind reaction breeds blind revolution; no law is more firm than
that which declares that the triumphant revolutionary party is the
mirror image of the police force it has had to overcome. Delay,
then, means neither blind reaction nor timid temporizing, but conscious, careful use of obstructive power to keep inevitable change
from having the most destructive, and the most avoidable, of its
side effects, to make it gradual and therefore subject to criticism or
modification on the basis of experience.

Apocalyptic revolutionaries are fond of "tying things together"
on the ancient eschatological principle that the forces of dark and
the forces of light are now pitted against one another in the world's
final Armageddon, from which will arise a new heaven on earth.
The fact that terror of one sort or another always follows a successful revolution is simply evidence, if evidence were needed, that it is
easier to raise such expectations than to satisfy them. Delay, dis-
crimination, and the deliberate encouragement of uneven social
development, all serve to implement a fundamental and healthy

mistrust of those people who promise lavishly to cure humanity's ailments, but gun down all free critical inquiry into whether they have actually done so. Of course such mistrust is not particularly Machiavellian, it is simply common sense operating on the premise that one has something to lose—whether belongings, or freedoms, or simply authority over one's own mind—by submitting to an omnipotent, armed bureaucracy.

Partly for simple ease of expression, the discussion has proceeded up to this point by way of a highly simplified rhetoric which implies that every thoughtful person conducts his own foreign policy, that he is, in effect, a Machiavellian prince. There's a grain of truth in this, but the preliminary to it must be a quick glance at the actual processes by which policy is made in a democratic society and some of the main anomalies involved in making it. Politicians are the basic makers of decisions within a democracy, and they are animals of two entirely different dispositions, depending on whether they are or are not running for office. A herd of wild elephants stamped- ing through the jungle is mild and reasonable compared to a group of politicians whose offices are at stake. What they need most of all is an Issue, comprehensible to the dimmest and most laborious mind among their constituents, on which they can occupy a posi- tion of unassailable virtue—vivid, noble, and very simple. Political image-making is a series of political morality plays involving Right versus Wrong, Good versus Bad, the seven cardinal virtues personi- fied in one candidate versus the seven deadly sins personified in the other. On the other hand, since they are largely lawyers by training, work in committees as a matter of instinct, and are quiveringly sen- sitive to their most useful constituents, politicians when they are not actually running for office tend to complications, entangle- ments, and mares' nests of legal verbiage. The United States Con- gress, for example, proposes to assume major responsibility for a for- eign policy that will have to be defended on the hustings before voters who have to depend more on their sound moral instincts than on their ability to distinguish Austria clearly from Australia. Yet the same United States Congress is directly responsible for a tax law of ultra-Talmudic complexity and opacity. The law is incomprehensibly complex, as everyone knows, because a body of lawyers calling themselves legislators have worked for years at scrib- bling and overscribbling special exceptions for the special interests of the special group that for some reason they have in mind at the moment. Politicians are thus easily drawn out of a long-range orbit to accommodate special interests; yet periodically they have to rep- resent themselves as the souls of inflexible moral principle and the chosen vessels of the Everlasting Law. Machiavelli would throw up his hands in despair at the thought that his Prince, or any other ruler, might have to operate through such a cumbersome and unwieldy instrument. Add to this that the American president must himself be a politician and curry regular favor with a vast, heterogeneous, and widely uninformed electorate, and the marvel is that we have a foreign policy at all.

And indeed we probably would not have even the rudiments of a foreign policy if things were done strictly by the book. But it is the saving grace of democratic government that the book tends to be one thing and reality another. (There is a way of saying this which implies that organized corruption is the saving grace of democratic government; but this is a little more cynical than I mean to be). At every level of government, from submunicipal to international, there is an official, flow-chart way of doing things which everybody knows is at wide variance with the manipulative way in which things are really done. In theory a legislator is responsive to his constituents, but in real life he is responsive to lobbyists, advisers, and pressures converging on him from all manner of different directions. So a modern democratic government, in making international decisions, gets unofficial input through a vast variety of channels apart from the bodies officially designated to give their "advice and consent." Some, perhaps most, of this input comes from interest groups; some comes from experts, whether holding official posts or not, who get to exercise influence in official and unofficial ways. The bureaucracy itself, either through initiative or lethargy, wields immense power over decisions which, in theory, it is supposed simply to execute. There are the vast, vague forces of "public opinion," and the even vaguer forces which to some indefinite extent manipulate it. Pluralism is thus the rule in all government decision making; and if this seems to blur and diffuse even further the responsibility which Machiavelli would locate so decisively in the Prince alone, it also means that we are all involved, that there is no longer much excuse for anyone to adopt the role of the aggrieved and betrayed innocent. If the making of princely decisions is diffused through the society, so too should be—must be—an awareness of the basic conditions, hard as they are, under which decisions have to be made.

This after all is the other aspect of the corrupt and irresponsible ruler, who usurps privileges and betrays the public trust. Wicked though this fellow is, he grows as naturally as a mushroom out of simple-minded citizens who think (or pretend to think; for in this twentieth century authentic innocence is rare indeed) that when they have elected to office a stuffed shirt with a high line of virtuous palaver, their civic duty has been done. Under this thin veil of fake idealism, we happily put crooked politicians in office so that they will soil themselves with the guilt we are not ready to accept for ourselves; when they are sufficiently smutted, we cast them out like scapegoats, to be replaced, Tweedledee by Tweedledum or (as the case may be) Tweedledum by Tweedledee. But in the painful world of adult life, as Machiavelli is still required to remind us, goodness or the pretense of goodness is not enough. Dogcatchers, perhaps, should be elected to office on the basis of a warm smile and a charismatic personality; but town clerks should know how to read and cipher. Presidents of great nations should have sharp, clear minds, and a gambler's instinct for figuring the odds. For public life at its best is a nasty thing, involving as it does taking chances with other men's lives. Ugly words must sometimes be spoken in the hope they will prevent even uglier events from occurring; some solemn promises must be broken so that others may be kept; the truth must be distorted or denied in one sector so that it may (perhaps) be fulfilled in another. There is no distinction between virtuous and evil political actors to compare with the difference between the aware and the deluded. The deluded think they can tell right from wrong, follow the right, and avoid the wrong; they imagine themselves philosopher-kings, and are perfectly capable of winding up like Robespierre, murdering everyone in sight. The aware are vital economists, whose personal agony is the only reason we have to gamble on their sense of what is and what is not necessity.

In this context I think it right to acclaim Machiavelli as a great moral conscience, and to urge, as the best token of his claim to that title, his exceeding bad reputation among the "unco guid." He resurrects what they are passionate to bury—the undying worm of man's bad conscience at pretending to rule his fellow man. But this is also the most powerful of motives for keeping alive the free market in critical ideas for as long as possible, as widely as possible, at any cost—because it makes us feel so bad. Awareness of the complexities of the world is a heavy burden, as Erich Fromm long ago pointed out in his classic study of Nazi motivation, *Escape from Freedom*. It is rendered heavier today by the frightful weight of modern communications, which make us instantly aware of all the evil in the world, while our power to do anything about that evil is smothered by mass governments and mass populations. Under the circumstances, one can understand the appeal of a movement representing itself as the climax of all history, which offers to resolve all complexities, relieve all responsibilities, assuage all guilts. But the price of relief is cutting out of the mind just that gnawing element of personal responsibility and personal decision which used to be located exclusively in the prince, and for which the mental marketplace is almost the last remaining theater. We are none of us princes in the theater of war or politics (far from it!), and even our princes are not much like princes any more; but in the private mind some element of freedom and decision remains, so long as we can have some confidence we are not dealing with a screened and pre-digested body of basic evidence. On the marketplace, we stand or fall by our own decision; what we decide to believe, we believe after hearing what can be said against it, and what we think we believe, we need believe no longer than it appeals to us as right. Exercising such judgment, and applying it with all the awareness we can muster to the preservation of free judgment under either of the competing groups of troglodytes which dominate our age, is at least one form of perhaps mythic Machiavellism, very appropriate to our circumstances as we advance at the usual rate on the year 1984. The interior prince of the twentieth century has no easier task before him than the exterior prince of the sixteenth century; but if we wish to avoid a society of doublethinking pigs, some shadow of this ancient elitist figure had better be able to survive.

A discourse pretending to logic which comes to no conclusion except that logic is a desirable procedure is bound to have some-what the look of a short circuit. Freedom can be, and often is, an appallingly empty and concentric concept; it cannot possibly survive unless it can be made to feel full. Apart from welfare, in other words, it's a verbal nothing. Making freedom feel full is an all-day, year-round business for practically everyone who has leisure to think and energy to act. "Too little and too late" is such an old story in the dealing of haves with have-nots that it's about time we noticed one of its contraries: "Less is enough if it comes early." For what men get when they need it abjectly only confirms their sense of slavery; what they get when they can make their own use of it con-firms their sense of self-reliance. At least in the modern world, a state defining its role in princely terms cannot hope to grow in power by creating clients or slaves; on the contrary, its role is fulfilled only in the sponsorship of other princely states. What could be done in this respect is hard to guess since so little has been tried; compared to some of the thinkable options, it doesn't seem the most desperate of ventures to foster independence and self-respect in those we need as friends.

Peripherica

FRIEDRICH NIETZSCHE

[Morals as Fossilized Violence]†

The late-nineteenth-century German philosopher Friedrich Nietzsche had a great admiration for Machiavelli; their styles, their temperaments, their estimates of human nature were much alike. More interesting for our purposes than a mere comparison is the way in which Nietzsche complements Machiavelli's political insights, by arguing that the "autonomous" moral values which the virtuous propose as a standard for judging politics, are not in fact heaven-descended. Morality, Nietzsche argues, is the product of acts of violence, repeated over and over again, till social and moral values are literally beaten into men. All religious and moral codes are tainted with cruelty; our search for an origin of moral codes and standards can only take us back to a long and terribly painful conquest as a result of which men gradually learned to interiorize their external compulsions in a conscience. Morals then are simply fossilized violence; and the truly autonomous conscience, like that of Machiavelli's prince, is one that imposes its own moral values on itself.

Our selection is from the second essay, titled " 'Guilt,' 'Bad Conscience' and Related Matters" in *The Genealogy of Morals*. Nietzsche has been describing the difficulty of breeding an animal (man) with the right to make promises—an animal capable of triumphing over his own deepest and healthiest instinct, which is to forget.

II

This brings us to the long story of the origin or genesis of responsibility. The task of breeding an animal entitled to make promises involves, as we have already seen, the preparatory task of rendering man up to a certain point regular, uniform, equal among equals, calculable. The tremendous achievement which I have referred to in *Daybreak*[1] as "the custom character of morals," that labor man accomplished upon himself over a vast period of time, receives its meaning and justification here—even despite the brutality, tyranny, and stupidity associated with the process. With the help of custom and the social strait-jacket, man was, in fact, made calculable. However, if we place ourselves at the terminal point of this great process, where society and custom finally reveal their true aim, we shall find the ripest fruit of that tree to be the sovereign individual, equal only to himself, all moral custom left far behind. This autonomous, more than moral individual (the terms *autonomous* and *moral* are mutually exclusive) has developed his own, independent, long-range

---

†From Friedrich Nietzsche, *Zur Genealogie der Moral* (1887), translated by Francis Golffing and reprinted as *The Genealogy of Morals* (New York: Anchor Books, 1956).
1. *Morgenröte*, published by Nietzsche in 1881.

will, which dares to make promises; he has a proud and vigorous consciousness of what he has achieved, a sense of power and freedom, of absolute accomplishment. This fully emancipated man, master of his will, who dares make promises—how should he not be aware of his superiority over those who are unable to stand security for themselves? Think how much trust, fear, reverence he inspires (all three fully *deserved*), and how, having that sovereign rule over himself, he has mastery too over all weaker-willed and less reliable creatures! Being truly free and possessor of a long-range, pertinacious will, he also possesses a scale of values. Viewing others from the center of his own being, he either honors or disdains them. It is natural to him to honor his strong and reliable peers, all those who promise like sovereigns: rarely and reluctantly; who are chary of their trust; whose trust is a mark of distinction; whose promises are binding because they know that they will make them good in spite of all accidents, in spite of destiny itself. Yet he will inevitably reserve a kick for those paltry windbags who promise irresponsibly and a rod for those liars who break their word even in uttering. His proud awareness of the extraordinary privilege responsibility confers has penetrated deeply and become a dominant instinct. What shall he call that dominant instinct, provided he ever feels impelled to give it a name? Surely he will call it his *conscience*.

III

His conscience? It seems a foregone conclusion that this conscience, which we encounter here in its highest form, has behind it a long history of transformations. The right proudly to stand security for oneself, to approve oneself, is a ripe but also a late fruit; how long did that fruit have to hang green and tart on the tree! Over an even longer period there was not the slightest sign of such a fruit; no one had a right to predict it, although the tree was ready for it, organized in every part to the end of bringing it forth. "How does one create a memory for the human animal? How does one go about to impress anything on that partly dull, partly flighty human intelligence—that incarnation of forgetfulness—so as to make it stick?" As we might well imagine, the means used in solving this age-old problem have been far from delicate: in fact, there is perhaps nothing more terrible in man's earliest history than his mnemotechnics. "A thing is branded on the memory to make it stay there; only what goes on hurting will stick"—this is one of the oldest and, unfortunately, one of the most enduring psychological axioms. In fact, one might say that wherever on earth one still finds solemnity, gravity, secrecy, somber hues in the life of an individual or a nation, one also senses a residuum of that terror with which men must formerly have promised, pledged, vouched. It is the past—the longest, deepest, hardest of pasts—that seems to surge up whenever we turn serious. Whenever man has thought it necessary to create a memory for himself, his effort has been attended with torture, blood, sacrifice. The ghastliest sacrifices and pledges, including the sacrifice of the first-born; the most repulsive mutilations, such as castration; the cruelest rituals in every religious cult (and all religions are at bottom systems of cruelty)—all these have their origin in that instinct which divined pain to be the strongest aid to mnemonics. (All asceticism is really part of the same development: here too the object is to make a few ideas omnipresent, unforgettable, "fixed," to the end of hypnotizing the entire nervous and intellectual system; the ascetic procedures help to effect the dissociation of those ideas from all others.) The poorer the memory of mankind has been, the more terrible have been its customs. The severity of all primitive penal codes gives us some idea how difficult it must have been for man to overcome his forgetfulness and to drum into these slaves of momentary whims and desires a few basic requirements of communal living. Nobody can say that we Germans consider ourselves an especially cruel and brutal nation, much less a frivolous and thriftless one; but it needs only a glance at our ancient penal codes to impress on us what labor it takes to create a nation of thinkers. (I would even say that we are the one European nation among whom is still to be found a maximum of trust, seriousness, insipidity, and matter-of-factness, which should entitle us to breed a mandarin caste for all of Europe.) Germans have resorted to ghastly means in order to triumph over their plebeian instincts and brutal coarseness. We need only recount some of our ancient forms of punishment: stoning (even in earliest legend millstones are dropped on the heads of culprits); breaking on the wheel (Germany's own contribution to the techniques of punishment); piercing with stakes, drawing and quartering, trampling to death with horses, boiling in oil or wine (these were still in use in the fourteenth and fifteenth centuries), the popular flaying alive, cutting out of flesh from the chest, smearing the victim with honey and leaving him in the sun, a prey to flies. By such methods the individual was finally taught to remember five or six "I won'ts" which entitled him to participate in the benefits of society; and indeed, with the aid of this sort of memory, people eventually "came to their senses." What an enormous price man had to pay for reason, seriousness, control over his emotions—those grand human prerogatives and cultural showpieces! How much blood and horror lies behind all "good things"!

IV

But how about the origin of that other somber phenomenon, the consciousness of guilt, "bad conscience"? Would you turn to our genealogists of morals for illumination? Let me say once again, they are worthless. Completely absorbed in "modern" experience, with no real knowledge of the past, no desire even to understand it, no historical instinct whatever, they presume, all the same, to write the history of ethics! Such an undertaking must produce results which bear not the slightest relation to truth. Have these historians shown any awareness of the fact that the basic moral term *Schuld* (guilt) has its origin in the very material term *Schulden* (to be indebted)? Of the fact that punishment, being a *compensation*, has developed quite independently of any ideas about freedom of the will—indeed, that a very high level of humanization was necessary before even the much more primitive distinctions, "with intent," "through negligence," "by accident," *compos mentis*, and their opposites could be made and allowed to weigh in the judgments of cases? The pat and seemingly natural notion (so natural that it has often been used to account for the origin of the notion of justice itself) that the criminal deserves to be punished *because* he could have acted otherwise, is in fact a very late and refined form of human reasoning; whoever thinks it can be found in archaic law grossly misconstrues the psychology of uncivilized man. For an unconscionably long time culprits were not punished because they were felt to be responsible for their actions; not, that is, on the assumption that only the guilty were to be punished; rather, they were punished the way parents still punish their children, out of rage at some damage suffered, which the doer must pay for. Yet this rage was both moderated and modified by the notion that for every damage there could somehow be found an equivalent, by which that damage might be compensated—if necessary in the pain of the doer. To the question how did that ancient, deep-rooted, still firmly established notion of an equivalency between damage and pain arise, the answer is, briefly: it arose in the contractual relation between creditor and debtor, which is as old as the notion of "legal subjects" itself and which in its turn points back to the basic practices of purchase, sale, barter, and trade.

V

As we contemplate these contractual relationships we may readily feel both suspicion and repugnance toward the older civilizations which either created or permitted them. Since it was here that promises were made, since it was here that a memory had to be fashioned for the promiser, we must not be surprised to encounter every evidence of brutality, cruelty, pain. In order to inspire the creditor with confidence in his promise to repay, to give a guarantee for the stringency of his promise, but also to enjoin on his own conscience the duty of repayment, the debtor pledged by contract that in case of non-payment he would offer another of his possessions, such as his body, or his wife, or his freedom, or even his life (or, in certain theologically oriented cultures, even his salvation or the sanctity of his tomb; as in Egypt, where the debtor's corpse was not immune from his creditor even in the grave). The creditor, moreover, had the right to inflict all manner of indignity and pain on the body of the debtor. For example, he could cut out an amount of flesh proportionate to the amount of the debt, and we find, very early, quite detailed legal assessments of the value of individual parts of the body. I consider it already a progress, proof of a freer, more generous, more *Roman* conception of law, when the Twelve Tables decreed that it made no difference how much or little, in such a case, the creditor cut out—*si plus minusve secuerunt, ne fraude esto.* Let us try to understand the logic of this entire method of compensations; it is strange enough. An equivalence is provided by the creditor's receiving, in place of material compensation such as money, land, or other possessions, a kind of *pleasure.* That pleasure is induced by his being able to exercise his power freely upon one who is powerless, by the pleasure of *faire le mal pour le plaisir de le faire,* the pleasure of rape. That pleasure will be increased in proportion to the lowliness of the creditor's own station; it will appear to him as a delicious morsel, a foretaste of a higher rank. In "punishing" the debtor, the creditor shares a seignorial right. For once he is given a chance to bask in the glorious feeling of treating another human being as lower than himself—or, in case the actual punitive power has passed on to a legal "authority," of seeing him despised and mistreated. Thus compensation consists in a legal warrant entitling one man to exercise his cruelty on another.

VI

It is in the sphere of contracts and legal obligations that the moral universe of guilt, conscience, and duty, ("sacred" duty) took its inception. Those beginnings were liberally sprinkled with blood, as are the beginnings of everything great on earth. (And may we not say that ethics has never lost its reek of blood and torture—not even in Kant, whose categorical imperative smacks of cruelty?) It was then that the sinister knitting together of the two ideas *guilt* and *pain* first occurred, which by now have become quite inextricable.

* * *

HANNAH ARENDT

[The Experience of Foundation]†

Machiavelli's unique position in the history of political thought
has little to do with his often praised but by no means unarguable
realism, and he was certainly not the father of political science, a
role now frequently attributed to him. (If one understands by political science political theory, its father certainly is Plato rather than
Machiavelli. If one stresses the scientific character of political science, it is hardly possible to date its birth earlier than the rise of all
modern science, that is, in the sixteenth and seventeenth centuries.
In my opinion the scientific character of Machiavelli's theories is
often greatly exaggerated.) His unconcern with moral judgments
and his freedom from prejudice are astonishing enough, but they do
not strike the core of the matter; they have contributed more to his
fame than to the understanding of his works, because most of his
readers, then as today, were too shocked even to read him properly.
When he insists that in the public-political realm men "should
learn how not to be good," he of course never meant that they
should learn how to be evil. After all, there is scarcely another political thinker who has spoken with such vehement contempt of
"methods [by which] one may indeed gain power but not glory."
The truth is only that he opposed both concepts of the good which
we find in our tradition: the Greek concept of the "good for" or
fitness, and the Christian concept of an absolute goodness which is
not of this world. Both concepts in his opinion were valid, but only
in the private sphere of human life; in the public realm of politics
they had no more place than their opposites, unfitness or incompetence and evil. The *virtù*, on the other hand, which according to
Machiavelli is the specifically political human quality, has neither
the connotation of moral character as does the Roman *virtus*, nor
that of a morally neutral excellence like the Greek ἀρετή. *Virtù* is
the response, summoned up by man, to the world, or rather to the
constellation of *fortuna* in which the world opens up, presents and
offers itself to him, to his *virtù*. There is no *virtù* without *fortuna*
and no *fortuna* without *virtù*; the interplay between them indicates
a harmony between man and world—playing with each other and
succeeding together—which is as remote from the wisdom of the
statesman as from the excellence, moral or otherwise, of the individual, and the competence of experts.

His experiences in the struggles of his time taught Machiavelli a
deep contempt for all traditions, Christian and Greek, as presented,

†From Hannah Arendt, "What Is Au-
thority?" in *Between Past and Future*   (New York: Viking, 1969), pp. 136–41.
The author's notes are not included here.

nurtured, and reinterpreted by the Church. His contempt was leveled at a corrupt Church which had corrupted the political life of Italy, but such corruption, he argued, was inevitable because of the Christian character of the Church. What he witnessed, after all, was not only corruption but also the reaction against it, the deeply religious and sincere revival emanating from the Franciscans and Dominicans, culminating in the fanaticism of Savonarola, whom he held in considerable respect. Respect for these religious forces and contempt for the Church together led him to certain conclusions about a basic discrepancy between the Christian faith and politics that are oddly reminiscent of the first centuries of our era. His point was that every contact between religion and politics must corrupt both, and that a noncorrupt Church, though considerably more respectable, would be even more destructive to the public realm than its present corruption. What he did not, and perhaps in his time could not, see was the Roman influence on the Catholic Church, which, indeed, was much less noticeable than its Christian content and its Greek theoretical framework of reference.

It was more than patriotism and more than the current revival of interest in antiquity that sent Machiavelli to search for the central political experiences of the Romans as they had originally been presented, equally removed from Christian piety and Greek philosophy. The greatness of his rediscovery lies in that he could not simply revive or resort to an articulate conceptual tradition, but had himself to articulate those experiences which the Romans had not conceptualized but rather expressed in terms of Greek philosophy vulgarized for this purpose. He saw that the whole of Roman history and mentality depended upon the experience of foundation, and he believed it should be possible to repeat the Roman experience through the foundation of a unified Italy which was to become the same sacred cornerstone for an "eternal" body politic for the Italian nation as the founding of the Eternal City had been for the Italic people. The fact that he was aware of the contemporary beginnings of the birth of nations and the need for a new body politic, for which he therefore used the hitherto unknown term *lo stato*, has caused him to be commonly and rightfully identified as the father of the modern nation-state and its notion of a "reason of state." What is even more striking, though less well known, is that Machiavelli and Robespierre so often seem to speak the same language. When Robespierre justifies terror, "the despotism of liberty against tyranny," he sounds at times as if he were repeating almost word for word Machiavelli's famous statements on the necessity of violence for the founding of new political bodies and for the reforming of corrupt ones.

This resemblance is all the more startling since both Machiavelli and Robespierre in this respect go beyond what the Romans themselves had to say about foundation. To be sure, the connection between foundation and dictatorship could be learned from the Romans themselves, and Cicero, for instance, appeals explicitly to Scipio to become *dictator rei publicae constituendae,* to seize the dictatorship in order to restore the republic. Like the Romans, Machiavelli and Robespierre felt founding was the central political action, the one great deed that established the public-political realm and made politics possible; but unlike the Romans, to whom this was an event of the past, they felt that for this supreme "end" all "means," and chiefly the means of violence, were justified. They understood the act of founding entirely in the image of making; the question to them was literally how to "make" a unified Italy or a French republic, and their justification of violence was guided by and received its inherent plausibility from the underlying argument. You cannot make a table without killing trees, you cannot make an omelet without breaking eggs, you cannot make a republic without killing people. In this respect, which was to become so fateful for the history of revolutions, Machiavelli and Robespierre were not Romans, and the authority to which they could have appealed would have been rather Plato, who also recommended tyranny as the government where "change is likely to be easiest and most rapid."

It is precisely in this double respect, because of his rediscovery of the foundation experience and his reinterpretation of it in terms of the justification of (violent) means for a supreme end, that Machiavelli may be regarded as the ancestor of modern revolutions, all of which can be characterized by Marx's remark that the French Revolution appeared on the stage of history in Roman costume. Unless it is recognized that the Roman pathos for foundation inspired them, it seems to me that neither the grandeur nor the tragedy of Western revolutions in the modern age can be properly understood. For if I am right in suspecting that the crisis of the present world is primarily political, and that the famous "decline of the West" consists primarily in the decline of the Roman trinity of religion, tradition, and authority, with the concomitant undermining of the specifically Roman foundations of the political realm, then the revolutions of the modern age appear like gigantic attempts to repair these foundations, to renew the broken thread of tradition, and to restore, through founding new political bodies, what for so many centuries had endowed the affairs of men with some measure of dignity and greatness.

Of these attempts, only one, the American Revolution, has been successful: the founding fathers as, characteristically enough, we still call them, founded a completely new body politic without violence and with the help of a constitution. And this body politic has at least endured to the present day, in spite of the fact that the specifically modern character of the modern world has nowhere else produced such extreme expressions in all nonpolitical spheres of life as it has in the United States.

This is not the place to discuss the reasons for the surprising stability of a political structure under the onslaught of the most vehement and shattering social instability. It seems certain that the relatively nonviolent character of the American Revolution, where violence was more or less restricted to regular warfare, is an important factor in this success. It may also be that the founding fathers, because they had escaped the European development of the nation-state, had remained closer to the original Roman spirit. More important, perhaps, was that the act of foundation, namely the colonization of the American continent, had preceded the Declaration of Independence, so that the framing of the Constitution, falling back on existing charters and agreements, confirmed and legalized an already existing body politic rather than made it anew. Thus the actors in the American Revolution were spared the effort of "initiating a new order of things" altogether; that is, they were spared the one action of which Machiavelli once said that "there is nothing more difficult to carry out, nor more doubtful of success, nor more dangerous to handle." And Machiavelli surely must have known, for he, like Robespierre and Lenin and all the great revolutionaries whose ancestor he was, wished nothing more passionately than to initiate a new order of things.

However that may be, revolutions, which we commonly regard as radical breaks with tradition, appear in our context as events in which the actions of men are still inspired by and derive their greatest strength from the origins of this tradition. They seem to be the only salvation which this Roman-Western tradition has provided for emergencies. The fact that not only the various revolutions of the twentieth century but all revolutions since the French have gone wrong, ending in either restoration or tyranny, seems to indicate that even these last means of salvation provided by tradition have become inadequate. Authority as we once knew it, which grew out of the Roman experience of foundation and was understood in the light of Greek political philosophy, has nowhere been re-established, either through revolutions or through the even less promising means of restoration, and least of all through the conservative moods and trends which occasionally sweep public opinion. For to live in a political realm with neither authority nor the concomitant awareness that the source of authority transcends power and those who are in power, means to be confronted anew, without the religious trust in a sacred beginning and without the protection of traditional and therefore self-evident standards of behavior, by the elementary problems of human living-together.

TRAIANO BOCCALINI

From *News Bulletins from Parnassus*†

Traiano Boccalini, who flourished in Italy during the last years of the six-teenth and first years of the seventeenth century, got his political experience as a Roman judge and administrator for three tough Renaissance popes, Sixtus the Fifth, Clement the Eighth, and Paul the Fifth. But when it came time to publish his great satirical work, *I ragguagli di Parnasso*, in 1612, he moved to the freer climate of Venice, and was careful to stay there for the rest of his life. The book is a set of imaginary newsletters from the kingdom of Parnassus, in which animals and books speak their minds and present their problems before the court of King Apollo, while authors, like Niccolò Machiavelli, are revived from the dead to be set on trial. Machiavelli, as the reader will see, is roundly condemned before this tribunal, but on grounds which suggest that Boccalini felt much more sym-pathy for him than for the court which in condemning him was so flagrantly serving its own selfish interests.

(1, 89)

Niccolò Machiavelli, who had been banished from Parnassus on pain of death, is discovered hiding in the library of a friend, and is sentenced to undergo the penalty previously pronounced against him, of death by fire.

Although Niccolò Machiavelli was banished many years ago from Parnassus and its territories under the very gravest penalties both to himself and to those who dared receive in their libraries a man of such pernicious principles, nonetheless last week, in the house of a friend who was secretly harboring him in his library, he was taken prisoner. The criminal judges at once took cognizance of his person, and this morning the fatal fires were about to be lit, when he asked His Majesty that some time be allowed him to say something in his own defense before the tribunal that had condemned him. Apollo, displaying his usual benignity, gave him to understand that he might send his solicitors to court, where they would be courteously heard. Machiavelli replied that he wanted to act as his own lawyer, and that Florentines had no need of lawyers to state their case. Everything he requested was granted. Machiavelli was therefore brought before the bar of justice, where he spoke in his own defense as follows:

"Behold, My Lord of the World of Letters, that Niccolò Machia-velli who has been condemned as a seducer and corrupter of the human race, and a disseminator of scandalous political ideas. I am not present in this court to defend my writings, which I here

---

†From *I ragguagli di Parnasso* (Venice, 1630). Translated by the editor.

denounce publicly, and condemn as impious and full of cruel and hateful instructions on how to govern states. So that, if what I have published in my books is doctrine invented by me out of my own head, if it is novel advice, then I demand immediate and unconditional execution of the sentence that the judges have been pleased to pass on me. But in fact my writings contain nothing more than political precepts and rules of state that I have derived from the actions of various princes whom, with Your Majesty's permission, I'll be glad to name in this court—men of whom it's as much as your life is worth to say an evil word. Now I ask you, what justice, what reason is there that they who invented that furious and desperate political process described by me should be held sacrosanct, while I, who have simply described it, am called a scoundrel and an atheist? I certainly can't see any rationale for adoring the original of a thing as sacred, and denouncing the copy as execrable. Nor do I see why I alone should be persecuted, when the reading of history, which is not only permitted but praised to the skies by everyone, is notoriously capable of converting into so many Machiavellis all those people who look at it through political glasses. Thanks be to God that people aren't all as simple-minded as some would like to think; so that the same people who with the brilliance of their intellects have been able to investigate the deepest secrets of nature, may yet have the wit to discover the true ends of princes in their actions, even though they use the greatest art to conceal them. And if the princes, in order to twist and turn their subjects as seems best to them, want to have them stupid and ignorant, then they will have to make up their minds to the same measures so brutally practiced by the Turks and Muscovites, that is, to prohibit good books. For books are what turn into Arguses those blind eyes that otherwise would never ferret out the true ends of princes' thoughts. Thanks be to God that the hypocrisy so familiar in the world today has power, like the stars, only to incline but not to force human minds to believe what the manipulators of that hypocrisy want us to believe."

The judges were much moved by these words, and it seemed that they were about to revoke the sentence when the Fiscal Advocate advised them that Machiavelli was not only deservedly condemned for the abominable and execrable precepts to be found in his writings, but should be severely punished for another reason, as well. It seems he had been found the other night in a fold full of sheep, to whom he was teaching the way to fit into their mouths the false teeth of dogs—with the evident peril that shepherds might be altogether exterminated, who are persons of such necessity in this world. What an indecent and troublesome thing it would be if this rascal made it necessary for the farmers to arm their breasts with plate mail and to wear iron gauntlets whenever they wanted to milk their sheep or shear them. The price of wool and cheese would rise sky-high if in the future it should become harder for the shepherds to guard themselves from the sheep than from the wolves. No longer able to keep the flock obedient with a whistle and a crook, they would need a regiment of soldiers to do it; and at night, to keep them in order, it wouldn't simply be a matter of stringing a few ropes: walls would be needed, with towers, and moats with counter-scarps, after the modern fashion.

These atrocious accusations appeared to the judges so important that they all voted to carry out the original sentence against such a vicious man; and they published it as a fundamental law for the future that any man would be considered an enemy of the human race who ever dared to tell the world such scandalous things. And they all confessed that neither wool nor cheese nor lamb, which derive from sheep, render that animal precious to man, but only its vast simplicity and infinite docility. And that it wasn't possible for a great number of such beasts to be governed by a single shepherd unless they had been deprived of horns, of teeth, and of wit. So that it would set the whole world ablaze if a man should try to make the simpletons clever, and bring light to those dim moles whom Mother Nature had with great circumspection created blind.

ANTONIO GRAMSCI

From *The Modern Prince*†

Antonio Gramsci (1891–1937) was one of the founders and chief theoretical spokesmen of the Italian Communist party. His writings, collected under the title *Note sul Machiavelli* and translated into English by Louis Marks under the title *The Modern Prince* (International Publishers, New York, 1959) are in fact only intermittently concerned with Machiavelli. In the first of his "noterelle" Gramsci deals at greatest length and most fundamentally with Machiavelli by arguing not only that the Communist party is and can be a kind of collective prince, but that Machiavelli himself meant his book to be read by those who did not know the game of politics and had to learn it to take advantage of the political institutions (princes and princedoms) made available to them by history. This is an old position, expressed nearly two hundred years ago by Rousseau, Foscolo, and Alfieri; but Gramsci, as one might expect, expresses it with a difference.

†From Antonio Gramsci, *The Modern Prince and Other Writings*, trans. Louis Marks (New York: International Publishers, 1959), pp. 141–42. Footnotes are by the editor of this Norton Critical Edition.

* * *

In this way the problem is posed of the significance Machiavelli had in his own times and of the ends which he set himself in his books, and especially in *The Prince*. Machiavelli's doctrine was not in his own time purely "bookish," a monopoly of isolated thinkers, a secret book which circulated among the initiated. Machiavelli's style is not that of a systematic writer of tracts, as was usual in both the Middle Ages and Humanism. On the contrary, it is the style of a man of action, a man who wants to encourage action, it is the style of a party "manifesto." The "moralistic" interpretation given by Foscolo[1] is certainly wrong; still, it is true that Machiavelli has *unveiled* something and not only theorized reality: but to what end? A moralistic or a political end? It is usually said that Machiavelli's standards for political behavior "are applied but not spoken about"; the great politicians—it is said—begin by cursing Machiavelli, declaring themselves anti-Machiavellians, just in order to apply his standards "sanctimoniously." Would not Machiavelli in this case have been un-Machiavellian, one of those who "know the tricks of the game" and stupidly teach them to others, whereas popular Machiavellianism teaches the opposite? Croce's assertion that, as Machiavellianism is a science, it can serve reactionaries as well as democrats, as the art of fencing helps both gentlemen and brigands, to defend themselves and to murder, and that Foscolo's judgment should be understood in this sense, is true abstractly. Machiavelli himself notes that the things he is writing are applied, and have always been applied by the greatest men in history; it does not seem, therefore, that he wants to advise those who already know; his style is not that of disinterested scientific activity, nor can he be thought to have arrived at this these of political science along the path of philosophical speculation, which in this particular subject would have been something of a miracle in his time, if even today it finds so much contradiction and opposition.

We can therefore suppose that Machiavelli had in view "those who do not know," that he intended to give political education to "those who do not know," not a negative political education of hatred for tyrants, as Foscolo seems to mean, but a positive education of those who must recognize certain necessary means, even if those of tyrants, because they want certain ends. The man who is born into the tradition of government through the whole complex of his education which he absorbs from his family environment, in which dynastic and patrimonial interests predominate, acquires

1. Ugo Foscolo, romantic and liberal poet of the early nineteenth century, sug- gested in his *Sepolcri* of 1807 a partially democratic interpretation of Machiavelli.

almost automatically the characteristics of the realistic politican. Who then "does not know?" The revolutionary class of the time, the Italian "people" and "nation," the citizen democracy which gave birth to Savonarola and Piero Soderini and not Castruccio and Valentino.[2] It can be considered that Machiavelli wanted to persuade these forces of the necessity for a "leader," who would know what he wanted and how to obtain it and to accept him with enthusiasm even if his actions might be or appear to be contrary to the widely held ideology of the time, religion. This position of Machiavelli is repeated for Marxism. The necessity is repeated of being "anti-Machiavellian," of developing a theory and technique of politics which can help both sides in the struggle, but which it is thought will end by helping especially the side "which did not know," because in this side is held to exist the progressive force of history. In fact one result is achieved immediately: that of breaking up the unity based on traditional ideology, without which the new force would be unable to gain awareness of its own independent personality. Machiavellianism has helped to improve the traditional political technique of the conservative ruling groups, just as has Marxism; but this must not conceal its essentially revolutionary character, which is felt even today and which explains the whole of anti-Machiavellianism from that of the Jesuits to that of the pietistic Pasquale Villari.[3]

* * *

Epigrams, Maxims, and Observations
from the Machiavellians

As with many hard substances, contact with Machiavelli often results in sparks; a random sampling of these brief illuminations is presented herewith. Unless otherwise indicated, translations (where called for) are by the editor.

In this godless world of Nature (Machiavelli thought), man was left alone with only himself and the powers Nature had given him, to carry on the fight against all the fateful forces wielded by this same Nature.[1]

—Friedrich Meinecke

The art of government is the organization of idolatry.

Liberty means responsibility. That is why most men dread it.

Vice is waste of life. Poverty, obedience, and celibacy are the canonical vices.

2. Gramsci distinguishes popular and democratic leaders like Savonarola and Soderini from princes and war lords like Castruccio Castracani, duke of Lucca, and Cesare Borgia, duke of Valentino.
3. Pasquale Villari's monumental biography of Machiavelli (1877) did not meet with Gramsci's approval.
1. From Friedrich Meinecke, *Machiavellism,* 1925; trans. Douglas Scott and published with introduction by D. W. Stark (New Haven: Yale University Press, 1957), p. 35.

Economy is the art of making the most of life.

The love of economy is the root of all virtue.

Political Economy and Social Economy are amusing intellectual games; but Vital Economy is the Philosopher's Stone.

If you injure your neighbor, better not do it by halves.[2]

—"The Revolutionist's Handbook and Pocket Companion"

Maybe the Tuscans are wrong about this, but slavery is always in their eyes a form of imbecility; intelligence and liberty being, in Tuscany, synonymous.[3]

—Curzio Malaparte

Machiavelli is no more the inventor of Machiavellism than Graves is the inventor of Graves's disease.[4]

—Mario Praz, "Machiavelli and the Elizabethans"

O the rare tricks of a Machivillian!

He doth not come like a gross plodding slave

And buffet you to death: no, my quaint knave,

He tickles you to death; makes you die laughing,

As if you had swallowed a pound of saffron.[5]

—*Loquitur* FLAMINEO in *The White Devil*

Nguien Van Luc, a local writer who was just finishing a book called "Machiavelli and the war in Indo-China" accompanied me very often. . . . He was fascinated by Machiavelli, and quoted *The Prince* continually. He used to say, "This is the textbook for all our politicians. Their behavior is always inspired by Machiavelli, in the South as in the North. Unhappily for them, and fortunately for us, the Americans don't know Machiavelli. They would have a lot to learn—how to protect themselves from us, I mean. One day or other, the war will end, with the victory of the Communists, of course, but it won't really be finished. Other internal struggles will start up, since power is the highest ambition of all the Vietnamese. As for the flotsam running the government now, all they want is to make money and get away to France, rich like Madame Nhu— they're not particularly afraid of communism, because they know that one day or another they will wind up on good terms with the North. . . . Leaders here and leaders in the North are of the same social class; they are often relatives, sprung from the same bourgeois

2. From "The Revolutionist's Handbook and Pocket Companion, by John Tanner, M.I.R.C. (Member of the Idle Rich Class)," an appendix to G. B. Shaw's play, *Man and Superman.*

3. From Curzio Malaparte, *Maledetti Toscani,* (Florence, 1956), p. 12.

4. From Mario Praz, "Machiavelli and the Elizabethans," in his book *The Flaming Heart* (New York: Doubleday Anchor Books, 1958)

5. From John Webster, *The White Devil.* act V, scene 3, lines 196 ff.

class, with the same French education. They know their Machiavelli, too; and in my opinion the difference between us and the Italians is not so great. We're both Catholic, we both know Machiavelli, both are naturally mafiosi. How can you expect the Americans to know anything about all that?[6]

—Goffredo Parise

The maxims of Machiavelli—liberals recite them while kings put them into practice.

—Alessandro Manzoni, in conversation

There is Machiavellism and Machiavellism; a real Machiavellism and a false Machiavellism; a Machiavellism deriving from Machiavelli and one deriving sometimes from his disciples, more often from his enemies. There are thus two or even three Machiavellisms, one of Machiavelli, one of the Machiavellians, and one of the anti-Machiavellians. But then there's also a fourth—that of the people who have never read a line of Machiavelli, but who freely misapply verbs, nouns, and adjectives derived from his name. Machiavelli surely cannot be held responsible for what the first or last comer since his day has made him say.[7]

—Charles Benoist

There is . . . a . . . great difference in kind between my world and Machiavelli's. We are discovering women. It is as if they had come across a vast interval since his time, into the very chamber of the statesman.

In Machiavelli's outlook the interest of womanhood was in a region of life almost infinitely remote from his statecraft. They were the vehicle of children, but only Imperial Rome and the new world of today have ever had an inkling of the significance that might give them in the state. They did their work, he thought, as the ploughed earth bears its crops. Apart from their function of fertility, they gave a humorous twist to life, stimulated worthy men to toil, and wasted the hours of Princes. He left the thought of women outside with his other dusty things when he went into his study to write, dismissed them from his mind. But our modern world is burthened with its sense of the immense, now half articulate, significance of women. They stand now, as it were, close beside the silver candlesticks, speaking as Machiavelli writes, until he stays his pen and turns to discuss his writing with them.[8]

—Herbert George Wells

6. From Goffredo Parise, "Dentro il 'calvario' del Vietnam," in *Corriere della Sera* (Milano) April 13, 1975, p. 3. Signor Parise's article was based on a visit to Vietnam made in 1968.

7. From Charles Benoist, *Le Machiavélisme* (Paris: Plon, 1907), Preface.
8. From H. G. Wells, *The New Machiavelli* (New York, 1911), p. 9.

True cynicism is a fault of the temperament of the observer, not a conclusion arising naturally out of the contemplation of the object; it is quite the reverse of "facing facts." In Machiavelli there is no cynicism whatever. . . . Such a view of life as Machiavelli's implies a state of the soul which may be called a state of innocence.[9]

—T. S. Eliot

The continuation of Machiavelli's thought need not be sought among the Machiavellians, who continue his politics of precept and casuistry by writing about "reason of state," often mingling this topic with moralistic trivialities; neither should it be sought among the anti-Machiavellians, auctioneers of the fusion, the identity of politics with morals, who devote themselves to thinking up states founded on pure principles of virtue and justice; nor, finally, among the eclectics, who juxtapose theories of morals and theories of politics, and instead of resolving the antinomies, soften and empiricize them, converting them into accidents and inconveniences which happen in life but can be given the character of accidental things. Instead, the train of Machiavelli's thought must be sought in those who try to clarify the concept of "prudence," of "shrewdness" in short of "political virtue," without mixing it up with "moral virtue" and without making it the mere negation of that quality: for example, among seventeenth-century writers, Zuccolo. And the same train may be found in some potent spirits who theorized that beyond the shrewdness and sagacity of the individual as conceived by Machiavelli lay the divine workings of Providence—such, for example, was Tommaso Campanella. But the true and worthy successor of Machiavelli, the powerful intellect who gathered up these scattered suggestions of the critics, and gave them power by combining them with the undying thought of the Florentine secretary, was another Italian (and indeed in these two Italians can be symbolized the entire philosophy of politics in its seminal form): and this was Vico. Not particularly well disposed toward Machiavelli, yet full of his spirit, he clarified and purified that spirit, integrating its conceptions of politics and history, resolving its hesitations, softening its pessimism.[1]

—Benedetto Croce

There are none more dangerous for the State than those who wish to rule the kingdom according to the principles which they have got from their books. By this means they often ruin it completely, because the past bears no relation to the present, and

9. From T. S. Eliot, "Niccolò Machiavelli," in *For Lancelot Andrewes* (Garden City, N.Y.: Doubleday Doran, 1929), pp. 50–51.

1. From Benedetto Croce, *Etica e politica* (Bari, 1945), book II, section 1, "Machiavelli e Vico," pp. 253–54.

because the relative disposition of times, places, and people is quite different.[2]

—Cardinal Richelieu

Altogether then the remarkable power of attraction which Machiavelli exerts on thinking men today rests on the fact that his thoughts often contain some concealed driving force which leads on beyond themselves, in such a way that he frequently offers much more than he is directly intending to offer.[3]

—Friedrich Meinecke

All the portraits of Machiavelli which survive, about a dozen of them, are more or less imaginary; the best may have been taken from a terra-cotta bust done during his lifetime or shortly thereafter. The only direct and authentic description of his person is a few lines written by his wife, Marietta Corsini, when their little boy was born —"so white of skin, with hair on his head like velvet, black like a little crow." She thought the baby beautiful because he was like her husband.

—R.M.A.

Machiavelli believed in democracy: it lay beyond his experience.[4]

—Ezra Pound, quoted by Donald Davie

Weakness is more opposed to virtue than is vice.
There are evil heroes as well as good ones.[5]

—La Rochefoucauld

We are much beholden to Machiavelli and other writers of that class, who openly and unfeignedly declare or describe what men do, and not what they ought to do. For it is not possible to join the wisdom of the serpent with the innocence of the dove, except men be perfectly acquainted with the nature of evil itself; for without this, virtue is open and unfenced; nay, a virtuous and honest man can do no good upon those that are wicked, to correct and reclaim them, without first exploring all the depths and recesses of their malice.[6]

—Francis Bacon

2. From Cardinal Richelieu, *Political Testament* (3rd ed., 1688), chapter VIII, section 2.
3. Meinecke, op. cit., p. 149.
4. From Donald Davie, *Ezra Pound, Poet as Sculptor* (New York: Oxford University Press, 1964), p. 92.
5. From La Rochefoucauld, *Maximes* (Classiques Garnier).
6. From Francis Bacon, *De Augmentis Scientiarum*, book VII, chapter 2. The translation is by F. R. Headlam.

Machiavelli, in his Histories and Discourses breathes with every word the spirit of liberty, justice, insight, truth, and supreme loftiness of spirit; hence anyone who reads him well, responds to him energetically, and immerses himself in this author, can only emerge from the experience a passionate enthusiast for liberty, and an enlightened practitioner of all the political virtues.[7]

—Vittorio Alfieri

Machiavellism is the geometry of politics.[8]

—Charles Benoist

When Mazarin tried to make use of M. de Fabert in a shabby deal, the marshal said to him: I hope, my lord, you'll allow me to decline this job of lying to the Duke of Savoy, particularly since it's over a trifling matter. The world knows that I'm an honest man; don't sacrifice my honor till it's a matter of saving France.[9]

—Albert Cherel

The first act of justice of any prince is to maintain himself as prince.[1]

—From the "Pseudo Prince," attributed to Fra Paolo Sarpi

. . . *Nicholas Machiavel's Prince,* who is a man, (though through the grand corruptions of the age and place in which he lived, and the safety of his own life, was forced as may rationally be judged to write in some kind of unhandsome disguises) I must call for the excellency and usefulness in corrupt times and places for his work's sake, *one of the most wisest, judicious, & true lovers of his country, of Italy's liberties and freedoms, and generally of the good of all mankind that ever I read of in my days.*[2]

—John Lilburne

7. From Vittorio Alfieri, *Del Principe e delle lettere* (Kehl, 1789; reprinted Bari, 1927), book II, chapter 9, unit 5.
8. From Charles Benoist, *Le Machiavél-isme*, III (1936), p. 379.
9. From A. Cherel, *La pensée de Machia-vel en France* (Paris, 1935), p. 82.
1. From the "Pseudo Prince" (ca. 1615), wrongly attributed to Fra Paolo Sarpi. This work was originally titled "An opinion on how the republic of Venice should govern itself," was probably by one of Sarpi's many enemies, and

got titled *The Prince* only because of its Machiavellian tone, long after Sarpi's death.
2. From John Lilburne, *The Upright Man's Vindication* (London, 1653), p. 7, quoted by Felix Raab, *The English Face of Machiavelli* (London: Routledge and Kegan Paul, 1964), pp. 173–4. The prose is not very neat, but the sentiment is obviously sincere, and "Free-Born John" Lilburne was one of the toughest, most vociferous agitators for freedom against both Charles I and Oliver Cromwell.

Bibliography

As one might anticipate, the enormous spate of books and articles about Machiavelli includes material written in a great variety of European languages—with the curious exception of Russian.[1] The bibliography is thus challengingly multilingual. Though a great deal of this material has been translated into English, a serious student of Machiavelli cannot go very far without Italian, German, and French. The following list of readings concentrates on works written originally in English or available through translation; but occasionally it is bound to stray into other languages. Even so, it remains a minimal approximation to a bibliography of the subject; so much has been written on or about Machiavelli that a vast volume would be required simply to name the various contributions to the various discussions that have waxed and waned over the centuries.

BIOGRAPHIES

For many years a standard biography on the grand scale, rich in details and relatively unadventurous in outlook, was that of Pasquale Villari, *Niccolò Machiavelli and his time*, published at Florence in 1877 and translated into English in 1878. A more recent *Life of Niccolò Machiavelli* incorporating later scholarship and elegantly written, is that of Roberto Ridolfi (Rome, 1954); it too has been translated into English (by Cecil Grayson, for the University of Chicago Press, 1963). Oreste Tommasini, *La vita e gli scritti di Niccolò Machiavelli* (Turin, 1883, with numerous later additions) is a vast and disorderly compendium of information. Edmond Barincou did an intimate study for the French series "So-and-so *par lui-même*"; it has been translated by Helen R. Lind under the simple title *Machiavelli* as Evergreen Profile Book 23 (New York: Grove Press, 1961). A more romantic, semifictionalized volume, which links Machiavelli with Savonarola, Castiglione, and Aretino as lawgivers of their age, is Ralph Roeder's *Man of the Renaissance* (New York: Viking, 1933); though a little florid in its rhetoric, it is still vivid and imaginatively compelling.

BACKGROUNDS

General accounts of the Renaissance and of Italy's peculiar destiny in the fifteenth and sixteenth centuries must always be headed by two old war

1. Sir Isaiah Berlin assures us that there was one significant study of our author by Kamenev, the political pseudonym of Lev Rosenfeld; when he was placed on trial for treason, his analysis of Machiavelli was made one of the charges against him by prosecutor Vyshinsky, and he was promptly shot. Nobody has tried the subject since—which is rather a shame, as the creators of the Gulag Archipelago clearly have some curious refinements to add to the theory and practice of political duplicity.

horses—Jacob Burckhardt's *Civilization of the Renaissance in Italy*, first published in 1860 and still going strong, with an English translation available in the Modern Library; and John Addington Symonds, *History of the Renaissance in Italy*, published in several volumes between 1875 and 1886. Symond's volumes hardly constitute a proper history, but are full of rich and curious information. Ferdinand Schevill has written, among other books, *A History of Florence* (New York: Harcourt Brace, 1936) with a useful introductory survey of the sources of Florentine history; in 1963 it was reprinted in two volumes as *Medieval and Renaissance Florence*. Garrett Mattingly, *Renaissance Diplomacy* (London, 1955) provides valuable standards for judging Machiavelli's theory and practice in the light of his own times. A fundamental study, which impinges only indirectly, but even so very importantly, on the life and thought of Machiavelli is Hans Baron's monumental *Crisis of the Early Italian Renaissance* (Princeton University Press, two volumes 1955, one volume 1966). A careful introduction to the social background is Lauro Martines, *The Social World of the Florentine Humanists*, 1390–1460; a fascinatingly intimate study of the political background is Nicolai Rubinstein, *The Government of Florence under the Medici 1434–1494* (Oxford University Press, 1960). More popular in its orientation, less accurate, and containing many specifics which the political historians take for granted, is a French study of *Daily Life in Florence in the Time of the Medici* by Jean Lucas Dubreton, tr. A. L. Sells (London: Allen & Unwin, 1960). One gets even closer to the world of mercantile Florence as it existed about a century before Machiavelli's time through *Two Memoirs of Renaissance Florence*, written by Buonaccorso Pitti and Gregorio Dati, translated by Julia Martines, edited by Gene Brucker, and published as Harper Torchbook TB 1333. Finally, although the student cannot go far wrong reading the articles of Felix Gilbert wherever he finds them, two call for particular mention: "Florentine Political Assumptions in the Age of Savonarola and Soderini" in the *Journal of the Warburg and Courtauld Institutes* XX (1957), 187–214; and "The Concept of Nationalism in Machiavelli's Prince," in *Studies in the Renaissance* I (1954), 38–48.

English books on the Borgias tend to be more lurid than accurate, like "Baron Corvo" 's general account of the family and Rafael Sabatini's popular biography of Cesare; in Italian, Gustavo Sacerdote and Clemente Fusero have both written detailed factual accounts of Cesare's career (Milan, 1950, 1958); they tend generally to support Machiavelli's contention that during his brief ascendancy the Romagna was well ruled.

POLITICAL THEORY

A major contribution to the study of Machiavelli as a political theorist was made by Augustin Renaudet, *Machiavel, étude d'histoire des doctrines politiques* (Paris, 1942). The standard study of Machiavellism is that of Friedrich Meinecke, *Die Idee der Staatsräson* (Munich, 1924), translated into lumpy English by Douglas Scott and published as *Machiavellism* (London and New Haven, 1957). Sharp, though dated, is "Luther and Machiavelli," by J. N. Figgis, in *Studies in Political Thought from Gerson to*

274 · Bibliography

Grotius (Cambridge, England, 1916), pp. 71–121. A recent symposium, one of several occasioned by the 500th anniversary of Machiavelli's birth, was edited by Martin Fleisher under the title, *Machiavelli and the Nature of Political Thought* (New York, 1972). Among the important articles are those of Hans Baron, "Machiavelli: the Republican Citizen and the Author of The Prince" in *English Historical Review*, 76 (1961), and of Myron Gilmore, "Freedom and Determinism in Renaissance Historians," *Studies in the Renaissance*, III (1956), 47–60. Garrett Mattingly's "Changing Attitudes Toward the State" in *Facets of the Renaissance* (Los Angeles, 1959), pp. 19–40, is more substantial than his "Machiavelli's Prince: Political Science or Political Satire?" in *American Scholar* 27 (1957–58) 482–91, which is an academic joke by a most distinguished man. For those with Italian, the three essays of Luigi Russo collected under the title *Machiavelli*, and reprinted as Universale Laterza 28, though perhaps a bit antiquated, are still vital and incisive. The same thing can be said of Russo's annotated edition of *The Prince*, which is a bit hard to find since Sansoni brought it out during the second World War.

Hostile critics of Machiavelli's morals are beyond number, and as most of them are frankly uninterested in Machiavelli, but are tilting at other windmills, we shall list only a few. Giuseppe Prezzolini's *Machiavelli anticristo* (Rome, 1954) carries its thesis on its title page; under the more subdued title of *Machiavelli* it has been translated into English (New York, 1967). Herbert Butterfield, *The Statecraft of Machiavelli* (London, 1940); Gerhard Ritter, *Die Dämonie der Macht* (Munich, 1948), translated by F. W. Pick as *The Corrupting Influence of Power* (Hadleigh, England, 1952); and Piero Conte, *L'errore logico di Machiavelli* (Rome, 1955) are all a little less extravagant in their views than Jacques Maritain, "The End of Machiavellianism," variously translated and reprinted but Englished in *The Review of Politics* IV (1942), 1–33. Father Leslie J. Walker, S.J., has translated the *Discourses* (London, 1950; Yale University Press, 1952) with a corrective introduction and cautionary notes.

LANGUAGE

Instead of thrashing over the morals that Machiavelli didn't have or the political visions that he did have, scholars of recent years have taken to analyzing the language he used as an index to the mind using it. An innovator in this field was Fredi Chiappelli, *Studi sul linguaggio di Machiavelli* (Florence, 1952); this book was shortly followed up by H. de Vries, *Essai sur la terminologie constitutionelle chez Machiavel* (Amsterdam, 1957), and by a great number of detailed studies. Among these we notice J. H. Hexter's study of the meaning of the word *stato* ("state") in "*Il principe* and *lo stato*," *Studies in the Renaissance* IV (1956), 113–38, which became chapter III in *The Vision of Politics on the Eve of the Reformation* (New York City: Basic Books, 1973). Words like *politica, ordini,* and *fortuna* have been discussed by J. H. Whitfield in *Modern Language Review* L (1955), 433–43; in the essay reprinted in this Norton Critical Edition, pp. 194–205; and by Sasso in the *Rivista storica italiana* LXIV (1952), 205. Regarding *virtù* there is a whole library of discussion: see the essay by Plamenatz in this Norton Critical Edition, pp. 217–26, and also essays by Whitfield in *Modern Language Review* XXXVIII (1943), 222–25 and Allan Gilbert in *Renaissance News* IV (1951), 53–54, with controversy in the following issue. In *Italian Renaissance Studies*, ed. E. F. Jacob (London, 1960), pp. 48–68, Denys Hay has an account of the complex word *barbarian*, bearing immediately on Machiavelli's use of the term. In Fleisher's symposium, noted above under the heading "Political Theory," there are three studies of Machiavelli's language as a structuring element in his thought, by Fleisher himself, by J. G. A. Pocock, and by Robert Orr. Chiappelli's *Nuovi studi* appeared in Florence, 1969. Finally, it should not be overlooked that Machiavelli himself wrote a little *Dialogo intorno alla nostra lingua*, confirming our sense that he was a literary artist very conscious of his tools and materials. It is set in context by an essay of Cecil Grayson in *Italian Renaissance Studies*, ed. Jacob, pp. 410–32. The text is in Blasucci, ed., *Opere letterarie* (Milano, 1964), pp. 212–28.

WAR

Machiavelli's ideas on war and its conduct have been discussed by Felix Gilbert, "Machiavelli and the Renaissance of the Art of War," in *Makers of Modern Strategy*, ed. E. M. Earle (Princeton, 1943) and by J. R. Hale, "War and Public Opinion in Renaissance Florence," in *Italian Renaissance Studies*, ed. Jacob, pp. 94–112. C. C. Bayley, *War and Society in Renaissance Florence* (Toronto, 1961) relates the much earlier ideas of Bruni on the subject of militia to those of Machiavelli. See also Piero Pieri, *Il rinascimento e la crisi militare italiana* (Turin, 1952).

CURIOSITIES

A handsome and copiously annotated Italian edition of *Il Principe* (though it is now very hard to locate and much merits reprinting) is that of L. A. Burd (Oxford, 1891). J. R. Hale has written a broad survey of *England and the Italian Renaissance: the Growth of Interest in its History and Art* (London, 1954). Peter S. Donaldson has edited and translated *A Machiavellian Treatise* by Stephen Gardiner. The manuscript was written around 1553–55 but never published; it draws directly on *The Prince* and the *Discorsi*. Since Gardiner was Bishop of Winchester and Lord Chancellor under (Bloody) Mary, this is a specific evidence of Machiavelli actually having influence, if not on a persecution, at least on a persecutor. An important and deeply skeptical critical statement by Benedetto Croce is "Una questione che forse non si chiudera mai" in *Quaderni della critica* 14 (1949), 1–16. George Eliot brings Machiavelli on the stage of her Renaissance-Florence novel *Romola*; T. S. Eliot delivers his verdict in the collection titled *For Lancelot Andrewes*. R. H. Buskirk, sensing that the true analogue to Machiavelli's city-state is not the nation any more, but the corporation, has written a potentially funny book, *Modern Management and Machiavelli* (Boston, 1974). Among the 500th anniversary collections, in addition to that of Fleisher noted above, there should be cited: *Studies on Machiavelli*, ed. M. P. Gilmore (Florence, Sansoni, 1972); *Italy: Machiavelli "500"* (Jamaica, New York: St. John's University Press, 1970), and

The Political Calculus, ed. A. Parel (Toronto, 1972). Frederick the Great's highly "Machiavellian" attack on Machiavelli (in writing which he was aided by Voltaire), the *Anti-Machiavel*, has appeared under the editorship of Theodore Besterman as volume V of *Studies on Voltaire and the 18th century* (Geneva, 1958).

FURTHER READINGS

A full and proper bibliography of Machiavelli is probably by now beyond the power of man or computer to compile. Certainly if one defines "Machiavellism" at all loosely, there is no end to the discussions of war, power, politics, authority, punishment, democracy, morality, leadership, personality structure, international law, freedom, responsibility, etc., etc., within which his name, and more rarely his ideas, may crop up. Still, a reader who is interested in Machiavelli himself, and wants to begin (as sensibly he should) with some fairly recent books, is not without help. Eric W. Cochrane has listed some studies from the years 1940–60 in the *Journal of Modern History*, XXXIII, 2 (June 1961), 113–36; and Sir Isaiah Berlin in a special supplement to the *New York Review of Books* for November 4, 1971, p. 20 ff. adds a little bit to it. And there are of course bibliographies, formal or informal, in most of the works listed above.

The lack of a compendious bibliographical guide would be more distressing, except that it's true of Machiavelli studies, more than almost any others, that reading one book about him leads you to three or four others that you feel compelled to read. Book-hopping, from Y's footnotes to X's text, from Z's review of F's howler to J's improvement of C's long-inadequate formulation, is the classic way to get into a subject. Adventurous minds will ask nothing better.

Index

277